Library of
Davidson College

Religion as Social Vision

This volume is sponsored by
The Center for South and Southeast Asia Studies
University of California, Berkeley

The Center for South and Southeast Asia Studies of the University of California is the unifying organization for faculty members and students interested in South and Southeast Asia Studies, bringing together scholars from numerous disciplines. The Center's major aims are the development and support of research and language study. As part of this program the Center sponsors a publication series of books concerned with South and Southeast Asia. Manuscripts are considered from all campuses of the University of California as well as from any other individuals and institutions doing research in these areas.

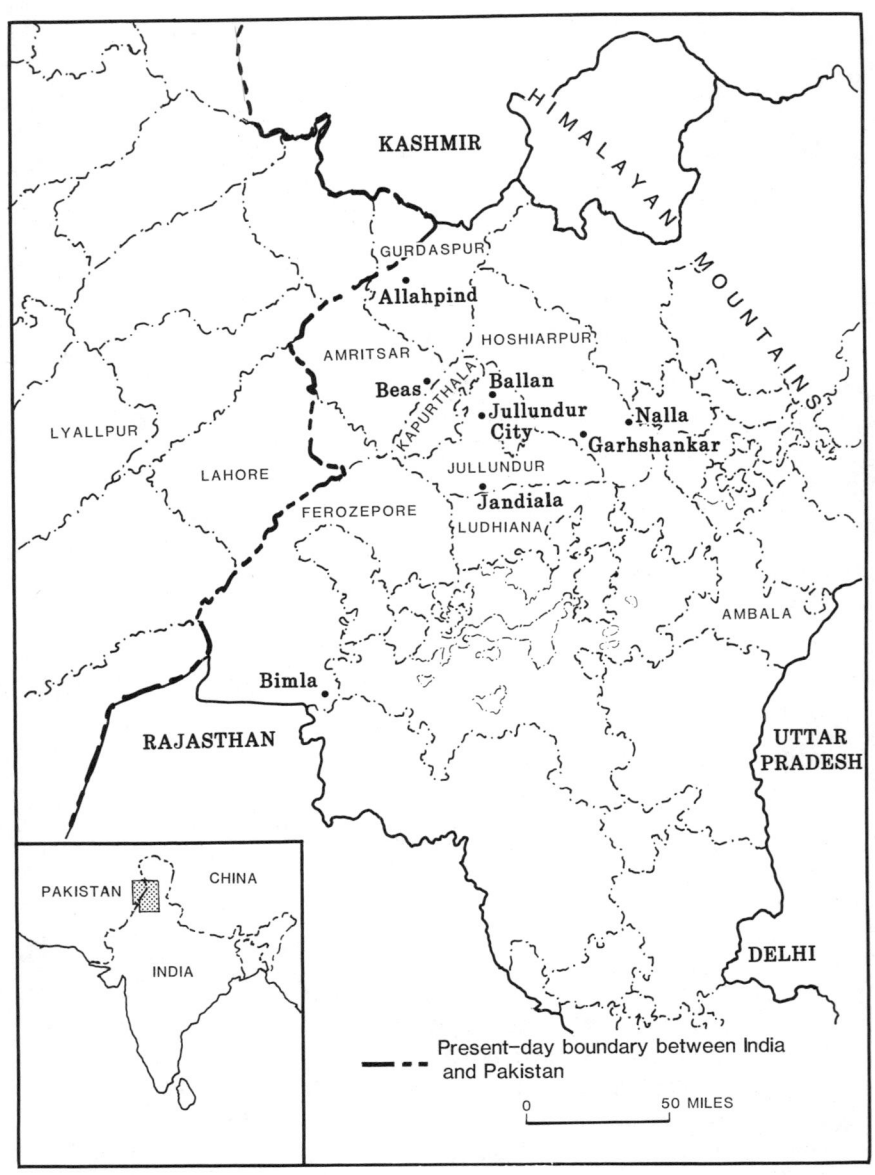

CENTRAL DISTRICTS OF THE PUNJAB BEFORE 1948. Names of districts are in small capitals.

Religion as Social Vision

The Movement against Untouchability in 20th-Century Punjab

MARK JUERGENSMEYER

University of California Press
Berkeley · Los Angeles · London

University of California Press
Berkeley and Los Angeles, California
University of California Press, Ltd.
London, England
© 1982 by the Regents of the University of California
Printed in the United States of America

Library of Congress Cataloging in Publication Data

Juergensmeyer, Mark.
 Religion as social vision.

 Bibliography: p.
 Includes index.
  1. Untouchables. 2. Punjab, India (State) — Religion. 3. Punjab, India (State) — Social conditions.
 4. Social movements — India — Punjab (State) I. Title.
 DS422.C3J83   305.5'6   80-24187
 ISBN 0-520-04301-4

1 2 3 4 5 6 7 8 9

CONTENTS

PREFACE vii

INTRODUCTION: Religion and Social Rebellion 1

PART I: The Setting 9

   1. The Experience of Untouchability   11
   2. The 1920s: A Time for Social Change   22

PART II: The Rise of Ad Dharm 33

   3. The Movement and Mangoo Ram   35
   4. The Ideology of a Political Religion   45
   5. Ideas into Action: The Organizational Character   55
   6. Responses to the Arya Samaj: Factions in Change   64
   7. The Great Census   72

PART III: Continuities and Encounters 81

   8. The Revival of Ravi Das   83
   9. The Religion of Village Untouchables   92
   10. Ad Dharm in the Villages   107
   11. The Urban Experience: Ad Dharm as New Dharm   115
   12. Mangoo Ram vs. Gandhi   124
   13. "Hope from God and Help from the King"   132
   14. Politics and the Decline of Ad Dharm   142

PART IV: Competing Visions 157

   15. The Ambedkar Alternative   159
   16. Rishi Valmiki: The Saint of Sweepers   169
   17. Christianity: The Sweepers' Revolt   181
   18. The Uncertain Appeal of Marxism   193
   19. Radhasoami and the Return of Religion   208

PART V: Revival Post-Independence 221
   20. The Ex-Untouchables of Post-Independence Punjab 223
   21. The Lonely Modernity of Model Town 234
   22. Ravi Das in Wolverhampton 245
   23. Ad Dharm Anew 258

EPILOGUE: The Social Vision of
             Religious Movements 269

APPENDIX A: The Early Life of Mangoo Ram 283

APPENDIX B: Report of the Ad Dharm Mandal,
              1926–1931 290

LIST OF INTERVIEWS 309

GLOSSARY OF INDIAN TERMS 315

BIBLIOGRAPHY 321

INDEX 347

PREFACE

Locating adequate materials for the study of lower caste social movements has been at many stages an exercise in invention. When I began, I found only a few documents of the sort with which a historian would feel comfortable. These I supplemented by interviewing approximately a hundred leaders of lower caste movements past and present, including the remarkable Mangoo Ram, founder of the Ad Dharm movement, whom I met almost by chance in retirement in the Punjab. To probe the social contexts of his and other recent movements and their effect on individual lives, I conducted surveys, case studies of village and urban localities, and still more interviews. In this way a project begun under the rubric of political analysis has turned frequently to the methodologies of social history, anthropology, even quantitative surveys; and the central issue, the relationship of religion to social change, leads directly into the realm of the sociology of religion.

From the beginning, I have held to the intellectual conviction that social movements, especially religious ones, are genuine acts of creativity, not merely responses to social pathology. That concern motivated my Ph.D. dissertation on this subject, written at the University of California, Berkeley, under the wise and able tutelage of Warren Ilchman, now vice-president of the State University of New York. As the study progressed, another issue surfaced and became central: the importance, in India, for social change to have a religious form. I discovered that the poorest of India's marginal people, the Untouchables, have for years been engaged in struggle against social oppression, but covertly so: their struggle has taken the form of cultural rebellion, expressed in the creation of new religious movements. This book, then, is the history of one such movement of Untouchables in the Punjab and its linkages to several others, and more broadly, an analysis of the role which religion commands in lower caste struggles for social change.

My initial involvement in India in 1966–1967, teaching at Punjab University and doing famine relief work in Bihar state, was under the sponsorship of the World Student Christian Federation's Frontier Intern program. Research for this study undertaken in India in 1970–1972, 1973, 1978, and 1979 was encouraged by my colleagues in the Center for South and Southeast Asian Studies and in the program in Religious Studies at the University of California, Berkeley, and by those in the Graduate Theological Union. Financial support came from an Indo-American fellowship and a National Defense Foreign Language grant, and a host of Indian scholars and leaders of lower caste organizations have provided insightful guidance. I have greatly appreciated the advice of B. S. Rangnekar and Victor d'Souza of Punjab University and the assistance of my Punjabi tutors, then graduate students at the university, Devinder Singh of Punjab University Evening College and Mohinder Singh of Khalsa College, Anandpur. Further help in translation came from Surjit Singh Goraya in Berkeley. As for intellectual stimulation and hospitality in India, I have been grateful above all to my friend and colleague, Manoranjan Mohanty of Delhi University and his delightful family.

Many of the leaders described and quoted in this study became in time both friends and helpful critics as they took a personal interest in the progress of this book. Particularly rewarding have been the hospitality and insight of L. R. Balley, Mangu Ram Jaspal, and Manohar Mehay of Jullundur, and Bhagwan Das of Delhi. And without the support and kindness extended to me by the indefatigable Mangoo Ram this study could scarcely have come to be. Alas, he and other Ad Dharm leaders interested in the project have passed away before its completion. I hope that his spirit, and those of Swami Shudranand, Sant Sarwan Das, Sadhu Ram, M.P., and Seth Kushi Ram, will in some way live on through their contribution to this study.

In organizing the material into a book, I chose short, compact chapters as the vehicle for presenting sections which, although related, are diverse, each section a small story in itself. As for style, I have tried to steer between the interests of the India specialists and the nonspecialists, although each may feel I have veered too far in the other's direction. I do not assume that the reader has any special knowledge of Indian religion, Untouchables, or the Punjab. For those who wish to pursue these topics further, and for the specialists who may be curious about my sources, I have included an extensive bibliography. Regarding the problem of transliterating words of Indic origin, I have decided, with some misgiving, to omit diacritical marks from the text. A glossary of Indian terms appearing in this book will be found at the end, providing for the specialist the proper transliterations of those words, diacritical marks intact, and providing, for the nonspecialist, relevant definitions.

In the final preparation of this book I was comforted (sometimes, it seemed, like Job) by advisors who challenged but ultimately strengthened the conceptions recorded here. Philip Lilienthal of the University of California Press persevered through change after change. John Webster of United Theological College, Bangalore, reviewed the chapter on Punjab Christianity. Several other friends have taken on the task of reading and improving the entire manuscript, for which I am deeply grateful: Ainslie Embree of Columbia University, W. H. McLeod of the University of Otago, and especially Jack Hawley of the University of Washington, who has shared my burden of preparing the final version, and with his marvelous facility for precise and fluid prose, breathed new life into many of these pages. Sucheng Chan of the University of California, Berkeley, has given to this project more than she realizes: her own high standards of intellectual discipline and social concern. By helping to provide a humane environment for the research and writing of this work, she—and the others in our affable but somewhat peculiar family—have helped to remind me that the study of society is always, ultimately, the study of the quality of life.

Those who have assisted and encouraged me in this project—and they have been many, more than I have room to cite—have been generous, not only for reasons of friendship, but because they share the conviction that the viewpoints of the lower caste people of the Punjab, which this book attempts to convey, need to be heard. As for a dedication, then, a simple one is appropriate: To those who, though oppressed, have conceived great visions, and have had the courage to make them live.

INTRODUCTION:
Religion and Social Rebellion

Some years ago in Delhi a casual street-side conversation with a group of Punjabi sweepers and municipal employees from Untouchable castes revealed their profound disaffection with the culture of the dominant society. The subject was social change and the sluggishness of its pace. As one might expect, they felt that their poverty was to blame for their limitations—that and the social stigmas of untouchability that linger still, despite the government's concerted efforts at reform. But then, with a surprising vehemence, they turned to religion. Because the concept of untouchability is a religious one, they explained, a change in religious concepts would have to accompany economic and social progress. "Besides," they continued, "Hinduism is not ours. It is the religion of the rich people and the upper castes."

I asked them what their own religion was, and their answers were curious. Some gave names of other religions, and some gave their caste names, indicating perhaps that theirs was a religion with no name. They told me that they were sweepers, Christians, and Chamars (leatherworkers), and one claimed that his grandfather had been in the Ad Dharm, a religious movement of Untouchables. But they were emphatic about one point: they were not Hindu.

It is clear that the religious identity of Untouchables is a complicated matter—but then, my phrasing of the question may have jarred. For my meaning of "religion" may not have been theirs, nor did their concept of religion necessarily agree with that of upper castes. I had used the word *dharm* to translate the Western notion of "religion," but in fact there is no good translation: the idea is alien in the Indian context. Scarcely anywhere in the subcontinent can one find a unitary creed and community such as the term implies, and in the Punjab, which has been the meeting ground and battlefield for a bewildering variety of cultural traditions, concepts of "religion" are particularly diverse.

The English word "religion," as a description of India's cultural affiliations, could mean any one of several things. I have heard it translated as *qaum*, a large religious community such as that of the Muslims. It could also mean *panth*, the fellowship of those who revere a lineage of spiritual authority. Or again it could mean *dharm*, customs and codes of social obligation and spiritual behavior such as those entailed by caste or ritual and implied in observing the polarity between pure and impure. In the West we are used to thinking of these three elements—tradition, church, and ethics—as fitting together in a coherent scheme, but in the Punjab they do not coalesce so predictably. People who claim to be Sikhs may be devoted followers of Muslim saints and regular observers of Hindu customs as well. They see no inconsistency in this, for the three elements of religious identity—*qaumik, panthik,* and *dharmik*— function independently.

Moreover, the relative importance of each element may shift over time. For example, one could argue that Sikhism was primarily a guru movement, a *panthik* form of religion, until the nineteenth century when a reform movement, the Singh Sabha, attempted to give it the credibility and coherence of a large, unified community, a *qaum*. Hindus too have altered their perceptions of their tradition. Before the nineteenth century Hindu religious life in the Punjab was almost solely a pattern of practices and customs, a *dharmik* form of religion, until the strong presence of the Muslim *qaum* in the Punjab encouraged many Hindus to conceive differently of their own religious identities. Through the Arya Samaj they gave Hinduism a unified and organized *qaumik* form as well. In Islam, as practiced by

Punjabis, the veneration of Muslim saints provided that fundamentally *qaumik* religion with a *panthik* form. And in the case of the lower castes in our own century, as this study will show, older *panthik* forms of religion were used as a basis for creating a *qaumik* form, in which the less agreeable *dharmik* customs of religion were discarded and replaced.

Therefore, when many lower caste people say that they are not Hindu, they mean that they are offended by the role into which they are placed in the *dharmik* world view of the Hindus. From the perspective of the lower castes "Hinduism" means Hindu *dharm,* the moral and social order that underlies the concepts and divinities of the tradition, and a "Hindu" is any person who belongs to the upper castes and accepts these concepts and their social and theological implications. There is an interesting paradox here, for renunciation of the world is a dominant theme in Hindu soteriology. Yet Hindus also believe, by and large, that one cannot begin the process of renouncing the world without first involving oneself in its social bonds and fulfilling the *dharmik* obligations that it imposes. Hindu concepts of salvation require that Indian society be essentially and fundamentally a religious society.

Hindu society is caste society, as Louis Dumont argues in *Homo Hierarchicus.* According to Dumont, the institution of caste, "a religious notion," upholds the social order and provides individuals with access to the social whole.[1] Caste as a social grouping falls somewhere between what other societies know as extended families and ethnic communities, with the critical difference that in India caste is the central fact of social organization, the fundamental category. There can be social change within castes, and castes can change position slightly in relation to one another; but one cannot conceive of a Hindu social order that removes caste altogether or radically alters the bases upon which castes are related without changing the basic values (which are religious values) that undergird the social system. To do so would be essentially to change the religion.

1. Louis Dumont, *Homo Hierarchicus: The Caste System and Its Implications* (Chicago, 1970), p. 47.

Some Western social analysts, in recognizing this fact, have despaired about the possibility of any basic change in India at all. Because of the caste system, Barrington Moore argues, "fundamental change" in India is "very difficult."[2] Caste "constitutes an obstacle to all effective political action."[3] Max Weber also held such a view, applying it with peculiar force to the Untouchables. Weber claimed that it was "precisely the lowest classes, who . . . never think of toppling the caste system through social revolutions or reforms."[4]

Yet there have been social revolutions in India: they have come in the guise of religion. The ancient heterodoxies of Hinduism—Buddhism and Jainism—gave expression to radical social visions through religious doctrines and communities that undercut the power of the then prevailing Brahmanical priesthood. During the medieval centuries in India, devotional *bhakti* movements provided at least the illusion of new religious societies in which the power of priests held no sway and all devout followers were regarded as spiritually equal, regardless of caste. In recent centuries the messages preached by "rebellious prophets" have been both political and religious,[5] and in our own time Gandhi conceived of an egalitarian and modern India in part by amending and shifting certain Hindu religious concepts.

Except for the Buddhist and Jain heterodoxies and Gandhian Hinduism, which were *dharmik,* these movements have been *panthik* forms of religion. Over the centuries the *panthik* movements have served as pressure valves for Hindu society: forms of social and religious expression which exist as islands in Hindu society but do not ultimately disturb it. In fact, one may argue that they play a functional role for Hindu society, providing an acceptable alternative to Hinduism's *dharmik* social structure.

2. Barrington Moore, Jr., *Social Origins of Dictatorship and Democracy: Lord and Peasant in the Making of the Modern World* (Boston, 1966), p. 341.
3. Ibid., p. 384.
4. Max Weber, *The Sociology of Religion* (Boston, 1964), p. 43.
5. Stephen Fuchs, *Rebellious Prophets: A Study in Messianic Movements in Indian Religions* (Bombay, 1965).

Indians in general find their social locations at any number of points along the spectrum between *dharmik* structure and *panthik* anti-structures, but Untouchables are not so broadly dispersed. For them the *dharmik* end of the spectrum holds no appeal. Despite Dumont's argument that Untouchables are vital to Hindu concepts and practices and are expected to be in attendance at many social and religious occasions,[6] they have been denied access to the scriptural tradition, the temples, and the priesthood of Hinduism. Moreover, as the butt of the social system, with the stigma of being outcaste compounded with the discomfort of poverty, they have been given every reason to wish for an alternative social structure and a reformulation of socio-religious ideas. Hence Untouchables have tended to cluster at the *panthik* end of the spectrum by following *bhakti* movements, or to leave the spectrum altogether by converting to alien religions such as Islam and Christianity.

In the Punjab the options for the lower castes have been especially varied. As Gandhi noted—and he was ordinarily very sensitive to such things—"caste has much less force"[7] in the Punjab than in other areas of India. A sociological and a religious reason explain that fact. The sociological reason is that over half the population of the Punjab is made up of Jats, a nomadic group that entered the Punjab some centuries ago and eventually became a caste. The presence of Jats modified the traditional caste structure by introducing another in which a large cluster of Jat subcastes were surrounded by a variety of servant and merchant castes. Thus the usual competition for status ranking in the caste hierarchy has come to be complicated by tensions between Jat and non-Jat castes. Untouchables usually fare better in the latter kind of competition, although they are sometimes caught in the middle in a collision between Jat and non-Jat.

The religious reason for the Punjab's social liberalism is that a large proportion of Punjabis are not Hindus. Prior to independence and the partition of the Punjab in 1947, over half of all Punjabis were Muslim. Only 30 to 40 percent

6. Dumont, *Homo Hierarchicus*, p. 55.
7. S. L. Malhotra, *Gandhi and the Punjab* (Chandigarh, 1970), 152.

were Hindus, and most of the remainder were Sikhs. After independence, when the Muslim-dominated areas were granted to Pakistan, the state was both Hindu and Sikh, and the restructuring of the Punjab in 1968 gave it a Sikh majority. Since Muslims and Sikhs theoretically do not have castes, this has a considerable influence on the social organization of the area. In fact, caste status divisions have become entrenched within the Sikh and Muslim communities of the Punjab too, but the concepts of ritual pollution and karmic retribution are not so strong in the cultures of these religious traditions. Consequently, caste in the Punjab does not have quite the same rigor or force of religious sanction as it has elsewhere.

For Untouchables, the presence of Muslims and Sikhs in the Punjab is proof that alternative models to *dharmik* Hinduism are viable. The Muslims represent a *qaumik* model, a large and organized community which elicits fierce loyalty and respect for central authorities. The Sikhs offer the model of a *panthik* group which has become established as a separate tradition. Untouchables had usually been regarded as *dharmik* Hindus, but many of them found that identity, like the social oppression that accompanied it, a burden. Their task, then, was a double one: to find some way of disengaging themselves from Hindu customs, and to choose some workable form of alternative religious community from the variety of models available. One group of lower class rebels illustrates the difficulty of this double task with particular clarity: the Ad Dharm movement. At times Ad Dharmis were baffled at the choices, at times bold in selecting among the options.

The Ad Dharm has been central among lower caste social and religious activities in the Punjab for most of this century. Its history reflects the development of Punjab's lower caste social consciousness: it incorporates elements of social awareness from an earlier religious tradition of village Untouchables, it records changes in the Untouchables' vision of themselves and their society, and it gives expression to the enlarged hopes and expectations that eventually outlived the movement itself. In this study we will trace the rise and fall of the Ad Dharm, survey the social forms that replaced it in time, and examine the attempt that was made to resuscitate the movement within the last decade. We will also consider the Untouchables' involvement in a variety of related movements—the Ravidas, Arya Samaj, and Ambedkar movements, the Valmiki Sabha, Christianity, Radhasoami—and investigate their flirtations with Marxism and several political parties. These various social expressions provided prisms through which the conditions and culture of Untouchables have been focused and refracted in new directions. Hence, throughout the study it will be necessary to look closely at the social contexts from which these movements emerged and on which they made their impact: traditional villages, changing Indian cities, and Untouchable communities abroad. We begin with the most basic context of all, the experience of untouchability itself, which provided each of the lower caste movements with its motive force.

PART I The Setting

1 The Experience of Untouchability

Like most social categories, the label of untouchability implies that we know more about the lives of the persons to whom it is applied that in fact we do. For we know more about untouchability as a concept than we know about Untouchables as a people. As a concept, untouchability connotes an attitude, a prejudice: it refers to a pattern of relationships seen from the point of view of a person of higher status. From that standpoint a person of much lower status is deemed impure: he or she literally cannot be touched. But Untouchables certainly are tactile beings, touchable among themselves and their peers. Only an upper caste perspective portrays them as persons potentially injurious to piety.

The religious concept on which the notion of untouchability is based is that of ritual impurity, according to which certain materials are thought to create adverse karmic effects when one comes into contact with them. Scholars have long debated what logic, if any, underlies this idea. The nature of the materials themselves provides a significant clue, for these articles—leather, dead animals, feces, cut hair, sweat, and so forth—share one property in common: they were once a part of living tissue and have now been severed or otherwise passed from life to decay. This in turn suggests that the force behind the concept of ritual impurity is the elementary fear of death itself and the horror of bodily decrepitude.[1]

---

1. This is my observation, but there is no consensus on why the polarity of purity and pollution is of such importance to Hinduism. According to Dumont, the polarity corresponds to the war between nature

There are degrees of pollution. Any person may become polluted temporarily while defecating; perspiring during work has the same effect. Women become polluted during menstruation. Each caste, furthermore, is to some degree "untouchable" from the perspective of a caste ranked ritually higher. And there is room for differentiation within potentially polluting occupations. A barber, for example, though necessarily in contact with cut hair, may be considered less polluted than a laborer who constantly perspires.

Some people, however, by virtue of their continual contact with polluting articles, become permanently and irrefutably affected in the eyes of everyone else. The most polluting occupations are those that involve continual contact with dead animals, feces, and the like—the occupations of the leatherworkers and the sweepers. These are the people who today are characteristically called "Untouchables," but the idea that certain groups of people are to be identified as the repository of untouchability seems to have come into common usage only in recent centuries: it is not a part of the ancient literature. Perhaps the term came from outsiders, such as the early British in India, when they observed a practice which seemed to them clearly to demarcate a special category of people as "untouchable."[2] The missionaries called such people "outcastes."

The notion that Untouchables are outcaste is not quite correct. It is true that no place is allotted them in the traditional division of Indian society into four *varnas*, but their

and the spirit in which "impurity corresponds to the organic aspect of man" (*Homo Hierarchicus* [Chicago, 1970], p. 50). There is also a Freudian suggestion that "purification is an overt imitation . . . of the infant's dependence on the mother" (Richard Lannoy, *The Speaking Tree: A Study of Indian Culture and Society* [New York, 1971], p. 156) and the structural anthropologists' explanation that the purity/impurity continuum in various cultures provides the function of "imposing system on an inherently untidy experience" (Mary Douglas, *Purity and Danger: An Analysis of Concepts of Pollution and Taboo* [London, 1966], p. 4).

2. Early uses of the word *achut* ("untouchable") seem to refer more to things than to people. Terms such as "outcaste" were clearly British inventions, and suggested biblical origins (see Psalms 147:2 and Isaiah 11:12). Ordinarily, in rural Indian society, lower castes are referred to by their caste names, rather than by the generic label "Untouchables." The

role at one end of the purity/pollution spectrum is as essential to the social whole as that of the Brahmans at the other. Indeed, the concept of untouchability is not only endemic to the caste system, it is its very basis, for as Louis Dumont explains, the opposition of purity and impurity "underlies hierarchy, which is the superiority of the pure to the impure, underlies separation because the pure and the impure must be kept separate, and underlies the division of labor, because pure and impure occupations must likewise be kept separate."³

Because the word "untouchable" betrays an attitude rather than constituting a descriptive label, it is technically incorrect to speak of Untouchables as a people, to dignify the term by using it as a social category. And in fact, since the Indian constitution, in Article 17, abolished the concept of untouchability "and its practice in any form," the term in present-day India is less frequently used than it once was. Yet, of course, the notion of untouchability persists, for it runs as deep in Hindu consciousness as the religious concepts from which the notion has evolved, and there continue to be "untouchable" castes. These castes, traditionally called Chamar and Chuhra in the Punjab, are the largest of those that have borne the stigma of being "untouchable." They are the leatherworking and sweeper castes, ubiquitous across North India, and in some areas of the Punjab they constitute 15 to 25 percent of the population, one of the highest concentrations anywhere. These groups exist, and one must call them something.

My own preference is for the term "lower castes." But I also continue to use the term "Untouchables" to describe the castes in question because it has been the term most commonly used over the years, even by the people to whom it refers, and because it draws attention to a fact of social prejudice which should not be disguised by more subtle terminology. Gandhi coined the name Harijan ("chil-

---

British were eager to locate people within broad social classes, and perhaps their use of the term was passed on to the Indians. (I am grateful to Professor Ainslie Embree of Columbia University for suggesting the latter possibility.)

3. Dumont, *Homo Hierarchicus*, p. 135.

dren of God") in an attempt to honor the lower castes. His term is the one most often used today by politicians and journalists, but one seldom hears it from members of the lower castes themselves, who consider it patronizing. The British suggested another alternative: in compiling a list of castes for welfare purposes they titled the list (or "schedule") with the simple, neutral term "Scheduled Castes." The schedule is not exactly coincident with the list of castes formerly considered untouchable, but it is close enough, and since the term holds no pejorative connotations, many of the former Untouchables prefer to be called Scheduled Caste. Still, the term "untouchable" remains, as do the groups of people and the social attitudes to which it refers.

Who are the Untouchables and what does untouchability mean to them? In the Punjab their experiences are widely varied. They live in the villages, and they live in the cities. They are mired in bitter poverty, and they relax in financial comfort. They profess variously to be Muslim, Sikh, Hindu, and Christian, and some deny any religious affiliation at all. Most members of the lower castes, however, share the stigmas of untouchability: they are frequently denied the chance to eat, smoke, or even sit with members of the upper castes, and they often must use separate wells from those maintained for the use of others. These injustices are sanctioned more or less by religion, but there are others, more extreme, that go entirely beyond religious approval: *begar*—forced labor—for instance, and the sexual abuse to which many lower caste wives and daughters are subjected.

While not all lower caste persons are poor, Untouchables share the oppression of poverty almost in the same degree as they share their social oppression. Clustering together upper castes and the Scheduled Castes as two comparable groups, I found that the average monthly per capita income of the Scheduled Caste members in 1970–1971 was forty-six rupees (about six dollars), whereas the upper castes on an average earned over three times that amount. Scheduled Caste members were crowded over four to a room, whereas the upper caste ratio was a more comfortable 1.5.⁴ In many Scheduled Caste families every member, from young children to aged grandmothers, engages in some form of employment in addition to the tasks of maintaining the household, simply to ward off hunger and the burdens of severe debt.

Yet these people are not simply poor folk: they are castes. And that makes them different from the "cultures of poverty" in various parts of the world which have many of these same elements—economic hardship and social ostracism,[5] the "mark of oppression" observed among people such as the Blacks in the United States.[6] It is sometimes argued that the concepts of caste and untouchability can rightly be applied to these other societies as well,[7] but the particularly religious sanctions which undergird that form of social segregation known as the caste system are peculiar to the Hindu tradition.[8]

Still, it is a subject of considerable debate even in India whether the lowest stratum of Indian society should be re-

4. The survey contained 93 questions regarding economic conditions, cultural attitudes, and political and religious affiliations. It was administered to approximately 150 upper caste and lower caste respondents in six locations (three villages, a town, and two sectors of a city) in 1970–1971. The questions and a statistical tabulation of the responses are in Mark Juergensmeyer, "Political Hope: Social Movements of North India's Untouchables, 1900–1970," Ph.D. Dissertation, University of California, Berkeley, 1974, Appendix A and Appendix B.

5. Oscar Lewis, *Five Families: Mexican Case Studies in the Culture of Poverty* (Boston: Beacon Press, 1962). The term "culture of poverty" is sometimes associated with a causative model in which cultural attitudes are allegedly responsible for the inability of the poor to rise from their conditions of oppression. This model does not apply to the Punjab Untouchables, whose cultural attitudes are those of defiance as well as submission. For a critique of the "culture of poverty" model, see Charles Valentine, *Culture and Poverty* (Chicago, 1968).

6. Abram Kardiner and Lionel Ovesey, *Mark of Oppression* (Cleveland: World Publishing Co., 1962).

7. Gerald D. Berreman, "Structure and Function of Caste Systems," in George DeVos and Hiroshi Wagatsuma, eds., *Japan's Invisible Race: Caste in Culture and Personality* (Berkeley and Los Angeles: University of California Press, 1966).

8. Dumont, *Homo Hierarchicus*, chap. 10, "Comparison: Are There Castes Among Non-Hindus and Outside India?" and the appendix, "Caste, Racism and Stratification—Reflections of a Social Anthropologist."

garded as an economic class or as a group of social castes. This issue is especially lively in the Punjab, where Hindu social values are moderated by those of other traditions. But the important matter for purposes of this study is not how the issue is debated, but how the lower castes regard themselves—whether they consider themselves to be castes, and hence a part of the Indian social system as a whole, or participants in a culture of poverty which marks them off as a separate society. To explore this question I turned to case studies of lower caste locales.

In some of these cases Untouchables carry a strong awareness of caste and caste restrictions. In Bhatinda district I spent some time in a village of moderate means in an area made profitable through irrigation. The lower castes there are usually engaged in their traditional occupations of sweeping and leatherworking except during harvest time, when they serve as agricultural laborers. They observe caste restrictions among themselves as strictly as do the upper castes. The Chamars refer to the Chuhra caste as "Harijan," but exempt themselves from that term, which Gandhi intended to embrace all Untouchables. The Chuhras, though they accept the word "Harijan" for themselves, reserve the label "Untouchable" for the vagrant castes: gypsies and nomadic tribes, whom they regard as even lower than themselves. The Chamars not only refuse to intermarry with the Chuhra caste, but have no other social relations with them, including eating, smoking the water-pipe, or even engaging in much conversation aside from what is necessary to conduct their working affairs. And the Chuhra keep the same distance from castes they consider more humble than they, the marginal Mirasis and Bazigars. In this Bhatinda village the Chamar and Chuhra call themselves Hindus and locate themselves somewhere in the middle of the caste hierarchy. Thus they ratify the legitimacy of the caste system and the concept of untouchability by acknowledging that they are lower than many castes but not lower than all.

In other locations in the Punjab the members of Chamar and Chuhra castes place less emphasis on their individual caste identities. Instead, they regard themselves collectively as *achut*, "Untouchables," sullenly accepting a term many resent, but accepting the word to distinguish themselves from the rest of society. The lower castes with this attitude are from two extremes: either they are better off than their caste mates in other sections of the Punjab or they are extremely disadvantaged. In the one case, their use of a single term to designate themselves represents their collective rebellion against observing the internal caste divisions that upper caste society ascribes to them; in the other, they all feel the brunt of their common social stigma so sharply that they dare not think of themselves in terms that would dignify them in comparison with any of the others. But the result is the same: they think of themselves collectively as "Untouchables."

The rebellious attitude is illustrated by a prosperous town in Ludhiana district, in central Punjab, where all the inhabitants, including the Untouchables, are less subject to exploitation from rich landlords than are their counterparts elsewhere in the Punjab. The lower castes, primarily Chamar, perform a variety of menial tasks, and a few have managed to launch a modest trade in raw leather hides. The significant thing, however, is that they see themselves principally as drones in a mercantile society. This is a town where social status is based on trading, the accretion and exchange of financial capital, and the lowest castes, unable to save enough to enter into even petty capitalism, feel that they are unfairly denied access to the system. Occasionally they agitate for higher wages, and they make a practice of casting their votes according to the economic policies of the candidates. They regard their leatherworking and other manual occupations not as acts of ritual impurity but simply as unpleasant, ill-paid labor. Any movement that will give their people a sense of unity and a degree of political leverage potentially claims their allegiance.

In another area of the Punjab, a tiny village in a semi-desert area of Ferozepur district near the Rajasthan border, where the economy is far more depressed, lower caste people also characterize themselves simply as "Untouchables." Their reasons for doing so, however, are diametrically opposite. In this area members of the lower castes are united by the fact that all of them, both Chuhras and Chamars, function as landless laborers. They even live together in compounds provided for them by large landlords. In this area of the Punjab, village society is stratified into three groups: a few landlords, primarily belonging to Jat Sikh subcastes; a small number of artisan and merchant castes (Hindus and Sikhs); and a large number of Untouchables (of indifferent religious affiliation) who provide labor for the farms. But in general the lower castes lump all of the upper castes together in talking about the dominance of "them" over "us," and speak of themselves for the most part simply as "Untouchables" or "poor people."

In the Ferozepur village, as in the Ludhiana town, class has replaced caste in the social consciousness of lower caste folk. The ritual observances of purity and pollution associated with caste, which are maintained by Untouchables in some other areas of the Punjab, have been forgotten in the competition between large economic divisions. From the point of view of these lower caste people in Ferozepur and Ludhiana, there are only the rich and the poor, the exploited and the exploiters. The upper castes, however, have a different view of the situation, perceiving social divisions as matters of caste rather than functions of economic class: in response to a survey question, the upper castes identified casteism and social discrimination as the cause of the Untouchables' plight. The Untouchables felt themselves, instead, to be victims of poverty and economic discrimination.[9]

Even though many lower caste people regard class as a more salient distinction than caste, some still continue to refer to themselves by their caste names—Chuhra, Chamar, and their many synonyms. And the vehicles they use to give expression to their sense of common identity, both in the Ludhiana town and the Ferozepur village, are those which have been shaped along caste lines. Particularly important are the caste associations, *panchayats*—governing bodies which tend in the Punjab to be stronger among the

9. I discuss these issues further in "The Cultures of Deprivation: Three Case Studies in the Punjab," *Economic and Political Weekly*, Annual number, February 1979.

lower castes than among the upper.[10] Other symbols of collective identity, however, do not explicitly reinforce old caste boundaries. As we shall see in the movements described in this study, attempts have been made among Untouchable groups to foster unity by means of symbols calculated to appeal to them all.

The most extreme interpretation one might make of the cultural differences that exist between the Untouchables and the upper castes of the Punjab would be to argue that these two groups occupy two separate societies. The differences between these two societies, one might argue, are not only the obvious ones that follow from prejudice and poverty, but also differences of custom—such everyday matters as eating habits, social mores, and family patterns. In general, the social habits of the Scheduled Castes are more flexible than those of the upper castes. Scheduled Castes are more liberal about taboos against eating meat of all kinds, even beef. They tend to consider divorce permissible, although not especially honorable,[11] and have a reputation for using country liquor, marijuana, and narcotics. The family patterns tend to be nuclear in contrast with the large joint families which usually characterize village society in the Punjab. Perhaps this is due to the possibility of divorce, but more likely it is caused by mobility: many Scheduled Caste nuclear families live apart from their joint families out of occupational necessity—in order to be near their places of work. When opportunities for employment become available in distant places the news spreads rapidly, and lower caste people move swiftly to places of advantage. Lower caste communities have communication channels of their own, facilitated through the *panchayat* networks, which span large distances between villages. In some areas,

---

10. This feature was noted in the 1911 census, which explained that "the higher castes are seldom subject to governing bodies; and where they are, the control is not very effective" (*1911 Census of India, Punjab*, part A, chap. 11, pp. 420–421).

11. The best description of marriage and family customs continues to be George W. Briggs, *The Chamars* (Calcutta and London, 1920), chap. 4.

in fact, the lower castes speak in an accent and an argot different from that of the upper castes.[12]

Much as all this seems to suggest that Untouchables live in a society all their own, one must remember that in India every caste has distinctive customs and traditions. Moreover, gradations exist between various strata of Untouchables, and a large gray area of "backward castes" provides a buffer between them and the upper castes—groups such as the washermen, the barbers, the carpenters, the basket-weavers, the makers of musical instruments, and others who are not usually regarded as Untouchables but who do not belong to the "twice-born" upper castes. It is not easy to decide, then, whether or not one ought to conceive Untouchables as composing a separate society defined along socioeconomic class lines. My own observation is that if one must choose between two extremes, it is more accurate to portray Untouchables as culturally and economically separate than to depict them as part of a larger, homogeneous continuum. But neither characterization is wholly inaccurate.

What really matters, however, is how Untouchables themselves see these things, and they tend sometimes to veer toward one position, sometimes toward the other. They are uncertain whether ultimately they should regard themselves as separate from, or a part of, Hindu society. This indecision, historically, has been critical, for it has given a fluidity to their identity which could be exploited in the interests of social change. At times, of course, it made them simply the victims of those whose interests were furthered by one position or the other, but it also provided the fallow ground in which their own social movements could take root. Such movements provided frameworks of iden-

12. Regarding Scheduled Caste dialects, and their distinct difference from that of the upper castes, see John J. Gumperz, "Dialect Differences and Social Stratification in a North Indian Village," *American Anthropologist* 60 (1958); also "Religion and Social Communication in Village North India," *Journal of Asian Studies* 23 (June 1964). For separate channels of communication among the Scheduled Castes, see Robert J. Miller and Pramodh Kale, "The Burden on the Head Is Always There," in J. Michael Mahar, ed., *The Untouchables in Contemporary India* (Tucson: University of Arizona Press, 1972).

tity which could convince Untouchables either that they were acceptable units within the total caste structure or that they were collectively outcaste and therefore reliant upon their own resources. The more conciliar movements did the former, the more radical ones the latter. New social values were provided by new religions. And timing was always crucial: in certain moments certain issues have so confronted this uncertainty which Untouchables feel about their own identity as to transform it from a lingering inner tension to something potentially explosive.

2 The 1920s: A Time for Social Change

Opportunities for ambitious social change come to the oppressed classes only in rare moments in history, moments in which change seems feasible and support for some sort of change seems available. In the recent social history of the Punjab, the 1920s presented such a moment: it was then that the Ad Dharm and several other movements like it began to flourish. Changes in British governing policies in India after World War I sent reverberations through the Punjab, which shifted alignments and made new opportunities seem possible to Untouchables. In the cacophony of political realignments in the early 1920s it became clear to the lower castes that their numbers were a commodity of political value, and that political organization was an arena in which they could compete. Moreover, they found that the ideology of equality which was paramount in both British and nationalist positions could advance their growing political aspirations.

The lower caste leaders in the Punjab did not have to discover these matters by themselves. In the 1920s these issues were brought before them from two directions: the active organizing of Untouchable groups in other regions of India, and the communal politics and unrest within the Punjab. The former provided an internal incentive for Untouchable organization, and the latter provided an external arena for action. The momentum of other Untouchable activities across India encouraged the Ad Dharmis to organize, and the stalemate of communal politics in the Punjab made that organization opportune.

Untouchables began to form political and social organizations early in this century. The first independent Scheduled Caste political movements in India appeared to have been launched in 1910, when the All-India Depressed Classes Association and the All-India Depressed Classes Federation were established under the encouragement of the Bombay Presidency Social Reform Association.[1] Their initial purpose was to pressure the Indian National Congress (later to become the Congress party) to include the removal of untouchability as one of its main planks, and they succeeded in the 1917 meeting of the Congress at Calcutta.

Soon afterward, however, the political climate changed substantially. The Government of India Act, which took effect in 1919, provided explicitly for communal representation in Indian parliaments. This stimulated the formation of new Scheduled Caste political organizations, which aimed not only to secure benefits for Untouchables but also to organize them into coherent political blocks.

Such political organizing was not seen as favorable to the interests of the Congress party, and Untouchables at the time were aware that it was not. Rumors spread among politically active Untouchables that at the 1923 meeting of the Indian National Congress in Cocanada some sort of deal had transpired between Gandhi (who was in prison) and the Ali brothers (Mohamed, who that year was Congress president, and Shaukat, who then was Khilafat Conference president), in which the sixty million Indian Untouchables would be neatly divided between Hindu and Muslim religious communities for census purposes. There is no record that such a deal was discussed, much less formulated, at the 1923 Congress.[2] But in the memories of some old Scheduled Caste leaders, resentment against the alleged Ali deal

1. R. C. Majumdar, *Struggle for Freedom* (Bombay, 1969), p. 1001.
2. In fact, the Cocanada Congress, aside from being "perhaps the grandest Congress ever held," was uneventful, and the issue of Depressed Class allocations seems not to have arisen. (B. Pattabhi Sitaramayya, *The History of the Indian National Congress*, vol. 1 [1885–1935], pp. 261–262.)

played an important role in solidifying Scheduled Caste political unity.³ Ali deal or not, there is no doubt that there was a general concern about political identity among the Scheduled Castes throughout India during the early 1920s and a desire to create political organizations that would reflect the autonomy of the Scheduled Castes.

In South India, the Nadars successfully petitioned the government for a change of their caste name in the 1920 census,⁴ and there had been an Adi Dravida movement in Madras since at least 1918.⁵ M. C. Rajah, its leader and the chief spokesman of the Madras Untouchables in the legislative council, was the best known Untouchable in India at the time. The Adi Dravida movement seems to have been the first to formulate the concept that the Scheduled Castes were the original inhabitants of India, and from there, apparently, the idea spread north and lent its name to the Ad Dharm movement in the Punjab and the Adi Hindu movement in what is now Uttar Pradesh (U.P.).⁶

The leaders of the Ad Dharm, however, denied this. They regarded themselves as having been first, and supported their claim for copyright on the "Adi" term by argu-

3. Interview with Lala Mohan Lal, former secretary of the Harijan Sevak Sangh of Punjab, 1932–1947, Jullundur, May 1, 1971. Mangoo Ram remembers the Ali deal to partition Scheduled Castes as being in 1922, reported in the *Nava Yug* newspaper in Ludhiana. "Reading this, we felt strongly that our *biradari* [brotherhood] needed a leader to speak for our rights and our *qaum* [community]; so I started the Ad Dharm." (Mangoo Ram, April 17, 1971, interview.)

4. Robert L. Hardgrave, Jr., *The Nadars of Tamilnad: The Political Culture of a Community in Change* (Berkeley and Los Angeles: University of California Press, 1969), p. 181.

5. British references to "Adi Dravidas" appeared during the Montague-Chelmsford tour, 1918.

6. There is a brief history of the *Adi Hindu Andolan* in a biography of the movement's leader, Swami Achutanand (Chandrika Prasad Jigyasu, *Shri 108 Svami Achhutananadji Harihar,* Lucknau: Hindu Samaj Sudhar Karyalay, 1960). According to Owen Lynch, the Swami also preached briefly in Agra, where "he was driven, some say stoned, out of Agra by the leaders of the Jatav-Kshatriya movement because of his radical doctrines" (Owen Lynch, *Politics of Untouchability: Social Mobility and Social Change in a City of India* [New York, 1969], p. 76).

ing that "Adi" is a word commonly in use only in North India, as in the title of the Sikh scriptures, the Adi Granth, from which the leaders claimed they borrowed the term. Nonetheless, there is no evidence that the term "Adi" was used by Punjab Scheduled Castes before 1925, and there is evidence of its usage in Madras in 1915 and earlier by Pandit Aiyodhidas, also a southerner, who had founded the Paraiyan Mahajana Sabha in 1895.[7]

Whether the northern movements were in contact with the Adi Dravidas and drew their inspiration from the South cannot be definitely said. What is clear, however, is that the Adi Hindus of U.P. were in contact with the Ad Dharm of Punjab. The leader of the Adi Hindu movement, Swami Achutanand, called a meeting in Delhi in early 1926, which some of the Punjab people attended.[8] Achutanand came from Kanpur, where with several other Scheduled Caste leaders he had published a small newspaper in Hindi entitled *Adi Hindu*.[9] Apparently the purpose of the meeting was to bring some unity among Scheduled Caste activists in Uttar Pradesh, Delhi, and the Punjab.[10]

The meeting displayed a certain amount of agreement regarding the need for a Scheduled Caste organizational identity separate from the upper castes, and some attempt was made to forge a united front. But there was disagreement

---

7. M. R. and S. Barnett, "Contemporary Peasant and Postpeasant Alternatives in South India," *Annals of the New York Academy of Sciences* 220, March 11, 1974.

8. The fact of the meeting is attested by Mangoo Ram (April 11, 1971, interview), Swami Shudranand (May 15, 1971, interview), Sohan Lal Shastri (interview in Delhi, June 25, 1971), Principal Ram Das, Dayanand Salvation Mission (interview in Hoshiarpur, April 18, 1971), and Gurvanta Singh, vice-president, Punjab Congress party (interview in Jullundur, May 9, 1971).

9. I am told that Achutanand's newspaper was literally small—it would fit in the palm of one hand. Other leaders of the Adi Hindu movement are identified in a deputation to the Simon Commission in Lucknow, December 6, 1928 (Great Britain, Indian Statutory Commission, *Selections from Memoranda and Oral Evidence by Non-Officials*, vol. 16, part 1 [London: H.M. Stationary Office, 1930]).

10. Interview with Mangoo Ram, founder-leader of the Ad Dharm movement, Garhshankar, April 17, 1971.

over the name of the movement and the significance behind it. According to the Ad Dharm leaders, Achutanand wanted the "Adi" movements all over India to unite behind the same name, whereas the Punjabis thought they should first attain regional strength under separate names, and then unite. In addition, the Punjab delegates to the meeting objected to using a name that would include the word "Hindu." Thus the names remained separate, as did their organizations, although the movements continued to maintain contact through meetings in Kanpur and Lucknow in 1927 and 1929.

The fact that a large number of "Adi" movements appeared at the same time is no reason to suppose that they were orchestrated by a central command. The simultaneity is more simply explained by the similarity of political and social issues which pertained throughout India at the time. Except for borrowing the name and sharing a similarity of purpose, each of the movements had only the most tangential organizational relationship to its "Adi" counterparts. India is not only vast but diverse, and the diversity is perhaps most acute among the lowest classes, who have little opportunity to create a national leadership elite. Thus M. C. Rajah, Dr. Ambedkar, and other national spokesmen for the lower castes based their support upon regional coalitions, just as Gandhi had. Each movement constituted one block in that base upon which lower caste claims were made nationally during the 1920s, the 1930s, and later.

But each of the regional movements also responded to regional issues as well as to national ones—often more acutely, in fact—and the peculiar situation of the Punjab made the movement there distinctly different from its sister organizations in other parts of India. One of these distinctive features had to do with the presence of the Hindu reform movement, the Arya Samaj. As members of the lower castes in the Punjab seized on Christianity as a means for creating a mass movement, the Hindus associated with the Arya Samaj began to fear that their own position would be significantly weakened. The Untouchables had been considered nominally Hindu by British census-takers. If they declared themselves Christian instead, the political leverage of the Arya Samaj, as spokesman for the Hindus, would be threatened. Because Hindus, hemmed in by Muslims and Sikhs, do not enjoy the easy majority in the Punjab that they do in other parts of India, this was a considerable threat, and the Arya Samaj took action.

By 1900 it had developed efficient procedures for *shuddhi*, a process of purification (as the name literally implies) or reconversion by means of which it intended to bring into Hindu acceptability those members of the lower castes who had been lured into the orbit of Islam and Christianity. By 1910, over 36,000 Meghs (a relatively high status Scheduled Caste) from the Sialkot area had become Arya Samajis.[11] At about the same time the Arya Samaj sponsored several Arya-affiliated organizations specifically concerned with the uplift of Scheduled Caste welfare. And in addition to the conversions and the welfare organizations, large numbers of Scheduled Caste young people began to attend Arya Samaj schools. The rapid growth of a network of intercaste D.A.V. (Dayanand Anglo-Vedic) colleges and high schools around the turn of the century provided a means for widening Arya Samaj influence among the Scheduled Castes. These schools, like Christian and government institutions established at the time, also had the effect of creating a new generation of educated Scheduled Caste youth, and there was no guarantee that they would remain favorable to the Samaj.

The Arya Samaj and the Christian church were not the only competitors for lower caste allegiance: in the three-way struggle for status and influence among Hindus, Muslims, and Sikhs the latter two also made their bids. In a famous incident in 1900, Sikhs rebelled at the Arya Samaj's practice of publicly shaving lower caste Sikhs and offering them *shuddhi*.[12] The Sikhs had just begun to reaffirm that

11. Kenneth W. Jones, *Arya Dharm, Hindu Consciousness in 19th Century Punjab* (Berkeley and Los Angeles: University of California Press, 1976), p. 212.
12. See Kenneth W. Jones, "Ham Hindu Nahin: Arya-Sikh Relations, 1877–1905," *Journal of Asian Studies* 32, no. 3 (May 1973).

they were "not Hindus,"[13] and were developing their own Singh Sabha.[14] This created an added dilemma for the Scheduled Castes, who had to decide not only whether to join an upper caste religious organization, but also whether it should be Hindu or Sikh. Some members of the Sikh Khalsa Diwan tried to create their own "depressed class movement" to encourage Scheduled Caste support,[15] and there were organized demands for *gurdwara* reform laws that would permit them unquestioned entrance to Sikh places of worship. Muslims were also active through the originally syncretist and mystical Ahmadiyya movement, which in the early 1900s vied increasingly with the Aryas and Sikhs in supporting the demands of Scheduled Castes.[16] The appearance of the Congress in the Punjab introduced yet another political force, and it too was eager to claim Scheduled Caste support.[17]

The Scheduled Castes were essentially bystanders in the competition among upper caste communal groups, but their considerable numbers were necessary to support the rival claims of these organizations. And as their allegiance was courted, their identities came into question. Previously no one had wondered about the religious preferences of the lowest castes; suddenly, it seemed that every group wanted to claim them as its own. Thus the Scheduled Castes were

13. Sardar Kahan Singh, *Ham Hindu Nahin*, Khalsa Press, Amritsar, 1899. The pamphlet was in reaction to the Arya Samaj insistence that Sikhs were Hindus (see Lala Thakar Das, *Sikh Hindu Hain*, Khatri Press, Hoshiarpur, 1899).

14. Before 1900, the Sabha worked closely with the Arya Samaj. See chapter 9 of Khushwant Singh, *History of the Sikhs*, vol. 2 (Princeton, 1966).

15. N. G. Barrier, *The Sikhs and Their Literature* (Delhi, 1970), p. xxxii.

16. The Ahmadiyyas did not solicit Scheduled Caste membership, however. See J. C. Archer, *The Sikhs in Relation to Hindus, Muslims, Christians and Ahmadiyyas* (Princeton, 1946); and Spencer Lavan, *The Ahmadiyah Movement: A History and Perspective* (Delhi, 1974).

17. The argument has been made that the appeal by the Congress and Gandhi for the abolition of untouchability was made in part to gain the numerical support of the Scheduled Castes. See R. C. Majumdar, *Struggle for Freedom* (Bombay, 1969), p. 999.

caught in the cognitive confusion of competing world views, an incendiary situation which frequently had spawned new social movements in other parts of the world.[18]

The British government exacerbated this competition among communal groups by holding out communal rewards, such as allotments to legislative councils, and by enacting prejudicial legislation. An example of the latter was the Land Alienation Act of 1900,[19] which limited the right to own land to a set list of agricultural castes. The object was reasonable—to prevent Hindu moneylenders from unjustly taking over large portions of farmland—but the effect was to enhance the wealth and status of many Muslim landowners, and to create massive dissension within an influential class of Hindus and Sikhs (and among a few Untouchables as well, who were also debarred from land ownership).[20] In 1909, the British government's Indian Councils Act (the so-called Morley-Minto Reforms) prepared the theater for further political competition in the Punjab by establishing provincial legislative councils with representation based on communal affiliations. The British did not invent communalism, of course, but nothing served better to reinforce communal politics than the principle of communal representation.[21] It was extended even further by the Government of India Act of 1919, which established the pattern of dyarchy (concomitant British and local rule) and stipulated that Indian representation be apportioned communally in accordance with the number of Sikhs, Hin-

18. The Mormons, for example, had their origins in an area of upstate New York called the "burned-over district" because of successive waves of revivals.

19. A discussion of the controversy in the Punjab surrounding the Land Alienation Act is in N. G. Barrier, "Punjab Politics and the Disturbances of 1907," Ph.D. dissertation, Department of History, Duke University, 1966. See also N. G. Barrier, *Punjab Alienation of Land Bill of 1900* (Durham, N.C., 1965).

20. Untouchables were excluded from owning land because they were not traditionally landowning, and also because they were sometimes used as foils for moneylenders, who would buy land through them.

21. See N. G. Barrier, "The Punjab Government and Communal Politics, 1870–1908," *Journal of Asian Studies* 27, no. 3 (May 1968).

dus, Muslims, and other communal groups to be found in the population at large.[22] The way in which one divided up the Scheduled Caste population under those headings, then, became a sensitive and critical matter.

The first provincial elections in the Punjab, in 1920, indicated two things to the Scheduled Castes. First, they learned that by virtue of sheer numbers, Muslims had a preponderance of electoral power; this made them potential allies for Scheduled Caste support. Second, they became aware that the Scheduled Castes—if unified—could use their numbers as a bargaining leverage among the political forces. According to some memories, one of the most critical issues at the time of the founding of the Ad Dharm was precisely that, the need for political mobilization of the Scheduled Castes.[23]

At the same time the turn toward nationalism had a direct effect on the government's relations with the lower castes. In the Punjab, as elsewhere, the government began to feel increasingly on the defensive in the face of a rising nationalist sentiment among the urban educated classes. Despite the impact of the massacre at Jallianwalabagh in Amritsar in 1919, the Congress was never overwhelmingly successful in mobilizing such sentiment, but the Arya Samaj did better—and managed to enlist the support of its lower caste members in doing so. Another force was the militant Gadar party, which was composed mostly of overseas Punjabis in the United States, but had made some attempts to organize in the Punjab.[24] Like the other nationalist movements, however, Gadar was almost exclu-

22. The categories of constituencies in 1921 were as follows: Mohammedan (Urban and Rural), non-Mohammedan (Urban and Rural), European, Sikh, Indian Christian, and Anglo-Christian.

23. Mangoo Ram, April 17, 1971, and Swami Shudranand, May 15, 1971, interviews. The Swami said, "We organized to fight elections since the Hindus and Muslims had their own parties and communal representation."

24. The Gadar party, which was most active from 1913 to 1918, had its international headquarters in San Francisco. For further information about this quixotic movement and the tragic attempt to return to the Punjab to foment revolution in 1915, see L. R. Mathur, *Indian Revolutionary Movement in the U.S.A.* (Delhi, 1970), and my articles,

sively upper caste,[25] and the lower castes appeared to have nothing more to gain by joining it than they had by making common cause with other nationalist movements. The government, by contrast, had a lot to gain by insuring that Untouchables did not join the nationalist cause. Constituting 10 to 25 percent of the population, they could have given a considerable impetus to the nationalist movements if they had supported them. It was in the government's best interest, therefore, to pacify the lower castes rather than do anything that would encourage them to join the nationalist forces. Their demands, after all, were modest and their loyalty was useful in maintaining the status quo.

In the opening years of the 1920s, the political atmosphere in the Punjab was charged with activity and change. Gadar cadres were still active in the villages, and in 1923 a new group of Sikh terrorists, the Babbar Akalis, began a series of violent attacks against the British in the central districts. The Congress noncooperation movement had begun, and Gandhi's tour of the Punjab in 1921 received enthusiastic crowds. The nationalist newspapers, the *Punjabee* and the *Tribune,* nurtured a growing nationalist educated elite. With the innovation of provincial elections in 1920 emerged the Unionist party, spokesman of Muslim landed interests, and the Sikh political party, the Akali Dal. And at the same time, the other communal organizations continued to solidify their organizational resources: Christianity was entering its last phase of mass expansion, and the Hindus' Arya Samaj turned its attention increasingly to the problems of numbers, the census, and elections for the legislative councils. It was a time for political movement generally, and it was especially ripe for political movement within the poorest classes.

Marginal groups have the opportunity to act meaningfully only when the dominant structures of society are

---

"Ghadar Sources: Research on Punjabi Revolutionaries in America," in Harbans Singh and N. Gerald Barrier, eds., *Punjab Past and Present: Essays in Honour of Dr. Ganda Singh* (Patiala, 1976), and "The Ghadar Syndrome: Immigrant Sikhs and Nationalist Pride" (Berkeley, 1979).

25. With the sole exception of Mangoo Ram (see Appendix A to this book, "The Early Life of Mangoo Ram").

under stress and change is possible. In the Punjab in the 1920s, upper caste communal groups were occupied with internal restructuring and with an intense competition among themselves which was further exacerbated by innovations in the political and electoral realm. Yet at the same time these groups provided models of corporate identity, and their organizations and educational institutions trained new leadership for the Scheduled Castes. And the government, defensive in a time of rising anti-British sentiment, appeared vulnerable to new demands and alliances from the poor. It is impossible to understand how the Ad Dharm and other movements like it were launched without appreciating the intensity of this turmoil. But these factors, external to the Untouchable community, should not obscure the importance of another element: a new social consciousness which was emerging among Untouchables themselves throughout the subcontinent, which a small but articulate group of Ad Dharm activists tapped in the Punjab.

PART II The Rise of Ad Dharm

3 The Movement and Mangoo Ram

In the early 1920s a handful of educated young Untouchable activists who had been meeting together in Jullundur began serious discussions about developing a circle of communication and political strength. The three key leaders were Vasant Rai, Thakar Chand, and a person who called himself Swami Shudranand.[1] They shared several characteristics in common aside from their youth and their education: their caste was Chamar, they were financially secure, many had been associated with the Arya Samaj, and they came from the same geographical area. All of them came from rural areas of central Punjab—districts Jullundur and Hoshiarpur, and the princely state of Kapurthala. This area is characterized by fairly small land holdings, a large number of Untouchables, and an almost even sectioning of the pre-partition population among Muslims, Sikhs, upper caste Hindus, and members of the lower castes.[2]

1. All of these leaders have used other names. Swami Shudranand's original name was Shiv Charan, according to Principal Ram Das, a Scheduled Caste leader in the Arya Samaj, who has known him since the early 1920s (interview with Principal Ram Das, Hoshiarpur, April 18, 1971). Vasant changed his name from Singh to Rai in order to disassociate himself from the Sikhs (interview with Swami Shudranand, Jullundur, June 10, 1971); he was also known as Basant, because of the usual transposition of v's to b's in the Panjabi language. Thakar Chand is known also as Thakar Das (interview with Sadhu Ram, New Delhi, June 24, 1971, and November 7, 1973; interview with Sant Ram, M.L.A., Jullundur Municipal Hospital, June 12, 1971).
2. Throughout pre-independence Punjab, Muslims had predominated, with Hindus and Sikhs, in that order, as the minority communities; the equality among the communities in the central districts

Most of the Indian immigrants to the United States and England originated from this area, and it was here that the Gadar party had its Punjab base.

The early Ad Dharm activists, unlike most of their caste fellows, were not field laborers. Some had land, or at least cultivating rights, but the Land Alienation Act of 1900 had excluded them from actual land ownership, a fact that made little difference in most cases, since village social pressure prevented them from owning a large amount of land even if they had the money to purchase it.

More important was their involvement in business, especially ventures related to the traditional caste occupation, leatherworking.[3] Swami Shudranand's father had come from the nearby town of Phagwara to set up a large bootmaking operation in Jullundur, where the British army cantonment had created a great market for boots and army shoes. The leather trade also attracted the families of the other early Ad Dharm leaders. The trade in raw skins suddenly became profitable, not only because of British army demand, but also because of the development of the leather-processing industry in India and an increased export market abroad. According to a 1911 government report, the growth of the skin trade had been "phenomenal":

> Only 6,482 persons lived by this trade in 1901, but as many as 29,762 now [1911] belong to the profession [skin trading]. A great impetus has been given to the export of raw hides by the imposition of heavy duties in European countries on tanned leather, while uncured skins are exempt from taxation. An idea of the way in which raw hides, etc., are being drained off

---

was a peculiarity in that respect. A further discussion of the significance of demography in the development of the new religious movements will be found in chapter 7.

3. During the first decades of this century, many of the Hindu castes traditionally involved in small business began developing factories in the cities, thus opening the business opportunities in small towns to the Scheduled Castes (*Punjab District Gazeteer*, vol. 9 (1935), part B, pp. cix–cxxii). The leather business is especially appropriate for the Chamars, since they are traditionally leatherworkers; hides are considered ritually polluting for the upper castes.

can be formed by a visit, at any time of the year, to the goods office of any of the larger railway stations in the Punjab province.[4]

The new-found wealth gave some Scheduled Caste men the mobility and leisure to be involved in organizational matters, and made them relatively independent of traditional economic and social ties.

With monetary success came education. The early Ad Dharm leaders were not all well educated, but at least they were literate, which put them in the upper 99.5 percentile of their caste.[5] At least three had become teachers in secondary schools.[6] Others had primary and secondary education, and a few had completed high school.

Most of the schools which the early Ad Dharm activists had attended were sponsored by the Arya Samaj. Swami Shudranand, after attending an Arya Samaj high school in Jullundur in 1914, became a missionary for the organization.[7] Other early Ad Dharm leaders also had affiliations with the Aryas. Thakar Das was called Pandit because of

4. *Punjab Census Reports,* 1911, chap. 12, p. 515. The report also remarks that the trade was "mostly in the hands of Khojas," a higher caste group who hired Chamars to do the actual handling of the hides; but a large number of Scheduled Caste merchants traded in leather as well. The only income tax assessed among Punjabi Chamars in 1911 was for those involved in trade (1911 *Punjab Census,* chap. 12, subsidiary table 12, p. 553). A European ban on the import of finished leather also favored Scheduled Caste traders; since only raw pelts were being shipped, the trade was considered offensive to many upper caste merchants (ibid., p. 502).

5. 1921 *Punjab Census,* chap. 8, p. 283.

6. Mangoo Ram, Sadhu Ram, and Gurvanta Singh. Vasant Rai and others used the honorific title "master" indicating they had been schoolmasters.

7. This is according to Mangoo Ram (interview at Garhshankar, April 17, 1971), Ram Das (April 18, 1971, interview), who claims that Shudranand was in charge of the Aryas' Hoshiarpur mission to the Scheduled Castes, and Sadhu Ram, M.P. (interview at New Delhi, June 24, 1971). Swami Shudranand denies that he was an Arya Samaj preacher (Swami Shudranand, June 10, 1971, interview). He claims that he was in contact with the Arya Samaj only until graduating from high school, and that it was his father who was a devotee of Dayanand. Moreover, Swami Shudranand denies that any of the early Ad Dharm leaders had anything to do with the Arya Samaj.

his association with them, and Vasant Singh had worked with the Arya Samaj as a teacher before taking up with the Samaj's orthodox Hindu opposition, the Sanatan Dharm. The Samaj provided an organizational model for a new social group to emulate, and for the Ad Dharm leaders it was initially something even more: it was the maternal context in which their movement was conceived, and from which it grew.

The Arya Samaj was first established far from the Punjab, in Bombay in 1875. It founder, Swami Dayananda Saraswati, had discovered in the Vedic writings of his ancient Aryan forebears some very modern social values: among them were the opposition to idol worship, the diffusion of Brahmans' priestly authority, and the treatment of women and Untouchables with humane regard.

The ideology caught on especially in the Punjab, and there particularly among urban Hindus of mercantile castes, who found that it fit well into their own needs for a progressive ideology based on traditional cultural values. From its first beginnings in the Punjab, at Lahore on June 26, 1872, the movement expanded rapidly. It was the new Hinduism for a new middle class. The Samaj translated the Vedas into the vernacular, de-ritualized the Hindu ritual, and perhaps most important, established a network of schools on primary, secondary, and college levels.

Lower caste people were welcomed into the Samaj, in large part for ideological reasons: to demonstrate the relevance of Vedic scripture to all. For bright, ambitious youths from the lower castes, the Arya Samaj's educational institutions provided a way out and up, and its organizational structure offered a training ground for leadership. Those who did not work directly with the Arya Samaj or attend its schools were associated with its service organizations for the Scheduled Castes, such as the Dayanand Dalit Udhar at Hoshiarpur and the Achut Udhar at Lahore.

The Ad Dharm would later claim that these were controlled by the upper castes, but some of the Samaj-related societies operated with a measure of independence. Before the founding of Ad Dharm, a Scheduled Caste member of the Arya Samaj from Hoshiarpur, Sant Ram, B.A., had begun a new movement for Scheduled Caste equality within the Samaj. Sant Ram's organization, the Jat Path Thorak Mandal (Society for the Abolition of Caste), begun in 1922, was involved by 1924 in a major conflict with the Arya Samaj organization, and eventually left it.[8] The Jat Path Thorak Mandal was not a model for the Ad Dharm, since its urban, reform Hindu, intercaste composition was quite different from what the Ad Dharm would embrace. But the fact of previous Scheduled Caste rebellion within the Arya Samaj was an encouragement for lower caste Arya Samajis who wanted to create an alternative organization: in the Ad Dharm they created an Arya Samaj of their own. And because of their participation in Arya organizations a new generation of Scheduled Caste youth became aware of one another and of the potential that existed for a larger network of association among the educated and active of their castes.

The first organizational meeting of the Ad Dharm occurred in Jullundur in 1925.[9] Speeches by Swami Shudranand to Scheduled Castes in Jullundur that year had struck a responsive chord in Vasant Rai, Thakar Chand, and other young lower caste members. The Swami was said to have been persuaded by the Ahmadiyya Muslim sect that the Scheduled Castes were being duped by the Arya Samaj.[10] The Ahmadiyya sect had looked upon the Samaj's seduction of the Scheduled Castes with some dis-

---

8. The central theme of the Jat Path Thorak Mandal was that of intercaste marriages, an idea supported by an Arya Samaji formerly associated with the Gadar movement—Bhai Parmanand (interview with Sant Ram, B.A., village Purani Bassi, Hoshiarpur district, April 18, 1971). See also the autobiography of Sant Ram, B.A., *Mere Jiwan Anubhav,* and the publications of the Mandal, which are on file at the Sadhu Ashram, Una Road, Hoshiarpur. The Mandal's reliance on upper caste Arya Samajis was a persistent problem. Plans to have Dr. Ambedkar address the Mandal in 1936 had to be cancelled. Ambedkar's speech, never given, was printed as *The Annihilation of Caste* (Amritsar: Ambedkar School of Thoughts, 1936).

9. Swami Shudranand (interview, May 15, 1971) claims that the first meeting was in Valmiki Mohalla of Jullundur, in 1925; Sadhu Ram (June 24, 1971, interview) claims that it was "in Atma Ram's Scheduled Caste Mohalla" in Jullundur in 1925.

10. Sadhu Ram, ibid.

favor, assuming that it wanted to recruit lower caste members only for the purpose of swelling its political strength. When the Samaj launched its programs for uplifting the Scheduled Castes, ostensibly out of social concern, the Ahmadiyyas voiced their disdain in the form of a pamphlet entitled *Achut Udhar ki haqiqat, ya Hindu Aksari ke Mansube* (The Truth about Untouchable Uplift, or the Schemes of the Hindu Majority).[11] According to the memory of some old Ad Dharmis, this pamphlet had a considerable influence on Swami Shudranand and the other Untouchable leaders who had been connected with the Arya Samaj.[12] Swami Shudranand, they say, left the organization at that point and began working in Gurdaspur district on behalf of the Ahmadiyya sect—not as an Ahmadiyya convert but as a supporter of the Ahmadiyya critique of the Samaj.[13] It was in the course of that involvement, in 1925, that the Swami came to Jullundur and, so they say, made the speech that crystallized the sentiments of a number of disgruntled Scheduled Caste members of the Arya Samaj.

  11. I am grateful to Mr. L. R. Balley, Ambedkar Mission Society, Jullundur, for showing me a copy of the original Ahmadiyya pamphlet. He claimed that a later, revised edition mentioned the Ad Dharm favorably.
  12. Sadhu Ram (November 7, 1973, interview) claims "We read the Qadiani Ahmadiyya book and decided they were right; we then wanted to be like them, only not become Muslim." Sadhu Ram says that the title of the book was *Critical Condition of Untouchables,* by Fateh Mahmood Sayal.
  13. Sadhu Ram, ibid. Swami Shudranand himself denies any direct involvement with the Ahmadiyyas (Swami Shudranand, May 15, 1971, interview) but does admit that he later conducted negotiations with other Muslim leaders for support of the Ad Dharm Mandal. Ahmadiyya support is also mentioned in the *Report of the Ad Dharm Mandal, 1926–1931* (in Urdu), Jullundur, 1932 (hereafter *Ad Dharm Report*), p. 57. The only copy of this report which I have been able to locate is in the possession of Mr. L. R. Balley, Ambedkar Mission Society, Jullundur. An English translation, by Mark Juergensmeyer and Surjit Singh Goraya, appears as an appendix to Mark Juergensmeyer, "Political Hope: Social Movements of North India's Untouchables, 1900–1970," Ph.D. dissertation, University of California, Berkeley, 1974 (the pagination of the original manuscript is retained in the translated version, so page numbers for the *Report* refer to both the Urdu original and the English translation). Translated selections from the *Report* appear in Appendix B of this book.

There are reports of several meetings in addition to the Jullundur gathering during the same year.[14] One continued for four days and ended only when the upper castes in the area attacked the participants for utilizing the village pond. These meetings grew larger in the course of 1925 as new people were brought in.

There are two competing accounts of how the circle of leaders began to take shape. According to one, the original Jullundur group, centered around Vasant Rai, Swami Shudranand, and Thakar Chand, thought it would be valuable to include Mangoo Ram, the young Chamar who had recently returned from travels abroad and had become something of a folk hero.[15] According to this account, Vasant Rai went to see Mangoo Ram, who was teaching at an Arya Samaj school in Mugowal, but failed initially to persuade him to become involved in helping to form a new organization. Later, in 1926 or 1927, when a delegation went to Mangoo Ram, he agreed. The other account of the way in which the group came together places the initiative on Mangoo Ram.[16] He is said to have communicated with Shudranand and the others while they were still members of the Arya Samaj, and in a series of secret meetings in late 1925 and early 1926 spirited them away from the Samaj and into the new organization.

The differences between these two accounts, though they are symptomatic of divisions that have plagued the Ad Dharm throughout its history, are not crucial, for a consistent thread runs through them both. Both versions agree

14. Meetings were held in the Valmiki Mohalla of Shamchurassi, a small town midway between Jullundur city and Hoshiarpur city, another at Nurmahal, a town twenty miles south of Jullundur city, and other meetings at Pandori Nijeran, the Jullundur district village which was the home of Vasant Rai (Mangoo Ram, April 17 interview).

15. Swami Shudranand, May 15 interview.

16. Mangoo Ram has a quite different list of the original founding members attending that first meeting: Hazara Ram from Pilanwala, Hari Ram from Pandori Bibi, Sant Ram Azad from Hoshiarpur, and Mangoo Ram himself. These names, mentioned by Mangoo Ram in an interview (April 17, 1971), and also cited by Chanan Lal Manik in "Ad Dharm Bari" ("About Ad Dharm") in *Ravidas Patrika*, no. 46 (December 29, 1970), made up a "Hoshiarpur group" within the early leadership. In 1929 the Jullundur and Hoshiarpur groups broke apart, but Mangoo Ram and his Hoshiarpur allies retained the office in Jullundur.

that a young, educated, lower caste elite had discovered itself through the aegis of the Arya Samaj and in some way was beginning to rebel against it. They also underline, from their differing perspectives, the critical role of one man, Mangoo Ram, in the early years of the organization. Indeed, the founding meeting of the movement was held at his school in village Mugowal, district Hoshiarpur, on June 11–12, 1926.[17] There Mangoo Ram was elected president of the organization, a title he never relinquished throughout the movement's history. And to a large extent the Ad Dharm movement reflected his personal perception of the needs and moods of his people.

What kind of man was Mangoo Ram? Like his early colleagues in the movement, Mangoo Ram was bright, young, educated, and financially independent.[18] His father, like other ambitious Chamars at the time, had developed a flourishing trade in raw hides for the leather market. Still, despite their economic achievements, Mangoo Ram and his family had to bear the stigma of untouchability. When he attended elementary school near his home village in Hoshiarpur district, he was the only Untouchable in the class and was not allowed to sit inside the building. He was forced instead to squat in the doorway, but he managed even so to keep pace with his class fellows and eventually graduated with the second highest marks.

None of this distinguished Mangoo Ram from his Ad Dharm colleagues; such experiences were common. But one feature was not common: he spent much of his early life abroad. In 1909, when Mangoo Ram was twenty-three years old, his father arranged through a labor contractor to have Mangoo Ram work in America and send money home. Part of the passage over was paid by the contractor, who was to be reimbursed when the young man began working. The network of connections was tight: Mangoo Ram's employer in the orchards of central California was the brother of a local landlord back home in the Punjab. Mangoo Ram was sent first to Fresno, then to various work camps throughout the central part of California.

17. *Ad Dharm Report*, p. 10.
18. Sources of information about Mangoo Ram's life history are cited in n. 1 in Appendix A, "The Early Life of Mangoo Ram."

The critical phase of his sojourn in the West, however, came when he discovered the Gadar movement, a militant nationalist band of young expatriate Punjabis who lived in California, printed seditious literature against British rule in India, and plotted their own quixotic rebellion. Mangoo Ram became deeply involved, accompanying a boatload of weapons from San Diego to what the Gadarites hoped would be a revolutionary conflagration in India. This part of Mangoo Ram's story develops into a complicated web of capture, escape, and intrigue (see Appendix A, "The Early Life of Mangoo Ram"). Suffice it to say that by 1925 he had found his way back to the Punjab, a man of almost forty. His first action was to establish a school for lower caste children with the help of the Arya Samaj, but almost immediately he became involved in the new politics of the Ad Dharm. By 1926 his personal charisma had placed him firmly in control of the movement, and a new career for Mangoo Ram had begun.

Mangoo Ram's Gadar adventures make an exciting story, but one hesitates to leap to any conclusions about their significance for the Ad Dharm movement. After all, Mangoo was the only one among his peers who had experienced these things, and the strength of his leadership depended far less on their fascination than on his ability to speak to the condition of his fellow Punjabis. Still, the American hegira made Mangoo Ram special: the lower castes of the Punjab could boast very few heroes of national—let alone international—proportions. But perhaps more significant was the effect of the experience on Mangoo Ram himself. For sixteen years abroad he had enjoyed a life in which he was treated as an individual rather than as a Chamar. No matter that racial sentiment in America at that time excoriated the Indian community. Within that community there was a sense of equality that contrasted markedly with Punjabi society at home, and to an Untouchable that was of no small importance.

Even more important was the camaraderie of the Gadar movement itself: it provided a standard of fellowship and equality that Mangoo Ram believed to be applicable to all societies. His social expectations had risen definitively. As with Gandhi, Sri Aurobindo, and many others whose leadership in India was prefaced by years of living abroad, Mangoo Ram's expatriate experience had made him bold, impatient. Moreover, again like Gandhi, Mangoo Ram returned to his homeland in middle age, ready to begin a new career—and found none waiting. Social activism provided a natural compensation, and in that sphere he rose swiftly to leadership stature.

Mangoo Ram was a restless, even ambitious man, socially sensitive and politically astute. One would probably not describe him as religious, certainly not pious, and on the face of it there is something unlikely in his founding and leading a religious movement. In India, however, piety in the modern Christian sense—intense, interior devotion—is not the commanding feature for most persons' religious identities. Outward observance of religious customs matters much more. Mangoo Ram considered himself neither saint, avatar, nor guru; but despite his lack of pretense to religiosity he did fulfill a religious role. He was something of a broker, making religious symbols and ideas accessible to ordinary people. And into those symbols he packed all the insight, skill, and vision he had amassed in his revolutionary years of living abroad.

4 The Ideology of a Political Religion

Mangoo Ram and the early leaders of the Ad Dharm perceived their first task to be the creation of a new religion. In their initial meetings, even before they developed an organizational structure, they labored over a basic ideological theme upon which they could build a system of religious ideas and symbols. Its central motif was novel: the idea that Untouchables constitute a *qaum*,[1] a distinct religious community similar to those of Muslims, Hindus, and Sikhs, and that the *qaum* had existed from time immemorial.

The following statement, written during their first year, trumpets the basic manifesto:

> We are the original people of this country, and our religion is Ad Dharm. The Hindu *qaum* came from outside and enslaved us. When the original sound from the conch was sounded, all the brothers came together—chamar, chuhra, sainsi, bhanjre, bhil, all the Untouchables—to make their problems known. Brothers, there are seventy million of us listed as Hindus, separate us, and make us free. We trusted the Hindus, but they turned out to be traitors. Brothers, the time has come: wake up, the government is listening to our cries. Centuries have passed, but we were asleep, brothers. Look at the lines that Manu has writ-

---

1. This is an Urdu word derived from Persian and is sometimes translated as "nation," but more accurately as "a people" or "community." Frequently transliterated as *qaum*, it can also appear as *quom, quam, kaum,* or *kuom.*

ten, but he is a murderer. There was a time when we ruled India, brothers, and the land used to be ours. The Hindus came from Iran and destroyed our *qaum*. They became the owners, and then called us foreigners, disinheriting seventy million people. They turned us into nomads. They destroyed our history, brothers. The Hindus rewrote our history, brothers. There is hope from God [*bhagwan*] and help from the king. Send members to the councils and start the *qaum* anew, brothers. Come together to form a better life.[2]

This was a myth of power addressed to a people without power. It was intended to communicate the sense of strength that Mangoo Ram felt belonged to his caste fellows by right. As he explained, partly stating a fact, partly expressing a hope, "The Untouchables have three powers: communal pride [*qaumiat*], religion [*mazhab*], and organization [*majlis*]."[3]

The hope was that these powers could be fostered and sheltered through force of ideology. The Ad Dharm leaders endeavored to convince their followers that they were part of a great *qaum*, and not simply village Chamars, by projecting a mythical past. In so doing they borrowed from other "Adi" movements of the early 1920s the idea that Untouchables were the original people of India—a conception that would later be treated at some length by Dr. B. R. Ambedkar,[4] and one that may have some grounding in fact,

2. "Mugowal Zila Hoshiarpur de Ad Dharm Skul: Wadda Bhwari Diwan" (Mugowal, Hoshiarpur District, in the Ad Dharm School: Huge Public Meeting, a poster announcing the first Ad Dharm conference), Jullundur: Kishan Steam Press, 1927 (in Punjabi). English translation by Mark Juergensmeyer and Surjit Singh Goraya, in Juergensmeyer, "Political Hope," p. 633.

3. Mangoo Ram, Garhshankar, April 17, 1971; also cited in *Ad Dharm Report*, p. 3.

4. Dr. B. R. Ambedkar, *The Untouchables: Who Were They, and Why Did They Became [sic] Untouchables?* (The grammatical mistake in the title was undoubtedly the fault of the printer rather than the author.) See also B. R. Ambedkar, *The Shudras: Who They Were and How They Came to Be the Fourth Varna of the Indo-Aryan Society.*

as a number of arguments from textual studies and physical anthropology now suggest.[5]

The Ad Dharm version of that theory, however, was colorfully unique. Liberally seasoned with appeals for *qaum* unity, government support, caste uplift, and opposition to the Hindus, it professed not only the antiquity of the Untouchable *qaum* but also its superiority over the upper caste *qaums* who had later come on the scene. The early leaders of the Ad Dharm envisioned a prehistoric paradise, a place somewhere in North India where the original *(adi)* inhabitants of the subcontinent dwelt in amicable equality:

> In the beginning, when nature created human beings, there was no discrimination. There were no differences and no quarrels. In particular, there were no such concepts as high or low caste. God [*ishwar*] was meditating; all was in harmony.[6]

According to certain versions of the Ad Dharm mythology—details sometimes differed[7]—these primordial beings were ancestors not only of the Untouchables but of the upper castes as well, and progenitors not only of the inhabitants of India but of the citizens of much of the rest of the world. Some of these original people, it was claimed, early migrated to Europe where they became the Aryans, the same Aryans who would later invade India and become the higher castes. These Aryans were a vastly ignorant and boorish folk:

> These people were primitive. They lived in trees and caves, ate bark and leaves, and had no spiritual life.

---

5. See Sir Herbert Risley, *The People of India*, 2nd ed., edited by W. Crooke, London: Thacker and Co., 1915 (originally 1905), chap. 6, in which Risley summarizes the arguments of Ibbetson, Senart, Nesfield, and Dill, on the racial origins of caste.

6. *Ad Dharm Report*, p. 6.

7. The differences between the versions in the *Report*, the early posters, and the memories of the leaders concerned primarily whether the Adi people were ancestors of both higher and lower caste people or only of the Untouchables.

They lived as shepherds and hunters, and had no sense of communal identities [*qaum*].[8]

These unfortunate apostates contrasted in every respect with the group of people who remained behind and became the forerunners of all present-day Untouchables. The latter, the *adi* people, were renowned throughout the ancient world for the heights of civilization to which they rose on the plains of northern India:

> Peoples of the world considered our land as the crown of success, and paid tribute to us and our achievements. They respected and bowed down to our kings. There was no enemy, no foe, no fear of foreign invaders, and no signs of internal dissension . . . during this time of our great achievement.[9]

But then the Aryans came and destroyed it all, scattering and subjugating the original people:

> There were many wars—six hundred years of fighting—and then the Aryans finally defeated our ancestors, the local inhabitants. Our forefathers, the inhabitants of our glorious motherland, were pushed back into the jungle, and into the mountains. Some of them stayed and asked for mercy; they were enslaved.[10]

The similarities between this story and some archaeologists' suggestions about what happened to the pre-Aryan Harappan civilization in North India in 1700 B.C. are striking. The site of Harappa was discovered by Sir John Marshall in 1921 in Montgomery district of the Punjab, and speculations about India's racial origins were common in the news of the time. Perhaps it is only coincidence that the Ad Dharm and the other Adi movements were founded soon after that, but there is a curious justice to the fact that Lyallpur district, near the Harappa site, became one of the strongest bases of support for the Ad Dharm movement.

The Ad Dharm myth continued beyond the arrival of the Aryans. It reported that the original people (later Untouch-

8. *Ad Dharm Report*, p. 7.   9. Ibid.   10. Ibid.

ables) were subjugated with "so much cruelty and injustice" that they "forgot their own identity."[11] This was the crucial and tragic denouement of the myth of origins. From there the story paused only briefly to denounce Manu, the legendary codifier of Hindu law, before advancing to the present period. And at that point it depicted what was simply a continuation of the terrible events of the Aryan conquest, showing how the Aryans' modern descendants, the upper castes, persisted in subjugating those who had descended from the original inhabitants of India, the Untouchables. The only ameliorating agencies in that long sweep of time were those that came from outside India: the British and Mughul governments, both of which are said to have attempted to help the original people. And an oblique compliment is thrown in the direction of Christianity for having challenged the control of Aryan Hindus:

> Christianity tried to attract all communities [*qaum*] and especially the low castes, because the Untouchables are an orphaned people. . . . Swami Dayanand realized that Christianity was digging a hole in the foundation of Hinduism which would destroy the entire building.[12]

The whole account receives its sharpest political focus when it deals with Swami Dayanand and his Arya Samaj, which it portrays as history's most devious attempt to control the original people. The name itself should have warned the world of the organization's true intent, for Arya Samaj means literally "the society of Aryans." From the perspective of the Ad Dharm myth, the chief function of the Arya Samaj was to keep the Untouchables from realizing their true nature as an original *qaum*. The device of *shuddhi*, "purification," was seen, not as an invitation to equality, but as a means of keeping the Untouchable *qaum* securely within the Arya Samaj's grasp:

> The sole purpose [of the Arya Samaj] was to bring all of the Hindu organizations together so the Untouch-

11. Ibid.   12. Ibid., pp. 9–10.

ables would not leave their ranks. . . . [Members of the Arya Samaj] seduced thousands of Untouchables in the net of reconversion [*shuddhi*]. They conjured up all sorts of hypocritical arguments, saying that untouchability was over and there was no discrimination. The poor Untouchable was trapped again by the Hindu Aryan, just like falling into the clutches of elephants' teeth.[13]

But the myth supplied an inner identity as well, justifying the Ad Dharm as a *qaum*. Ad Dharm was not, it showed, the religion of a caste group, it was the religion of a people, and "we should distinguish among Hindus, Ad Dharmis, and the other *qaum* of India." [14] A number of critics of the Ad Dharm, including members of lower castes, have attacked this concept, feeling that to initiate a religion of Untouchables would simply buttress and perpetuate the concept of untouchability.[15] But for those in the Ad Dharm it was a matter of central concern to distinguish between the notion of caste and that of *qaum* religion, even if the latter drew attention inadvertently to the former. The Ad Dharm claimed a *qaum* identity precisely in order to undermine the notion of caste: as a *qaum* they would enter into society as equals. The Muslim, Sikh, and Hindu *qaums* may have been a quarrelsome lot, but these religious groups maintained a certain respect for one another. In building his *qaum*, furthermore, Mangoo Ram hoped to attract other constituencies than those comprising the Scheduled Castes.[16] One of the movement's reports, indeed, listed twenty Brahmans and two Jains among the membership.[17]

13. Ibid., p. 10.
14. Ibid., p. 38.
15. Interview with Prithvi Singh Azad, M.L.A., Kharar, Rupar district, Punjab, April 13, 1971; and Principal Ram Das, President of Dayanand Salvation Mission, Hoshiarpur, April 18, 1971.
16. Interview with Mangoo Ram, Garshankar, January 29, 1971. He emphasized that the Ad Dharm promoted humane virtues and social justice, and that in that sense it was a universal religion: "We call ourselves a *qaum* only if the others do."
17. *Ad Dharm Report*, p. 70.

To these basic ideas propounded in the myth of origin, the Ad Dharm leaders added other theological concepts. They adopted a nontheistic notion of divinity, one that was consistent with many of the beliefs of lower caste people: the role of God is played by Nature.

> Nature [*Qudrat ka Mela*] created human beings from the original source [*adi*] at the time that it created all beings in the earth. The knowledge of moral behavior [*karm-dharm*] was also given to them at that time by Nature. Nature made humans superior to animals. But among humans, all were equal. . . . Everyone believed in one *dharm* which Nature had given them through intellect and knowledge.[18]

Occasionally there is mention of God in a more formal sense: "God [*Ishwar*] was meditating; all was in harmony."[19] And Mangoo Ram made a practice of using the name *Adi Purkh* for the divine—literally "the Originator," or "the Original Being."[20] All these designations, although they are theistic terms, are impersonal in intent, reinforcing an emphasis that was congruent with the teachings of many of the medieval saints *(sants)* whose poetry saturates the early rhetoric of the Ad Dharm. There were frequent references to Kabir, whom many would regard as the greatest of these poet-saints, but it was Ravi Das, himself a Chamar, who became the particular patron of the Ad Dharm.

To many in the Punjab it may have appeared that this reverence for Ravi Das was part of an effort to create a sort of Sikhism for the lower castes, with Ravi Das playing a role like that of the Sikh gurus. In Hindu areas, by contrast, the praise of Ravi Das would have been understood as an attempt to mediate between Ad Dharm and the Hindu tradition. And some of those who became members of the movement may indeed have shared these perceptions. But to the leaders of the Ad Dharm, Ravi Das was neither of these things: they saw him as having preached a basic morality that was beyond the province of either Sikhism or Hinduism, the kind of universal vision of social

18. Ibid., p. 6.   19. Ibid.   20. Mangoo Ram, April 17, 1971.

virtue that made it possible for them to urge that "all Ad Dharmis should follow the rishis, the gurus, the bhagats, the mahatmas—all the great religious leaders. True worshippers of these saints will not believe in idol worship, the caste system, or superior and inferior practices."[21] On the other hand, the Ad Dharm was quite specific about what religious practices should not be included in their faith—namely, those of upper caste religions which denigrated the Scheduled Castes: "The granths and sastras which show Untouchables as slaves should be boycotted. To follow the teachings of such books is a mortal sin."[22]

The *satsang* ("worship services") of the Ad Dharm followed a pattern very much like those of the Sikhs: there were readings from the scriptures of the Ad Dharm gurus, a few hymns, some poetry, a homily, a silent meditation.[23] Like the Sikhs, the Ad Dharm intended to have its own scriptures, and for that purpose the writings of Ravi Das and other lower caste teachers began to be compiled. The project was never finished, but it is worthy of note that it did reach the stage where a title was chosen for the corpus, and that the title took the form of a phrase borrowed from the Arya Samaj: *Ad Prakash,* meaning "the Original Light." Another borrowing from the Arya Samaj may have been the Sanskrit phrase *soham,* which the Ad Dharm used as a *mantra* and employed as an insignia on its publications.[24]

The traditional veneration of Ravi Das and the other lower caste gurus on the part of the Scheduled Castes was taken over wholesale. Ad Dharm urged its followers to continue their devotion to the gurus, perhaps as a way of insuring that they would not easily be taken in by the beliefs and practices of the upper caste religions or by Christianity. The leaders of Ad Dharm exhorted the people to meditate regularly—every morning—and to worship one

21. *Ad Dharm Report,* p. 12.
22. Ibid.
23. Mangoo Ram, December 1, 1970.
24. The sacred phrase appears prominently at the top of all official newspapers, reports, and posters of the Ad Dharm Mandal. *Soham* is found in the Upanishads as a term meaning "I am that," and was interpreted by Ad Dharmis as implying the basic unity and equality of the world.

The Ideology

of the gurus: "to live without a guru is a sin."[25] They used the term "guru" to refer to living holy men from lower caste communities, as well as the legendary ones:

> A guru should be someone who knows the teachings of the previous masters with truthfulness and good knowledge. He should be able to distinguish between falsehood and truth. He should be able to bring peace and love within the community.[26]

Through the mediation of local, village gurus, all of the traditional lower caste gurus were to be honored, and were to be included within the new definition of the faith, the Ad Dharm.

Each of the major religious communities in the Punjab has its own greeting: "Salam" for the Muslims; "Sat Sri Akal" for the Sikhs, and "Namaste" for the Hindus. The early leaders of the Ad Dharm recognized that to be a *qaum* they needed a greeting too, and they adopted the salutation "Jai Guru Dev" ("victory to the divine guru") to which the response was "Dhan Guru Dev" ("blessed be the divine guru"). In this case the guru was understood as Ravi Das or one of the other lower caste saints.[27] More visible signs of spiritual identity were created as well. Just as Sikh Akalis were identified by their beards and blue turbans, Muslims by their distinctive turbans and caps, and Hindus by their dress and sacred threads, the Ad Dharm attached special significance to the color red and urged that it be widely worn:

> Red color is the symbol of the Ad Dharm. It is the color of the original inhabitants; the Aryans took it and prohibited Untouchables from wearing it. We request the government to allow us to wear red colors. In fact, we insist on it: red is our rightful color.[28]

---

25. *Ad Dharm Report*, p. 37.
26. Ibid. If one chose one's guru from history, it was assumed it would be Ravi Das, Rishi Valmiki, Gogapir, or other figures from lower-class traditions whom the Ad Dharm wished to claim within the framework of its faith.
27. Mangoo Ram, April 17, 1971.
28. *Ad Dharm Report*, p. 15.

In the areas of the Punjab that bordered on Rajasthan the wearing of red by Untouchables was understood as a matter of direct affrontery, since the upper caste Rajputs there considered red to be the color of their own military royalty; and this was true to a lesser extent in other regions as well. Near Rajasthan the Rajputs made a habit of beating lower caste villagers who dared to wear red.[29] A willingness to shed blood on behalf of the people, in fact, came to be remembered by some Ad Dharmis as the most basic meaning of the color.[30] Most frequently, red was worn in the form of turbans, but older men sometimes preferred to wear the more traditional white turbans instead, and they were allowed to don red armbands.[31] With red turbans, the sacred word *soham,* and their own special greeting, the Ad Dharm visibly demonstrated its characteristics as a separate movement and as a separate *qaum.*

Through several means, then, the Ad Dharm presented to its followers a vision of a world which both confirmed and transformed the rude experience of Untouchables. It gave meaningful shape to the situations in which they already lived by extolling the power of *qaumiat* and *mazhab,* projecting the notion of a separate community understood as a new religion. And in doing so it implied that a different sort of world was coming into being, for the separate identity so defined signaled hope for a society in which social groups carried no inherent mark of judgment and in which the benefits of progress could be shared by all. But the ideology of the Ad Dharm was only a vision; it remained the task of the Ad Dharm as an organization to present that vision as something real, to give it force and cogency. Indeed, the very enormity of the vision became for the organization a challenge, a burden difficult to bear.

29. Mangoo Ram, April 17, 1971. Mangoo Ram said he first learned about the restrictions on the use of red in Lahore, when a Muslim gave him a book on Rajasthani history.

30. Interview with Rullia Ram, former Ad Dharmi, and his son, J. C. Badhan, Jullundur, March 28, 1971.

31. Mangoo Ram, April 17, 1971.

5 Ideas into Action: The Organizational Character

The Ad Dharm as an organization was faced with a quite different task from that of the Arya Samaj and the Singh Sabha. Those groups clothed in an organizational form a communal identity that had already existed, at least to some extent, among urban Hindus and Sikhs before. The founders of Ad Dharm, by contrast, had to create that sense of identity as well as express it; like the Christian missionaries, they had to invent the very community they intended to lead. The collective identity of being Untouchables had existed long before the Ad Dharm came on the scene, of course, but the notion of Untouchables as a religious nation, a *qaum*, had not. Hence, at the same time that the leaders of the Ad Dharm were fostering a sense of intercaste identity and giving it voice, they were also required in some way to *be* that identity, emulating in their own organization a community they had as yet only envisioned—a challenge of Himalayan proportions—and it is vastly to their credit that for at least a few years it appeared as if the organization actually would succeed.

In November 1926, after the organizing conference at Mugowal, Mangoo Ram and his colleagues opened an office in Jullundur city, and the movement became a *mandal*, an established organization. The building that they constructed near the railroad tracks was large enough to include living quarters for the permanent staff: Mangoo Ram and his associate, Hari Ram, and the two persons in charge of the publications of the movement, Ram Chand and Sant

Ram Azad.[1] In addition, there were three permanent clerks: one for correspondence and mass mailings for the rallies, one to assist the executive committee, and one for keeping records and monitoring financial arrangements. There was also a managing committee of influential and moneyed members of the Scheduled Castes. Mangoo Ram was president of the executive committee, and initially the other members of the original circle were in leadership positions as well: Thakar Chand was the executive secretary, Hans Raj was vice-president, and Swami Shudranand and Vasant Rai were members of the executive committee.

The bureaucracy was intended to provide a structure of support for the activities and networks of communication that made the movement what it was. Yet the bureaucracy itself was extremely prominent in this fledgling movement—there was so little else—and its style communicated more vividly than anything else what the movement stood for.

The distance between the central staff of the movement, housed in Jullundur, and its village constituents was great: geography symbolized a broader reality. The movement's newspaper, the *Adi Danka* (Drum of the Adi People), which was printed in Urdu and read by a growing number of literate Untouchables, projected an image of progressive modernity.[2] By far the greater part of the movement's total constituency, however, still could not read, and depended on Ad Dharm representatives in the villages for their contact with the ideas emanating from Jullundur. These representatives were the human embodiment of the movement,

1. Mangoo Ram, April 17, 1971. Further information on the organization of the movement described in this chapter comes from this interview and from the *Ad Dharm Report*.

2. There is no complete run of the *Adi Danka* still available, to my knowledge. A few copies may be found among the memorabilia of Mangoo Ram. A former missionary to the Punjab, Clinton Loehlin, made a comparative sociological analysis of the contents of some of the issues in the 1930s, and found that like the Negro newspapers in the United States, the *Adi Danka* was a mixture of national news, reports on the progress of the community, and inspirational religious articles. The unpublished results of that study are with Dr. Loehlin in Marysville, California.

bridging the gap between the city elite and the village masses. Eight full-time workers traveled throughout the region and gave the major speeches. They were called *updeshak* ("missionaries"), and their subordinates were *pracharak* ("preachers"); both terms were borrowed from the Arya Samaj. The major local leaders—some fifty-seven of them, in every area of the Punjab—were given the title Honorary Pracharak. According to Mangoo Ram, there were also seventy-five part-time *pracharaks,* only thirty of whom were paid; the rest served as volunteers. When they were paid, the full-time *updeshaks* and *pracharaks* received thirty rupees per month. Many of them had been doing the same sort of work for the Arya Samaj, so the role came easily.

The advantage of this impressive organizational staff was that it enhanced Ad Dharm's image as a real entity, a coherent and progressive *qaum* capable of an effective organizational network. The problem with all of this bureaucracy was that it was, indeed, a bureaucracy: it was capable of sapping the movement's energy simply in the task of keeping itself alive and, in the process, of alienating the masses from a bureaucratized leadership that often operated at a considerable distance from them. Several features of the leadership style, however, were designed to ward off these potential dilemmas: the Jullundur office was simple and accessible, and the organizational network was sufficiently large to include many of the local leaders. Furthermore, Mangoo Ram and his cohorts spent much of their time traveling through the districts, and they made their decisions collectively.

This is a point worth looking at more closely. According to Mangoo Ram, decisions were never made unless they were approved unanimously. Pressed on this point, Mangoo Ram explained that he meant all of the followers, not simply the leaders, when he used the term "unanimous."[3] At the local level, he said, all of the local lower caste members who were interested would gather, debate, and decide a given issue. On the central level the leaders

3. Mangoo Ram, April 17, 1971.

would bring the important issues before mass rallies, and the decisions would be made by acclaim, with varying points of view argued by their separate defendants. This device for making decisions was faulted, however, by de facto decision-making on the part of the small leadership elite surrounding Mangoo Ram; and factional disputes arose in this group, as they would in any party clique. The illusion of collective decision-making was important, however, for developing a sense of immediacy, loyalty, and participation on the part of the followers. The masses at the rallies, in shouting their "ayes" and their "nays," felt the power of influencing decisions that would affect their lives and shape their social destinies.

Financial support, however, was another matter. Some critics of the movement suspected it was financially supported—and controlled—by the Muslims, the Christians, or the British government.[4] In the *Ad Dharm Report*, written in 1931, all of those accusations are called a "blatant lie."[5] Because of those rumors from outside and because of internal suspicions as well, the Ad Dharm Mandal kept close check on its books. The *Report* goes so far as to provide detailed information on such diverse and peripheral items as "food and kitchen," "musical instruments," "pictures," and "clothes for the *pracharaks.*"[6] It was tempting to think that money for such items as clothes and musical instruments must have come from the British or the Muslims, considering the poverty of most of the movement's members. Mangoo Ram claims, however, that most of it came from the masses themselves at the Ad Dharm rallies, where collections were taken and offering songs were sung. Some local units of the movement sent contributions of grain in addition, and the leader of each local unit was supposed to collect eleven rupees annually from every village group supporting the Ad Dharm.[7]

 4. Interview with Prithvi Singh Azad (former M.L.A.), Kharar, April 13, 1971; and Principal Ram Das, Hoshiarpur, April 18, 1971.
 5. *Ad Dharm Report*, p. 69.
 6. Ibid., pp. 72–79.
 7. Ibid., p. 78; Mangoo Ram, April 17, 1971; and Swami Shudranand, May 15, 1971. The *Report* claims that the movement also appealed to a variety of organizations for financial aid, but received a favorable re-

But there were large contributors who marred the otherwise popularist image of the movement's financial support, and the largest contributions came from outside the Punjab altogether. According to Mangoo Ram, Punjabi Chamars from New Zealand—especially one Dasandha Singh, originally from Dhada—gave over twelve thousand rupees in the initial years and an additional one to two thousand rupees annually thereafter.[8] Punjabi Chamars in Singapore and the United States also sent money. Another large source of financial support for the Ad Dharm movement was in India, but on the other side of the subcontinent: Calcutta. Punjabi Chamars who had gone there to seek their fortunes continued to have some influence on the community back home by contributing to the Ad Dharm. One Mali Ram is said to have sent almost forty thousand rupees.[9] The largest single contributor, however, was an occasional resident of Calcutta, Seth Kishan Das, originally from Jullundur, who provided the original headquarters for the Ad Dharm and whose continued support kept the movement going from year to year.[10] Seth Kishan Das had made his money in the leather market and continued to be active in Punjab politics even after setting up a branch of his business in Calcutta and spending much of his time there. Largely because of his influence, a special branch of the Ad Dharm movement was established in Calcutta. On the local committee in charge were several Chamars who were sufficiently proud of their new industrial positions to change their last names to Machinwala ("one skilled in

---

sponse only from the Jat Path Thorak Mandal. This money they refused because "it would not be fair to take money only from them" (*Ad Dharm Report,* p. 16).

8. Mangoo Ram, April 17, 1971. The concluding paragraph of the *Ad Dharm Report* is a message of appreciation to the New Zealand financial support (*Ad Dharm Report,* p. 80). W. H. McLeod of the University of Otago, New Zealand, informs me that Dasandha Singh was not an immigrant to New Zealand, but in all likelihood had settled in Fiji.

9. Receipts from Seth Kishan Das dating from this time are to be found among Mangoo Ram's collected memorabilia in Garhshankar. Seth Kishan Das also affirms that he was the major contributor to the Ad Dharm, and built the headquarters (interview with Seth Kishan Das, Jullundur, November 16, 1973).

10. *Ad Dharm Report,* p. 50.

machines"),[11] and they kept alive their Untouchable ties at home through the novel, progressive means that the Ad Dharm afforded.

It was important for the ideology of the movement that it appear inclusive, and although special efforts to involve members of higher castes from various parts of the Punjab almost inevitably met with failure, there was greater success in making the Ad Dharm a movement representing all major Untouchable groups. Almost all of the original leaders had been Chamar, but they quickly began to recruit members of the other large caste of Untouchables in the Punjab, the Chuhra (sweepers). In 1927, soon after the movement was founded, a special branch of the organization was established in Ferozepur district, the Balmik Ad Dharm Mahasabha Akalianwala, especially for the Chuhra caste, and several Chuhra leaders who were prominent in their own organizations (the Valmiki Sabhas) were temporarily a part of the Ad Dharm.[12] The rank and file of village Chuhras, however, identified with the Ad Dharm only in a few areas, despite the fact that the publications of the movement unwaveringly promoted ecumenism among all of the Untouchable castes.

Efforts were made to make the movement geographically inclusive too. A special branch of the Ad Dharm was established rather early in the mountain areas of Chamba and Kangra,[13] and though many of the Untouchables who joined the Ad Dharm there belonged to subcastes that were considered broadly Chamar, they were in fact quite different from Chamars living on the plains. The conditions under which the Scheduled Castes lived in the mountain areas were particularly oppressive, in part because of the

  11. Ibid.
  12. The names of Chuhra caste leaders Chunni Lal and Bakshi Lal have been mentioned by Ishwar Das Pawar as being Ad Dharmis (interview with Ishwar Das Pawar, Punjab Civil Service, retired, Chandigarh, April 9, 1971). Current Valmiki Sabha leaders claim that Mahatma Fakir Chand and Gandu Ram, Valmiki leaders, were also leaders in Ad Dharm (interview with R. L. Gill, president of the Valmiki Sabha, Charan Das group, Jullundur, May 28, 1971). Mangoo Ram denies that any of them were in the Ad Dharm inner circle (Mangoo Ram, April 17, 1971).
  13. *Ad Dharm Report*, p. 51.

isolation of the mountains and in part because one caste, the Rajputs, was dominant, and autocratically so. According to one account, when local Scheduled Caste leaders requested Mangoo Ram to hold rallies there, the upper caste Rajputs drove them out of the village, and they were forced to hide in the city of Pathankot to escape reprisals. Only after Mangoo Ram appealed to the government and the Rajputs were rebuked was it safe for the Ad Dharmis to return to their homes.

On the other side of the Punjab, in the extreme west, another special branch of the movement was established in 1931, both to solidify support in that area and to counteract factional disputes within the Ad Dharm movement.[14] In this area, Lyallpur district, there was increasing dissatisfaction with the Jullundur leadership, and some members were threatening to break away from the movement. Mangoo Ram reacted by establishing a youth organization, Ad Dharm Naujawan Santokh Sabha, in part to mollify the dissent. The very title, in fact, says as much: it was "the organization for the satisfaction of Ad Dharm youth." Seven other regional associations were established at the same time,[15] mostly in order to organize Untouchables for the census of 1931. One of these branches contributed to the geographical dispersion of the movement by being established in Benares, but this group, like the one in Calcutta, consisted of expatriate Punjabi Chamars from whom the Ad Dharm had a right to expect a modicum of support. Benares was the home city of Guru Ravi Das, so the Ad Dharm also had sentimental and ideological reasons for wanting to establish a base there.

The *Ad Dharm Report* of the same year claims for the movement an organizational structure linking together five hundred presidents of local chapters, each of them allegedly presiding over five hundred followers. As if to

14. Ibid., p. 52.
15. The branches were in Mahalpur, Hoshiarpur district (Mangoo Ram's home area); Wagah *tehsil*, Moga, Ferozepur district; the state of Bahawalpur; the city of Montgomery; Patekhera, *tehsil* Fazilka, Ferozepur district; Raikot, Ludhiana district; and the city of Benares, in distant U.P. (ibid, pp. 50–52).

prove to skeptics that the Ad Dharm did, indeed, have five hundred local leaders, Mangoo Ram listed each of them by name as participants in the central "administrative committee."[16] There is no way of determining how active these "local leaders" in fact were, but this organizational network, to the extent that it had existed, had both strengths and weaknesses. On the one hand, it was a large group, which tapped the local leadership structure of the village caste communities and in that sense represented a collective unity. On the other hand, this unity had definite limits, because most of the local presidents were from the Chamar caste, and the overwhelming number of them were from three districts: Hoshiarpur, Jullundur, and Lyallpur.

Even limited unity, however, was sufficient to justify Ad Dharm's claims to being a *qaum*, and for a few years after 1931 the network expanded and was carefully maintained. According to the Ad Dharm rules, the leaders of each local unit, in most cases the local elders of the caste, were reelected each year.[17] They received from the Ad Dharm organization a red armband with the word *pradhan* ("leader") in Punjabi written in black; leaders of particular eminence received sashes with the word written in gold.[18] The very fact of local leadership elections, red armbands, gold lettering, visits from the Jullundur command, and the persistent mailings (perhaps the only mail many of the local leaders ever received) meant a great deal to the villagers. These organizational trappings began to give reality to a long-standing dream: a society in which village Chamars would have a role in framing the decisions that affected their lives.

For most rural members of the Scheduled Castes who participated in it, the Ad Dharm was an entirely novel form of association. It presented a complete contrast to the closed and parochial society they had always known, and as such it stimulated hopes and generated allegiance. But it contained a fatal flaw. For, although its ideological vision spoke of a united *qaum*, the organizational reality gave

16. Ibid., pp. 16–30.
17. Mangoo Ram, April 17, 1971.
18. Ibid.

evidence of sharp differences between the movement's educated progressive leadership and the illiterate traditional following; between Jullundur, Hoshiarpur, and Lyallpur regions; and between Chamar and Chuhra castes. The organizational structure was firm enough to obscure these differences during the initial years, but in time the tensions increased, and the precarious unity showed signs of breakage.

6 Responses to the Arya Samaj: Factions in Change

One of the reasons for tension within the Ad Dharm was the persistent attraction of the Arya Samaj, which had earned the crowning opprobrium in the Ad Dharm's myth of origin not only because its ideology stood genuinely opposed to that of the Ad Dharm but because in certain respects its position was so similar. It was a contempt bred by familiarity, and there was always the threat that the closeness of the tie would swamp the Ad Dharm. The Samaj, after all, was also a reform movement, and one dedicated to returning Hinduism to a purer form in which the more unpleasant features of caste prejudice would be alleviated. This received practical expression in the Samaj's gestures of benevolence to the lower castes, including associations for their social uplift and in some cases invitations for them to participate in *shuddhi* so that they could be admitted to full membership in the Hindu fold.[1] To the leaders of the Ad Dharm this generosity seemed to be deviousness of the worst sort, seducing Untouchables into accepting a religious tradition that would always, whatever the guise, relegate them to a lower status.

Still, the Arya Samaj and its social uplift organizations continued to be models for important segments of the Ad Dharm movement. Because of the educational training that many of the early Ad Dharm leaders had received in Arya

1. For the development of the Arya Samaj in the Punjab in the years immediately preceding the establishment of the Ad Dharm, see Kenneth W. Jones, *Arya Dharm* (Berkeley, 1976).

Samaj schools, and the leadership training they had had in the various Arya-sponsored organizations, it is not surprising that many organizational aspects of the Ad Dharm were patterned after those of the Samaj. Moreover, the two movements actively competed on the village level to receive the support of the lower caste constituencies. And the Arya organizations lured away disaffected leaders of the Ad Dharm when there was disagreement in its ranks, offering alternative careers in social service and lower caste uplift. For individual Ad Dharmis the Arya Samaj was an opportunity as well as a threat, but to cast one's lot with the Samaj involved a reorientation more fundamental than many realized, a choice between two mutually opposed world views. One buttressed the Hindu hegemony, the other undercut it.

Four Arya Samaj social uplift organizations were especially threatening to the Ad Dharm movement: Patat Udhar, Antaj Udhar, Achut Udhar, and especially the Dayanand Dalat Udhar in Hoshiarpur.[2] These were the "false fronts" which Ad Dharm accused the Arya Samaj of using "to keep the foundations of the Hindu caste system together,"[3] and the Ad Dharm tried to undercut their influence by questioning the motives of their leaders:

> These organizations are run by high caste Hindus. They collect the money like beggars, but then spend it for themselves. They do not spend it for the Untouchables. Ninety-nine percent of the Untouchables do not even know the names of these organizations. But if you read their reports, they give exaggerated claims of their achievements. The truth is that these organizations are composed of selfish people.[4]

---

2. *Ad Dharm Report*, pp. 2, 10. These four Arya Samaj organizations are also listed by Mangoo Ram, April 17, 1971. Their names may be translated as "Uplift of the Untouchables," "Uplift of the Lowborn," "Untouchables' Uplift," and "Swami Dayanand's Uplift of the Oppressed," respectively.
3. *Ad Dharm Report*, p. 10.
4. Ibid., p. 55.

The Ad Dharm had no sympathy for expressions of guilt and regret on the part of the Samaj for the repression that the Scheduled Castes had endured, doubting their sincerity: "These high caste 'Untouchable' organizations . . . simply shed crocodile tears over the Untouchables."[5] The problem was, however, that to ordinary villagers this deception was not apparent, for in outward aspects the Ad Dharm and Arya Samaj movements appeared very similar indeed. Both held conferences and sent out *pracharaks;* they even championed much the same slogans for social reform.[6]

To the Ad Dharm, then, the Arya Samaj was a threat of the most serious proportions, and the Ad Dharm no less a danger for the Samaj. It insulted the Samajists' pride in social reform and assaulted their political aspirations by threatening to drain off much of the numerical support they needed to increase Hindu political power. Lower caste leaders involved in Arya Samaj organizations felt this most acutely: their personal influence would suffer a drastic blow if the Ad Dharm succeeded in wresting village support from their hands. But it was a general threat as well, challenging the possibility of a reformed Hindu society. As one lower caste leader in the Arya Samaj explained,

> We in the Arya Samaj actively opposed the Ad Dharm and tried to make it fail. It stood for everything we disliked—separating our people from the Hindu society. A good deal of Arya Samaj energy was spent in fighting the Ad Dharm and preaching against them. Every newspaper and preacher of the Arya Samaj carried the fight against them.[7]

In areas where the Ad Dharm had begun to make progress the Arya Samaj movements increased their activity, and in areas dominated by Sikhs, there was a parallel response: Sikh organizations similar to the Arya Samaj movements made appeals to the villagers to dissuade them

5. Ibid., p. 2.
6. Principal Ram Das, April 18, 1961.
7. Ibid.

from falling under the influence of Mangoo Ram and his "Achut qaum." The following reminiscence about the whole situation comes from an Ad Dharmi who had been active in Lyallpur district:

> During the first three years, we made much progress and gathered a large following. But then other *qaum* began obstructing us. Christians sent Bibles to the houses of our people and tried to lure us with education; the Arya Samaj wanted to "purify" us; and the Sikhs attempted *amrit prachar* [preaching Sikh baptism].
>
> The Hindu *qaum* tried to get back at us, and the Arya Samaj spread their messages through our neighborhoods. They had adult education programs at night, and taught us Hindi and the alphabet, and gave us writing boards and inkpots. Sikhs started teaching us Gurmukhi. The upper castes, to woo us, and because they were afraid of the rise of Ad Dharm, suddenly started drinking water from our hands, and opened their schools to us.[8]

Among those lower caste members of the Arya Samaj who had left to join the Ad Dharm there were many who maintained a certain sympathy for the Samaj. After all, it had done much to bring enlightenment and egalitarian beliefs to urban and backward areas.[9] And to a significant number of Ad Dharm leaders in the late 1920s Mangoo Ram's ideology seemed too strident, since its extreme emphasis on separatism cut off possibilities for meaningful compromise and coalition with the upper castes. Such people recognized that the Arya Samaj comprised the liberal and progressive elements within Hindu society, and

---

8. Chanan Lal Manik, "Adi Dharm Bari" ("About Ad Dharm"), in *Ravidas Patrika* 2, no. 1 (January 5, 1971).

9. Appreciation for the Arya Samaj has been noted by several former Ad Dharm leaders, including Sadhu Ram, M.P., June 24, 1971; Swami Shudranand, March 15, 1971; and Ishwar Das Pawar, interview at Chandigarh, April 9, 1971 (Pawar was not an official leader because of his position with the government service).

they feared that if the Ad Dharm could not get along with them, they probably could not get along with anyone else. Indeed, they challenged the ultimate theoretical cogency of Mangoo Ram's position, denying that the Ad Dharm was intended as a separate religion and seeing in it only a means to an end:

> The purpose of Ad Dharm was simply to give us some organization. We were not in Hindu culture previously, so we had to form our own movement to proclaim ourselves a part of Hinduism, so that we could get back into Hindu society.[10]

The dissatisfaction which these Ad Dharmis felt was quickly exacerbated by another facet of Mangoo Ram's leadership: his indifference to the nationalist cause. Just at the time when the Arya Samaj and other upper caste Hindu and Sikh leaders were growing more militantly nationalistic, the Ad Dharm was entering into a significant collusion with the government. As early as 1928 it was sending formal delegations.[11] This loyalism deepened the rift between the Ad Dharm and the Arya Samaj and put considerable pressure on Ad Dharm leaders, who felt themselves being uncomfortably separated from the rest of the Indian population in the Punjab. As a result, a number of them were lured back into the Arya Samaj; this in turn alarmed Mangoo Ram:

> They [the Arya Samaj reform movements] have seduced and bribed some of our preachers [*pracharaks*]. But the Ad Dharm Mandal's roots go too deeply; we cannot be shaken by this.[12]

The issue came to a head around 1929, when many of the Ad Dharm leaders returned to the Arya Samaj movements. The exodus included founding members of the movement, such as Thakar Chand, Vasant Rai, and Swami Shudranand. According to Mangoo Ram, they left, not because

10. Sant Ram, M.L.A., June 12, 1971.
11. Mangoo Ram, April 17, 1971.
12. *Ad Dharm Report*, p. 3.

of disagreements over strategy, but rather because of moral indiscretions:

> Thakar Chand, . . . because of his misdoings and corruption, was removed [from the position of general secretary], and the *qaum* and the *baradari* boycotted him. The whole proceedings were published in the Adi Danka, and everyone knows what happened.[13]
>
> The former *pracharak*, Basant Singh [Vasant Rai], . . . worked for the Mandal for two years. On February 15, 1929, the administrative committee of the Mandal met and decided that the monthly allowance of every missionary should be 15 rupees. Basant Singh got upset over this and criticized the committee; the committee felt insulted, and he was suspended from the Mandal. From here he went to *tehsil* Dasua in Hoshiarpur district and started fooling poor and innocent people there, and collecting money from them for a few months.
>
> His corruption was brought to notice, and responsible people there held a meeting and asked to see his accounts. They determined that he had been embezzling money for himself, misusing funds, so the whole community boycotted him. From there he ran away to Dayanand Dalat Udhar Mandal, Hoshiarpur. Everyone knows about this because it was published in the Adi Danka.[14]

Swami Shudranand seems to have eased his way out more gently. He was elevated to the post of general secretary sometime after Thakar Chand left, but then decided to leave the movement himself. The *Ad Dharm Report* of 1931 described his defection as follows:

> Shuddra Anand, who was previously a preacher, and an honest one, who was with the Dayanand Dalat Udhar Mandal in Hoshiarpur, became secretary for

13. Ibid, p. 59.   14. Ibid, p. 44.

eight months, but he was not of a settled nature—he did not like to stay in one place more than a year. He was blessed with a restless nature, so he did not stay. He requested to leave. He is working with the Dayanand Dalat Udhar Mandal, Hoshiarpur.[15]

It is worth noting that the matter of strategy was not the only concern in this affair: there were human issues as well. Almost all the leaders who left the movement were from Jullundur district, whereas most who stayed were from Mangoo Ram's home district, Hoshiarpur, so the exodus of 1929 reflected a victory for the Hoshiarpur faction in leading the movement. Disaffected leaders formerly active in the Ad Dharm started their own organization, the All-India Ad Dharm Mandal, established in 1930 with headquarters in Lyallpur. The disgraced Vasant Singh served as its president, and Sadhu Ram as its general secretary.[16] The organization was limited primarily to an office in Lyallpur from which it tried to negotiate relationships with the government and other organizations such as the Arya Samaj, to which it was more conciliatory than Mangoo Ram had been. The group survived for only three years, disbanding in 1933 to merge forces with Dr. Ambedkar,[17] and never represented a serious threat to Mangoo Ram's leadership. Indeed, his mass following throughout the Punjab not only continued but expanded.

The crisis of 1929, then, left the Ad Dharm shaken but very much intact. It allowed the movement to emerge with a closely knit and compatible leadership team and an ideology that clearly emphasized the distinctive separateness of the Untouchables as a *qaum*. The ideology and the organization of the movement were more or less consistent with each other, both reflecting an extreme position. Mangoo Ram had made the choice which many leaders of oppressed movements elsewhere in the world have had to make: to stand firm on issues of ideological position and organiza-

---

15. Ibid, p. 45.
16. Sadhu Ram, June 24, 1971, and November 7, 1973. Sadhu Ram is my only source of information regarding the Lyallpur group.
17. Ibid.

tional unity, rather than to risk diffusing the momentum of the movement through compromise.

But there was something else involved. A momentum *had* begun, and with it the appearance of reality in the illusions they had created. The ideology and mythology of the Ad Dharm movement had begun to take on an air of truth. The myth of origin, the superiority of the Adi people over the Aryan invaders, the claims to status as a *qaum* with the power of its own tradition and its own integrity—all these ideas combined to produce a great myth of identity, which perhaps no one believed more strongly than the leaders of the Ad Dharm themselves. It was as if they had made a myth and stepped inside it. Once having proclaimed the concept of their *qaum* they could not retreat from the total commitment that it implied. To have accepted the Arya Samaj's support for Untouchables would have been, from their point of view, to accept the Arya Samaj itself, and not only that but the religious assumptions about human nature and the notions of pollution, purity, and karmic retribution upon which the social constructs of caste are based. To have accepted those concepts not only would have forfeited their strategic position of separatism, it would have negated their own neatly constructed social identities and their vision of social order. Mangoo Ram and his colleagues had no choice but to stay upon the narrow path that they had charted. They were caught inexorably in their images of themselves.

7 The Great Census

The momentum of the Ad Dharm movement was building toward the census of 1931, the first one to be held since the Ad Dharm was formed. A good showing in the census would establish the Ad Dharm's legitimacy and publicly proclaim the strength of its following. But the census was more than that. It was an event for the movement, a seminal event, in Erik Erikson's construction of the term. Like Gandhi's first major *satyagraha,* the census of 1931 would be remembered by the Ad Dharm as the time when everything came together: all the actions and ideas of that moment were rich with meaning.

It may seem odd that a census should become the object for such an effusion of energy and emotion, but its importance was very real. The reasons may be found in the census statistics themselves, for although the relative numerical strengths of the religious communities in the Punjab vary according to region, in the central Punjab, where the Ad Dharm had had its greatest impact, there were almost equal numbers of Muslims, Hindus, and Sikhs.[1] This balance was especially close in the Jullundur and Hoshiarpur districts, the *doab* area between the Beas and Sutlej rivers. This area has another peculiarity, as the census reveals: it houses an abnormally large number of Untouchables, approximately 23 percent of the population.[2] If

1. Amritsar, Ludhiana, Jullundur, and Hoshiarpur districts, and the princely state of Kapurthala (see Map 1 in this book). All statistics are from Government of India, *1931 Census, Punjab* (hereafter *Punjab Census Report*), vol. 20, chap. 11, sec. 4.
2. Ibid., p. 310.

Untouchables, for some reason, were removed from the census categories in which they were formerly listed—as Sikhs, Muslims, or Hindus—and counted together as a separate group, they would be almost exactly equal in number to each of the other three major communities. When one keeps in mind that legislative seats were apportioned by the British according to communal representation, the numbers that each community claimed could be translated into political force. In that sense the real "elections" occurred, not in the polls cast for this candidate or that, but in the apportionment of candidates which was determined through the census results.

If the lower castes were removed from their old places on the census rolls and regrouped under a new category—such as Ad Dharm—the greatest losers would be the Hindus, since up until then the census takers had been instructed to use that category if their Untouchable respondents were uncertain about the matter of religious affiliation. The code read:

> All Chuhras who are not Muslims or Christians, and who do not return any other religion, should be returned as Hindus. The same rule applies to members of other depressed classes who have no tribal religion.[3]

In 1909 when the census commissioner, Edward Gait, issued a circular suggesting that the "depressed classes" ought to be listed separately from the upper caste Hindus, the response from Hindus had bordered on panic.[4] The suggestion was not adopted, but the tremors lingered on, and the Ad Dharm's proposed entry into the 1931 census revived those fears. In particular, it exacerbated tensions between the Ad Dharm and the Arya Samaj, many of whose members were sensitive to the political repercussions of the census issue. This may have been one reason for the British government's joy over the appearance of the

---

3. These instructions were in the guide for census takers, reprinted in the *Punjab Census Report*, chap. 11, p. 289.

4. R. C. Majumdar, *Struggle for Freedom* (Bombay, 1969), p. 1001. See also the discussion of the Gait circular in Kenneth Jones, "Religious Identity and the Indian Census" in *The Indian Census: A New Perspective*, edited by N. G. Barrier (Columbia, Mo.: South Asia Books, 1979).

Ad Dharm: it had the potential of adversely affecting the political resources of Hindu organizations such as the Arya Samaj, which had taken nationalistic stances.

Opposition could be expected, then, when the Ad Dharm appeared as a category on the census rolls under "religious communities," for to do so was a sizeable achievement. In addition to implying a certain legitimacy, it gave the Ad Dharm leverage for negotiating with other organizations and with the government. Furthermore, and perhaps most important, it represented a victory for the internal ideology of the movement, which required that the Ad Dharm be recognized as a *qaum*, equal to that of Muslims, Sikhs, and Hindus. It seemed to herald the wider recognition of what had been resolved at the very first Ad Dharm conference:

> We are not Hindus. We strongly request the government not to list us as such in the census. Our faith is not Hindu, but Ad Dharm. We are not a part of Hinduism, and Hindus are not a part of us.[5]

It was on October 10, 1929, that the Ad Dharm leaders brought before the government the notion of having Ad Dharm listed as a separate religion on the census. The suggestion was readily accepted, in a move that many upper caste observers in both that day and this have regarded as purely cynical in intent, calculated to separate the Untouchables from their Hindu comrades.[6] The government, for its part, was at pains to make clear how the change had taken place. In the Census Report of 1931 it was explicitly stated that it had come as a response to representations made by Mangoo Ram and the Ad Dharm

---

5. *Ad Dharm Report*, p. 14.
6. Interview with Prithvi Singh Azad, M.L.A., Kharar, Rupar District, Punjab, April 13, 1971. Prithvi Singh Azad himself believes that the inclusion of Ad Dharm was a government device, and reports that a similar opinion was widely held among the upper castes at the time. S. L. Malhotra, a historian at Punjab University at Chandigarh, believes that the British used Ad Dharm to help break up the Hindus (interview with S. L. Malhotra, Professor of History and Gandhian Thought, Punjab University, Chandigarh, April 28, 1971).

Mandal, and not, by implication, at the government's own caprice:

> The Punjab Ad-Dharm Mandal had petitioned the Punjab Government before the census operations started in 1930, representing that the depressed classes should be permitted to return Ad-Dharm as their religion at the time of the census as they were the aborigines of India and while the Hindus kept them at a respectable distance they did not believe in the Hindu religion. The President of the Punjab Ad-Dharm Mandal was informed that a clause was being provided in the Census Code requiring that persons returning their religion as Ad-Dharm would be recorded as such.[7]

Once Ad Dharm had been entered on the census lists, great effort was expended in making sure that a massive number of respondents declared it as their true religion. The organization was expanded with branch offices and scores of village workers to secure that end. It was a time of great tension as the Ad Dharm attempted to capitalize on one of the few resources of the poor, their large numbers, and to withdraw that strength from other communities. The *Ad Dharm Report* chronicled the events of the time:

> During the census count, if anyone even mentioned the word Ad Dharmi, they wouldn't let us. These people say they are our brothers, but they treat us like cats and dogs. Especially the Akali Sikh people would start making trouble for us during the census if we said we were Ad Dharmis. They would trap us in our houses with thorny branches placed in our doors. They wouldn't let us go to the wells for water. They wouldn't let us buy goods from shops. They called us names, harassed us, and wouldn't let our cattle out to feed. Our young daughters out on the roads were raped and insulted. Sometimes they burned our houses, looted and plundered. They wouldn't give us our wages for six months to a year. They took our

---

7. *Punjab Census Report,* 1931, part A, chap. 11, p. 289.

cattle. They threw straw into our houses, ignited it, tried to burn us alive, and wouldn't let us drink the dirty water from the village pond. Around the ponds, there would be Sikh volunteers to guard the dirty pond. Without reason, they would have trumped up legal charges, and threatened us with guns, pistols, swords, etc. Our children were starving without food or water, but these upper class people had no mercy. Their fathers would go to the wastelands [*jangal*] and cut grass for food. Then the Sikh volunteers would break our cooking utensils. But in spite of all this harassment during the census-taking, the Ad Dharmi people still broadcast their message.[8]

As this report indicates, the Sikhs took the threat from Ad Dharm more seriously than the Hindus. As one old Ad Dharmi was later to explain, "The Hindus [treated] the Sikhs badly, by taking some of their people into Hindu census rolls, so the Sikhs took it out on us."[9] The Sikhs allegedly broke up an Ad Dharm rally at Nankana Sahib by destroying the kitchen where the meals for the rally were being prepared, throwing the hot rice at the participants, and beating up several of the Ad Dharmis.[10] In other places, two Ad Dharm organizers allegedly were killed.[11] These incidents were widely publicized by the movement to illustrate the importance of the census, and every effort was made to steel the Untouchables' will for the occasion, as in the following song:

> Leave the bickering behind,
> And tie your turban red;
> We do not have to record
> Any qaum other than our own;
> So, Ad Dharmi, be strong.[12]

This was certainly the movement's most active hour, and it may have been the high-water mark of its popularity.

8. *Ad Dharm Report*, pp. 55–57.
9. Chanan Lal Manik, "Adi Dharm Bari," January 5, 1971.
10. Ibid. Nankana Sahib is in West Punjab, forty miles from Lahore.
11. Ibid.
12. Ibid.

The final total of Ad Dharmis reported in the 1931 Punjab Census was 418,789.[13] That number was roughly equal to the number of Christians in the Punjab, and as Mangoo Ram pointed out, Christianity had been converting Punjab Untouchables for over fifty years, whereas the Ad Dharm had been active for only five. In Jullundur district 80 percent of the lower castes reported themselves as Ad Dharmi, and in Hoshiarpur the figure was almost as high. A half dozen other districts registered at least half of their lower caste population as Ad Dharm. But the number of Ad Dharmis in the total population was not overwhelming, only about 1.5 percent, perhaps only a tenth of the total number of lower caste people in the Punjab. The Ad Dharm leaders claimed that the widespread intimidation of those wanting to record themselves as Ad Dharmi had prohibited more names from being amassed, and there are newspaper reports and comments in the Census Report itself which support the allegation.[14] Consequently, some Ad Dharm leaders feel that the actual number of those who wanted to record their names as Ad Dharm may have been four times that of the actual tabulation—two million instead of less than a half million.[15]

Who were these half million or two million Ad Dharmis? Since the census statistics are given by district as well as by caste, it is possible both to map out their demographic distribution and to chart their caste differences. The demographic distribution reveals rather dramatic contous. On map 2, two epicenters of Ad Dharm support are immediately apparent: one in the Jullundur *doab* area (including districts Jullundur and Hoshiarpur and the state of Kapurthala), and the other in the area of Lyallpur (including districts Sheikhapura, Multan, and Montgomery). The reason for the strength in the Jullundur *doab* is obvious—that was the center of the movement—but it is not so plain why the Lyallpur area returned such encouraging figures. One explanation would be that the new canal colonies

13. *Punjab Census Report*, 1931, part A, chap. 11, subsidiary table 1, p. 318.
14. Ibid., p. 335.
15. Mangoo Ram, April 17, 1971.

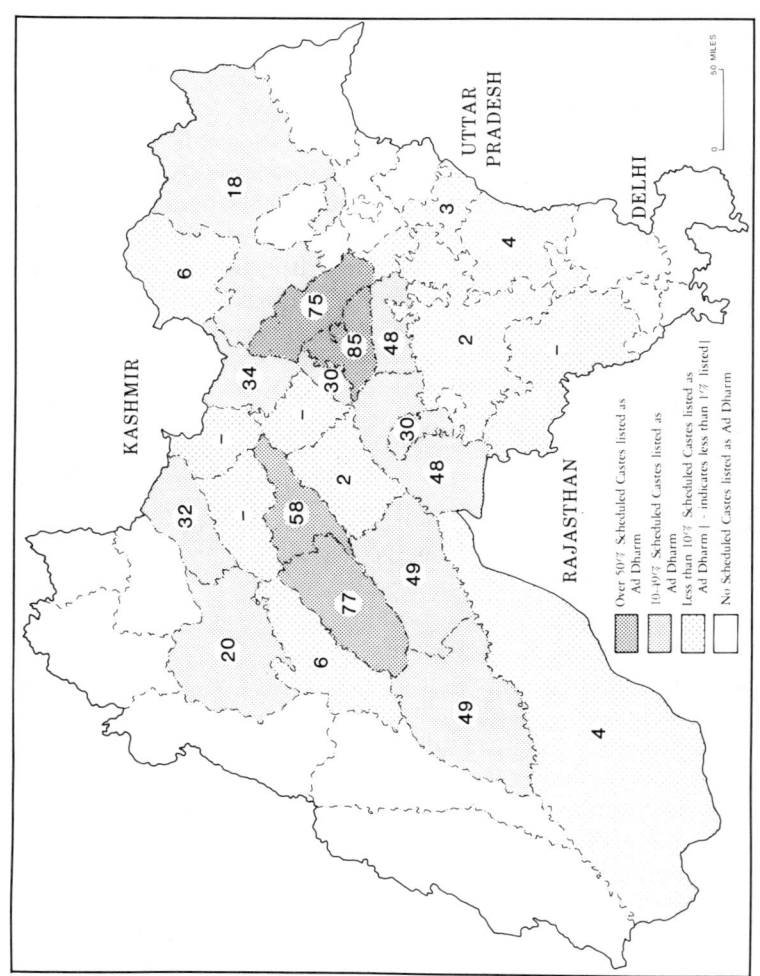

DISTRIBUTION OF AD DHARMIS IN DISTRICTS OF THE PUNJAB

Source: 1931 Census of India, Punjab, Chap. 11, Sec. 4, Par. 236, p. 310. Percentages calculated from the census figures.

there brought large numbers of immigrants to the area, many of them Chamars from Jullundur district. Other sources of enthusiastic support were the mountain areas of Kangra (18 percent Ad Dharmi) and the northwestern areas of Shahpur and Gujarat. In these regions the Ad Dharm had engaged in vigorous organizational activity to mobilize the resentment of the large numbers of lower caste people living there against the oppressive domination of the Rajput castes. It is striking, however, that so few Ad Dharmis were enrolled in Amritsar and Lahore districts, for these two are sandwiched in between the Ad Dharm strongholds of Jullundur and Lyallpur. The simplest explanation for this apparent anomaly is that the Scheduled Castes are less numerous there, proportionately and in absolute numbers—about 30,000 in Amritsar and 50,000 in Lahore, compared with 135,000 in Jullundur.[16] Moreover, Scheduled Castes in the Amritsar and Lahore districts are mostly Chuhra rather than Chamar, and the bulk of Ad Dharm support came from the Chamar castes.[17]

Aside from their areas of residence, the census returns also tell us something about the social characteristics of the persons who named the Ad Dharm as their religion. For example, the literacy of the Ad Dharm followers was over twice that of other members of lower castes. This is also probably an indication of age, since the young had greater access to new educational opportunities. They were probably better off financially as well, since their numbers were greater in the wealthier areas of the Punjab. Finally, the census results indicate that although Ad Dharm followers came from a variety of castes, the overwhelming number were Chamars. Although some Chuhras listed themselves as Ad Dharmis, this happened for the most part only in specific areas,[18] and with a significant difference. By comparison with Chamars, as the Census Report shows, "among Chuhras a larger proportion of illiterates have returned themselves as Ad-Dharmis."[19] This indicates that

16. *Punjab Census Report*, 1931, vol. 20, chap. 11, appendix 1, p. 317.
17. Ibid., p. 310.
18. Ibid., p. 334–335.
19. Ibid., p. 334.

the younger educated elite of the Chuhra caste did not see in Ad Dharm the same attraction as their Chamar counterparts, and had begun to form organizations of their own.

With the census of 1931 the Ad Dharm had carved out a niche for itself. In the public world of the Punjab at that time—the world of the Arya Samaj, the Singh Sabha, and the various movements for communal identity, nationalism and reform—the Ad Dharm had made its mark. It had established a fact which previously had been unproved: that the Untouchable castes were capable of mobilizing for their own benefits, and of organizing in ways that permitted them to compete under the conditions that governed the sociopolitical arena at large. The time had been ripe for such an achievement, but an achievement it was, and the Ad Dharm deserved whatever glory it conferred. The year 1931 and the great census would be remembered as the movement's crowning moment.

PART III Continuities and Encounters

8 The Revival of Ravi Das

Even though the Ad Dharm had largely contrived to win its victories of 1931 through strategy and organization, its rapid success as a movement would not have been possible unless it had touched some deeply held elements of identity and self-awareness that already existed among its village constituents. Ad Dharm did much to highlight the oppression of Untouchables in the Punjab and to accelerate their growing self-consciousness and transform it into an effective political force; it made their common identity more visible than it had ever been before. But it did not create that identity. That had been expressed long before in the veneration of Ravi Das and in other, more general features of the religion of the lower castes. The Ad Dharm might win the allegiance of a small coterie of leaders by imitating the Arya Samaj or adopting a modern lifestyle, but what mattered to the masses was the continuity between the Ad Dharm and these old and familiar realities.

When the Ad Dharm appropriated the figure of Ravi Das, the sixteenth-century poet-saint *(sant)*, and used his picture as their emblem, his sayings as their sacred texts, and stories about his life as illustrations of lower caste pride and power, it was touching the heart of the cultural tradition of lower caste Punjab. For centuries the memory of Ravi Das had been kept alive by a loose network of shrines and pilgrimage centers (called *deras*) dedicated to his devotion. Other medieval *sants* were revered by members of all castes, and the Sikh gurus themselves were part of this *sant* tradition.[1] But for the lower castes Ravi Das was special: he was himself a Chamar. Hence *deras* dedicated to him not only provided foci for the spiritual life, they functioned as lower caste cultural centers as well.

Seven miles north of the city of Jullundur there is a particularly splendid Ravi Das *dera*. The resident holy man, Sarwan Das—who in the popular use of the term in contemporary Punjab is also called a *sant*—is a Chamar, and his following is drawn primarily from that and other lower castes. One finds the figure of Ravi Das prominently displayed throughout the temple and the other buildings of the *dera*, and his writings form the basis of its liturgy. Ravi Das is regarded as more than a saint in this *dera*: his figure and his writings take the place of the gurus and the Granth of Sikhism, and the gods and the scriptures of Hinduism. The *dera* has all the appearances of being a temple in the religion of Ravi Das.

Sarwan Das, the religious leader of the *dera*, sits on a small pedestal beside an electric fan in the center of the compound, where he receives the many guests who come on pilgrimage. He wears sunglasses, a flowing white beard, and an orange turban folded in a manner similar to that of the Sikhs. Sarwan Das explains to visitors that his father, Pipal Das, established the *dera* at that location, near village Ballan, around the turn of the century while wandering in search of truth.[2] When he encountered the place, he found a pipal tree, which appeared to be dead, but after he watered it, it sprang back to life. Pipal Das understood this as a clear indication that truth was to be obtained on that spot, so he solicited nearby villagers to donate the land and began constructing his *dera*. It soon became the goal of pilgrimage for lower caste and other villagers from all over

---

1. V. Raghavan, *The Great Integrators: The Saint-Singers of India* (New Delhi: Publications Division, Ministry of Information and Broadcasting, Government of India, 1966). See also Karine Schomer and W. H. McLeod, eds., *The Sant Tradition of India*, Berkeley: Berkeley Religious Studies Series, 1981.
2. Sant Sarvan Das, spiritual leader of Ravi Das Dera, village Ballan, Jullundur district, interview on April 15, 1971 (in Punjabi).

central Punjab, and from its inception it was a center for the veneration of Ravi Das.

According to Sant Sarwan Das, Mangoo Ram had gone to Pipal Das in the early stages of the Ad Dharm movement for information about the writings and teachings of Ravi Das; he also visited another *sant*, Hiran Das, with the same mission. These two were charged to fashion a body of scripture for the Ad Dharm under the title "Sri Guru Ad Prakash Asankh Deep Granth" (The Lord's Original Scriptures of Infinite Light), but for most of the movement's history this document remained only a name. In the interim Ad Dharmis resorted to a collection of poetry that Hiran Das had already published, in 1908, comprising verse of his own and some of the sayings attributed to Ravi Das.

The stamp of Ravi Das was also felt in the piety the Ad Dharmis expressed at the *deras* of Pipal Das and Hiran Das, the one located at Ballan and the other in village Hakim, near the town of Phagwara. These became objects of pilgrimage for members of the Ad Dharm and points at which the movement's connection with the tradition of Ravi Das was especially affirmed. But they were never exclusively Ad Dharm sites: they remained the separate institutions they had been before Mangoo Ram visited them, and they survived long after the movement declined. The same holds true for the veneration of Ravi Das in general: the Ad Dharm gave it a special prominence, but it certainly did not exhaust its appeal. Long after the demise of Ad Dharm, *deras* such as that of Sarwan Das remain popular destinations for pilgrimage in the Punjab.

Ravi Das appealed to the lower castes for obvious reasons, since he was one of their own. This did not mean that his message differed in any essential respect from that propounded by Kabir, his Benares compatriot, or by the man who is alleged to have been their common teacher there, Ramanand. All of them preached *bhakti*—spiritual union with the divine accomplished through devotion, chanting, and meditation—and all of them held that spiritual fulfillment depends entirely on an individual and interior search. None believed that this search was related in any way to ascetic or ritual practices or to the obligations of caste. In this sense all of them, together with most other *bhakti* poets of the time, presented a challenge to the religious basis of social hierarchy in India, one that had special meaning for members of the lower castes. But Ravi Das was set apart by his own Untouchable background, and the occasional poems in which he alluded to it were held in special esteem by activists such as the Ad Dharm leaders. The following is an example:

> And I, born to be a carrier of carrion, am now
> the lowly one to whom the Brahmans come
> And lowly bow. They seek
> the shelter of my name, Servant of the Sun,
> Whose service is the service of the Lord.[3]

Ravi Das was not the only medieval *sant* to have come from a humble background—Kabir and Dadu were both weavers—and he was not the only one to become the focus of a lower caste *panthik* movement. There are Dadupanthis in Rajasthan[4] and two separate branches of the Kabirpanth, one in Benares and one in Madhya Pradesh,[5] in addition to the Satnamis of Madhya Pradesh[6] and the Shiv Narayans of Uttar Pradesh;[7] all of these are movements whose social base is in some places largely Chamar. Those who took Ravi Das as their special patron are almost entirely Chamar—they are called Raedasis in Uttar Pradesh, where they first developed,[8] and their movement was very much on the rise throughout North India in the first two decades of this

---

3. Trans. by J. S. Hawley and M. Juergensmeyer, in Wm. T. deBary, ed., *Sources of Indian Tradition* (New York: Columbia Univ. Press, 1982, rev. ed.).

4. W. B. Orr, *A Sixteenth-Century Indian Mystic: Dadu and His Followers* (London, 1947). The lower caste adherents were called Gharibdasis and Ghisapanthis.

5. G. H. Westcott, *Kabir and the Kabir Panth* (Calcutta: The Association Press, 1907, reprinted by the Bhartiya Publishing House, n.d.).

6. Lawrence A. Babb, "The Satnamis: Political Involvement of a Religious Movement," in J. M. Mahar, ed., *The Untouchables in Contemporary India* (Tucson, 1972).

7. G. W. Briggs, *The Chamars* (London, 1920), pp. 211–214.

8. Ibid., pp. 207–211. See also William Crooke, *Tribes and Castes of the North-Western Provinces and Oudh*, vol. 2 (Allahabad, 1890), pp.

Swami Shudranand

◀ Mangoo Ram reading an old copy of *Adi Danka*

First edition of *Ravidas Patrika*, showing a picture of Ravi Das on the cover

Master Charan Singh at the Radhasoami Dera, Beas, overseeing the work project undertaken by his devotees

Devotees at the Radhasoami Dera, Beas, performing service by helping to build a dam

Jandiala, where some members of lower caste have joined the Communist parties

Attendant at the Ambedkar Bhawan, Jullundur

Rev. Y.C. Mal, lower caste pastor of Jullundur city church

Ravi Das pilgrimage site at village Ballan

Healing of a snake-bite wound by a Gogapir holy man in village Bimla

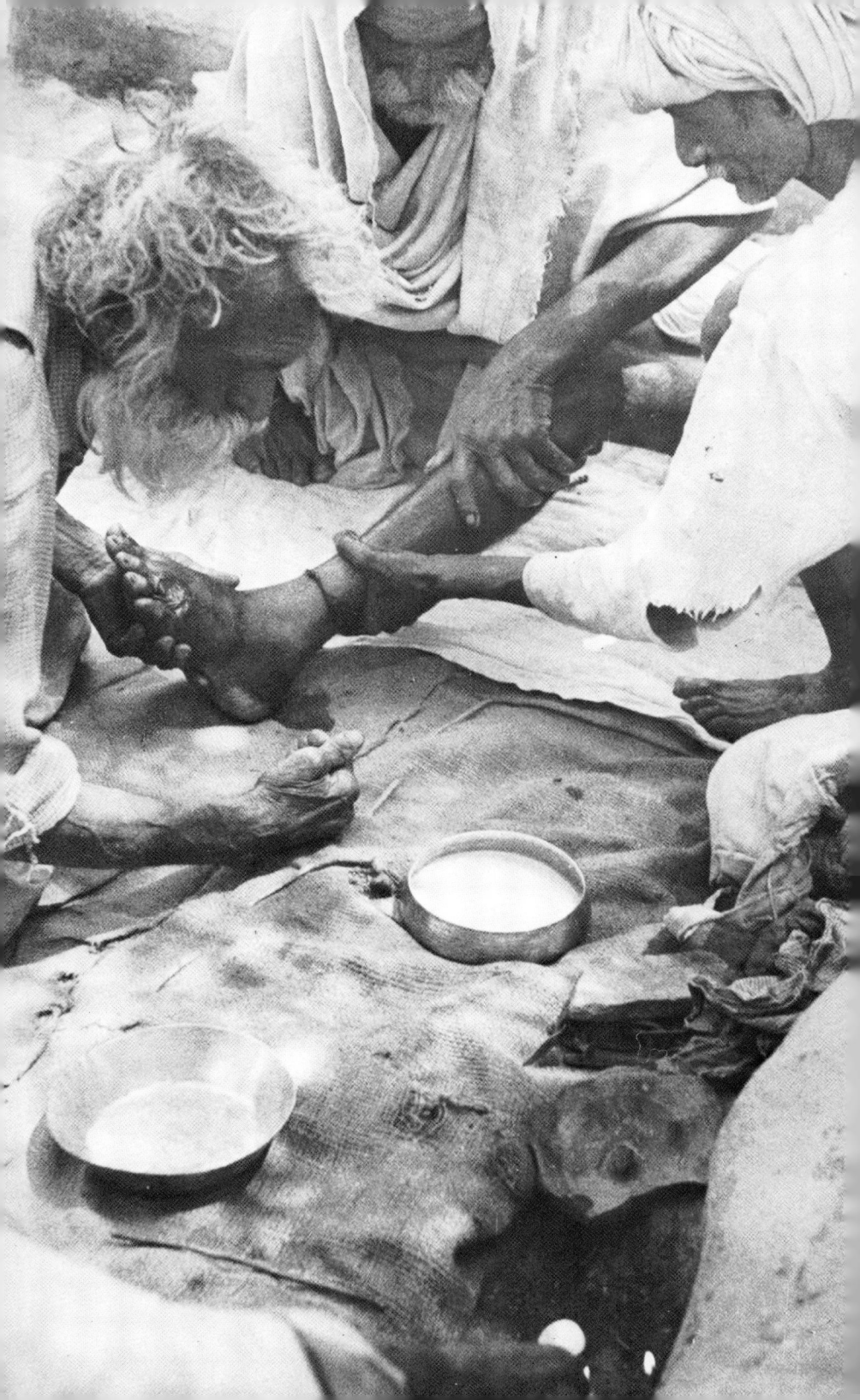

century, in the years immediately before the founding of the Ad Dharm.[9]

Sant Hiran Das played a role in this expansion when he established his Ravi Das Sabha, in 1907, in village Hakkim,[10] and a year later published his collection of Ravi Das's sayings.[11] Several other *deras,* including that of Pipal Das, were founded soon afterward, among them another near Jullundur and three in Hoshiarpur district. Pipal Das's *dera* at Ballan remained the largest, but out of a total of sixty *deras* a dozen are of considerable size.[12]

The term "sect," which is often applied to the Ravi Das *panth,* is somewhat misleading, for it implies a closed society with a sharp division between its members and those outside. In fact, nothing of this sort existed: in India the different levels of religious identity allow for multiple religious affiliations. For the followers of Ravi Das the word *panth* is the appropriate one: it is cognate with the English word "path," and conveys a similar meaning of a "way," a movement of like-minded sojourners, rather than a well-defined organization.[13] The *dera* of Pipal Das is typical as an expression of the Ravi Das *panth* in this respect, since it has no formal structure, either of organization or of beliefs. Nothing unites the groups of devotees who come there on pilgrimage except their common veneration of Ravi Das and their common sharing of legends about him.

One must look to these myths to discover what Ravi Das means to his followers as a religious and social symbol. A current myth among Chamars has the effect of enno-

---

185ff; Denzil Ibbetson, E. D. MacLagan, H. A. Rose, *Tribes and Castes of the Punjab and North-West Frontier Province* (Lahore, 1911), p. 306; and *The Religious Sects of the Hindus* (Christian Literature Society, 1904), p. 57. In the Punjab the Raedasis were also called Ramdasis.
9. Briggs, *The Chamars,* p. 210.
10. Swami Shudranand, June 10, 1971.
11. *Rae Dasi Ki Bani* (Allahabad: Belvedere Press, 1908).
12. Sant Sarvan Das, April 15, 1971.
13. W. H. McLeod has mounted a persuasive argument for using the term *panth* rather than "sect" for the Sikhs, and the argument would apply to the Ravidasis as well. (W. H. McLeod, "The Sect and Nation of the Sikhs: A Problem of Terminology and Definition," unpublished paper, 1978).

bling the profession of trading in dead animals. It tells how God *(bhagwan)* asked Ravi Das to remove a dead cow, which he did, as befitted his social role. But Ravi Das saved part of the animal—its heart—and planted it in the ground, whereupon a certain bush promptly arose bearing a flower with the form and color of a heart.[14] In addition to honoring the tanner's role, this story attributes a magical or divine origin to a plant that is important to the Chamars. And it depicts Ravi Das as playing a harmonious role among the unseen forces, connecting the realm of humanity with that of nature.[15]

The upper caste myths about Ravi Das are different from stories such as this in that they link the saint with the high Brahmanical tradition. In one of these, a Brahman disciple of Ramanand purchases sacrificial food from a merchant who had once had money-dealings with a Chamar, thereby polluting the food. Ramanand in his anger causes the Brahman to be reborn as a Chamar, a fact which becomes apparent when the baby (Ravi Das) refuses to suckle his own Chamar mother for fear of becoming ritually polluted.[16] In another myth, after Ravi Das performs a miracle in the court of a king, the jealous priests of the court slash into his chest, only to discover a Brahmanical thread that has been retained from a previous life.[17] Each of these myths has the virtue of making the Untouchable, Ravi Das, more acceptable to the upper castes.

Both sorts of stories, the lower caste and the high caste, might be termed "integrative myths." They integrate the *bhakti* tradition either downwards or upwards: with the traditions of the lower castes or with the higher, Brahmanical tradition. And both sets of myths contain motifs which perform the function of reconciling a social anomaly: that an Untouchable should be gifted with vast religious pow-

14. Briggs, *The Chamars*, p. 210. This myth was also related to me at the Ravi Das Dera, village Ballan, April 15, 1971.
15. Ibid., pp. 126–127.
16. Ibid., p. 208.
17. Ibid., p. 209. Posters at the Ravi Das Dera, village Ballan, which portray this myth are called "Brahman posters" by the devotees, since they assume that only a Brahman would have portrayed Ravi Das in such a manner.

ers. The "cow-heart" myth does this strictly from within the Chamar perspective, dignifying the caste occupation in the process, while the "reborn Brahman" myth attacks the problem by making Ravi Das at once a Chamar and a Brahman. The anomaly is perceived rather differently in the two cases, but the solutions are similar in that they integrate a strange reality into a social world view.

The Ad Dharm took the integrative myths and the Ravi Das symbol and appropriated them for a separatist identity. His picture, his name, and his stories were salted throughout the literature and events of the movement. The "integrative" aspect was still there—Ravi Das was still seen as the Chamar hero who was able to pull his weight among the Brahmans—but in developing their own interpretations of the myths, the Ad Dharm leaders placed more emphasis on Ravi Das's Untouchable defiance than upon his Brahman acceptability. In songs, illustrations in their speeches, and articles, the Ad Dharm showed the lower castes that this folk hero, whom they held to be as good as the Brahmans, was in fact better than the Brahmans—and of a different tradition. Ravi Das was an Ad Dharmi.

The Ad Dharm's use of Ravi Das as a symbol allowed the movement to emphasize the separate religious tradition of the lower castes and at the same time to utilize a familiar figure who was identified with the high Hindu tradition. Moreover, in the Punjab, where the Sikhs were as important a religious community as the Hindus, it was significant that Ravi Das had also been associated with the Sikh tradition. Verses written by Ravi Das appear in the Sikh scriptures, and he had further been identified with Sikhism through a curious confusion over names.

Perhaps because of his contributions to the Sikh Granth, Ravi Das's name was easily confused with that of one of the ten gurus of Sikhism, Guru Ram Das. Hence it became the convention to call Chamars who converted to Sikhism "Ramdasis." These Ramdasis frequently discarded the occupation of tanning in favor of weaving, and they wore the insignia of the Sikhs. Neither of these was an entirely novel practice. Some of the members of the Raidasi movement had also advanced their occupational status—often more so, in fact, than these Sikh Ramdasis, though the latter were usually accorded a higher social status—and they too had sometimes adopted the characteristic marks of the Sikhs. This double precedent provides the easiest explanation as to why Guru Ram Das's name should have been linked with Chamar converts to the faith: "Raidasi" and "Ramdasi" sounded measurably the same. Ibbetson, however, the early census director and ethnographer, found the situation genuinely baffling and stated that the confusion was not his alone:

> The Census gives us no idea of the numbers of the followers of Ravdas because there are Ramdasi or Ramdasi Chamars, as well as Ravdasi or Raidasi Chamars, and the two have become hopelessly mixed in the returns. The Ramdasi are true Sikhs, and take the *pahul* [initiation vows]; the Ravdasis are not Sikhs, or, if Sikhs, are only Nanakpanthis, and do not take the *pahul*. Among the people themselves the two terms are by no means clearly distinguished.[18]

Another ethnographer suspected that the confusion was intentional, providing a way to justify the inclusion of Chamars among the Sikhs by suggesting that the association had been traditional.[19]

When the Ad Dharm movement appropriated the figure of Ravi Das, then, it was connecting itself with an old and complex symbol. On the one hand, Ravi Das had stood for the cultural and religious identity of the lower castes, particularly the Chamars, both traditionally and in the form of the Raidasi movement. On the other hand, his name had been linked, through the stories about his being a Brahman and through his indirect association with the Ramdasis, with efforts to bridge the gap between Untouchables and upper caste society. When the Ad Dharm claimed Ravi Das as part of its heritage it altered these alignments. It had the effect of muting the assimilationist tendency while connecting the figure of Ravi Das with something modern and

18. Ibbetson et al., *Tribes and Castes*, p. 306.
19. G. Fagan, quoted in ibid., p. 307.

dynamic. The prestige of Ravi Das among common folk encouraged their participation in the new movement, and in the eyes of the educated the reputation of the movement as a modernist force wiped away whatever associations the veneration of Ravi Das may have had with an oppressed past. Thus Ravi Das was not only reclaimed by the Ad Dharm; he was revived as well.

9 The Religion of Village Untouchables

When the census described the Untouchables first as Hindu, then as having abandoned the faith for a new religion, Ad Dharm, it was doubly inaccurate. As we have seen, the Ad Dharm was not altogether new, for it marshaled in its support the Untouchables' long-held allegiance to Sant Ravi Das. Moreover, the Untouchables' previous beliefs were only marginally "Hindu." Indeed, one should question the appropriateness of that term, or any other category associated with the high tradition, for describing the religious beliefs and affiliations of the lower castes.

The labels of the major communities—Hindu, Muslim, and Sikh—have been applied to Untouchables by upper caste people very loosely. In the Punjab, those terms are appellations for members of upper castes, whereas the Untouchables are described as that, Untouchables, or as Chuhra-Chamar, or as members of special categories of upper caste religions reserved for the low, such as Mazhabi Sikhs or Achut Hindu. Untouchables seldom describe themselves as Hindu, Muslim, or Sikh, except when political or social reasons make it expedient to do so. In areas dominated by Sikhs, for instance, all the Untouchables in those areas will affect Sikh signs and habits. Some lower caste people use different names on different occasions: in the presence of Hindus a person may identify himself as Ram Chand, among Sikhs as Ram Singh, and with Christians, John Samuel. The British census-takers, in noting this phenomenon, spoke of the lower castes' "fickleness" with regard to religion,[1] and the determination of the correct apportionment of lower caste followers among Hinduism, Sikhism, and the other major religions was one of their knottier problems. The numbers would shift peculiarly from one census to another, to the embarrassment of the statisticians.[2] During politically active periods, such as the 1920s and later, post-independence, members of upper castes would vie with one another over the right to claim Untouchables within their religion. It is clear that the Untouchables were not considered normatively Hindu.

But except in the Punjab, where the issue has become political, one seldom hears anyone described as a Hindu, for the term is foreign both conceptually and etymologically. Etymologically, the term came from travelers from the West who described those people who lived east of the Indus river as Sindhus (Hindus).[3] The religion, Hinduism, is the name for what those people believe, assuming they all believe the same thing. But the notion of religion as the doctrinal faith of a culturally unified community—a centrally organized and theologically consistent entity—derives from Christian, Islamic, and Jewish usage, and does not fit comfortably with the patterns of belief and behavior which are India's "religion." In fact, one might question whether Hinduism is a religion at all, in the Western sense. The term has meaning only as the name one gives to India's eclectic religious culture, or more specifically, the *dharmik* customs and practices associated with the upper castes and the veneration of the main deities in the tradition.

In that broad sense, Untouchables are Hindus, but Hinduism in the *dharmik* sense has been explicitly rejected by many modern members of the lower castes, and may have been rejected, less obviously, though as firmly, by the generations that preceded them in village India. Traditions of

1. Government of India, *1931 Census,* Punjab, vol. 20, chap. 11, sec. 4, p. 311.
2. I have charted the variations in census statistics from 1881 to 1931 regarding the religious preferences of the lower castes. A rise in numbers of Hindus matches roughly a decline of Sikhs, and vice versa (Juergensmeyer, "Political Hope," p. 48).
3. The word "Hindu" is an old Persian variant on the Sanskrit *sindhu,* one of whose meanings refers to the Indus River.

beliefs and practices exist in villages, especially among lower caste villagers, which parallel those of the high tradition, and may constitute their own alternative to *dharmik* Hinduism. Perhaps much of the uncertainty over the Untouchables' religious identity may be due to that fact: they have had a religious tradition of their own. Yet it has never been clearly defined, for the Untouchables wove that element of religion into a complex fabric of religious involvement which also included participation in *panthik* movements, devotion to the deities, and a lingering adherence to *dharmik* customs. And they gave it no name.

The religion of lower caste villagers defies any single characterization. The central and consistent feature of their religious life is an awesome respect for the vitality of the spirit world, and a conviction that its presence is ubiquitous in special people, natural objects, remarkable events, and potent signs and symbols.[4] Rocks, stones, and large natural outcroppings have special significance, and are sometimes decorated and worshipped much like the deities in Hindu temples. Certain trees are also held in special regard, pipal trees and banyans being among the more auspicious. A totemic significance is ascribed to some of these objects; subcastes *(gotras)* of the lower castes take on the names and emblems of certain trees, plants, and animals.[5]

The spiritual power that is invested in certain objects of the natural world is not neutral. It has either benign or

    4. This and most of the following characterizations of the religion of village Untouchables come from my village studies in the Punjab in 1970–1971, with emphasis on the locales indicated on map 1, in the frontispiece: village "Nalla" in the Sivalik foothills of Hoshiarpur district, village "Bimla" in Ferozepur district near the Rajasthan border, village "Allahpind" in Gurdaspur district near the Pakistan border, Scheduled Caste areas in and near the town of Jandiala in Jullundur district, the Valmiki Mohalla section of old Jullundur city, and the newer Boota Mandi section on the outskirts of Jullundur city. The names in quotation marks are pseudonyms. Similar observations about the religious life of village Untouchables, in considerably greater detail, are found in Briggs, *The Chamars* (London, 1920), chap. 6.
    5. Briggs and the ethnologists list *gotras* (subcastes) of Chamars named after seeds, grain, fruit, sheep, goats, and buffaloes (ibid., p. 127); see also the article on Chamar, Chuhra and other lower castes in Denzil Ibbetson et al., *Tribes and Castes of the Punjab* [Lahore, 1911]).

malevolent effects on the lives of individuals. It expresses itself in vital forces that constantly interact in human affairs. Much of the skill of a spiritually aware person is aimed at discerning these powers, predicting their effect, and maneuvering them in propitious directions. Things that are useful in warding off bad spirits (or rather, the potentially bad effects of spirits) include iron and other metals; fire and various elements associated with it, such as smoke, ashes, charcoal, and flames; and blood, or the color red as a sort of surrogate blood. Commotion of various sorts is thought to have the power of distracting bad spirits and scaring them away. Fluttering flags have a similar effect and are frequently posted near sacred places for that reason. Sheer volume can also disturb and banish bad spirits, so the loudness one typically encounters on special occasions and at special places has a spiritual as well as a festive value. Certain symbols also have a prophylactic effect on demonic spirits: circles, crossed lines, and swastikas are prominent among these. The major effect of all these is to keep pernicious spirits away, but there are also practices designed to lure good spirits into one's affairs. Giving a child a sacred name, for example, holds out the possibility of attracting good spirits, as does the presence of light and the smell of incense.

Spirits emanate from the souls of the dead. Not all souls become disembodied spirits permanently, but for some days after death every soul lingers on in this world. The special potency that inheres in the souls of the heinously evil and the heroically good makes it especially likely that their spirits will endure even when their bodies have been taken away, and a similar fate is apt to befall those grievously wronged by circumstances.[6] Such spirits, accessible precisely because they are disembodied and can make their influence felt in various places, are thought to reside in rocks, trees, and the like, but their activities are oriented toward the affairs of humans. Souls of witches and very

6. Devious persons are particularly likely to live on as malevolent spirits, but the souls of persons dying in catastrophic or unfortunate circumstances, or without the benefit of proper funeral rites, may be equally threatening.

bad persons become evil spirits, and the souls of saints and the generously good become their benign counterparts. To have one of the latter as an ancestor is quite useful, and many venerate such ancestors, praying for their intercession in the affairs of the present. The fate of a soul at death is not always certain. Sacred rites at the time are most important in helping to ease the soul through a potentially dangerous passage.[7] It is not altogether clear where the safely dispatched soul goes if it avoids becoming either a good or an evil spirit; the Hindu notion of transmigration is sometimes invoked, but one also hears notions of a pleasant afterlife, a sort of old soul's home, a heaven.

Two questions can be raised about these beliefs: Do they form a coherent religious system? And are they solely the province of the lower castes? At first glance, the answer to the second question is easy enough, for it is clear that these notions are found to some degree among all villagers, regardless of caste. Hinduism, as a pattern of practices and moral order—that is, as a *dharmik* religion—can tolerate many of these ideas without doing damage to the Hindu world view.[8] Astrology, the auspiciousness of dates and places, and the positive and negative effects of certain foods are all part of the spiritual outlook of most Indians, including those who fit most firmly in the Brahmanical, *dharmik* tradition.[9]

    7. The practices of the funeral rites appear to be deliberately eclectic. For example, in Malerkotla, in central Punjab, the Chuhras bury their dead, as do Muslims, but on their way to the grave the carriers of the bier change places, as in Hindu custom. Moreover, there is a *faqir* who accompanies the burial party and recites verses of Guru Nanak, in the manner of a Sikh funeral (Ibbetson et al., *Tribes and Castes*, p. 198 n.).
    8. Marriott suggests that the dual processes of universalization and parochialization in village religion knit the great and little traditions together (McKim Marriott, "Little Communities in an Indigenous Civilization," in McKim Marriott, ed., *Village India: Studies in the Little Community* [Chicago, 1955], p. 211); and Babb observes that "cultural elements of both textual and local provenance are drawn into a single overall pattern of relationships" (Lawrence A. Babb, *The Divine Hierarchy: Popular Hinduism in Central India* [New York, 1975], p. 26).
    9. Marglin, in a recent study of the auspiciousness of kings, suggests that the polarity between the auspicious and the inauspicious is parallel to that *dharmik* polarity between purity and pollution, but—in

Yet these universally popular forms of spirituality do differ from the range of practices and beliefs common among the lower castes in the Punjab. In part the difference is one of degree: the lower castes follow these practices and cherish these concepts largely to the exclusion of those of the higher tradition. But the difference is more basic than that. In recognizing naturalistic powers and locating the source of spiritual power in the good and evil spirits that originate from the souls of the dead, the lower castes project a complete cosmology of the spiritual world that contrasts fundamentally with the occasional nature of upper caste practices of divination and goes well beyond the regarding of certain things as more auspicious than others. The lower castes appear to ground their religious practices and convictions in a completely alternative religious structure.

This structure is at odds with two groups of assumptions included in the *dharmik* Hindu world view: those comprising Hindu notions of reality and those making up Hindu concepts of the self. The lower castes' world, populated with good and evil spirits, is an ethically dualistic world, and one in which the ultimate realities are present and immediate. The realm of the spirits is in this world; it is here that the wars of the spirits are waged. Like a civilian caught within a battle, the individual self is both an onlooker and a participant in such conflicts, and his or her spiritual goal is not so much to transcend the world as it is to survive within it. This notion runs counter to a basic tenet of *dharmik* Hinduism, the notion that karmic merit accrued during this life is directed toward a future and distant goal, the release of the soul *(moksha)* after many cycles of rebirths. For the lower castes the possibility of salvation—or rather, of divine protection—is much more immediate, and the idea of *karma* is irrelevant.

It is an important issue whether one accepts the proposition that lower caste people believe in karmic rebirth, not only because the idea is fundamental to *dharmik* Hinduism and would have a direct bearing on whether one considers

---

agreement with Louis Dumont—she finds the former polarity encompassed by the latter (Frédérique Appfel Marglin, "Wives of the God-King: A Study of the Rituals of Some Temple Courtesans in India.")

Untouchables rightly Hindus, but also because it has sometimes been suggested that Untouchables accept their lot in life with passivity on account of this belief.[10] They are fatalistic about their low status in life, the argument goes, because they recognize that their own misdeeds in a previous life have caused their degradation in this one. Since it was my impression that the idea of *karma* was less important to Punjabis in general and to the lower castes among them in particular, I raised this question to a sampling of both lower caste and upper caste Punjabis. The results are shown in table 1.[11] Less than half of all respondents believed in the karmic cycle of birth and rebirth, but an even lower proportion of lower caste respondents expressed such a belief.[12] When the question was asked whether they believed that the present conditions were the result of *karma* from a previous life, a question to which the response should logically have shown a high correlation with the other, there was even less assent, especially among the upper castes, as is shown in the table. But the significant figures are the first ones, which demonstrate that

---

10. For a recent example of this position, see Stephen Fuchs, "The Religio-Ethical Concepts of the Chamars in Northern India" *Missiology: An International Review* 4, no. 1 (Jan. 1976). It is implied also in Max Weber, *The Sociology of Religion* (Boston: Beacon Press, 1964), p. 43. Briggs (*The Chamars,* pp. 200–201) also makes this observation, although he finds it less prevalent where *panthik* movements have influence.

11. Tabulation of the answers is given in Juergensmeyer, "Political Hope," Appendix B.

12. Similar observations about the absence of the idea of karmic retribution among the lower castes are made in Bernard S. Cohn, "Changing Traditions of a Low Caste," in Milton Singer, ed., *Traditional India: Structure and Change,* Bibliographical and Special Series, vol. 10 (Philadelphia: American Folklore Society, 1959), p. 207; Gerald Berreman, "Caste in Cross-Cultural Perspective," in G. deVos and H. Wagatsuma, eds., *Japan's Invisible Race: Caste In Culture and Personality* (Berkeley and Los Angeles, 1966), p. 311; Andre Beteille, "Pollution and Poverty," in Mahar, ed., *The Untouchables in Contemporary India;* and Pauline Kolenda, "Religious Anxiety and Hindu Fate," in E. Harper, ed., *Religion in South Asia* (Seattle, 1964); and Kathleen Gough, "Harijans in Thanjavur," Kathleen Gough and Hari P. Sharma, eds., *Imperialism and Revolution in South Asia* (New York: Monthly Review Press, 1973).

TABLE 1. ACCEPTANCE OF KARMIC CONCEPTS

	Belief in rebirth	Belief that one's condition resulted from a previous life
Lower caste respondents	39%	29%
Upper caste respondents	47%	15%

fewer lower caste respondents affirmed the idea of *karma* at all.[13]

The lower castes' disbelief in *karma* has implications for an understanding of their attitudes toward another fundamental *dharmik* Hindu concept: pollution. In great measure Hindus avoid impure things, actions, and persons in order to prevent the accretion of bad *karma,* and they undertake purifying acts to increase their good *karma.* Without the concept of karmic retribution, matters of purity and pollution become seemingly unimportant, and it would be odd if the Untouchable castes accorded them significant attention. It is true that, by and large, Untouchables observe the social customs regarding eating, smoking, and fraternizing with other castes, but these customs do not require acceptance of the concepts behind them; only compliance is necessary. One finds that they have few compunctions about pollution in more private matters, such as eating meat, handling dead animals, and touching other supposedly contaminated objects, even those not necessary for their traditional caste roles. On this point it is clear that distinctions between purity and pollution have less force among them than among the upper castes. Indeed, because others consider that everything they touch is polluted by that very act of touching, the distinction between pure and impure becomes hardly relevant to them.

13. The responses from the villages were somewhat different from those in the towns and cities. The more sophisticated urban members of lower castes tended to affirm belief in the karmic cycle (whereas among upper caste urban respondents it was the reverse, since city folk tend to be more secular), indicating that belief in the karmic cycle was for lower caste people an affectation adopted in the city, perhaps for reasons of status, to appear more "Hindu."

In this sense the stigma of Untouchability has liberated them from the concept of ritual pollution altogether.[14]

Moreover, as we have seen earlier, their own religious beliefs in spiritual powers do not require the concept of ritual pollution. In the lower castes' world view, objects and events are indeed charged, but with moral force rather than degrees of ritual cleanliness. And that moral valence is not necessarily the sort that Hinduism's karmic morality implies, since it follows not from individual actions but from the living presence of good and evil spirits. The presence of the spirits, and the requirements it places on human activity, not only vitiates Hindu *dharma*, it replaces it.

Other elements of the high tradition are also replaced. Lower caste religion provides parallels to the legendary figures, the divinities, and the holy men of the high tradition. In general, the great divinities of Hinduism do not figure prominently in lower caste religion. The term "Ram," for example, refers to a benign cosmic force, a sort of heavenly father, rather than to a specific incarnation of Vishnu rich in mythological significance.[15] Local gods, by contrast, entirely strange to the high tradition, are considered to be specific and powerful, capable of influencing the realm of the spirits. These are the recipients of frequent petitions, as are certain legendary figures. Ravi Das, for example, in addition to his prominence as the legendary founder of a *panthik* movement, is generally regarded among the lower castes as a helpful divine spirit.[16] An Untouchable will pray for his benevolent intervention much as a Mahayana Buddhist might pray to a *bodhisattva*, or a Roman Catholic Christian to a saint.

14. I pursue the matter further in my article, "What if Untouchables Don't Believe in Untouchability?"

15. The high god was also described as *bhagwan, ishwar*, and *parameshwar;* even Mohammed and Jesus occasionally appeared in lower caste mythology (Ibbetson et al., *Tribes and Castes*, vol. 1, p. 202), and Briggs reports that some Chamars worshipped Indra, an ancient Indian god who is infrequently worshipped by present-day upper caste Hindus (*The Chamars*, p. 198).

16. Ravi Das is called "Dev" (God) in some urban areas of the Punjab, although this is partially in imitation of those Sikhs who insist on using that term for their own Guru Nanak.

Some of these legendary figures are unique to the lower castes. The most widely followed are Lal Beg and Bala Shah, who are sometimes described as if they were two separate realities, sometimes as two names for the same figure.[17] In either case the composite Lal Beg/Bala Shah is regarded as having once lived on earth; he has now attained divine status, however, and is available to be called upon by members of the Chuhra caste for whatever spiritual or personal advantages a supplicant may wish to obtain. One form of worship is to make a small shrine of earth, putting a stick over it with a piece of cloth in the form of a small flag; *ghi* (clarified butter) or grain is then offered as a sacrifice, and prayers can be said in front of the shrine for the alleviation of hardship. Clearly Lal Beg/Bala Shah plays an intercessory role in regard to the spirit world, but there are also legends which show him as providing linkages to the high tradition in various forms.

According to some of the British ethnographers, the name Lal Beg came from a legend in which Shiva rubbed his hand on a red stone, Lal Batta, producing Lal Beg.[18] The name Lal Beg has also been described as a corruption of Lal Bhikshu, "The Red Monk," referring to Shiva himself. Other legends link Bala Shah to Vaishnava, rather than Shaiva Hinduism, by relating the name Bal to Balmik, the Punjabi pronunciation of Valmiki, the author of the Ramayana epic, who in Punjab is thought to have been of lower caste. Finally, as the term Shah would suggest, there are several legends linking Lal Beg/Bala Shah to Muslim traditions. In one of these Lal Beg is portrayed as the son of a Moghul woman who was barren until the intercession of Rishi Balmik (Valmiki) enabled her to bear a son. Another legend makes Lal Beg the son of a Shaikh from Multan who conquered Kabul and Kashmir, but renounced all of this in order to found the religious tradition that bore his name and produced five sects, otherwise known as five Chuhra subcastes.[19]

17. The issue is discussed in Ibbetson et al., *Tribes and Castes*, vol. 2, pp. 20–24.
18. Ibid., p. 20.
19. Ibid., p. 21.

Another legendary figure venerated among the lower castes in the Punjab is Gogapir, a personage active in communicating with the serpentine world. A lineage of lower caste holy men claim to have special access to Gogapir's power, and thereby are able to cure snakebites. I observed such a cure in Bimla, a remote village near the Rajasthan and Haryana borders of Punjab, where the Gogapir holy man was a Chamar named Bhagat Singh. In a private room Bhagat Singh first played a tune on his one-stringed musical instrument, the *iktar,* and while singing a song about Gogapir, he fell into a trance. Then, shaking and trembling, his eyes closed, he threw aside his *iktar,* raced outside, sucked the wound of the person who had been bitten and spat the material into a pan of milk and *ghi* which his wife had heated on a fire for the purpose. Bhagat Singh then drank the solution, pouring some of it on the fire as a sacrifice to the spirits of the snakes.

The powers of this holy man and other followers of Gogapir are not limited to curing snakebites, but that is the basis on which their other claims to power are made.[20] Snakes are regarded as agents of demonic spirits of various sorts, hence to control snakes is to demonstrate the ability to control a wide range of malevolent forces. And even when lower caste holy men cannot demonstrate their powers in such vivid ways as the Gogapir adepts, their caste fellows tend to defer to them out of a general feeling that holy men have special access to the world of the spirits. Many of the traveling *sadhus* who beg throughout the Punjab succeed because of the fear that they might conjure up some evil act if alms were denied them. Lower caste *sants*—who follow in the tradition of medieval *sants* like Ravi Das and Kabir, are often installed at *deras,* and perform a teaching function—are regarded somewhat differently, but even they are thought to be able to placate evil

20. References to Gugapir are found in the Punjab *Census Report* for 1891 (in which Guga is described as "the most popular object of worship . . . in the east of the Punjab," p. 104); Briggs, *The Chamars,* pp. 123, 143, 151–152, 170–171; Temple, *Legends of the Punjab,* nos. 6 and 52; and Crooke, *Popular Religion and Folk-Lore,* p. 133. For a more recent study of this tradition among the Scheduled Castes, see Ram Ratan, "A Study in Magic and Medicine: Treatment by Poison-Sucking Among the Bhangis," in *Vanyajati,* vol. 3, 1955.

spirits and attract good ones. Brahmans likewise have such powers.

The role of Brahmans within lower caste religion is something of a peculiarity. A Brahman, by rights, ought to have nothing to do with Untouchables, since Brahmanhood is the manifestation of ritual purity and Untouchables embody pollution, and most Brahmans keep their distance. There is, however, a class of Untouchable Brahmans in the Punjab, and the early ethnographies could only speculate as to whether they were fallen Brahmans or members of the lower castes taking on the role.[21] In either case their presence might appear to indicate that Untouchables have taken the structures of Brahmanical Hinduism seriously—though the very idea of an "Untouchable Brahman" is abhorrent to Brahmans themselves—but one ought not accept this conclusion too readily. The very propounding of a notion so offensive to Hindu sensibilities may well represent an act of protest rather than acceptance, and the duties assigned to these Untouchable Brahmans are not only lax by Brahmanacal standards but often of a different order from what Hindus expect. These Brahmans are intercessors as much as ritual specialists, engaged in fending off evil spirits and supplicating good ones, and as such form a consistent part of the village religion of Punjab Untouchables.

Elements of the Untouchables' traditional village religion are shared with several minority traditions. Perhaps the most obvious parallel is with the animism and naturalism of the tribal societies which preceded the Aryans in ancient India, and which persist in mountainous areas of eastern and central India.[22] Their belief of the presence of spirits in persons, events, and natural objects provides one area of

21. Ibbetson et al., *Tribes and Castes,* vol. 1, pp. 131–142.

22. Fürer-Haimendorf finds the concept of *karma* nonexistent in tribal religion: "In none of the tribal societies did we encounter the idea that moral choices affect a person's fate in a future existence" (Christoph von Fürer-Haimendorf, *Morals and Merit: a Study of Values and Social Controls in South Asian Societies,* Chicago: University of Chicago Press, p. 168). See also David Mandelbaum, "Transcendental and Pragmatic Aspects of Religion," *American Anthropologist* 68: p. 1174–1191; and Martin Orans, *The Santal: a Tribe in Search of a Great Tradition* (Detroit: Wayne State University Press, 1965).

evidence in support of the theories of the Ad Dharm and Dr. Ambedkar to the effect that there was a direct line between today's Untouchables and the aboriginal inhabitants of the subcontinent.

Less obvious but possibly more significant areas of similarity are to be found in the Nath Yoga tradition. The Nath Yogis embody many of the ancient tantric elements of esoteric Hinduism, and express as well much of Shaivite Hinduism in its stress on the interior search for mystical union, the awesome and destructive power of the realm of the gods, and the relative unimportance of external forms of ritual behavior. The Nath Yogis, much more influential in medieval times in the Punjab than they are today, maintain a spiritual tradition said to have been founded by the semilegendary Gorakh Nath in North India sometime between A.D. 800 and 1000. They are practitioners of Hatha Yoga, and have renounced the world of *dharmik* Hinduism, caste and all.[23]

The links between the Nath Yogis and the religion of the lower castes are both direct and indirect. A large number of lower caste people are followers of Gorakh Nath, and there is a lower caste temple (specifically for the Chuhra caste) erected at a Gorakh Nath shrine in the Punjab near Amritsar. Furthermore, most of the ubiquitous lower caste *sadhus* make selective use of the practices and appearance of Nath Yogis in their own cults. (There are separate upper caste and lower caste groups of Yogis, a distinction which theoretically should not exist.) A particular connection has been established in legend between the popular figure of Gogapir and Gorakh Nath: Gorakh Nath allegedly assisted Gogapir in achieving mastery over the serpentine world.[24] Snakes are important to the Naths as conveyors of destructive powers, so the Nath-Gogapir relationship is understandable even without the legendary accounts of an actual meeting. Finally, the *sant* tradition itself, embracing such

23. G. W. Briggs, *Gorakhnath and the Kanphata Yogis* (Delhi, 1973). Gorakh Nath is also discussed by Mircea Eliade in *Yoga: Immortality and Freedom* (London, 1958).
24. The Nath/Gogapir relationship is discussed in Ibbetson et al., *Tribes and Castes*, vol. 1, p. 397, and Briggs, *The Chamars*, p. 150.

lower caste figures as Ravi Das and Kabir, was the product of an earlier medieval synthesis between Nath Yoga and Vaisnava *bhakti,* so Nath ideas were conveyed to lower caste religious consciousness through that route as well.[25]

The main conceptual area of agreement between the Nath Yogis and lower caste religious beliefs is their common emphasis on the immediate accessibility of spiritual power, a power that is mysterious, and that is malevolent as well as benign. Another area of agreement is the conception of God. In the Nath tradition God is formless *(nirguna),* and the overarching concept of God held by the lower castes (though not necessarily the most potent, as the strong ties to local gods and divinized legendary figures show) is also one in which God is understood as having no physical attributes. The lower caste concept of Ram, like that of many of the medieval *sants,* is a case in point. The Nath tradition affirms that spiritual power can be augmented by a concentration on sacred words; similarly, words, especially the names of persons and things, are thought to transmit spiritual power in lower caste religion. Holy men too form an essential part of the Nath tradition, as they do in the religion of the lower castes. Brahmans, of course, play a major role in neither (although, as we have seen, one finds a certain sort of Brahman in Untouchable religion), nor do the *dharmik* social customs which they epitomize, beginning with caste itself. These similarities do not prove that Untouchable religion was borrowed from the Naths or vice versa; another possibility would be that these are two branches of a common and pervasive North Indian folk tradition.

Other strands of popular religion which entered the culture of lower castes may have come from the Shakta cults, which are common in the nearby mountainous areas of the Punjab. Similarities with Shakta practices include the emphasis on the spiritual power of iron and other metals, the efficacy of the color red, and the notion of divine entities as

25. The hypothesis of a *"sant* synthesis" between Nath Yogi and Vaishnava *bhakti* ideas is set forth in Charlotte Vaudeville, *Kabir,* vol. 1 (Oxford: Clarendon Press, 1974), pp. 117–118, and W. H. McLeod, *Guru Nanak and the Sikh Religion* (Oxford, 1968), pp. 151–158.

being capricious, destructive, and linked with the forces of nature. But in the main the religion of lower caste Punjab villagers could be characterized as built upon a basis of early, perhaps aboriginal concepts of good and evil spirits, to which a number of features were added which it holds in common with the Nath tradition—the idea of a formless God, the availability of spiritual power, a distaste for *dharmik* Hinduism, and a respect for holy men and their spiritual practices. This religion of lower caste villagers may not, until the Ad Dharm, have had a name. But it had a vitality and a coherence that marked it as a religious tradition of its own, distinct from the *dharmik* Hinduism of the upper castes.

10 Ad Dharm in the Villages

As the Ad Dharm moved into the villages of the Punjab, it encountered a complex pattern of religious attachments. The lower caste villagers to whom it wished to appeal adhered to their own traditional beliefs, remained loyal to the gurus of the *panthik* movements that had touched their lives, and at the same time participated in many aspects of the religious life of the upper castes—joining certain of their festivals, imbibing their legends and mythologies, using their names and language, and wearing their emblems of affiliation. The Ad Dharm had to compete at each of these levels. It had to embrace the traditional beliefs and customs peculiar to the lower castes, extol their *panthik* gurus, and gain these villagers' confidence that it could provide a genuine substitute for the roles that Hinduism and Sikhism had historically played in their lives.

The many facets of this encounter are captured in personal stories, recollections of the original village followers of Ad Dharm. One such person was Hari Lal. He is now in his seventies, a strong, distinguished man with a full white beard and a white turban folded in the style of Sikhs, who is employed in his caste occupation as a cobbler in the village of Nalla, in the foothills of the Himalayas.[1] Nalla has a population of some 350, 12 percent of whom are Untouchables, all of them Chamar. The Chamars live by themselves at the downhill side of the village, where they are compelled to use a separate well. They have a few animals, and

---

1. The name Nalla is a pseudonym.

some land, but their steady income is from shoemaking for the surrounding villages. Hari Lal is considered to be the spokesman and leader of the Chamar community.

Hari Lal describes his religious affiliations variously. He wears the Sikh turban, long hair, and beard, and explains that the Chamars are allowed inside the Sikh *gurudwaras,* have access to all of the Sikh shrines, and observe the Sikh holy days. His knowledge about the Sikh religion, however, is less than precise. He thinks that Guru Nanak and Guru Gobind Singh are divinities, somewhat like Rama and Krishna, whom he reveres as well.

Regarding practical religious matters, Hari Lal is quite convinced that there are spiritual forces in natural objects, and can point toward certain rock formations and peculiar trees which he knows to have especially potent spiritual powers. Certain people also possess strange powers: his wife, in fact, was only now recovering from an illness caused by a harmful gaze she had received from a demented lady in a neighboring village. All of these matters, Hari Lal explains, are not really matters of religion *(dharm),* but simply everyday matters for which there are no easy explanations. Thunderstorms and hail come into a similar category. As for religion, Hari Lal regards himself as an "Ad Dharm Hindu."

By "Ad Dharm Hindu," Hari Lal explains, he means that the Chamar people are not part of the Sikh community *(qaum).* The Sikh *qaum,* he says, is only for the upper castes, primarily Jats; so Hari Lal's people cannot be Sikhs, therefore they must be Hindus. Yet they are Hindus of a special kind, exemplifying a Hinduism reserved for Chamars. That, he explains, is what the word "Ad Dharm" means. But he uses the term "Ad Dharm" as his caste name as well, just as the upper castes are called Jat Sikhs or Gujjar Muslims—one term designating caste, the other religion. For Hari Lal, the term "Ad Dharm" means something more than caste, yet it does not quite replace the term "Hindu." It fills a lexical void.

Hari Lal and the other Ad Dharm families of the Chamar neighborhood of Nalla frequently visit a Ravi Das temple located several miles away. Every year this *dera* hosts a fair that attracts Chamars and other members of lower castes from a radius of ten to fifteen miles. This event provides a large fellowship in which the beliefs and customs of the lower caste traditions are preserved, and keeps alive a large network of associations. Hari Lal looks forward to these occasions as a "renewal of the *qaum*."

Hari Lal has at least three religious identities: *qaumik, dharmik,* and *panthik*. He accepts the high traditions of Sikhs and Hindus, at least sufficiently to know who some of the religious figures are, to keep the most obvious of their customs, and to attend the temples and observe festive occasions. These contribute to a *qaumik* identity in which Hari Lal has fused Ad Dharm, Sikh, and Hindu culture. On a day-to-day level, however, his *dharmik* world is governed by spiritual forces and powers which have little relevance to his social identities. And a third level provides Hari Lal with beliefs, practices, and associations which he identifies with his caste and his community. This third kind of religious identity, the *panthik,* he nourishes in the Ravi Das temples and the myths associated with them, in the legends about the Ad Dharm, and in the festive events it has organized over the years.

It was at such an event that Hari Lal first met Mangoo Ram and became familiar with the Ad Dharm movement during the 1920s. The Ad Dharm was holding a large rally several miles away from the village Nalla, one of hundreds that they held during those years, and Hari Lal, then a young man with much curiosity, attended with some of his friends. Thereafter, he participated in several more of these rallies and proudly recorded his name in the Ad Dharm category in the census of 1931. That summarized Hari Lal's involvement with the movement. As with most of the village followers of the Ad Dharm, the rallies and other events staged by the movement were what the movement was all about.

A typical rally would be something as follows. The news would come early: perhaps two weeks to a month before the rally was held, an Ad Dharm *pracharak* ("preacher") or *updeshak* ("missionary") would appear in the area with a bundle of posters under his arm which announced a Huge

Public Meeting for the Ad Dharm *qaum*. In addition to giving the particulars of the meeting arrangements, the poster took the opportunity to set the tone of the meeting— a vigorous call for *qaum* unity and uplift in the face of Hindu oppression.[2] The advance man would visit each village in the area, conferring with the caste *panchayat* leaders. If the local Scheduled Caste leaders had never heard of Ad Dharm before, the *pracharak* would nominate one of them to be the local Ad Dharm representative, and he was placed on the mailing list.[3] The advance visit also typically included a sharing of information—local troubles and regional news.

The actual day of the meeting was usually fixed on a weekend, but during the agricultural slack seasons any day of the week would do. Since people had to come some distance to attend, the meetings would often begin in the late afternoon of the first day and continue until the morning of the next. Each person brought his or her own bedroll,[4] and women were as frequent in attendance as men. The food was provided free by the Ad Dharm organization, although donations of food and money were encouraged in order to make the free food distribution possible.[5] As the crowd gathered in vacant land near the village, the first signs of the rally were the red turbans, the red armbands, and songs extolling the glories of Ad Dharm. In the area where the speakers would stand, a large red banner with the word *soham* was unrolled as a backdrop for the event.[6]

When a sufficient crowd had gathered, a local Scheduled Caste leader would welcome the visiting Ad Dharm dig-

---

2. Posters such as this are among the personal possessions of Mangoo Ram. I am grateful to him for allowing me to copy them.

3. Interview with Mangoo Ram, Garhshankar, November 13, 1973.

4. Instructions for the participants were given on posters like this one: Mugowal Zila Hoshiarpur de Ad Dharm Skul: Wadda Bhwari Diwan ("Mugowal, District Hoshiarpur, in the Ad Dharm School: Huge Public Meeting"), a poster announcing the first annual conference of Ad Dharm on June 11–12, 1927; English translation in Mark Juergensmeyer, "Political Hope."

5. Ibid.

6. Chanan Lal Manik, "Adi Dharm Bari" ("About Ad Dharm"), a series of reminiscences in the *Ravidas Patrika* (in Punjabi), Jullundur, beginning in the issue of December 29, 1970.

nitaries from Jullundur. Verses were recited from the poetry of Ravi Das and the other *bhakti* saints, and a number of new, specifically Ad Dharmi songs were sung, filled with lively lyrics and peppered with calls for unity, bravery, and struggle. A sample is the following song by Munshi Jhandoo Ram, one of the more popular singers of the movement, a stirring exhortation to himself and to his *qaum:*

> Ad Dharmi, lions, brothers,
>   Come join the organization;
> Wherever you hear your brothers are harmed,
>   Stand fast, dig in, and right the wrong;
> We prefer death more than a dismal life,
>   Make a sweetheart of death, Jhandoo.
> Leave behind dependence on others,
>   Make a friend of higher powers.
> Ad Dharmi, stay with your religion,
>   Though an army marches against you;
> Be brave, not cowardly or insincere—
>   You are descendants of lions;
> The body can even be destroyed;
>   The soul, made noble, will always stay.
> News of the meetings have come,
>   Jhandoo, why look behind?
> Some people flirt with selfish motives,
>   They are only playing games of chess;
> Beware of those treacherous ones,
>   For the swords of the enemy are drawn.
> The raga is clear only at the beginning,
>   As they tune the *sarangi* and the *mirdang*.
> Jhandoo, victory for Ad Dharm!
>   The dust of misery will pass with the wind.[7]

There were speeches as well, usually intended to confirm the Scheduled Castes' worst suspicions about the Hindus and bolster their best hopes about themselves. If the rally was an important one, Swami Shudranand or Mangoo Ram might be there personally. Shudranand especially had the

---

7. Ibid. March 9, 1971, issue; translated with the assistance of Devinder Singh, Punjab University, Chandigarh.

reputation of being an awesome orator,[8] who juxtaposed homey anecdotes with religious poetry, frequently ending his speeches with these lines:

> What is your religion? Truth. Who is your guru? Ravi Das, Rishi Valmik. Who are the Hindus? The Aryans from outside. We are not Hindus.[9]

Once the main address was complete, the meeting drew to a close with a public vote on a series of resolutions. These resolutions were solicited from the crowd. People shouted out their complaints and concerns, and these were transformed into proper-sounding phrases that seemed to simple villagers almost to have the force of law.[10]

In the cities the rallies were a bit different. A large procession began the affair, winding through the Scheduled Caste neighborhoods with banners and posters, chanting the slogan:

> Tie a red turban on your head—
> Fight for your *qaum* unto your death.[11]

The speeches in the city generally offered a little less poetry, a little more politics, but it was possible both in city and village for a rally to conclude with an immediate and active attempt to redress local grievances. There were efforts to use upper caste wells, enter Hindu temples and Sikh shrines, and bathe in village ponds.[12] Violence sometimes ensued on these occasions—sometimes even when the crowds were relatively docile—and upper caste vigilantes would try to break up the rallies and beat the leaders.[13] Finally the rallies would disperse with cries of "Jai Ad Dharm" and "Jai Guru Dev."

8. Interview with Principal Ram Das, Hoshiarpur, April 18, 1971; interview with Sadhu Ram, M.P., New Delhi, June 24, 1971.
9. Interview with Swami Shudranand, Jullundur, June 10, 1971.
10. *Ad Dharm Report,* p. 16.
11. Interviews with Rullia Ram and J. C. Badhan, Jullundur, March 28, 1971.
12. Interviews with Mangoo Ram, Garhshankar, December 1, 1970; see also *Ad Dharm Report,* p. 56.
13. Manik, "Adi Dharm Bari," *Ravidas Patrika,* January 5, 1971.

The impression Hari Lal gained from these rallies was that a new generation had emerged within the Scheduled Castes. It was a generation which some viewed as dangerously brazen, others as proudly heroic. And beyond that, the rallies made them proud of who they were. When Hari Lal was asked whether Ad Dharm replaced their old beliefs in the spirit world or were integrated into them, he seemed puzzled. The world of the spirits had nothing to do with Ad Dharm, he said, nor did the movement, in turn, have anything to do with the high tradition of Hindus and Sikhs. Ad Dharm was something new. Yet, he continued, as if contradicting himself, "it was *our* religion."

In Hari Lal's eyes the Ad Dharm succeeded in affirming the validity of his own religious culture without having explicitly to embrace those beliefs and practices as its own. Similarly, it managed to stand up to the Hindus without having to be exactly the same sort of religion that Hinduism was: its integrity as a religious movement was rooted in village culture instead. The Ad Dharm was a *panthik* movement consistent with Hari Lal's traditional religious practices (his *dharmik* religion), and it was potentially a religious community (a *qaum*). Thus Ad Dharm fitted into each level of his religious identity in some satisfactory way.

As a religion, Ad Dharm existed in the villages only now and then. The events of the Ad Dharm rallies were its moments of sacred time, extraordinary moments in which the affairs and concerns of the participants' ordinary lives were elevated to a level of spiritual validity, humane concern, and social power. But these events also managed to create elements of sacred place and sacred community. The fields near the villages on which the rallies were held were sometimes compared to the fields of Kurukshetra, the battlefield of the Bhagavad Gita: the very act of coming together in such an assemblage involved risk and offered a special excitement. And the community of people who gathered, although they may have gathered for many a Ravi Das *mela* in outwardly similar ways, assembled for the Ad Dharm occasions with the knowledge that this movement had an organizational force and a sense of social strategy which other religious associations did not have. So on this occasion they were a community of expectation and hope as well as a community at worship. Without wholly transforming it, the Ad Dharm rallies affirmed a religious culture that was rooted in the ancestral village past, but at the same moment they announced a decisive change and offered a bold but precarious vision of a new age.

11 The Urban Experience: Ad Dharm as New Dharm

In the villages the Ad Dharm had offered an idealistic vision, a hopeful fantasy. But in urban areas the vision seemed more palpable, for it matched an already changing, modern lifestyle. Many of the lower caste people who had left the villages for the cities had also abandoned the traditional beliefs in the world of spirits that form the backbone of the religion of rural Untouchables, but they were scarcely willing to embrace the *dharm* of Hindus and Sikhs as a substitute—or the concept of caste that went with it. For such people Ad Dharm provided a new *dharm*. From the first its ideology and organization had been closely linked with the experience of newly urban people undergoing great moments of social change, so for them it was able to do more than stimulate a vision of what could be: it described and prescribed a habit of life.

Perhaps nowhere in the Punjab was the Ad Dharm more integrally a part of an "ideology of transition"[1] than in the Boota Mandi settlement near the city of Jullundur. Today the area gives the impression of having brought that ideology to fulfillment, answering the Ad Dharm movement's most ambitious hopes. Its cultural symbols, such as Ravi Das, and its egalitarian social values are those propagated by the Ad Dharm, and they appear to have had much to do with making Boota Mandi what it is today. Indeed, the founders of Boota Mandi were Ad Dharmis. As the movement and the community grew, the strengths of one re-

---

1. The phrase is that of Thomas O'Dea.

inforced those of the other and their identities became intertwined. The residents of Boota Mandi, when asked about their caste, appropriate the name of the Ad Dharm itself, and the ubiquitous portraits of Sant Ravi Das are constant reminders of the heritage that the Ad Dharm revived.

Boota Mandi, like the movement to which it is related, is a proud, self-sufficient, financially strong, and socially conscious community. Stacks of hides piled along the side of the road signal that the leather trade is prominent here and has contributed greatly to Boota Mandi's growth and success. When one talks with some of the residents and visits their homes, one discovers how prosperous that trade can be: one of the families has a television set, a son-in-law (from the same caste as they) who has gone to England and become a film maker for the BBC, and a son who is a banker, married to a Punjabi woman (also within his caste) from Kenya. In the streets a number of motor scooters are in evidence, and several families own automobiles.

Boota Mandi is as vigorous in the cultural sphere as in the economic. Education has played an important role in its development, Untouchables learning from higher-caste or foreign teachers, and now a group of young Boota Mandi college graduates have established their own school, specializing in educating the young ladies of upper caste families. But Boota Mandi displays a cultural orientation of its own: pictures of Sant Ravi Das are everywhere, and he is remembered in the names of a number of community buildings. There is a Ravi Das Gurdwara, a Ravi Das library, a Ravi Das community center, even a Ravi Das youth club, a sort of social fraternity for high school and college age boys. A Ravi Das school operates out of the Gurdwara, educating 350 children, an impressive 90 percent of the school-age population; and over 50 percent of both boys and girls go on to attend high school.

It was not always that way, of course. Until about 1930 there was nothing along Nakodar Road where Boota Mandi now stands except for scrub brush and eroded fields. In that year Seth Kishan Das and his four older brothers, who were tenant cultivators in nearby Nangal village, five miles away, came with the intention of setting up a wholesale cloth business to cater to the British army cantonment in Jullundur.[2] There had been caste tensions between the Chamars and landholders in his village, and the brothers came with hopes for a new beginning. Kishan Das and his brothers soon discovered that more money was to be made in the sale of leather for military boots than in cloth, but the Muslims in Basti Gujan of Jullundur city had cornered the leather market and were not hospitable to competition. Since they were themselves Chamars, however, the brothers had better access to the sources of supply, the Chamars who collected the hides from the village hide-collectors and who did the rude tanning. Thus Kishan Das and his brothers were able to compete in the market despite all the Muslims' attempts to drive them out by intimidating their sources of supply and causing prices to fluctuate. It was the market *(mandi)* for boots, or at least for the leather which the British army had made into boots and other supplies.

Soon another Chamar, Sundar Das, came to Boota Mandi from village Dhanal, four miles away. Sundar Das had saved money selling leather to the Chinese shoemakers in Calcutta, so he also was able to enter the leather business. His became the second major family of Boota Mandi: various uncles and cousins migrated from the villages to join him, as Kishan Das's family had already begun to do, and even today much of Boota Mandi's population of 2,000 are either relatives of Kishan Das in the Klare subcaste or relatives of Sundar Das in the Mehay subcaste. The remaining residents come from the other Chamar subcastes that are found in villages within a twenty-mile radius: they provide the labor supply for the tanning and leather-transporting operations instituted by the Klares and Mehays. Fifty percent of Boota Mandi's residents are involved in small-scale rough tanning, which they do on contract; 30 percent are wage labor for the various tanning enterprises, and 20 percent are involved in the more lucra-

2. My information on Boota Mandi, its history, and its leading citizens, comes from extensive interviews in the area in 1970–1971, 1973, and 1978. I am especially indebted to Seth Kishan Das and to Manohar Lal Mehay, grandson of Sundar Das.

tive trading business. The merchants are organized into four syndicates which trade in tanned leather; the Klares and Mehays account for more than 20 percent of the trade in rough tanned leather and 70 percent of the rawhide sales to industries. The average worker does fairly well by lower caste standards, making between Rs. 200 ($25) and Rs. 300 ($37) per month, and the main merchant families are extraordinarily well off, in some cases earning thousands of rupees per month. Boota Mandi is no slum. Neither is it entirely a ghetto: a large number of its former residents have moved into the comfortable middle-class surroundings of the new residential colonies in Jullundur, where they draw government salaries in many cases comparable to those of other groups.

The leather merchants of Boota Mandi have provided leadership and financial support for several Scheduled Caste movements. In fact, the original pioneers, Seth Kishan Das and Sundar Das, were active in the Ad Dharm even before they founded Boota Mandi. Since Sundar Das was chairman of the Ad Dharm advisory committee, the Mehay family is especially proud of his role and has captioned his picture, prominently displayed on their office wall, with the words "Founder of the Ad Dharm Mandal."[3] Swami Shudranand, another of the Ad Dharm founders with connections in Boota Mandi, continued in the 1970s to spend much of his time there: the old bachelor activist was given a room to live in and generous regard.

The careers of the Ad Dharm, of other Scheduled Caste movements, and of the colony of Boota Mandi itself, are all intertwined, and behind them all stand the financial successes of the Boota Mandi patriarchs, Seth Kishan Das and Sundar Das. Both of them were ambitious, aggressive, firm. Seth Kishan Das was the more volatile and restless of the two, but both traveled frequently, especially to Calcutta, which was important to the leather trade, and both of them enjoyed politics. They both had had some education, but had mastered only the rudiments of writing, reading, and

3. *The Ad Dharm Report* lists Sundar Das as the first president of the executive committee of the movement and goes on to say that "due to personal circumstances" he resigned and was replaced by Seth Labu Ram of Sochi Pind, Jullundur district.

arithmetic. This was sufficient, however, for business purposes, and their ventures were visibly successful. Yet it was not their wealth but their philanthropy that made an enduring mark on the social character of the Punjab, through their support for lower caste movements such as Ad Dharm and for cultural activities associated with Ravi Das.

Seth Kishan Das and Sundar Das could have kept their money to themselves, but for several reasons they did not. One reason was quite patently self-interest. The Chamar handlers of hides in the villages were Boota Mandi's main source of raw material, and provided labor for its tanneries as well. It was simply good business for the entrepreneurs of Boota Mandi to promote the cultural symbols of their caste, since it encouraged loyalty from their workers and helped them solidify a network of business associations. In that sense the Boota Mandi businessmen supported the Ad Dharm and contributed to various Ravi Das efforts out of the same motives that encourage Western businessmen to support a businessmen's eating club or a civic charity.

But there were other factors involved. The Ad Dharm and the Ravi Das activities were not just clubs or charities, they were movements, emblems of changing values. Seth Kishan Das and Sundar Das endorsed those values, not only because it was good for business, but because it was good for themselves. It buttressed and ennobled their image of themselves and of the caste community of which they were a part. In general, these values embraced the goals of modern society: equal opportunity, reward based on merit, reverence, temperance, and reason. And the means of achieving these virtues also became charged with value: hard work, self-discipline, and education. All of these were the hallmarks of the Ad Dharm, repeatedly broadcast in its songs and poems and slogans; collectively, they constituted the movement's new *dharm*. More than just a moral code, they were aspects of an integrated ideal of social and personal behavior, undergirded with religious concepts. The *dharm* of Ad Dharm was egalitarian, and the ideological basis it claimed was truth itself: it aimed at orienting action toward the attainment and realization of knowledge, the highest form of human consciousness. Hindus had spanned their *dharm* between purity and pollution; the Ad Dharm chose the polarity of knowledge and ignorance instead.

According to the theology of the Ad Dharm, to achieve salvation was to attain the realm of *sachkhand* (a term used by Guru Nanak to describe the highest state of god-consciousness). *Sachkhand,* the realm of truth, could be reached only through knowledge, and knowledge, in turn, was not the religious knowledge of traditional Hinduism, but the knowledge provided by modern classrooms and textbooks. An Ad Dharm slogan puts the point succinctly: "Education leads us to where the truth resides [*sachkhand*]."[4] In the songs that were sung during the Ad Dharm worship services, education became almost an article of religious faith, as one can see in this verse sung during the collection of offerings:

> Knowledge shows the way to truth:
> > in order for our people to improve,
> > I beg these offerings from you.
> You can worship the goddesses and the gods,
> > but they won't solve the problems
> > that you have in your homes.
> You can plead for magic and magical spells,
> > still your actions may be bad
> > and your crops may not be good.
> So teach the truth and do good works,
> > for the sake of yourself, your *qaum* and kinfolk,
> > I beg these offerings from you.[5]

The following verse, sung as the oath of commitment, was a call to action mixed with religion and moral exhortation; again, education is a prominent part of the vision:

> Ad Dharm brethren, don't be lazy,
> > make every effort your very best.
> Taking our heads in our palms,
> > we will sacrifice ourselves for our *qaum.*

4. Interview with Mangoo Ram, Garhshankar, April 17, 1971.
5. This poem and the ones following were recited from memory by Mangoo Ram (April 17, 1971), who claims to have written them. They were translated with the assistance of Mohinder Singh and Devinder Singh, Department of Panjabi, Punjab University, Chandigarh.

> What if you've been born lowly—
>   we will show them how high we are.
> And those who have left our fold
>   are welcome to return again.
> We will educate our children—
>   fifth year, tenth year, up to B.A.,
> And preparing our scriptures, Ad Prakash,
>   we begin; our religion, Ad Dharm.

Many of these modern moral virtues were similar to those preached by the Arya Samaj, the Christian missionaries, and other reforming forces in the Punjab in the years when the Ad Dharm was forming. The role of women, for example, was held in higher esteem than in traditional society: "There should be great happiness on the birth of boys and girls."[6] Bride money was prohibited.[7] Primary education was recommended for girls as well as for boys;[8] and the dignity of women was generally honored.[9]

Other moral emphases were those that the Ad Dharm intended as correctives to loose living:

> Ad Dharmis should abstain from theft, fraud, lies, dishonesty, looking at someone else's wife with bad intentions, using anything which brings intoxication, gambling, and usurping other persons' property or belongings. All of these things, which are against the law of nature, are against the law of Ad Dharm.[10]

Yet all of this moralism was put in the context of religious commitment and the uplift of the whole community. The following verse, from a song that was sung when offerings were taken at rallies, was able to mix the high vision of a better society with the stern injunction against use of the hallucinatory drugs *bhang* ("marijuana"), *afin* ("opium"), and *post* ("raw opium"):

> Give us some offerings—body, mind, and money—
>   these, brothers, we expect from each of you;

---

6. *Ad Dharm Report*, p. 39.   7. Ibid., p. 40.
8. Ibid., p. 41.   9. Ibid., p. 39.   10. Ibid., p. 37.

> The time has gone when they called us high or low,
>   now is the time to build our *qaum* anew.
> We will leave drugs behind, for the betterment of us all;
>   brothers, I call for offerings from you.[11]

Most important of the modern virtues, of course, was that of casteless equality. Those who shaped the movement stated categorically that the "Ad Dharm does not believe in the caste system, or any inferiority or superiority of this sort."[12] And in this way they meant to include caste restrictions practiced among the lower castes themselves, as well as those within the total hierarchy. The leaders were proud to point out instances of marriages between an Ad Dharmi Chamar and a Christian convert from a Chuhra subcaste, even though they admitted that such instances were rare.

Finally, there was a group of injunctions intended purely to promote the general uplift and self-respect of the community:

> Cleanliness is important; it guarantees good health.
> Young girls and boys should not be sent out for
>   cutting grass and cutting wood.
> It is not good to cry and beat oneself at a death
>   or funeral; one makes the Guru Dev angry by
>   this act.
> To eat the food served at [upper caste] marriages is
>   legal, but the food should be decent, not leftovers.
> Each Ad Dharmi should help his fellow Ad Dharmi
>   in need.[13]

There was a genuine concern for the community, its image, and the mutuality of support within the "brotherhood," and these were immediate, personal concerns, calling for reforms in individual habits and relationships. Such principles, like all of the virtues the movement espoused, reinforced the same central point: to be a part of the Ad Dharm was a commitment to an encompassing lifestyle and a new social order.

11. Recited by Mangoo Ram, April 17, 1971.
12. *Ad Dharm Report*, p. 37.
13. Selections from the fifty-six "Ad Dharmi Commandments," *Ad Dharm Report*, pp. 39–43.

In the villages such a program had a futuristic ring, but in the cities the very same teachings were perceived as applicable in the present day. The leaders of the Ad Dharm had certainly not intended to reinforce such a cleavage: they thought of the stable *dharmik* community they had spawned in the cities and the more temporary sacred communities that they fostered in the village as parts of a single whole. And they had the conceptual resources to do so, since they conceived of the movement as a *qaum*, a broad-based religious organization. But in reality the differences between rural and urban contexts meant that the Ad Dharm comprised two rather distinct movements, two forms of religion. In the villages it was a movement whose main thrust was to accord pride and integrity to an established leadership by honoring a spiritual past and projecting a constructive future. In the cities, by contrast, the Ad Dharm was not suspended between a re-created and a visionary future to the same degree: it meshed into a genuine present, albeit a present in transition, by providing symbols of identity and ethical standards for a new species of lower caste entrepreneur. Such persons were no longer Untouchables, and they refused to tolerate a world view that would characterize them or anyone else in such a way. For Seth Kishan Das, the Klares, the Mahays, and other residents of Boota Mandi, Ad Dharm portrayed a new world in which they could believe, a world that was already half reality. It functioned as a new *dharm*, presenting a coherent set of values and obligations and laying the basis for a community of vision and trust. Mangoo Ram stood between these two cultures, rural and urban; although he was more a product of the modern than of the village lifestyle, his leadership, for the sake of consolidating his growing political strength and in the interest of maintaining his own ideological integrity, depended on both.

12 Mangoo Ram vs. Gandhi

In both villages and cities, Ad Dharm was more than a movement for change, it was an alternative way of looking at the social whole. But that did not make it unique. One could say as much for the Arya Samaj during the early years of the Ad Dharm movement—that fact caused much of the tension between them—and the world view that increasingly offered the most attractive competition was that of Gandhi and his nationalistic movements for reform. Like the Ad Dharm, Gandhi's reinterpretation of Hinduism affirmed modern cultural values, proposed a nonhierarchical view of society, and subscribed to a religio-scientific understanding of the self. And because Gandhi conceived of means and ends as a united whole, his movement was intended, like the Ad Dharm, to be itself a harbinger of the new society it envisaged. Gandhi's movement, perhaps even more than the Arya Samaj, posed a threat to the Ad Dharm because the ideology was so closely similar to its own, and Ad Dharmis regarded Gandhi and his movement in much the way they had perceived the Samaj—as subversive ploys of the upper castes.

Outwardly, it seems paradoxical that the Ad Dharm should have been so hostile to Gandhi, since Gandhi is remembered in Indian history as a great friend of the Untouchables. In his own personal habits he defied caste prejudices by welcoming Untouchables into his home and at his dinner table. It was he who coined the term "Harijan" in order to banish the use of the word "Untouchable." And after 1932, when Gandhi was eager to implement the notion that social transformation was necessary if India was to be genuinely free and not simply independent from British rule, he directed his efforts particularly to the uplift of the Untouchables.

All of this, however, did little to mute the Ad Dharm's hostility. In fact, it exacerbated it, making Gandhi an ideological competitor. But there were other reasons for the Ad Dharm's opposition as well, matters of temperament—Gandhi's pacifist moderation did not sit comfortably with the restless, angry mood of the Ad Dharm—and of political alliance. Gandhi and the Congress party were anti-British; and the British had become Ad Dharm's friend. Moreover, the Congress was dominated by upper caste Hindus, who the Ad Dharm feared would ultimately use whatever power they amassed to extend their domination over the lower castes. The Ad Dharm wanted no part of independence if independence meant government by upper caste Hindus; they preferred to take their chances with the British. The *Ad Dharm Report* said as much:

> As long as India's weak minorities—especially Ad Dharmis and the Mohammedan people—are not given full representation, and there is no guarantee of their proper treatment, there should be no change in the central government.
>
> India should not be given independence until the Untouchables are free and equal. Otherwise, it would be a disgrace to the British rule.[1]

Thus there was no love lost between the Ad Dharm and the Congress. The Congress had its own Scheduled Caste movement, the All-India Suppressed Classes Federation, which held processions through Lahore as early as 1924, primarily to protest the practice of *begar*, forced labor.[2] This group, subsequently renamed the Depressed Classes Mission, Lahore, sent a delegation to the Simon Commission hearings in 1928, not to condemn the caste Hindus but

1. *Ad Dharm Report*, pp. 63, 14.
2. Interview with Lala Mohan Lal, former secretary, Harijan Sevak Sangh, 1932–1947, in Jullundur, May 1, 1971.

to oppose the Land Alienation Act, which, they said, "reduced us to serfs," and to castigate the British government, which, they claimed, "more than caste Hindus [was] responsible for [their] poverty, illiteracy and backwardness."[3] This was a far cry from Mangoo Ram's position, and it is not surprising that Mangoo Ram had little use for the Scheduled Caste participants in these organizations.[4]

The nadir in relations between Gandhi and the Ad Dharm was undoubtedly reached in an encounter between a group of Ad Dharmis and a salt *satyagraha* in Jullundur in 1930.[5] The Punjab branch of the Indian National Congress, in sympathy with Gandhi's salt *satyagraha*, decided to boycott imported salt and make their own. Sometime that year, it seems (the date is not certain), the Ad Dharmis, led by Mangoo Ram, marched in protest against the Congress and on behalf of the British.[6] Apparently, there was some taunting on the part of the disgruntled Congress men, then some pushing and shoving, and before the day had ended the Ad Dharmis had vandalized the heavy kilns for making salt, beaten several of the Congress men, and stolen some pots and kettles.[7]

That incident was the culmination of a series of milder confrontations that ensued when the Ad Dharm made efforts to obstruct the goals of the Congress. In 1928, for example, they had reacted to Motilal Nehru's call for the abolition of separate electorates (except for Muslims) by

3. Lahore *Tribune* 48, no. 257 (Nov. 6, 1928).
4. Interview with Mangoo Ram, April 17, 1971.
5. Swami Shudranand claims also that it was one of the largest events of the Ad Dharm, involving thousands of their members in opposition to the Congress (interview on May 15, 1971).
6. This story was told essentially in the same form by several old Ad Dharmis during interviews: Mangoo Ram (April 17, 1971), Rullia Ram (March 28, 1971), Swami Shudranand (May 15, 1971), Seth Kushi Ram (May 15, 1971), and Seth Kishan Das (November 16, 1973). It was also confirmed by one member of the Congress party who was there at the time, Prithvi Singh Azad (interview on April 13, 1971). I have placed the date of the event in 1930, since that would correspond with Gandhi's largest salt *satyagraha*. My informants could not remember the date with accuracy; Mangoo Ram dated the event in 1933 and Swami Shudranand dated it in 1935.
7. Prithvi Singh Azad, interview on April 13, 1971.

declaring: "We hope that . . . the ghost of Untouchability will be sunk, along with the Nehru Report, in the River Ravi."[8] When the issue was raised at the Round Table Conference in London (1930–1932), the Ad Dharm was again staunch in its opposition to the Congress position. Mangoo Ram sent telegrams pledging the Ad Dharm's support for Dr. Bhim Rao Ambedkar, the Untouchables' representative at the conference, and continued to stand behind him and against Gandhi when the talks collapsed in disagreement over the issue of separate electorates for the Untouchables.[9]

Gandhi's response to the attempt to impose a system of separate electorates for the Untouchable community was as dramatic as it was strong. For Gandhi the issue was whether the Untouchables should be regarded as separate communities with their own representatives or whether they were to be considered part of the whole society; Ambedkar and Mangoo Ram were of the former view, Gandhi was of the latter. Gandhi vowed to "fast unto death" for his position and began, on September 20, 1932, an "epic fast" against separate electorates.[10] It had the effect of precipitating for the first time a crisis of national proportions that centered on the plight of the Untouchables. As one contemporary historian observed, "It threw the country into a state of alarm, consternation and confusion."[11]

Gandhi sincerely believed that his position was in the best interest of the Untouchables: he felt that separate electorates would only prolong the division of society between

8. *Ad Dharm Report*, p. 54.
9. Lahore *Tribune* 51, no. 240 (October 11, 1931). Mangoo Ram has a copy of one of the telegrams in his possession. It reads, in part, "Dr. Ambedkar is sole representative of all India depressed classes. We demand separate electorate. Joint electorate is detrimental to our interests." Mangoo Ram signed the telegram as "President of the Ad Dharm (Untouchables) Mandal." A similar telegram was sent by Basant Rai, the leader of the rival Ad Dharm headquarters in Lyallpur (Chanan Lal Manik, "Adi Dharm Bari," *Ravidas Patrika*, Dec. 29, 1970).
10. The best account of Gandhi's fast is written by his personal secretary, Pyare Lal, *The Epic Fast* (Ahmedabad, 1932).
11. B. Pattabhi Sitaramayya, *The History of the Indian National Congress*, vol. 1 (1885–1935) (Bombay, 1935), p. 533.

upper and lower castes. Some lower caste leaders, including the venerable M. C. Rajah, sided with Gandhi, convinced that "our regeneration is the fundamental aim of his life."[12] Dr. Ambedkar, however, and the Ad Dharm with him, were of a different mind, holding that without a guarantee of separate representation the Scheduled Castes would have no representation at all. To the leaders of the Ad Dharm, then, there was nothing saintly in the Mahatma's "epic fast." They saw his much-vaunted self-sacrifice as an underhanded trick, something he resorted to in time of extremity, the cynical ploy of a master politician.

Mangoo Ram was quick to respond by declaring a fast of his own.[13] This counter-fast, admittedly something of a publicity ploy itself, was one of a series of efforts he made to gain support for the Ambedkar position. Mangoo Ram went to Simla and raised his demands there,[14] he wrote an open letter to King George,[15] and he threatened the British with massive disturbances throughout the Punjab if the Scheduled Castes were not granted separate electorates. He later recalled that he told the British he had complete control over the Untouchables of the Punjab: "They were willing to die for me if necessary."[16] In Mangoo Ram's mind, certainly, the issue was just that critical, for it was the political manifestation of all that the Ad Dharm stood for as a separate *qaum*. From his point of view it would have been political and ideological suicide to attempt representation through Hindu seats in a legislature. It would have meant stepping backward into the very Hindu society from which the Ad Dharm was trying to liberate itself.

The Poona Pact, reached on September 26, 1932, solved the problem. Ambedkar and Gandhi agreed on a compromise in which the Untouchables would forfeit their

12. Statement by M. C. Rajah, "Politically 'Untouchables,'" reprinted in Pyare Lal, *The Epic Fast*.
13. My only sources of information on Mangoo Ram's counter-fast are interviews with him (April 17, 1971) and another Ad Dharmi, Gurvanta Singh (May 8, 1971). There is also mention of the counter-fast in Chanan Lal Manik, "Adi Dharm Bari," March 23, 1971.
14. Mangoo Ram, interview on April 17, 1971.
15. Ibid.
16. Ibid.

claim to separate electorates provided they were given reserved seats in open electorates. This meant that there would be no constituencies made up entirely of Untouchables, but in their place would be established districts in which only Untouchables could become candidates for office. The electorate in such districts, however, was to remain mixed, so that everyone would have a chance to determine which of the candidates would be seated. This system still prevails in India. When it was introduced in 1932 it was regarded as a great victory by the Ad Dharm, since it had the immediate effect of ushering Untouchable political candidates into the general elections with the assurance that some of them would take office.

The Poona Pact itself, however, did not guarantee how many seats were to be allotted to Untouchables, and Mangoo Ram continued his fast and his threats of further disturbances in order to assure an adequate number of seats in the Punjab. His actions, he felt, were responsible for securing the desired number of allocations (eight),[17] and when they were granted he broke his fast at a large rally in Jullundur. Reflecting on his fast later, Mangoo Ram explained that it had been a way of dramatizing what he said to the Mahatma at the time: "Gandhi, if you are prepared to die for your Hindus, then I am prepared to die for these Untouchables."[18] It was a personal gesture, and support for it came primarily from his own people: Seth Kishan Das, the wealthy Boota Mandi merchant, made all the physical arrangements and handled the public relations. Mangoo Ram received some help from the Unionist party, but apparently no direct financial or administrative aid came from Ambedkar,[19] and with the exception of a police guard, none from the government.

This personal vendetta which Mangoo Ram waged against Gandhi is touched with a special poignancy, for it highlights by contrast the broad areas of concern that the

17. Ibid.; and Manik, "Adi Dharm Bari," March 23, 1971.
18. Mangoo Ram, interview on November 13, 1973.
19. Mangoo Ram said that Sikandar Hyat Khan, the Unionist party chief minister of the Punjab, suggested that he undertake the fast (interview on April 17, 1971).

Ad Dharm and the Gandhians in fact held in common: both were struggling to improve the condition of Untouchables and to realize an egalitarian society. Yet the two camps were divided on issues of strategy and, on a deeper level, by genuine differences of social vision. Gandhi's understanding of the ideal social order was communitarian. He held that social harmony would be achieved through a collective seeking after truth that resembles in many respects the Quaker notion of consensus. The basic units in this striving after consensus were villages and urban neighborhoods—the social collectives that allowed for personal interaction among their members. If India was to be genuinely free, thought Gandhi, each of those units would have to be self-sufficient, equal, and harmonious—both in respect to its own membership and in relation to the other units of society. It followed that the major obstacles to such a state of harmony were the great social divisions, primarily those which separated religious communities and castes from one another. As Gandhi perceived the matter, these divisions had to be destroyed before there was any hope of an egalitarian social order.

The Ad Dharm, though it also maintained an egalitarian vision of the ideal society, saw matters quite differently. Perhaps their vision was simply not as radical as Gandhi's; or perhaps it was more realistic. It seemed to the Ad Dharmis that there was no possibility of achieving general social equality without first securing a measure of power and respect for those sectors of society currently being denied such equality—namely, the lower castes. And it was essential that that power and respect be granted to the lower castes as a whole: only then could individuals within those castes expect to earn the true respect of upper-class persons. This communalistic vision of the basis for social equality put Ad Dharm political strategy directly athwart Gandhi's, just as Gandhi's communitarian vision put his policies athwart those of the Ad Dharm. Each perceived the other as an obstacle to achieving intercaste harmony. Gandhi thought that the Ad Dharmis through their militant separatism were reinforcing the concept of caste divisions, and the Ad Dharmis thought Gandhi was trying to whitewash existing differences in a superficial harmony.

These are differences that persist to the present day between Gandhians and militant Untouchables. The Harijan Sevak Sangh, which Gandhi founded, is predominantly an upper caste affair; lower caste members are not encouraged into its leadership. The main purpose of the organization is to provide a way for upper caste people to aid the lower castes, providing them a means of expiating their sense of guilt for generations of abuse perpetrated against the lower castes.[20] Such a position is regarded as paternalistic nonsense by the more militant Untouchable activists, who in turn are regarded by the Gandhians and other social reformers as interested only in their own political ambitions. The Gandhians accuse them of building a separate constituency in order to create a base for their own political power. Thus the old issues of strategy, and the differing concepts of social harmony which lie beneath them, are still alive among those who are concerned to achieve social uplift for the lower castes.

20. Interview with Rabindra Nath Chawla, Secretary of Harijan Sevak Sangh, Kingsway Camp, Delhi, June 26, 1971.

13 "Hope from God and Help from the King"

In many ways the enlightened British ideal for India was more appealing to the Ad Dharm than Gandhi's. The Ad Dharmis had much to gain from the British politically, and they felt comfortable with them ideologically. Indeed, one senses an implicit admiration of Western politics and social values in Ad Dharm. The significance of this admiration, however, should not be exaggerated, for even though the American hegira of Mangoo Ram and the educational experience of the other Ad Dharm leaders had exposed them to Western notions of individualism and social homogeneity, the major factors that molded the movement as a whole were largely Indian: the example of Arya Samaj, the *qaum* models of Sikhs and Indian Muslims, the traditional religious identity of the lower castes, and the communal egalitarianism of the *panthik* movements. Nonetheless, there was a kinship between the Ad Dharmis' vision of a casteless meritocracy and the social ideals of British reformers that endeared one to the other. And circumstances bound them closer. The British were in power, but that power was under attack, and this meant that both groups had something to gain from the other's friendship.

There is no evidence that there was any direct encouragement from the British in the organizing of the Ad Dharm movement. Nevertheless, the creation of a friendly organization of Untouchables, one hostile to the Arya Samaj and other organizations from which anti-British sentiments had originated, was an event too fortunate for the British not to arouse suspicion in some quarters. There were upper caste observers in the Punjab who doubted that it was all coincidence and were convinced that if the Ad Dharm was not a British front per se, at the very least it must have received government money.[1] The Ad Dharm, of course, claimed that this was "a blatant lie," and regarded these accusations as simple indications of jealousy on the part of the upper castes:

> The world is changing; they do not realize that we are trying to change ourselves with the world. Everybody else is fighting for freedom; why shouldn't we? Why are the upper castes so envious and jealous of our progress? The Hindus and Sikhs just want us to be their faithful and loyal dogs. We tell them in ringing terms: neither government, Mohammedans, or Christians have any influence in our movement. We are simply asserting ourselves. We see the speed at which things are changing in the world today, so we simply ask for our rights.[2]

The friendship between the Ad Dharm and the government was understandable in light of the general purposes of the Ad Dharm movement. There was something a bit peculiar, however, in the camaraderie of Mangoo Ram, since in his earlier youth he had been actively opposed to the British. As an agent for the Gadar party who claimed to have been twice condemned to death by the British, it seemed unusual that he should become so solicitous toward them in such a short period of time. The British, for their part, apparently had no knowledge of Mangoo Ram's previous revolutionary activity; there is no investigatory file on him in government records. And Mangoo Ram justified his collusion with a former enemy on the grounds stated above: "The world is changing . . . [and] we are trying to change ourselves with the world."

One of those changes was the government's receptivity toward the appeals of the lower castes, which may have

1. This position was stated to be "common knowledge" by an historian at Punjab University, Professor S. L. Malhotra (interview, Chandigarh, April 28, 1971).
2. *Ad Dharm Report,* p. 69.

been a factor in the formation of the Ad Dharm movement in the first place. In a poster for one of the first Ad Dharm conferences in Mugowal in 1927, the government's name was invoked along with that of God to assure the Untouchables that the time had arrived to form a new movement for social change:

> There is hope from God [*bhagwan*] and help from the king [*badshah*]. Send members to the councils and start the *qaum* anew, brothers. Come together to form a better life. Destroy caste and creed, brothers. We have a generous government above us, brothers, so get together and save the Ad Dharm *qaum*. Those who are murdering us will not listen to our complaints. Brothers, get together and pray to God that the British rule may be eternal.[3]

As we observed earlier, the high point of many of the Ad Dharm conferences and rallies was the collective listing of demands to take to the government. The demands were of several kinds, including the appeal to recognize Ad Dharm as a separate religion, equal in status to the other *qaums*. The census listing accomplished that aim. There were other demands, however, that were not as easy to satisfy through government fiat. The Ad Dharm wanted to receive the political representation which the other *qaums* received, from state to village level.[4] In addition to the usual requests for proportionate representation in government jobs, the Ad Dharm made a special request regarding participation in the army, in which Punjabis have had a traditional interest, and in which the lower castes had previously served almost entirely in a very restricted role, primarily as bootmakers and menial servants.[5] The economic demands ranged from general requests to relieve unemployment to

---

3. "Mugowal Zila Hoshiarpur de Ad Dharm Skul: Wadda Bhwari Diwan." Translation in Juergensmeyer, "Political Hope," p. 633.
4. *Ad Dharm Report*, p. 14.
5. Ibid., p. 62. Some of the lower castes had served in higher positions. The Sikh Chuhras (Mazhabis) were utilized in the Sikh armies, and the British had regiments composed entirely of Mazhabis and Chamars. See Stephen P. Cohen, "The Untouchable Soldier: Caste, Politics and the Indian Army," *Journal of Asian Studies* 28, no. 3 (May 1969).

this very specific request, directed to the government procurement officers:

> If they have need of shoes and boots for their army, police, and industry, and if they want the best kind of leather, they should come directly to us, the Ad Dharm Mandal of Jullundur city, and not deal with some middleman. The government will save money and get better quality leather.[6]

A more typical economic request, however, is contained in these excerpts from a letter of Mangoo Ram to the governor of the Punjab, written in his own rustic English:

> I beg your Excellency to consider about [the Untouchables'] pitiable conditions and allow them to settle in some uncultivated piece of land, which they will cultivate, and thus relieve them from the severe clutches of the cruels. They will be most thankful to Your Excellency and pray for the prosperity of the benign Government throughout their lives.[7]

There were also requests for more schools, reserved seats for Scheduled Caste children, and special scholarships to allow the children to attend school. One demand went even further, requesting separate schools to be attended only by lower caste students because, it was claimed, "in Hindu schools our children are being ignored or are forced to learn Hindu ideas."[8] Other demands called for an end to forced labor,[9] and to the government's practice of regarding the Scheduled Castes as "castes" rather than "the laboring class."[10] There were also miscellaneous demands against harassment, prejudice, and the like.

Some of these demands appear to have been met. Or more accurately, some of the conditions to which Mangoo Ram referred were alleviated, and the Ad Dharm took

6. Ibid., p. 66.
7. The letter written on August 2, 1930, is in the possession of Mangoo Ram.
8. *Ad Dharm Report,* p. 64.
9. Ibid.
10. Ibid., p. 63.

credit for having prompted the government into increasing allowances for Scheduled Caste positions in government councils, government jobs, and educational scholarships. Mangoo Ram was quick to announce victory at each government concession:

> At least 50,000 Ad Dharm children are getting education in various schools. We want to thank the Education Minister from our hearts. Because of our countless requests, he paid attention, and granted free concessions for school tuition. . . . The Ad Dharm *qaum* will always be grateful to him; even the little Ad Dharm children will sing his praises:
> If I had as many tongues in my body as hair,
> I could not thank you enough.[11]

The Ad Dharm movement presented its demands to the government in special delegations and on the occasions of government commissions and public hearings, hearings which were themselves political events. The hearings stirred communal and parochial interests by presenting a forum in which they could be expressed.[12] Perhaps the most significant of the commission hearings were those of the Indian Statutory Commission, called the Simon Commission after Sir John Simon, the chairman. The commission was the British government's attempt to inquire into the workings of the Government of India Act of 1919, to see whether the patterns of dyarchy, communal representation, and the like were satisfactory. The Simon Commission was touted as the forerunner to even more sweeping reforms than these and was seen as the harbinger of semiautonomy for the Indian government, but because only British sat on the commission the hearings were boycotted by the Indian National Congress and other nationalistic elements.

On February 24–27, 1928, on the eve of the hearings, there was a meeting of the All-Indian Depressed Classes Conference in Delhi, led by M. C. Rajah of Madras, who was on the Indian joint committee working with Simon. The purpose of the Delhi meeting was to decide what

11. Ibid., p. 53.
12. N. Gerald Barrier, *The Sikhs and Their Literature* (Delhi, 1970), p. xl.

united approach the Scheduled Castes should take in regard to the hearings.[13] It is not certain whether the Ad Dharm leaders went to those meetings, but they went somewhere in late February of that year, a delegation of 150 of them, to "meet the Simon Commission."[14] Since the Simon Commission was not in India at the time, I suspect that the Ad Dharmis either met an advance arrangements party which was then active in Lahore[15] or went to Delhi to meet M. C. Rajah and the other Untouchable leaders gathered there. Later the Ad Dharm was to renounce Rajah for his role in the Simon hearings, and it is possible that some of the antipathy may have been generated when they met in Delhi, if indeed they did. Whether or not an Ad Dharm delegation attended, it is a matter of historical record that Rajah's pre-commission meeting in Delhi registered no visible support for the Ad Dharm. Quite the opposite, it nominated a committee of three, including no representation from the Ad Dharm, to "look into the Punjab Scheduled Caste problem."[16] Even so, Rajah's position prior to the hearings themselves and that of the Ad Dharm were not far apart. Neither planned to boycott the Simon Commission hearings as the Congress had urged them to do; both intended to make as much use of the event as possible.

The Ad Dharmis who flooded into Lahore in November 1928 made up "the biggest and grandest procession of the Ad Dharm's history."[17] Estimates vary about the size of the crowd, but it probably was in the thousands.[18] Mangoo

13. Lahore *Tribune* 48, no. 31 (Feb. 7, 1928). The *Tribune,* a nationalist newspaper, headlined the report of the conference "Adi Dravida Reactionaries."

14. *Ad Dharm Report,* p. 48.

15. In an interview Mangoo Ram gave this explanation (April 17, 1971) and placed the number of Ad Dharmis in the delegation as only fifty.

16. *Tribune* 48, no. 51 (Feb. 29, 1928). This was one of ten resolutions, the remainder of which were calls for social reform, so the Punjab situation must have presented a special problem to the Delhi meeting. What sort of problem is not clear.

17. Swami Shudranand, interview, May 15, 1971.

18. The *Ad Dharm Report,* p. 48, states the number as around 5,000. The Ambedkar leader, L. R. Balley, said that there were 2,000 there (interview, April 1, 1971), and Swami Shudranand remembers the size at 20,000 (interview, May 5, 1971).

Ram had made certain that the assemblage came from a variety of Scheduled Castes, and from disparate parts of the Punjab;[19] once in Lahore, they turned the event into a festive occasion, with red banners and red turbans and, of course, the Ad Dharm songs.[20] The appearance of the Ad Dharm delegation never attracted the attention of the newspapers at the time, but some of the upper caste organizations did take note. A member of the Indian National Congress, for instance, remembers the Ad Dharm's role at the Simon Commission hearings with some disdain: "There we were with our big procession, chanting 'Simon Commission Murdabad,' and there was Mangoo Ram with his procession, chanting 'Simon Commission Zindabad.'"[21]

According to the *Ad Dharm Report,* Mangoo Ram and the delegation presented a list of demands to the Simon Commission in "written form and in speeches,"[22] and printed their memorandum in two multilingual editions (English, Urdu, and Gurmukhi), which circulated in thousands of copies.[23] Considering all this effort, and the importance which the Ad Dharm accorded the event, it seems a pity that apparently the Ad Dharm delegation did not actually meet the commission. The official record of the hearings printed in full the memoranda of those delegations that appeared and the discussion that ensued, but the Ad Dharm is not among them.[24] This is all the more curious in light of the fact that groups similar to the Ad Dharm appeared before the commission in other parts of India— Bombay, Lucknow, and Madras, for example.[25] But not in the Punjab.

19. Mangoo Ram, interview, April 17, 1971.
20. Chanan Lal Manik, "Adi Dharm Bari."
21. Prithvi Singh Azad, interview, April 13, 1971.
22. *Ad Dharm Report,* p. 48.
23. Ibid., p. 49.
24. Great Britain, Indian Statutory Commission, *Selections from Memoranda and Oral Evidence by Non-Officials,* part 1, vol. 16 (London: His Majesty's Stationary Office, 1930).
25. Ibid. Ambedkar spoke before the commission in Bombay. The Lucknow delegation of Depressed Classes included the leaders of the Adi Hindu organization, and there were deputations from the All-India Adi-Dravida Maha Jana Sabha in Madras.

There seems to have been some display of unhappiness over the absence of any Scheduled Caste delegation at the Lahore hearings of the Simon Commission. The newspapers report that a man called Sunder Singh complained about the matter and received the reply from the commission that time was short, and that since M. C. Rajah was on the central committee, the voice of the Untouchables would be heard sooner or later.[26] It is also possible that the commission may have omitted lower caste delegations in the Punjab because they, like Gandhi, felt that in the Punjab Muslim-Sikh-Hindu communalism overshadowed the problem of Untouchability. Another reconstruction would accept the report of Mangoo Ram that the Simon Commission believed that Arya Samaj activities had virtually eradicated the problems of Untouchables in the Punjab. Mangoo Ram held M. C. Rajah accountable for this attitude on the part of the commission and claimed that when the Ad Dharm was apprised of the commission's position it broke with Rajah and decided to boycott the commission after all.[27] Whatever the reality, it is clear that from that time on the Ad Dharm claimed that M. C. Rajah was playing into the hands of upper caste Hindus, and turned instead to Dr. Ambedkar for their national leadership.[28]

Later Mangoo Ram would again apply to send a deputation with memoranda to a government commission—the Indian Franchise Commission of 1932—and this time the delegation was officially accepted and Mangoo Ram's name entered in the list of witnesses.[29] But this was not the grand occasion that the Simon hearings had been. Other, less formal delegations were also dispatched from time to time—to the governor of the Punjab or other provincial officials[30]—and the content of the deputations was much the same. There were specific demands of the sort earlier described, pleas for support of the Ad Dharm's argument

26. *Tribune* 48, no. 256 (Nov. 4, 1928).
27. Mangoo Ram, April 17, 1971, interview.
28. Manik, "Adi Dharm Bari," January 5, 1971.
29. Great Britain, *Indian Franchise Commission Report*, 1932.
30. Mangoo Ram, April 17, 1971, interview. One such deputation to the governor was on October 12, 1931.

for *qaum* status, and assurances that, as quid pro quo, there would be Ad Dharm support for the crown.[31] On occasion, indeed, the Ad Dharm went to almost pusillanimous lengths to demonstrate its loyalty for the government:

> God has certainly helped the Ad Dharmis, for when we were at the lowest pit of degradation, God sent to us Lord Montmore, the Governor of Punjab, so kind and loving a ruler. All the rights and hope we are being given is due to this angel of mercy which God has sent to us, in the form of the Governor of the Punjab. We pray earnestly for his long life.[32]

Support of the British had a double logic. On the one hand, there were direct and positive benefits to be gained from government policy, and on the other hand, the government could be used to assert the Untouchables' independence from the upper castes. And the government, in turn, had something to gain from supporting the Ad Dharm. It guaranteed the loyalty of a substantial segment of the population, the Untouchables, and kept them from aligning with the hostile, nationalist forces of the Arya Samaj and the Congress.

The Ad Dharm's attitude to the government was shaped, of course, by strategic motives. But more was involved than that—an attitude toward government itself, a conception of the natural relation between the governed and their governors. It is true that the Ad Dharmis attempted to manipulate the British by approaching them with a mixture of complaint and praise, demand and supplication, but this mix of messages did not arise from selfishness, cynicism, or civic irresponsibility. It was, rather, a coherent and natural form of communication built on a mind-set that conceived of government as a distant and alien thing, something toward which one could only send messages—messages al-

---

31. Letters of appreciation for the Ad Dharm's letters of loyalty and encouragement are found among the memorabilia of Mangoo Ram: May 21, 1931, from the Viceregal Lodge at Simla, dated May 21, 1931; from Lahore, May 29, 1939; from the Viceroy, May 4, 1936; from the Governor of the Punjab, April 10, 1946.

32. *Ad Dharm Report*, p. 63.

ternatively of honor and petition, as one might send prayers, sacrifice, and praise to a distant and potentially dangerous deity. Indeed, the language of the Ad Dharm's communications seemed sometimes to betray precisely this religious association, as above, when the British governor of the Punjab was styled as an angel of mercy.

The nationalist position must have appeared inconceivable to the lower castes: to them, the government was an ally, a friend, even a benign spirit. To do away with it, and to help one's enemies vault into power in the chaos that would surely ensue, must have seemed absurd. How much safer and constructive to flatter the government in one moment, like the gods, and petition it in the next. As with the vagaries of the spirit world and the caprice of nature, one was never certain what the results would be. Sometimes the supplications worked and sometimes they did not. But there were times when the government was indeed gracious, and one owed it a debt of gratitude. After all, before its arrival things had been considerably worse, and without government, things could be worse again.

14 Politics and the Decline of Ad Dharm

One could argue that the Ad Dharm was as political as it was religious, and that led to its undoing. The differences with Gandhi, and the movement's friendliness toward the British, signaled a shift increasingly toward issues of public policy and away from those cultural matters that launched the movement originally. It was a path laden with compromises, and indeed, the ultimate failure of Ad Dharm as a broad-based movement can be traced back to that departure. Yet the political and cultural elements had been jumbled together in some measure from the very beginning, and what happened to the movement was more complicated than simply a displacement of cultural elements with those political. As the Ad Dharm changed, its political and social contexts changed as well. Ultimately then, the difficulty with the movement was not only that it was becoming more political, but that it was having to change from one form of politics to another.

The word "politics" is of course used here quite broadly. Like "religion," the term needs to be reconsidered before it is used to describe the behavior of lower caste Punjabis, or for that matter, any other group in Indian society. In the West we are accustomed to thinking of politics as the organized articulation of interests competing for the attention or the control of a central authority.[1] In India, however,

1. See, for examples, David Easton, *The Political System* (New York: Knopf, 1953); Earl Latham, *The Group Basis of Politics* (Ithaca, 1952); and David Apter, *The Politics of Modernization* (Chicago: University of Chicago Press, 1965).

there has traditionally been very little organized articulation and not much of a central authority, especially from the perspective of villages. But there has been politics. If one thinks of politics as a concern with "who gets what, where, when, and how,"[2] then traditional India has always been political. In most instances, however, the political competition has taken place between rival groups—castes, regions, religious communities—and not necessarily in the arena of central authority. It was that sort of politics into which the Ad Dharm was born, but in the early decades of this century the shape of politics was subject to change.

By the mid-1930s there had been a shift—not in the reality of communal competition, but in its political expression. The Poona Pact laid the principle, and the Government of India Act of 1935 set the stage. Politics in the Punjab, as elsewhere in India, was moving from the interaction of social movements and communal organizations to direct competition in electoral politics. In the early 1930s the Ad Dharm had labored diligently to establish itself as a *qaum*, a separate religious community similar to that of the Muslims, Hindus, and Sikhs, and the point had been won in the 1931 census. But the victory was short-lived. No sooner had the movement become a *qaum*, at least in the eyes of its leaders, than the shift in politics rendered that sort of religious organization unimportant. The Ad Dharm was immediately faced with the need to create a kind of identity that would supersede the *qaum* by forming a political party or by some other means entering into the realm of political representation. The change was baffling to the old Ad Dharm leaders. Even when they reminisced about the Ad Dharm years later they seemed uncertain about what had happened to the movement in the years after 1935. The enthusiasm that overcame them when they discussed the earlier years dissipated as they at-

---

2. The phrase is that of Harold D. Lasswell, *Politics: Who Gets What, When, How* (New York, 1958). My understanding of politics is also aided by Sheldon Wolin's *Politics and Vision* (Boston: Little, Brown, 1960), in which it is argued that in the history of Western thought, politics refers to those concerns that arise in the realm of public affairs (p. 2.).

tempted to sort out the tangle of political choices that had faced them later.

At first the Ad Dharm movement had emulated the Arya Samaj. The Aryas provided an example of the way in which an organization could encourage a sense of religious unity, social coherence, and political influence. But by the mid-1930s the Arya Samaj had become badly divided within itself, and it no longer had the image and influence that it once compelled. Two other models for social organization and political influence had taken its place. One of these was the example set by Muslim nationalists who demanded a separate territory of their own. The other was provided by political parties and networks of religious communal support for electoral candidates.

The leaders of the Ad Dharm felt the lure of both these models and sensed the prestige and effectiveness they seemed to offer. But these new political forms took their sustenance from reliable constituencies of support, and in that realm it was difficult for the Ad Dharm to compete. It had to devote continuing efforts simply to sustain its constituent identity at the same time that it attempted to engage politically in the wider society. However, the Ad Dharm found it increasingly difficult to do both, as it was faced with new political exigencies. The leaders occupied themselves less and less with the tasks of maintaining their own community and turned their attention instead to creating levers of political influence. They were somewhat uncertain, however, about which direction to turn.

One of the models of new political activity, Muslim separatism, led to the notion of "Achutistan." During the early 1930s, the poet Sir Muhammad Iqbal had made popular the idea of a self-contained Muslim homeland in the Indian northwest, an area which came to be called Pakistan, and when Muhammad Ali Jinnah took over the Muslim League and transformed it, the Pakistan movement became an appealing model for the Ad Dharm. Just as radical Sikhs were later to seize upon the idea and demand a separate "Sikhistan,"[3] so members of the Scheduled Castes

3. The Sikh Akali Dal made such a demand in 1946; and apparently there was also a demand by members of the Jat caste for a "Jatistan."

in the Punjab adopted the concept and came up with the notion of Achutistan, a geographically distinct "Land of the Untouchables." The idea was never worked out in any systematic way, nor to my knowledge was there even a suggestion as to which areas of India might be incorporated into such a nation. But several old Scheduled Caste leaders were familiar with the concept,[4] and Mangoo Ram, according to his own report, broached the idea regularly at conferences during the mid-1930s.[5]

The road to Achutistan, however, seemed a long and difficult one, and the path to legislative representation more readily at hand. This too, however, was a tortuous route in its own way. A system of reserved seats had been established to guarantee certain positions for the Scheduled Castes, but any candidate put forth by the Ad Dharm for one of those seats would have to compete with others proposed by the Congress and the political organizations of the Sikhs and the Muslims.

The first election to incorporate the stipulations of the Government of India Act of 1935 took place in 1936, and the Ad Dharmis supported independent candidates in the eight constituencies reserved for Scheduled Castes. They mounted a campaign reminiscent of the great days of the 1931 census, and to their own surprise, they swept all but one of the seats.[6] In the urban Jullundur constituency, in

---

(Richard Lambert, "Hindu-Muslim Riots," Ph.D. dissertation, University of Pennsylvania, 1951).

4. There is common agreement that the notion of Achutistan circulated freely, but opinions differ as to its origins. Mangoo Ram said that it was his idea, in response to Pakistan and the idea of Sikhistan (Mangoo Ram, January 29 and April 17, 1971, interviews). Sant Ram, M.L.A. (June 12, 1971, interview), said the idea came from Hazara Singh Gill; Chanan Ram (former president of the Republican Party of Punjab, August 4, 1971, interview) said the idea came from a friend of Jagjivan Ram's; L. R. Balley (April 3, 1971, interview) said Dr. Ambedkar considered the idea, but rejected it; Seth Kishan Das (November 16, 1973, interview) said the idea came from Bihar; and Ram Das (April 18, 1971, interview) said that it was never a specific demand, but everyone talked about it.

5. Interview with Mangoo Ram, April 17, 1971.

6. Chanan Lal Manik, "Adi Dharm Bari," *Ravidas Patrika*, May 11, 1971; and interview with Swami Shudranand, May 15, 1971.

fact, they defeated the Congress rival by a resounding 1,400 votes.⁷ The victorious candidate was none other than Seth Kishan Das, the wealthy Boota Mandi leather merchant who had supplied the building for the Ad Dharm headquarters and served as Mangoo Ram's press agent during the Gandhian counter-fast.⁸

Seth Kishan Das's victory and those of the other six winning candidates were not as complete an endorsement of the Ad Dharm as one might have thought, for none of these men had actually been selected for candidacy by the Ad Dharm's central leadership. Instead, they were local figures who had worked with the Ad Dharm in some connection, decided to run for office, and subsequently received the movement's blessing. Its control over these men was no greater after the election than it had been before. The Ad Dharm had gained electoral strength from the fact that, in the villages particularly, it was simply an amalgam of local leadership, but this diffusion of authority made it difficult for the Ad Dharm to capitalize on its success.

Indeed, the elections had the effect of making more visible what factions already existed in the movement. In the Jullundur-Hoshiarpur area there was a division between supporters of Seth Kishan Das and other families of Boota Mandi who supported Master Gurvanta Singh.⁹ Both groups were loyal to Mangoo Ram, but each had its own following. Gurvanta Singh had been general secretary of the Ad Dharm in 1929, briefly, after the ungracious exit of Thakar Chand; he served "enthusiastically and honestly" but quit the position within a few months "because he had left college [in order to serve and] wanted to return."¹⁰ Gurvanta Singh ran for office in the 1936 elections, unsuc-

    7. Seth Kishan Das, November 16, 1973.
    8. The other six victories were those of Master Harnam Das from Lyallpur, Bhagat Hans Raj from Sialkot, Gopal Singh Khalsa from Ludhiana, Chaudhry Fakir Chand from Rohtak, Juggal Kishore from Jagadhri, and Chaudhry Prem Singh from Gurgaon. Mullan Singh from Hoshiarpur was the only Scheduled Caste victor supported by Congress, beating the Ad Dharm's general secretary, Hazara Ram, by a very narrow margin (Chanan Lal Manik "Adi Dharm Bari," May 11, 1971).
    9. Ibid.
    10. *Ad Dharm Report*, p. 44.

cessfully, and the Ad Dharm gave its official backing to Seth Kishan Das instead.[11]

Family rivalries and personal disputes had always separated these two camps, and the election had the effect of deepening these differences—ultimately at the expense of the Ad Dharm. It was not many years after the 1936 election that Seth Kishan Das and Master Gurvanta Singh bypassed the Ad Dharm altogether in expressing their opposition to each other: one took up a central position in Ambedkar's organizations and the other became a principal figure in the Congress.[12] The pattern was not very different in some of the districts of West Punjab, where dissensions within the Ad Dharm were also exacerbated by the elections.[13] The lure of office, with all the power and status that it seemed to imply, magnified the personal ambitions of those who had up until then been content with the political arena that the Ad Dharm provided, and aggravated their rivalries. As one Ad Dharmi put it: "The people who were elected to office suddenly considered themselves better than everybody else—better, even, than Guru Ravi Das."[14]

Mangoo Ram, from the movement's "headquarters" in Jullundur, viewed the elections with pleasure and satisfaction, but he was neither king nor kingmaker in the politics of the Untouchables. The apparent influence of the Ad Dharm was only that—an appearance—and it was not long before Mangoo Ram had to seek additional means of access to power. He did so by moving in the direction of the Muslims, who had originally inspired the vision of Achutistan, but now it was party politics that drew him rather than the vision of a separatist state.

In the early 1940s he entertained the idea of joining forces with the Unionist party—a group dominated by

11. Interview with Master Gurvanta Singh, vice-president, Congress party, Punjab, in Jullundur, January 31, 1971. According to Sadhu Ram (June 24, 1971, interview), Gurvanta Singh did not join Ad Dharm until 1935; previously, he taught in an Arya Samaj high school.
12. Seth Kishan Das was the first president of Dr. Ambedkar's Scheduled Caste Federation, and Master Gurvanta Singh became vice-president of the Congress party, Punjab.
13. Manik, "Adi Dharm Bari," May 11, 1971.
14. Ibid.

large Muslim landlords—which had so consistently controlled Punjab politics since the late 1920s that it took on some of the aura of government itself. The Ad Dharm had done well with the government before, and that helped to make Mangoo Ram feel comfortable with the idea.[15] But there were other factors as well. A consistent pattern of friendship had developed between Muslims and Ad Dharmis which dated back to the very beginning of the movement. The Muslim Ahmadiyya movement had been one of the models, and perhaps the impetus, behind Swami Shudranand's notion of establishing an independent movement of Untouchables.[16] According to the *Ad Dharm Report*, indeed, the Ahmadiyyas provided the only strong external support during the early years.[17] The Ahmadiyya movement had a history of being pro-British and seriously opposed to the Sikh and Hindu reform movements;[18] thus it was no surprise that it would favor the separatist and loyalist tendencies of the Ad Dharm. Ahmadiyya pamphlets praised the Ad Dharm openly.[19]

Swami Shudranand appears to have been the major link between the Ad Dharmis and the Muslims. He was responsible for establishing ties with a man he identified as Khasa Jusid Nizamuddin, who edited a newspaper in Delhi, the *Munadi* (Advertiser). Nizamuddin supported the Ad Dharm in print as a result of his meeting with Shudranand, and the Ad Dharm in turn promised to support him.[20] Later, however, when Swami Shudranand was expelled from the Ad Dharm during the factional disputes of 1929 and 1930, his

15. Mangoo Ram interview, April 17, 1971.
16. Interview with Sadhu Ram, M.P., June 24, 1971.
17. The *Ad Dharm Report* singles out for special appreciation Dr. Feroz-ud-din Ahmed, president of the Hamdard Hindu Injamin Ahmadiya (Ahmadiyya's Hindu-Sympathizers Organization), of Kath Garh, Batala, Sheikapura, Ludhiana, Lyallpur, Gurdaspur, and Jullundur (p. 57).
18. J. C. Archer, *The Sikhs in Relation to Hindus, Muslims, Christians and Ahmadiyyas* (Princeton, 1946). The Ahmadiyya leader Mirza Ahmad said of the British, "They brought peace and tranquility, but above all, religious liberty, and checked the 'plundering career of those marauders'—meaning Sikhs." Ibid., p. 290.
19. Mangoo Ram, November 13, 1973, interview; and L. R. Balley, April 3, 1971, interview.
20. Swami Shudranand, May 15, 1971, interview.

Muslim associations were held against him. He was accused of "work[ing] with the Muslims, and . . . trying to start riots and fights."[21]

Mangoo Ram did accept support from the Muslims, but it is not clear how much, nor of what kind. According to one old Ad Dharmi, the Muslims "helped with government appointments, gave us space for our meetings and rallies, and helped publish our pamphlets."[22] Those opposed to the Ad Dharm claimed flatly that the support went deeper: the Ad Dharm newspaper, *Adi Danka,* they claimed, was published by the Muslims, and the Muslim leader Zafarulla Khan wrote the checks for the Ad Dharm.[23] Mangoo Ram angrily denies these allegations. He argues that since the *Adi Danka* was printed in a Hindu shop (the Kishan Steam Press), it could scarcely have been supported by Muslims.[24] And on the whole, indeed, it seems that the only real support received from the Muslims was indirect: the Muslims treated the Untouchables with civility and welcomed them into a political party which they dominated, the Unionists.

The Ad Dharm's relationship with the Unionists began to develop during the 1930s. It was an odd affair built on negative interests that the wealthiest and poorest strata of Punjab society held in common: both the Unionist Muslim landlords and the members of the Ad Dharm opposed upper caste Hindus, Sikhs, and the Indian National Congress. Not all the Ad Dharmis favored the development of a liaison with the Unionists,[25] but Mangoo Ram had received support from the Unionist leader, Sikandar Hyat Khan, for his counter-fast against Gandhi in 1932,[26] and he felt obligated to support Sikandar as chairman of the legislative council in 1934.[27] After the Government of India Act

21. Mangoo Ram, November 13, 1973, interview.
22. Interview with Ishwar Das Pawar, April 9, 1971.
23. Interview with Prithvi Singh Azad, April 13, 1971.
24. Interview with Mangoo Ram, April 17, 1971.
25. According to Sadhu Ram, the issue was one of the reasons for dissension after 1935 (interview on June 24, 1971).
26. Mangoo Ram, April 17, 1971, interview.
27. A letter of appreciation from Sir Sikander Hyat Khan is among the collected memorabilia in the possession of Mangoo Ram (dated March 7, 1934).

in 1935, when the Unionist party began to organize for the elections in Lahore, they invited Mangoo Ram to be present.[28] The friendship bore fruit, for the Ad Dharm candidates in the 1936 elections received help from the Unionists, and partly for that reason were victorious.

The Unionist party was the resounding winner in the 1936 elections, and Sikandar Hyat Khan became the chief minister. If there had been reason for the Ad Dharm to support the Muslim party before in the effort to fend off common enemies, the Unionists' new role as rulers of government only enhanced their attractiveness. Mangoo Ram continued to support them, and with their sponsorship he was appointed to the Jullundur District Board in 1940. Soon afterward the political climate began to change again, as independence loomed near and no resolution to the Muslim-Congress disputes was apparent. In the Punjab the Muslim League, more aggressively Islamic than the Unionists, gained power, and demands for Pakistan filled the air.[29] In the crucial elections of 1945–1946, on the eve of independence, the Punjab Legislative Assembly results were as follows: the Muslim League won 79 seats, Congress won 51, the Panthic League won 22, and the Unionists and Independents, 10 each. Mangoo Ram was one of the Unionists' ten.

Even though the Unionists no longer dominated the politics of this era, Mangoo Ram's coalition with them probably remained a prudent choice, if indeed any coalition was advisable in the maelstrom that overtook Punjab politics in the years immediately before partition. The Ad Dharm could not align with any of the upper caste Hindu- or Sikh-dominated political parties without vacating most of its principles; with the Unionists they only had to moderate some of them, and the liaison obviated the need for

28. An invitation to the opening of the Unionist party headquarters is among the collected memorabilia in the possession of Mangoo Ram (dated April 19, 1936).

29. The Unionists joined the Muslim League in a proclamation in Lahore calling for geographical centers of Muslim political dominance in any settlement for independence. Sikandar Hyat Khan tried to modify the statement by saying that it did not necessarily imply the need for Pakistan.

them to make common cause with the more militant of the Muslim political groups. The Ad Dharm leaders adamantly insisted that they were not compromised by this relationship: "We used the Unionists, but we were not used by them."[30] Mangoo Ram and others claimed that the more extremist Muslim leaders, Jinnah and Sir Khizr Hayat Khan of the Muslim League, offered them large sums of money, land, and cabinet positions if the Ad Dharm would support them in their move toward Pakistan.[31] But Mangoo Ram refused to be enlisted in a cause in which he and the Ad Dharm had no direct interest: he was content to be a Unionist legislator.[32]

The motives of the Ad Dharm politicians in all this were undoubtedly mixed. Certainly there was an extent to which Mangoo Ram and the others had simply become used to power. But they may also have felt, and with some justification, that the best way to bring benefits to their people was to be situated inside the government, rather than storming the barricades. And in fact one of Mangoo Ram's first actions as an M.L.A. was to demand greater Scheduled Caste representation in government jobs.[33] But whatever the reasons for Ad Dharm's coalition with the Unionists, it was not a coalition built on strength: the Ad Dharm as a movement had all but disappeared. "Absorption" rather than "coalition" might be a better word to describe the new arrangement, and by 1946 the relationship between the Unionist party and the few remaining leaders

30. Ishwar Das Pawar, April 9, 1971, interview.
31. Mangoo Ram, April 17, 1971, interview.
32. Mangoo Ram was not the only Ad Dharm Unionist. Gopal Singh, Prem Chand, and Mulla Singh (who had been elected previously through the Congress) were also elected as M.L.A.'s on the Unionist ticket in 1946. Gurvanta Singh assumed office in the same elections, beating his old foe, Seth Kishan Das, who was running with the support of Ambedkar's Scheduled Caste Federation. Gurvanta Singh in an interview on May 8, 1971, claimed he was an Independent in that election; others claimed he ran with Unionist support.
33. A letter dated February 18, 1947, from Akhtar Husain, chief secretary to the governor of the Punjab, in response to Mangoo Ram's demand for greater Scheduled Caste representation in menial posts, is among the collected memorabilia of Mangoo Ram. Husain argued that the Scheduled Castes already exceeded their 2-1/2 percent quota.

of the Ad Dharm was strictly a matter of personal ties, not a yoking of political constituencies. The Ad Dharm had encountered electoral politics, and politics was the victor. Electoral politics has room for individuals and their factions of supporters, but it has no interest in religion as such. In abandoning religion for politics the Ad Dharm leaders had abandoned the Ad Dharm and the strength of its unifying symbols.

In June 1946, Mangoo Ram closed the office of the Ad Dharm in Jullundur city. That, however, was only the official demise of the movement; in fact, the organization had dissolved many years earlier. There was no grand moment of collapse. The movement had simply fragmented and dissolved as events and other social movements had overtaken it. In the final years of the Ad Dharm movement, the high hopes and great expectations had been replaced by factionalism and petty ambitions.

One could argue that the movement had not really dissolved, it had changed. It had become an arena for internal politics among newly politically-conscious groups of Untouchables, rather than a united front within the larger Punjab society. After all, with the shifting of politics in the 1930s to noncommunal parties and secular interests, the concerns of the Ad Dharm leaders changed too. Or one might regard the Ad Dharm as a phase in the leaders' own development. Having been trained in leadership skills under the Ad Dharm, they no longer needed the collective association it provided. But however one might perceive the aging of the Ad Dharm, it is hard to view the fragmentation of its energies and the exploitation of its symbols for personal advantage without a touch of sadness.

The demise of the movement's headquarters, like that of the movement itself, is a story of factions and personal ambition.[34] Eventually, the building became the Ravi Das High School, which continues to exist, a thriving institution for Scheduled Caste children. It is one of three legacies

34. Seth Kishan Das had given most of the money to construct the building. Yet when the building was vacated by the Ad Dharm, it was his rival, Master Gurvanta Singh, who eventually stepped in as custodian of the property and as chairman of the Ravi Das high school board.

of the Ad Dharm movement that continue to exercise an influence in the Punjab. The second is the name itself, which has become the Chamar's caste name in parts of Jullundur and Hoshiarpur districts. And the third is the movement's reverence for Guru Ravi Das.

This continued emphasis on Ravi Das worship, even after the discontinuation of the political organization of Ad Dharm, was a conscious decision on the part of the Ad Dharm leaders. In 1946 Sant Ram Azad wrote to Dr. Ambedkar, telling him that the Ad Dharm Mandal had decided to change its name to the Ravi Das Mandal and to leave the politics to Ambedkar and his All-India Scheduled Caste Federation. This elicited a reply from Ambedkar's headquarters which congratulated Mangoo Ram on his decision to "confine the activities of the Ad Dharm Mandal to social and religious matters affecting the Scheduled Castes and to entrust the political work to the All-India Scheduled Castes Federation in conformity with the rest of India."[35] The Ad Dharm's offer of support to Ambedkar was restricted to issues arising at the national level: Mangoo Ram and his associates had no intention of merging the Ad Dharm with the Punjab unit of the Scheduled Caste Federation. Even so, their letter to Dr. Ambedkar is significant, because it amounted to a recognition that they had neglected to nurture the cultural aspect of the movement. They had become politicians, and something had been lost.

Something else, however, had been gained: the creation of politicians was a signal achievement of the movement. Seth Kishan Das helped to found the Punjab Republican party, and Master Gurvanta Singh became a leader of the Congress, serving first in the Punjab cabinet of Pratap Singh Kairon and then as vice-president of the Punjab Congress party. Sadhu Ram also joined the Congress through the Scheduled Caste Federation, subsequently becoming a member of parliament in the central government, and after independence Mangoo Ram followed suit. He

35. Letter from D. B. N. Shivaraj, president, All-India Scheduled Castes Federation, New Delhi, to Mangoo Ram, president, the Punjab Ad-Dharm Mandal, Jullundur, dated June 24, 1946; in Mangoo Ram's personal collection.

supported the Bhargawa interim ministry in the Punjab in 1947–1952, not because he especially favored it, but because "without Congress, I realized that we could no longer do anything."[36]

Mangoo Ram afterwards went into semiretirement on a plot of land near Garhshankar, which some claim had been given to him by the British in gratitude for his support during World War II. After independence the Congress government allowed him to keep the British bequest in recognition of the allegiance he now extended to them.[37] Mangoo Ram functioned as a Congress legislator for only a brief period of years, but the evidence indicates that he used his position to aid the lower castes in a variety of ways. He pressed for land redistributions,[38] urged that

36. Interview with Mangoo Ram, April 17, 1971.
37. This version of how Mangoo Ram received his land is corroborated by Swami Shudranand (interview on May 15, 1971). Chanan Ram, former president of the Republican party of the Punjab (interview on August 4, 1971, in London) claims that Mangoo Ram received the land from the Zamindara League. Mangoo Ram's own version of the story is that he received the land from the British for serving them: "At the call of Mahatma Gandhi, I supported the British government during the war. But Kairon and Bhargawa [chief ministers of the Punjab after Independence] were against me, and after I had the land for only a year or so, they snatched it from me. Luckily the District Commissioner of Hoshiarpur was my friend, and wrote a letter to Rajendra Prasad and to Nehru. They said that if you take away what the British have given to Mangoo Ram, then the government will take away what they gave to others. So Nehru told Bhargawa that I had served the country for fifteen years, and my land should not be taken." (Interview with Mangoo Ram, April 17, 1971.) Recently Mangoo Ram has received an attractive citation for his struggles against the British as a "freedom fighter," in reference to his activities with the Gadar party, presumably, and not with the Ad Dharm.
38. Letter from Akhtar Husain, chief secretary to the governor, Punjab, to Mangoo Ram, February 18, 1947, in reference to Mangoo Ram's request regarding land redistribution. Also, letter from K. H. Henderson, secretary, Punjab Civil Service, Lahore, to Mangoo Ram, February 18, 1947, in response to Mangoo Ram's complaint that *zamindars* were preempting land that should be available for the Scheduled Castes. The boldness of this latter complaint is all the more striking in light of the fact that Mangoo Ram had just joined the party of those very *zamindars,* and the letter was addressed to him at the office of the Zamindara League, Hoshiarpur. Both letters are in Mangoo Ram's private collection.

more government jobs be set aside for them,[39] tried to establish holidays on the birth dates of lower caste gurus,[40] and interceded for members of his constituency when personal difficulties arose.[41]

Even in the case of Mangoo Ram, however, participation in a political party and in the government brought an end to the close identification between Scheduled Caste leaders and the majority of their followers in the villages. Many villagers felt that even if such politicians continued to fight for lower caste rights, they did so as outsiders, like the reformers of the Arya Samaj. Politics, they felt, had entered the Ad Dharm and seduced its leadership away. Still, the Ad Dharm would be remembered by the Scheduled Caste masses of the Punjab as a movement which created the possibility of power for the poor and gave dignity and integrity to their everyday cultural and social experiences. Mangoo Ram summed up its achievements as follows: "We helped give them a better life and made them into a *qaum*. We gave them gurus to believe in and something to hope for."[42]

39. The letter from Akhtar Husain to Mangoo Ram refers to Mangoo Ram's request for more government positions for Scheduled Castes.

40. Letter from D. A. Bryan, secretary to the premier, Punjab, to Mangoo Ram, January 29, 1947, regarding celebrations for the birth dates of Scheduled Caste gurus. Bryan's ignorance of the fact that Ravi Das is the patron saint of Chamar caste and Rishi Balmik is the patron saint of the Chuhra caste is made evident in his reply: "In the last paragraph of your letter you suggest that the birthdays of the Gurus of the Scheduled Castes—Guru Ram Dass and Rishi Balmik—should be recognized by the grant of gazetted holidays. The Premier has directed me to ask you which of these two Gurus is regarded with greater respect and veneration by members of the Scheduled Castes."

41. Letter from revenue minister to Mangoo Ram on February 17, 1947, regarding the "Gurbax Rai case," which Mangoo Ram says pertains to injustice done individual members of Scheduled Castes. The letter is in Mangoo Ram's private collection.

42. Interview with Mangoo Ram, April 17, 1971.

PART IV Competing Visions

15 The Ambedkar Alternative

Long before the formal dissolution of the Ad Dharm movement, something new had developed among the lower castes in India which threatened to make the Ad Dharm and regionally based movements like it obsolete: a militant national movement of Untouchables led by a remarkable man, Dr. Bheem Rao Ambedkar. There had been movements with a national network before, the best known of which was the Depressed Classes Mission, but they were affiliated with the Congress and other organizations that discouraged lower caste autonomy and militancy.[1] Previous national leaders from lower castes, such as M. C. Rajah, who also allied with the Congress, were regarded by the growing numbers of lower caste militants as having compromised themselves. Before Ambedkar there was no lower caste leader of national stature who could speak the language of the educated elite without being too closely identified with them.

Ambedkar's outspoken and brilliant statements on behalf of his people thrust him ahead of M. C. Rajah in popularity and soon earned him an unassailable position of national leadership that lasted his lifetime. Like Martin Luther King, Jr., Ambedkar's name has come to be identified with the struggles for justice among an oppressed sector of society. Ambedkar is also remembered in India's history for his service to independent India: he was chair-

1. For a discussion of the early organizations of Untouchables, see chapter 2.

man of the drafting committee of India's constitution and law minister in Nehru's first cabinet. But it is Ambedkar the militant Untouchable who endures in the memories of all.

Ambedkar was born in 1891 as a Mahar (a traditional laboring caste similar in status to the Chamars of the Punjab) in the state of Maharashtra.[2] His high marks at Elphinstone College, Bombay, brought him to the attention of the Maharaja of Baroda, who was keen on encouraging talented members of the lower castes; the Maharaja's support allowed Ambedkar to come to America, where he received his Ph.D. at Columbia University, and to pursue advanced studies at the London School of Economics. Ambedkar returned to India to practice law, and soon undertook the first of a series of essays on caste and the practice of Untouchability.[3] In 1925 he began organizing rallies and conferences in Maharashtra, and his national leadership among those of Untouchable castes became assured in 1930 when the British selected him and a South Indian, R. B. Srinivasan, to represent the Untouchables at the Round Table Conference. Ambedkar continued to be the most prominent member of Untouchable castes until his death in 1956.

Although Ambedkar is regarded as a political leader of Untouchables—he founded a labor party early in his career and the Republican party shortly before his death—he considered the problem of Untouchability to be a cultural and religious matter which had to be challenged on those fronts as well as on political ones. One of his first acts of protest against Untouchability was a public burning

2. The authorized biography of Ambedkar is C. B. Khairmode, *Dr. Bhimrav Ramji Ambedkar,* in five volumes, written in Marathi, each volume published by separate entities. See also Jeanette Robbins, *Dr. Ambedkar and His Movement* (Hyderabad, 1964); and Chandra Bharill, *Social and Political Ideas of B. R. Ambedkar* (Jaipur, 1977). In preparation is the revision of an excellent Ph.D. dissertation by Eleanor Zelliot, "Dr. Ambedkar and the Mahar Movement" (University of Pennsylvania, 1969).

3. Some of Ambedkar's best known essays are *Annihilation of Caste* (Bombay, 1936); *What Congress and Gandhi Have Done to the Untouchables* (Bombay, 1946); and *The Untouchables* (New Delhi, 1948).

of the sacred Hindu codes, the Manusmrti, which justify and detail the Hindu caste system;[4] and one of his last acts before his death was his conversion to Buddhism, an act that was tantamount to establishing a new religious movement, for there are scarcely any Buddhists in India today except for those who followed Ambedkar into the tradition. Thus, as both a cultural movement and a political strategy, Ambedkar's national alternative—although based upon regional movements such as Ad Dharm, competed with them as well. And in the end, Ambedkar appeared to have won.

By the early 1930s Dr. Ambedkar's new organization, later called the Scheduled Caste Federation, had expanded beyond the state of Maharashtra, where it was founded, and had begun to make an impact in the north. The Ambedkar movement appealed primarily to educated Untouchables in urban areas, so it never threatened the mass base of the Ad Dharm; but it did attract some of the Ad Dharm leaders. Chunni Lal Thapur, one of the few Ad Dharmis from the Chuhra sweeper caste, became active in the Scheduled Caste Federation, as did Ad Dharm's financial supporter from Boota Mandi, Seth Kishan Das, and several of his colleagues.[5] The Ambedkar movement also appealed to Sadhu Ram, who had been part of the rival Ad Dharm faction, which had set up its headquarters in Lyallpur. In fact, with the advent of Dr. Ambedkar's Scheduled Caste Federation, the Lyallpur branch of the movement dissolved.[6]

The rivalry between the Scheduled Caste Federation and the Ad Dharm movement in the Punjab, at least on a leadership level, continued for a number of years until 1940. As Mangoo Ram put it, "we passed each other; Ambedkar

4. Ambedkar organized his own Satyagrahis ("militant nonviolent activists," a term he borrowed from Gandhi), who held demonstrations demanding that the lower castes be allowed to use the public pond in the town of Mahad. It was there that the texts of Manu were burned on December 25, 1927. Bharill, *Social and Political Ideas*, p. 14.
5. Interview with Seth Kishan Das, Jullundur, November 16, 1973.
6. Interview with Sadhu Ram, M.P., New Delhi, June 24, 1971.

went up and we went down."⁷ The Scheduled Caste Federation had the advantage of being a national organization at a time when national politics in India was beginning to overshadow regional concerns. Even though village Untouchables may not have been very conscious of wider issues or appreciated the value of national organizations, the urban, educated people were sensitive to both, and recognized the importance of having a national spokesman. The Ad Dharm was caught in a bind. It had become too elitist, too political for the interests of the masses of lower caste villagers, but for the sophisticated and growing Scheduled Caste elite the movement was not political enough, and could never be viable on a national scale. So they turned more and more toward Ambedkar.

Mangoo Ram claimed that for a time he had hoped for a merger between the Ad Dharm and Dr. Ambedkar's movement and encouraged Dr. Ambedkar to take over the name and religious tradition of Ad Dharm and merge it into his own political strategy.⁸ Long before Dr. Ambedkar became a Buddhist in 1956, there had been talk of his joining some religion other than Hinduism as a way of demonstrating that the Untouchables were not a part of the religious tradition that sanctioned caste divisions. The Ad Dharm offered a solution, Mangoo Ram thought, since it was a religion expressly for Untouchables: it honored them by describing them as the original people and venerated the legendary figures of the Untouchables' traditions. That, however, seems to have been precisely the reason why Dr. Ambedkar did not favor Ad Dharm. He wanted to join, not a separatist religious tradition, but rather an egalitarian one, which would embrace the whole of society. For a while Ambedkar expressed interest in Sikhism, and he is said to have explored the idea in discussions with Sikh leaders in 1936.⁹ Mangoo Ram also welcomed that idea, since he felt that if Ambedkar became a Sikh he would also ven-

7. Interview with Mangoo Ram, Garhshankar, January 29, 1971.
8. Mangoo Ram interview, April 17, 1971.
9. Ambedkar's 1936 statement on the possibility of joining Sikhism is printed in N. N. Mitra, editor, *The Indian Annual Registrar,* July–Dec., 1936 (Calcutta: Annual Register Office), pp. 277–278. Ambed-

erate Ravi Das, who is included in the Sikh scriptures, and that would at least indirectly enhance the standing of Ad Dharm.[10] But Ambedkar ended up doing neither, and it was some years before he recognized the importance of placing religious symbols at the center of social identity and began encouraging mass conversions to Buddhism.

On national issues Mangoo Ram was supportive of Ambedkar. In that sense the Ad Dharm was the Punjab regional unit of a national network of support for Dr. Ambedkar and his strategy for social reform. After all, Mangoo Ram had stood behind Dr. Ambedkar in the Poona Pact issue and had joined him in his fast against Gandhi when Gandhi was fasting against Ambedkar's position. But within the Punjab, Mangoo Ram preferred to be regarded as the Untouchables' spokesman, and that placed him in direct competition with the Punjab unit of Ambedkar's Scheduled Caste Federation. Ultimately, he was not very successful. The Punjab seemed unable to sustain more than one vital movement at a time, and money and leadership were lured increasingly toward Ambedkar and away from the Ad Dharm. And when the Ad Dharm met its demise the movements that were its survivors and heirs were largely those associated with Ambedkar.

But that raises an issue: did the Ambedkar movements provide a continuation of the Ad Dharm's vision and constituency, or were they essentially new efforts to consolidate the social identity of lower castes? According to Lahori Ram Balley, editor of *Bheem Patrika,* a journal published in Jullundur and dedicated to the ideas of Dr. Ambedkar, the Scheduled Caste Federation in the Punjab was essentially an outgrowth from the Ad Dharm.[11] It was not

---

kar sent his son, Yeshwant Rao, and fifteen other Mahars to Amritsar for negotiations, which were apparently encouraged by the Sikhs. It is said that the Sikh establishment of a Khalsa College in Bombay was related to the Ambedkar discussions (Bharill, *Social and Political Ideas,* p. 49).

10. Mangoo Ram interview, April 17, 1971.

11. My information on the history of the Ambedkar movements in the Punjab comes primarily from interviews with leaders of the movements: Lahori Ram Balley, interviews in Jullundur on December 17, 1970; April 1, April 3 and May 3, 1971; November 14, 1973; and August

formally organized until July 1942, when Ambedkar called for organization on a national scale, and when the Ad Dharm was no longer capable of providing an organized political base for Ambedkar in the Punjab. In British India the Punjab was divided into two units, the princely states and the rest of Punjab, and the new Scheduled Caste Federation was divided along those lines as well. Seth Kishan Das became its first president in the Punjab proper, where his Jullundur home was located, and Sadhu Ram became president of the princely states' branch, with jurisdiction over his native Kapurthala. Both had been leaders of Ad Dharm, and both felt that the time had come for a national movement, one with political clout. The primary issue that agitated them and other members of the Scheduled Caste Federation was the one over which Ambedkar and Gandhi had differed in 1932: political representation. Under the terms of the compromise they had reached in the Poona Pact, Untouchables had gained electoral concessions, but not their own representatives. The Scheduled Caste Federation insisted now on separate electorates, which would have given them and other Untouchables organizations considerable power, for they, rather than the political parties, would have become the major agents in choosing lower caste representatives.

During the final struggle for independence and the trauma involved in the partitioning of the Punjab, issues regarding the lower castes were all but forgotten in the chaos of migration and resettlement. The Ambedkar movements began to be active again in the 1950s, when it became clear to the followers of Dr. Ambedkar that the new government was not going to be as useful as they had hoped in eradicating the difficulties of the lower castes. At that point the two Punjab units of the Scheduled Caste Federation were merged into one. In 1956, shortly before his death, when Ambedkar created the Republican party of India and his new Buddhist movement—political and cultural articulations, respectively, of his approach to social

16, 1978; Chanan Ram, interview in London on August 4, 1971; Sadhu Ram, M.P., interview in New Delhi on June 24, 1971, and November 7, 1973; and Seth Kishan Das, interview in Jullundur, November 16, 1973.

change—the Punjab branches of these movements became among the most active outside of Ambedkar's home state itself, Maharashtra. According to both Chanan Ram, who was president of the Republican party from 1956 to 1962, and Balley, who was president from 1962 to 1963, those were optimistic years: the party ran candidates of its own and sometimes supported candidates from other parties.[12] Where they ran independent candidates they were almost invariably defeated, but when they supported candidates in other parties or convinced other parties to support theirs, they met with success. According to Balley, however, the most exciting days of the party's history in the Punjab had nothing to do with elections, but centered around the widely publicized agitations it organized from December 1964 through February 1965 on behalf of greater rights for the lower castes.[13] The success of this venture, following as it did the party's repeated electoral defeats (except through coalition), sharpened internal disputes over strategy. Soon afterward there was a split in the national Republican party of India over the issue of whether the party should form electoral coalitions, especially with the Congress. The Gaikwad group was in favor, the Kobragarde group opposed. The Punjab Republican party split along these lines as well, with the majority favoring Kobragarde and organizing itself under the leadership of Duni Chand Chopri, another of the original leaders of the Ad Dharm.

After the schism neither branch of the Republican party fared very well anywhere in India, and the Punjab was no exception. The strategy of cooperation followed by the Gaikwad group led to assimilation into the Congress, while the militant separatism of the Kobragarde branch kept them from being effective in any electoral contest because they were never able to marshal more than a fraction of the votes. This latter fact did not disturb leaders such as Balley, who saw the whole enterprise of political parties and elections as educational devices rather than battles of strength. Balley thought that improvement for the lower

12. L. R. Balley, May 3, 1971, interview; and Chanan Ram, August 4, 1971, interview.
13. L. R. Balley, April 1, 1971, interview.

castes would not come until there was a more general social change, and for that he was appreciative of the work of the Marxists. In the meantime, however, he felt that education and the widening of political consciousness among the lower castes was a useful task.[14]

Whether or not the Republican party was useful for the educational purpose Balley hoped it would serve, it and the Scheduled Caste Federation before it were clearly instrumental in consolidating the identity of an urban circle of lower caste activists and effective in articulating their interests. Much the same could be said about the new Buddhism as well, the cultural arm of Ambedkar's movement, whose leaders tended to be the same as those of the party.

L. R. Balley, who operates out of a tiny one-room office in the industrial area of Jullundur, exemplifies the dedication of that leadership. Although he is nominally only the editor of the *Bheem Patrika* and a member of the board of the Republican party of India (Kobragarde faction), his role in the lower caste community is much more multifaceted than that: he is a counselor, ombudsman, political organizer, spiritual leader, historian, and educator. The tiny office is always crowded with visitors. But his ambitions are tempered by financial restrictions. He and other Ambedkarites have purchased a plot of land near Boota Mandi, where they eventually hope to build some sort of memorial to Dr. Ambedkar; to date, however, there is only a cement wall around the property and a gate with the words Ambedkar Bhawan (Ambedkar Building).

The membership of the Buddhist movement in the Punjab has in recent years been restricted to Balley and his circle of urban activists and has never numbered more than a few dozen.[15] This is due in large part to the strictness of their regulations. Converts are expected to be totally commit-

14. L. R. Balley, May 3, 1971, interview.

15. My information on Buddhism in the Punjab comes from interviews with L. R. Balley, cited previously; Bhagwan Das, Ambedkar Mission Society, in New Delhi, April 1, June 21, and June 24, 1971, and November 14, 1973; and with J. C. Badhan, Ambedkar Mission Society, March 28 and May 16, 1971. See also Adele Fisk, "Scheduled Caste Buddhist Organizations," in J. M. Mahar, ed., *The Untouchables in Contemporary India* (1972).

ted, are allowed to marry only within their own religion, and may not participate in the ceremonies of any other religious traditions even for social purposes; there is usually a long waiting period before a new member is admitted into the group.

After some years of variously patterned growth across the subcontinent, the Ambedkar Mission Society, founded by Bhagwan Das in New Delhi in 1969, has tried to introduce an element of organizational uniformity. Das, an articulate and educated man who frequently writes for Balley's journal, organizes Ambedkar rallies and conducts weekly Buddhist services. The services include readings from Dr. Ambedkar's books, a homily expounding social issues, the singing of *bhajans* ("religious folk tunes") which have been adapted to include stories about the Buddha and Ambedkar, and ends with a reciting of the traditional three refuges of Buddhism. In all aspects of the new Buddhist society Bhagwan Das is dedicated to removing the "anarchy" that he sees as pervasive: "everybody follows his own inclinations."[16] For example, wedding ceremonies have often varied, depending upon the whim of the parents; some adherents marry in temples, some in court, some in their homes. And social mores are problematical: the Ambedkar Mission Society has devised regulations to avoid the mixing of Buddhist practices with those of other religious traditions. All this is in answer to the justifiable fear that without the charismatic figure of Dr. Ambedkar the new Buddhism might begin to look more and more like the village religious practices which the lower castes have always followed.

The existence of the Ambedkar Mission Society also helps to give this Buddhist revival a worldwide visibility which it otherwise might not have had; in 1970, for example, Bhagwan Das represented it at a world conference of religions in Japan, and in 1979 he attended another in America. The Society hopes that with an organized structure it may be able to attract money from Buddhist countries in other parts of the world to help expand and routinize the Buddhist tradition in India. To date, how-

16. Bhagwan Das, June 21, 1971, interview.

ever, outside of Maharashtra the following has been quite small.

There is a certain irony in the fact that Ambedkar's great vision of mass movements of Untouchables has been reduced, at least in the Punjab, to small groups of elites for whom the name of Ambedkar is a matter of personal pride. Some followers have defended the situation by arguing that Ambedkar advocated a cadre strategy which made the participation of great masses inessential. Ambedkar taught them to "educate, agitate, and organize,"[17] roles for a small, Scheduled Caste avant garde. These coteries of Ambedkarites are political cadres. They keep alive Ambedkar's name, his image, and the ideals he expressed for a transformed India, and because of the enthusiasm of their commitment they have become the new symbol of lower caste defiance.

At least in some sense they have succeeded in replacing the Ad Dharm as the organizational expression of lower caste interests. At the same time, however, they have replicated the Ad Dharm's final error, becoming alienated from their own constituency. Two images of Ambedkar have been projected: Baba-sahib Ambedkar, the semidivine popular figure, and Dr. Ambedkar, the inspiring colleague of a new, educated class.[18] In the Punjab only the latter image has caught on, and without the aura of familiar religious symbols, Ambedkar and his movements remain alien from the life of Punjabi villages.

17. This slogan was promulgated by Ambedkar in the establishing of his first organization, the Bahishkrit Hitkarini Sabha (Society for the Welfare of the Excluded), in July, 1924 (Bharill, *Social and Political Ideas*, p. 19). The slogan is still frequently used by Ambedkarites, including L. R. Balley.

18. An interesting study of the mythic image of Ambedkar within the lower caste communities of the city of Agra is found in Owen Lynch, "Ambedkar: the Man and the Myth," pp. 97–112 in Mahar, *The Untouchables in Contemporary India*.

16 Rishi Valmiki, The Saint of Sweepers

The Valmiki Sabha also could be regarded as a direct replacement for the Ad Dharm, and like the Ambedkar movements, it also had gained its momentum long before the Ad Dharm's demise. In fact, it could in some ways be regarded as a parallel Ad Dharm movement, created especially for members of the lowest of the Untouchable castes, the Sweepers (Chuhras). Like the Chamars, who constituted much of the membership of the Ad Dharm, active members of the Sweeper caste also chose religious forms for their social protests, but except for a brief flirtation with Ad Dharm and a continuing alliance, their leaders did not choose Ad Dharm's formulation, preferring to fashion one of their own. The reasons for that preference, and their acceptance of a religious form of protest in the first place, has much to do with the social character of their caste and the cities in which they predominate.

In the cities, surprisingly, the Sweepers play a more traditional role than they do in the countryside. Mercantile Hindu castes such as the Khatris and Aroras dominate Punjab's urban life, giving the cities more of a Hindu character than is found in the countryside and reinforcing concepts of caste and untouchability. Moreover, the Sweepers in the cities are actually employed in their traditional roles, as sweepers, whereas their Chuhra caste fellows in the villages serve largely as landless laborers (the availability of fields for sanitary purposes having made sanitation tasks largely unnecessary). It is understandable, then, that when urban Sweepers began to form cultural and political organizations, they utilized symbols from Hindu tradition, but this did not mean that their organizations lacked a significant element of protest.

The Chuhras of the cities took Rishi Valmiki, the author of the classical Hindu epic, the *Ramayana,* as their patron saint and adopted his name as their own. Valmiki was said to have come from a lower caste, hence served as an appropriate symbol of lower caste cultural integrity as well as a link with the high tradition. In Punjabi his name is pronounced "Balmik," thus the Chuhras called themselves Balmikis. The Balmikis began to organize early in this century, and early became involved in the Ad Dharm movement.[1] But their alliance with the Ad Dharm, which married their interests to those of the Chamars, who were largely rural, did not last long. In about 1932 the Sweepers left the Ad Dharm to continue their own cultural associations and start new political movements for the benefit of their own caste.

The first Valmiki Sabha was constituted in Jullundur; references were made to it as early as 1910.[2] It was alleged at the time that the Arya Samaj encouraged the Sweepers to use the term "Valmiki" to indicate their agreement with Hindu traditions and values.[3] Whether or not that was precisely the case, the Valmiki Sabha in Jullundur did give the impression of being a Hindu sect, since it linked the worship and beliefs of the Sweepers to the higher tradition. At

  1. Interview with Mangoo Ram, Garhshankar, April 17, 1971; interview with Gurvanta Singh, Jullundur, May 8, 1971. The Balmiki role in the Ad Dharm is also indicated by the involvement of Chunni Lal Thapar and other Balmiki leaders mentioned in the *Ad Dharm Report,* 1931.
  2. The reference to the Valmiki Sabha in Jullundur was made in the *Indian Social Reformer* and the *Punjabee,* the latter cited in J. N. Farquhar, *Modern Religious Movements in India* (New York, 1924), pp. 369–370.
  3. The same allegation—that Lala Mulk Raj, brother of the Arya Samaj leader Lala Hans Raj, created the name and the movement in 1910 to discourage the Chuhras from converting to Christianity—was made voluntarily and separately by four persons: an upper caste former member of the Arya Samaj (interview with Lala Mohan Lal, former secretary, Harijan Sevak Sangh, in Jullundur, May 1, 1971) and by three lower caste members of the Arya Samaj (interview with Sant Ram, B.A., founder of the Jat Path Thorak Mandal, at village Purani Bassi,

the same time, however, it provided a focus for the coherence and pride of Chuhras as a caste by sponsoring fairs and festivals, organizing demonstrations to secure greater public recognition of Rishi Valmiki's importance, and encouraging educational and cultural improvements in the Sweeper community.[4]

If the Arya Samaj was instrumental in stimulating the growth of the Valmiki Sabha, it must have been disappointed with the direction it took, for at least two of the old-time leaders in the Jullundur Valmiki Sabha made a point of distancing themselves from the Samaj and the social customs of the upper castes. Mahatma Fakir Chand, who was considered by some to be the founder of the Jullundur Valmiki Sabha and presided over meetings at which Gandhi himself was present, renounced the values of Hindu society.[5] He and another early Valmiki Sabha leader, Gandu Ram (whom others claim to be the founder), were members of the Ad Dharm Mandal and supported the Ad Dharm's struggle against the Arya Samaj.[6] During those years the Valmiki Sabha was in close alignment with the Ad Dharm,[7] but apparently it always remained an independent movement with religious notions and concepts of communal identity of its own.

Although the Chuhras' traditional veneration of Bala Shah and Lal Beg persisted in various domestic religious

---

Hoshiarpur district, April 18, 1971; interview with Principal Ram Das, President of Dayanand Salvation Mission, in Hoshiarpur, April 18, 1971; and interview with Sohan Lal Shastri, former Arya Samaji, in New Delhi, June 25, 1971). Other versions of this story place the dates of Arya Samaj influence at 1928 and 1932.

4. My information on the Valmiki Sabha in the Punjab comes primarily from interviews with the following former and present leaders of the movement: Om Prakash Gill, Jullundur, May 5, 1971; R. L. Gill, president of Valmiki Sabha (Charan Das group), Jullundur, May 1 and 28, 1971; Hari Krishan Nahar, former president of Valmiki Navyuk Mandal, Jullundur, May 4, 7, 15, and 27, 1971; Yashwant Rai, former leader of Valmiki Sabha, Chandigarh, April 7, 1971; and Sant Ram, M.L.A., Jullundur, June 12, 1971.

5. R. L. Gill, May 28, 1971.

6. Interview with Swami Shudranand, Jullundur, May 15, 1971.

7. All of my Valmiki Sabha informants, and Mangoo Ram, agree that the Valmiki Sabha supported the Ad Dharm, at least prior to 1932.

practices and occasionally even in temple worship, the Valmiki Sabha was Hindu in all formal respects.[8] Rishi Valmiki was sometimes represented in pictures as an historical person, the author of the *Ramayana,* and sometimes as a sort of god; the main Balmiki temples in the major cities of the Punjab portrayed him in both modes and set his picture alongside images of the usual Hindu deities. As for religious leadership, a number of Balmiki holy men were associated with the major Balmiki pilgrimage center, Baba Gian Nath's Valmiki Ashram at Ram Tirith, near Amritsar. The Valmiki Ashram is at the side of a clean, attractive, bathing tank and near other ashrams occupied primarily by higher caste holy men. People of various castes stop at the small Valmiki temple there, which includes representations of various Shaiva and Vaishnava deities as well as an icon of Rishi Valmiki. Comfortably settled among the gods, Valmiki receives garlands and offerings of food, incense, and money in the Hindu manner.

The Valmiki *sabhas* are largely cultural affairs promoting the veneration of Rishi Valmiki, but they are also concerned about social reform. This concern, however, is almost entirely directed toward the moral betterment of their caste members, not toward the large issues of social and economic change. Such matters have become the specific

---

8. A discussion of Lal Beg and Bala Shah is found in chapter 9. In general, the religious and cultural background of the Chuhras (also known as Bhangi in other parts of North India) has not been studied as fully as that of the Chamars, but there is one older work, Col. R. Greevens' *Knights of Brooms* (Benares, 1894), and some recent articles, including Pauline Moller Mahar, "Changing Religious Practices of an Untouchable Caste" (*Economic Development and Cultural Change* 8 [1970]); and Ram Ratan, "The Changing Religion of the Bhangis of Delhi: A Case of Sanskritisation," in L. P. Vidyarthi, ed., *Aspects of Religion in Indian Society* (Meerut, 1961). Other studies have come from missionary scholars, including H. J. Strickler, "The Religion and Customs of the Chuhra in the Punjab Province, India" (M.A. thesis, University of Kansas, 1926). Helpful ethnographical material is also found in the writings of the missionary-scholar H. D. Griswold, and reports appearing in the Christian Missionary Society's *C.M.S. Movement Quarterly* from 1918 onward. Several other works will be cited in the following chapter, when the emergence of the Christian community out of the Chuhra caste in the Punjab is discussed.

province of another organization, the Sweepers Union, which was founded in 1937 with the name Safai Muzdoor Sangha (Sanitation Workers' Society) and appears to have been preceded by a similar organization called the Raksha Dal (Defense party).[9]

According to a Balmiki leader in Jullundur, Sant Ram, the cofounders of the Sweepers Union included Chuni Lal Thapar, Bal Mukand, Mohtan Singh, and himself, all of whom had had a certain amount of education and some prior experience in other movements.[10] Two of those who were said to be founders—Sant Ram and Thapar—were involved with the Ad Dharm movement in its formative stages, and left it in order to concentrate their efforts on the betterment of their own caste community.[11] The union staged its first major event in the Jullundur Sweepers' Strike of 1938, led by Sant Ram.[12] The agitation spread to other cities in the Punjab, and Sant Ram was jailed in Amritsar in the following year. That initial period of activity established what was to be called the Sweepers Union—then still the Safai Muzdoor Sangha—as the bargaining agent of the Sweepers, and it agitated from time to time over specific issues. Sant Ram himself, like other early leaders of the Ad Dharm, used the political base of the Sweepers Union to move on into other forms of politics, and in 1945 he joined the Congress party and became its parliamentary secretary under Chief Minister Sachar. In 1946 he was elected to the legislative assembly on the Congress slate and continued to serve until 1962.[13]

The Sweepers unions and Valmiki *sabhas* came to be established in most cities of the Punjab after 1940 and saw a significant expansion in the years following independence, especially in Chandigarh, Ludhiana, and Amritsar.[14] But the largest and most active chapters of both the Sweepers

9. Sant Ram, M.L.A., June 12, 1971, interview.
10. Ibid.
11. Ibid., and Mangoo Ram, April 17, 1971, interview.
12. Sant Ram, M.L.A., June 12, 1971, interview.
13. Ibid.
14. Yashwant Rai, April 7, 1971, and current leaders of the branches of the Valmiki Sabha in the Punjab.

Union and the Valmiki Sabha remained those that had been founded where the movement began, in Jullundur. The Balmiki sections of that city show clearly how religion and politics are mixed together in the social identities and political activities of Sweepers.[15]

The Balmikis in Jullundur are concentrated in two adjacent sectors *(mohallas)* of the old walled city. Some of them live in Ali Mohalla, an area now dominated by merchant caste Hindus, and most of them live in an area almost exclusively populated by members of the Sweeper caste, an area that formerly was called Darwaza Kobra (the Sweeper's Gate), indicating that it was next to the entrance to the old city reserved exclusively for members of the lower castes. After partition, when the Muslims in Jullundur were replaced by refugees from West Punjab—primarily Hindus from Khatri castes and a smaller number of Arora Sikhs—the Sweepers changed the name of their gate and the *mohalla* adjoining it to something more Hindu: now it is Balmiki Gate.

The Ali Mohalla/Balmiki Gate area is called the Madras area of Jullundur, suggesting the cosmopolitan, polyglot character it retains, even after the departure of the Muslims. It is a market area, the narrow lanes crowded with cloth shops, booksellers, and stacks of brass pots and kettles. A huge *gurdwara* stands beside a magnificent, but after partition unused, mosque, and there are several temples, including two large edifices constructed by the Valmiki Sabha, one in Ali Mohalla and the other along the main road next to Balmiki Gate. These Valmiki temples serve as community centers for local gatherings and political meetings. Since there are no Scheduled Castes in the immediate area other than Balmikis, their community is naturally self-contained.

15. This information on Balmiki Mohalla, Jullundur city, is based on field studies conducted there in 1970–1971 and updated in 1973, 1978, and 1979. Hari Krishan Nahar helped translate documents and assisted in the conversations conducted in Hindi. A complete description of the community in its Jullundur Scheduled Caste context is given in Juergensmeyer, "Political Hope," pp. 130–143.

The name of the community as a whole is not the only one that identifies it with upper caste traditions: subcastes too have received upper caste names, borrowed for the most part from social designations used by Jats and Khatris. In Balmiki Gate the Gill subcaste is the largest, and in Ali Mohalla, the Kalyana. Other subcastes are the Nahar, the Sabbarwal, and the Sondhi, of which the last is much the richest, since some Sondhis have shops. But the great majority of Balmikis do what their caste has always done: they provide sanitation services for the city. After independence these came to be administered by the municipal offices of the city, so many Balmikis became de facto government servants, subject to all the frustrations that an impersonal government bureaucracy entails, but to all the opportunities as well. The expansion of municipal services after independence meant that great numbers of Balmikis could be employed. By 1971 Jullundur had 1,300 municipal scavengers (the term for sweepers who are specifically involved in removing rubbish and excrement). About 70 percent of that number were women, and most families involved in scavenging work had more than one member employed, with the minimum age fixed at nineteen. The standard salary at that time was Rs. 150 per month, plus a variety of benefits, including maintenance support for the Sweepers' donkeys, health insurance, a provident fund, on-leave pay, and new implements—shovels, brooms, and the like. These conditions were remarkably good for the Punjab and for India generally, and they remain so today; but they did not come about automatically.

Perhaps the most important force in improving the economic welfare of Sweepers in Jullundur was the Sweepers Union, led in recent years by Om Prakash Gill. Gill led the Sweepers Union through a series of strikes that established its active posture and enhanced his own political reputation at the same time. In 1960 there were strikes for higher wages (the scale was then only Rs. 95 per month), and in 1964 another series was directed, among other things, to securing greater representation for Sweepers on the Jullundur Municipal Council. Soon thereafter Om

Prakash Gill was elected to the council, and he served on it as the only Balmiki member for many years. Strikes since 1964 have included demands for donkey charges to maintain the sweepers' animals, and for the formation of a new work gang to ease the growing work load. In March 1971 a group within the Sweepers' Union seized a vacant plot of land in demonstration of their demands for new government-supported residential quarters; they built their own huts there and called the makeshift camp Indira Colony, invoking the name and, they hoped, the sympathy of the prime minister. The government, however, quickly tore it down and the demand has yet to be fully met. Like any group, the Sweepers Union has had its factions, and not every strike has been a unified endeavor, but on the whole there has been a remarkable coherence and a surprising record of success.

If the Sweepers unions have been active in expressing the economic aspirations of the Balmikis, the Valmiki *sabhas* have been no less vigorous in the cultural realm. Central to the *sabhas*' activities are the veneration of Rishi Valmiki, and the propagation of myths that link him and his reputation with Chuhras and their subcastes. To many persons from upper castes, it comes as a surprise that the author of Hinduism's great epic, the *Ramayana*, is touted to be a Chuhra, even though there are many stories popular throughout North India which trace his legendary ancestry to a band of brigands. Nevertheless, robber bands often came from the poorest of castes, so it is only a short mental jump from those myths to the ones told exclusively by the Chuhras in which he is securely identified as one of their own. The Chuhra myths sometimes confuse Rishi Valmiki (Balmik) with the lower caste deity, Bala Shah; and other myths, although retaining Valmiki's role within Hindu tradition, tell how current-day customs and names used by the Chuhras are explained by the amazing events in the Rishi's legendary life. The more miraculous of the myths are told only among themselves, but the enhancement of Valmiki's name in general is a matter of great public pride, and consumes much of the Valmik *sabhas*' attention.

The Valmiki *sabhas* have had political concerns as well, interlocking with those of the Sweepers unions in what for the lower castes is a natural meeting of religion and politics. Since independence there have been two Valmiki *sabhas* in the city, and they are separated along the same political lines that divide the two factions within the Sweepers Union, both in Jullundur and in other areas of the state. A significant part of what separates these two groups has to do with their attitudes to the two major parties supported by upper caste Hindus, the Congress and the Jan Sangh. The faction of the Valmiki Sabha which favors the Congress is the old guard and includes the established leadership of the Sweepers Union among its members.[16] Sweepers employed by the city also tend to align with them.

The opposing group, which leans toward the Jan Sangh, made its final break with the old Valmiki Sabha in 1969, but frictions had long before been evident and involve issues that extend beyond party alignment. This group is composed of white-collar municipal government servants, and tend to be better educated and younger—Balmikis on the way up. According to one of their members, a young man from Balmiki Gate, this Valmiki Sabha has a different strategy: "The old group thinks the way to improve is raw politics, dirty deals and grabbing what you can. We think it's education, getting better occupations, and living a higher style of life."[17] Since many members of the new *sabha* are government servants, raw politics is not an option for them in any case: government servants are barred by law from being active in party politics.

16. Om Prakash Gill, Jullundur municipal councilman, belonged to this Sabha, as did Sant Ram, former M.L.A. from Balmiki Gate, and Shadi Lal, one of the city's sanitary supervisors. The Congress-supporting group was of a particular stripe, for there were two main Congress factions in Jullundur, one camp associated with the name of the former chief minister, Pratap Singh Kairon, and the other with Congress leader Darbara Singh. The Chamars, lead by Jullundur's old Ad Dharm leader Gurvanta Singh, tended to follow the Kairon group; and the Valmikis, including all of the Congress-supporting Valmiki Sabha, followed Darbara Singh.
17. Hari Krishan Nahar, May 4, 1971.

Two members of the Jan Sangh–supporting faction, Ram Lal Gill and B. L. Patanga, typify the interests of their circle. Gill, a clerk in Jullundur's main post office, and Patanga, a sign painter from Ali Mohalla, like to think of themselves as exemplars of the direction in which urban India is moving: they live a modern lifestyle, house their nuclear families in small, clean apartments, and boast of television sets. They travel frequently on organizational trips for their Valmiki Sabha throughout the state. Their link with the Jan Sangh is both an attempt to emulate the higher tradition of upper caste city dwellers, and to make contact with the merchant caste Hindus who lead the party. Gill and Patanga claim that the Jan Sangh exercises only an indirect influence on their group, however, since the party sponsors its own Scheduled Caste organizations, and does not, they claim, need to co-opt theirs to gain Scheduled Caste support.

The Jan Sangh's official auxiliary organizations for Scheduled Castes are largely constituted from one caste, the Balmikis. The party has an uplift society, the Harijan Social Forum; an organization of lower caste workers, the Bharati Muzdoor Sangh; and a working group within the party proper, the "Harijan Wing" of the Jan Sangh. The latter, along with the state headquarters of the entire party, is located adjacent to the Balmiki areas of Jullundur. When one visits the headquarters, one is greeted by a young Brahman who despite his own caste is active in campaigning for Balmiki support. Working along with him in full-time paid positions are Balmiki political organizers. One of these, R. K. Nahar from Batala, also served as state president of the Jan Sangh–affiliated Valmiki Youth Association. Nahar was also an active and dedicated member of the R.S.S. (the Rashtriya Swayamsevak Sangh, a right-wing Hindu organization which has the reputation of discouraging any sort of social change, especially that involving the traditional lines of caste and religious custom). Nahar admits that the numbers of Balmikis in the R.S.S. are very small, and that for most Balmiki supporters of the Jan Sangh, their emulation of upper caste Hindu positions does not go quite so far.

Some of the most interesting members of the Balmiki Gate community are those who are no longer in evidence, people whose talents or ambition gave them access to a better society or who developed allegiances that encouraged them to live elsewhere. Before independence, opportunities in the British army allowed many Balmikis to travel, and some settled in England. A few others, since independence, have been able to move to the Jullundur suburbs. Changes in government hiring policies have provided them with comparatively high-paying employment. These defections, however, have had only a negligible effect on community morale in Balmiki Gate, and relatives there feel no embarrassment in joining a marriage party in the fancier sections of the city or receiving Christmas packages from Birmingham. A greater threat to Balmiki community solidarity lies closer at hand, for there is a form of escape from Balmiki society much more common and much more easily accessible to the community at large than traveling abroad or buying into the middle class: one could become a Christian.

"Sure, they are resented," a young resident of Balmiki Gate told me, "because they move out of our *mohallas* when they are converted and they think they're better than we are."[18] But the same fellow has a brother who attends church, not because he is Christian but because "he made a little money, and he thinks it gives him status." R. L. Gill, the leader of one of the Valmiki *sabhas,* is indifferent about the matter. His own mother-in-law is a Christian, and he claims that although Christianity offers some educational advantages, it tends to separate its adherents from the special benefits assigned by the government to those who still identify themselves as belonging to one of the Untouchable castes. Christian-Balmiki marriages are frequent—"we're all in the same community"—but most Christians live in separate areas, near the Mission Compound, in Basti Bawa Khol, and in Jullundur cantonment, where many of the Chuhras were converted to Christianity around the turn of the century while employed in the British army as

18. Ibid.

servants. When the British departed, the advantages associated with Christianity were diminished, and many fewer Balmikis joined. But the Christian community remains a sort of half-brother to the Balmikis, a source alternately of challenge and of pride.

Despite the challenge of Christianity, the Valmiki *sabhas* continue to be the central cultural and social focus of the Sweeper caste. The appropriation of the figure of Valmiki doubtless reveals a desire to emulate Hindu ways and gain respect from the upper castes, but it also provides the cultural unity necessary to sustain the sweepers' struggle for dignity and to support the political claims of the Sweepers Union. No doubt the Balmikis' religious identity and political flexibility made them ripe candidates for co-optation and compromise, but it also gave them considerable room for maneuver in prosecuting their own ends. It is interesting in this regard that the working-class sweepers chose religious symbols to satisfy their cultural identity and tighten their social organization. Rishi Valmiki and the myths surrounding him could be used now in assimilationist, now in separatist strategies. And when sweepers came to envision a more radical avenue of social change, that too had a religious focus—the alternative society of Christendom.

17 Christianity: The Sweepers' Revolt

The first convert in the great surge of conversions to Christianity that swept the Punjab in the late nineteenth century was reported to be a Chuhra, a man named Ditt, who was described by one of the early missionary reports only as "a lame, dark man."[1] Ditt was baptized in Sialkot in 1873 by the Reverend S. Martin, who brought him into the church, "not because he saw his way decidedly clear to do so, but rather because he could see no scriptural ground for refusing."[2] To the surprise of the missionaries, Ditt was followed by hundreds of thousands of others from the lower castes, and Punjab Christianity became de facto a movement for the uplift of Untouchables, perhaps the first one in modern history. When a newspaper article reported that the rate of conversions would soon turn the Punjab into a Christian region,[3] a tremor of fear ran through the upper caste Hindu and Sikh elite.[4] It has been plausibly argued that this fear acted as a stimulus to the growth of the Arya Samaj in general;[5] certainly it encouraged the Samaj to develop many of its social service institutions, which were intended to offset what was regarded as the missionaries' religious seduction of the lower castes.

1. Andrew Gordon, *Our Indian Mission* (Philadelphia, 1888), p. 422.
2. Ibid.
3. The Lahore *Tribune,* October 19, 1892, p. 4. The *Tribune* was editorially commenting on the 1891 census returns, which listed almost 10,000 Christians in Sialkot district, whereas less than 300 had been registered in the preceding census (1881).
4. Jones, *Arya Dharm* (Berkeley and Los Angeles, 1976), p. 144.
5. Ibid., and *passim.*

The fear was excessive, as it turned out, but at the time it seemed justified, since the church did indeed have a manifold appeal for the lower castes. Its religious tenets presented attractive alternatives to Hindu concepts, especially the element of social concern and the promise of instant and easy access to salvation for all. But more than that, Christianity offered a model of an ideal social order and the means of achieving it. It challenged the caste system conceptually and provided, through its missionaries, access to the educational skills that would lay the basis for an egalitarian society capable of replacing it. It was a total alternative, as total as that which the Ad Dharm would offer the lower castes in the 1920s and 1930s.

There is no indication that the Ad Dharm consciously mimicked the church. Since most converts to Christianity were Chuhras, whereas the Ad Dharm movement appealed primarily to Chamars, there was little direct competition between them. It is true that at the time of its founding the Ad Dharm had hoped to gain a wider following and had viewed with disfavor the rate of Christian conversions among the Chuhra. This had led the early leaders of the Ad Dharm, in elaborating their myth of origin, to draw a parallel between latter-day Christian incursions and the much earlier invasions of the Aryans: Christians also were portrayed as outsiders bent on robbing the Adi people of their true identities.[6] But this hostility never became fundamental: time mellowed whatever tensions had been felt at the beginning.

By the middle of the 1930s both movements, the Ad Dharm and the Christian, had stabilized. Christian conversions had abated, and the missionaries turned the bulk of their attention to the education and social betterment of those who were already within the fold. The Ad Dharm ceased to expand at the same time, and it became increasingly clear that it would probably never include great numbers of Chuhras. In fact, since both movements were primarily concerned with the problems of social uplift and education and with securing government benefits for the

6. *Ad Dharm Report*, p. 9.

Chamar field-workers near village Bimla

A lower caste family servant in village Bimla

A shoemaker, Hari Lal, in village Nalla, with his grandson

Seth Kishan Das and L.R. Balley in Boota Mandi, Jullundur

Sant Sarwan Das, Master of the Ravi ▶
Das Dera, village Ballan

lower castes, there were several occasions on which the Ad Dharm and Christian communities worked together.

On July 7 and 8, 1937, a rally was held at the mission compound in Jullundur city, jointly sponsored by the Ad Dharm and the Presbyterian church. The Reverend Clinton Loehlin, who was then the district missionary in Jullundur, served as its chairman, and Mangoo Ram offered resolutions on behalf of the Ad Dharm. The perspectives of the two groups about the purpose of the conference and what it accomplished, however, were widely different. According to the Reverend Mr. Loehlin, the gathering had been sponsored in order to encourage the Ad Dharm to convert en masse to Christianity.[7] Similarly, the *United Church Review,* reporting on the event at the time, stated that the lower caste members "felt most friendly toward the Christian community and desirous of entering into their fellowship."[8] Mangoo Ram's view of the conference, however, was diametrically opposite. He held that it had been convened in order to encourage the Christian community to support demands which the Ad Dharm was making to the government on behalf of the lower castes. Whichever perspective more accurately represents the historical facts, the resolutions passed at the conference make it plain that a political alliance was formed. It was declared that "for the welfare of both the communities, the Achhuts [Untouchables] and Christians, in respect to political views, will in and out of the Legislative Assembly work together."[9] An Ad Dharm resolution also requested the Presbyterians to be more lenient in accepting children from Ad Dharm families into their educational institutions.

For Mangoo Ram, Christianity in the Punjab was as a movement among the lower castes similar to his own. Whether competitive or cooperative, it was a lower caste movement, not something alien. The missionaries, conscious of the international and transnational dimensions of

7. Interview with Clinton Loehlin, Marysville, California, August 10, 1972.
8. "Conference on the Uplift of Lower Castes," *United Church Review,* October 1937, p. 17.
9. Ibid.

Christendom, saw things differently: for them, if not perhaps for their lower caste charges, Christianity in the Punjab was something that rose above caste, hardly an instrument of caste identity and mobility. It is highly unlikely that the missionaries thought of themselves as partners in a lower caste social movement.

In fact, however, it was the Untouchables who had originally sought out Christianity, not the other way around. Originally, the missionaries of the Punjab had only attempted to convert the upper castes, since they regarded others as beyond the reach of the methods they preferred—intellectual argument and moral suasion. The enthusiasm of the first convert, Ditt, and the subsequent lower caste requests for conversion not only baffled the missionaries but embarrassed them: they saw no sensible or moral reason for keeping the lower castes out, yet feared that allowing them in would sully the church's reputation. In a brisk exchange of letters between the mission field and various denominational head offices, a number of missionaries warned about the consequences of "raking in rubbish into the Church."[10] But in the end the opportunity to swell Christian numbers seemed to be too great to miss, and suspicions about the motives of the new converts and their potential as Christians were abandoned.

These suspicions were not easily allayed, for the missionaries, although hoping for large numbers, were adamant about what they regarded as quality in their catches as well. The church stumbled upon a compromise: the notion of a "nurturing" Christian. The uneducated lower caste converts would be accepted into the Christian community, but in the same way that one might baptize a child into the faith. There was no expectation that the convert or the child would know much about the faith at the time of entering the church, but through proper nurture he or she would develop in the fullness of Christian faith and commitment as the years went on. This concept not only

10. J. C. R. Ewing, letter to Dr. Gillespie, March 19, 1894, cited in John C. B. Webster, *The Christian Community and Change in North India* (Delhi: Macmillan, 1976), p. 60.

created a justification for accepting the hundreds of thousands of lower caste converts into the fold, it also changed the directions of the missionary enterprise itself. It had the effect of shifting the church's attention away from elite education for an upper caste few to an enormous organization aimed at disseminating church materials and facilitating education for the masses. Within a few brief decades at the end of the nineteenth century, Christianity in the Punjab shifted from an elitist to a popular enterprise.

The missionaries soon became enthusiastic about the new situation. They justified the mass conversions as "acts of the holy spirit, working through the group instinct of the Indian."[11] The task of the missionary in this altered circumstance, they came to believe, was to take the raw material that had been given by the Holy Spirit and mold it so that it yielded proper Christians. One missionary, in attempting to recruit funds and new missionary personnel from his home church warned, "If the movement gets out of hand and beyond the church's proper control, then the end might be a disaster. . . . [I]t would damage the church for generations."[12] The nurture of the lower caste converts became the primary focus of the church in the Punjab, and the missionary forces swelled with teachers in the new secondary and technical schools, directors of Christian education, experts in adult literacy, church organizers, and experts in public health.

Thousands of missionaries arrived from England, Europe, and America, during the great years of the mass movement, from the 1880s through the 1940s, and these were exciting years. There were, after all, very visible evidences of the missionaries' achievements. Within a few years their efforts at recruitment had gone from yielding only a handful of upper caste converts to gathering almost a half million Christians from the lower castes. Moreover, many of the new converts—although not as many as one might expect—responded well to the educational and social services which the church provided. Morale was high. Although the mis-

11. W. S. Hunt, *India's Outcastes: A New Era* (London, 1924), p. 6.
12. W. Noble, *Floodtide in India: An Eyewitness Account of the Mass Movements* (London, 1937), p. 88.

sionaries were seldom explicitly supported by the British government (indeed, some governmental officials regarded them as a nuisance), the sympathy of much of the government for their enterprise was bountiful. Buttressed by this tacit governmental sanction and the great prestige of Western civilization, they had the run of India. In those remarkable years the global vision of victory for Christendom seemed achievable, and the enthusiasm of the missionaries in hastening its advent must have been infectious. The titles of their books say as much: *Gospel Romance Among the Huts of the Punjab, Floodtide in India,* and *Reap the Mighty Harvest.*[13]

It was a matter of only fleeting embarrassment that the mighty harvest in the Punjab was reaped almost entirely from among the lower castes. In some cases reports from the mission field preferred to obscure this fact by describing Punjabi Christians as "common villagers" or "illiterate menials" and ignoring the factor of caste. In other cases, however, there were efforts to understand and ennoble the culture of the lower castes through field studies of lower caste communities. It was argued, for example, that Bala Shah and the other lower caste religious figures were evidence of a primitive monotheism among the lower castes; in the eyes of the missionaries this elevated their religious beliefs above the polytheistic tendencies of upper caste Hindus.[14] Then too, the mere fact that the lower castes had been wise enough to select Christianity was seen as indication of their prescience and special destiny. One early missionary report celebrated the fact that the lower castes "are being transformed by Christianity" and "appear to be especially chosen for a divine purpose in Indian history."[15] Finally, the missionaries were often steadfast in viewing their lower caste converts in terms not of their past but of their future: once within the church they were regarded no

13. Howard E. Anderson, *Gospel Romance in the Huts of the Punjab* (New York, 1925); W. Noble, *Floodtide in India; Reap the Mighty Harvest,* a pamphlet of the Christian Missionary Society, c. 1927.

14. Hunt, *India's Outcastes,* p. 61, and Henry Madras, "The Mass Movement Towards Christianity in the Punjab," *International Review of Missions* 2 (1913), p. 444.

15. J. F. Burditt, *Work Among the Depressed Classes and the Masses* (Bombay, 1893), p. 17.

longer as Hindu Untouchables but as nurturing Christians who were at least potentially equal to Christians anywhere else in the world. Still, the missionaries continued to hope that this mass Christianity would be only the first phase in the expansion of the faith in the Punjab: that it would soon reach upward into the other levels of society as well. This never happened, of course—the church in the Punjab remained a predominantly lower caste institution—but the hope was tenaciously maintained for many years.

A few of the lower caste converts shared the missionaries' expansive vision. For those who became leaders and teachers in Christian institutions the great appeal of the faith was precisely its social promise: its commitment to creating a society, both in India and around the world, in which all persons would be equal. The masses of lower caste Christians, however, were lured instead by the more immediate prospect of escaping from Hindu social customs and receiving a number of tangible benefits at the same time: education, health care, employment within the church, and leadership training. Still, it would be a mistake to call these "rice Christians." Few of them joined the church for material gain alone. Rather, they responded to the same force that had impelled the missionaries: the transforming power of religious commitment. Behind their tangible gains lay a symbolic one—a new identity that provoked them into changing their names, their clothing, and their eating habits, and to take advantage of the new opportunities for self-betterment which the missionary institutions provided.

Even in the face of all this, the old caste distinctions persisted within the Christian community. The small number of caste Hindus who joined the Punjab church were dignified with the title of "convert," whereas recruits from the lower castes were known instead as "mass movement Christians" or simply "Christians."[16] It was only these lower

16. Interview with E. Y. Campbell, former missionary-sociologist in the Punjab, New Delhi, October 20, 1970. This and the observations which follow are corroborated by a variety of interviews among Punjabi Christians, and by my observations of lower caste Christian communities in the Punjab. Also see E. Y. Campbell, *The Church in the Punjab: Some Aspects of Its Life and Growth* (Nagpur, 1961).

caste Christians who left behind their family names and adopted foreign names such as John Samuel, Paul Masih (Masih meaning "Messiah"), and the like; upper caste converts retained their ties to the caste system by continuing to use their Hindu or Sikh names. The ritual of eucharist presented a special problem in the Indian setting, since all communicants ordinarily take the chalice and bread together, which would violate intercaste eating restrictions. The church could not acknowledge that prohibitions against commensality were still observed within the church, but managed to accommodate upper caste sensitivities nonetheless. The problem was solved in two ways: by establishing separate worship services for those who spoke English and those who spoke only Punjabi, which de facto eliminated the lower castes from English-speaking services; or, failing this, by ensuring that upper caste converts would sit at the front of the church so that they would use the communion implements first, before they became polluted by the Christians of lower castes.

Thus the egalitarian vision of a new society in Christendom was eroded somewhat by the fact that upper caste members who remained in the church were frequently accorded special privileges. But such converts were few indeed, and it became clear to many of the lower caste church leaders, if not to the missionaries, that Christianity in the Punjab was a lower caste religion and should be regarded as such. There was a growing demand within the church for the leaders of the Christian community to take more responsibility in the uplift of the lower castes and make appeals to the government for that purpose.[17] Some of the district missionaries found that they and their pastors were frequently agents of intercession to government and court officials—so much so that foreign missionaries often reported they felt more like lawyers and government liaison personnel than like ministers of the gospel.[18] More overt

17. Interview with S. F. Din, Christian leader and former deputy chairman, upper house of Punjab government, Chandigarh, June 5, 1971.
18. E. Y. Campbell, October 20, 1970, and interview with Clinton Loehlin, former missionary in the Punjab, Marysville, California, June 12, 1972.

attempts at political organization within the Christian community, until independence, were always discouraged by the missionaries.[19]

After independence the Christian church in the Punjab changed considerably. The missionaries began to leave in large numbers, which meant that the Christian community had to fend for itself in the face of a new government, which was less congenial to their interests than the British colonial government had been. The missionary exodus did, however, create a vacuum of leadership that fostered a new group of lower caste church leaders; previously, most of the indigenous leadership of the church had come from a small, upper caste minority. With greater Scheduled Caste participation came a greater emphasis on the social facts surrounding the Christian community as a whole, and the need for improving the economic and social conditions that beset the lower castes.

An example of a rather successful shift from the old missionary era into the new situation is provided by the Christian church in the old mission compound in Jullundur city. When the missionaries left, the pastorate of the church was transferred to a lower caste convert, Reverend Y. C. Mal, a spry and cheerful villager who managed to keep together a varied congregation of upper and lower caste converts. In recent years both segments of the community have expanded, and on Sunday morning expensive automobiles are parked alongside rickshaws outside the gates of the church. Although missionary money is no longer available, the members of the church are sufficiently prosperous to support the salary of the Reverend Mr. Mal and the activities of the community.[20] Most of the other enterprises of the Jullundur mission compound—the schools and training centers—have had to be abandoned, but nearby in the town of Suranassi a thriving complex of technical schools has sprung up, largely since independence, on the basis of

19. Amar Nath Singh, general secretary, Bharatiya Masihi Dal, Saranassi, Jullundur, April 26, 1971. Some early forms of political organization erupted before independence despite the missionaries' disapproval.

20. Interview with Y. C. Mal, pastor of the United Church of North India, Jullundur, December 10, 1970.

financial contributions from church agencies abroad. Indian Christians provide the administrative leadership and teaching staff, and the absence of missionary personnel seems a matter of little consequence.

In the villages the Christian church has not fared so well since independence. In the village of Allahpind, for example, approximately a fourth of the population is Christian, and their situation differs little from what it otherwise would have been, as measured by the lot of their caste fellows in other villages who have not converted to Christianity.[21] If anything, the Christians in Allahpind suffer an even lower status and less material resources. They are a ragtag lot alleged by the other villagers to be addicted to thievery and wine. Aside from their names, which are either foreign or otherwise clearly Christian, there is little to indicate their separate identity. They do not attend church, and church officials in a town eight miles away seem unaware of their existence, even though church records indicate that at one point the Christians in Allahpind maintained an active affiliation with their neighbors. Moreover, none of the Allahpind Christians whom I visited were able to identify any of the tenets of Christianity; the only aspect of Christianity they knew was "Lord Jesu Masih," Jesus Christ, who sometimes replaces the local gods as the subject of the folk tunes they sing at night.

It is chiefly in the cities, then, that the legacy of the great missionary era in the Punjab is apparent. Yet the need for greater organization among the Christians in the villages and for greater attention to the social and economic uplift of the lower caste constituency of the church generally has impelled some young Christian activists into a revival of the idea of village-based networks of Christian political organizations in the Punjab. One such Christian party is the Bhartiya Masihi Dal, the Indian Christian party, which was hastily organized in time for the 1967 elections and has put forward candidates in several elections since then.[22] Its purpose, like that of similar Christian parties recently con-

21. Allaphind is one of six locales described earlier; it is in Gurdaspur district near the Pakistan border. The name has been changed.
22. Amar Nath Singh, April 26, 1971.

stituted in the Punjab (the Masihi Sangat, the Masihi Sevak Sangh, and the Christian League) is to publicize the problems and demands of the Christian community through political candidates and to exert pressure on the elections through political alignments. Its platform includes demands for land for landless Christians, reserved places for Christians in government jobs and government schools, protection from intimidation by the upper castes, and assurances that the government will no longer adopt the practice of taking over church lands that have been in the hands of the missionaries. In addition, there are general demands that Christians be given social welfare benefits similar to those that other lower caste people receive, and that the Christian community be free from governmental harassment inspired by antimissionary sentiment.

In the 1971 election, the Bhartiya Masihi Dal candidate for an assembly seat from Amritsar, one Samuel Mal, owner of a scrap-metal shop, received 874 votes out of a total 350,000 cast in his constituency. Mal was obviously no threat to his opponents. He felt, however, that his purposes had been served simply by running in the election, because considerable press coverage had been given to his party's demands regarding the needs of lower caste Christians.[23]

In Pakistan the Christians have not organized into political parties, but in some ways their political influence has been greater.[24] Before the partition of India most of the lower caste converts to Christianity were from the Chuhra caste, and the Chuhra were most populous in the Western part of the Punjab, that portion which is now in Pakistan. Therefore the Christian community in Pakistani Punjab was sizeable, encouraging most other lower caste persons

23. Interview with Samuel Mal, Amritsar, December 14, 1970.
24. My information on Punjab Christianity in Pakistan comes from a variety of interviews there in 1971, 1973, and 1979, including especially Dr. Masih Barkat, Principal of Foreman Christian College, Lahore, June 28, 1971, and Dr. M. A. Q. Daskawie, Director of the Christian Study Centre, Rawalpindi, July 2, 1971, and their colleagues. See also Alfred A. Asimi, "Christian Minority in West Punjab," Ph.D. dissertation, New York University, 1964; and Pieter Streefland, *The Sweepers of Slaughterhouse* (Assen, 1979).

who remained in Pakistan at partition to become Christian. In Pakistani Punjab the Christian community and the lower caste community have become virtually synonymous, which has enabled the church to speak quite directly on behalf of the lower castes. The government of Pakistan, in initiating programs for educational and social reform to benefit the lower castes, has been able to avoid the issue of caste—for it would be embarrassing for a Muslim nation to acknowledge the persistence of caste identities—by dealing with the matter as one relating to the treatment of a minority religious community, the Christians.

Thus in recent years, both in India and in Pakistan, the concerns of the Punjab Christian church have again been directed to matters that made the church strong there in the first place: the social needs of the lower castes. Christianity never fully substituted for movements like the Ad Dharm, the Valmiki Sabha, or those of Dr. Ambedkar in championing the Untouchable cause, but like them it did provide a new social vision and a new social identity for the lower caste people. All four answered a common need, but Christianity, unlike the other movements, was only by accident a religion of the lower castes. Even in the cheeriest piety of church fellowship there were tensions between the global perspective of the missionaries and the parochial concerns of village Christians, and in the end the illusion of Christendom as a new society remained mostly that, an illusion. Illusions, however, can be vital, and the cogency of Christian symbols, institutions, and visions added significantly to the momentum of change for lower castes in the Punjab.

18 The Uncertain Appeal of Marxism

Where can one turn when the illusions of religion wear thin? Many former Ad Dharmis, Ambedkarites, Christians, and followers of the sweeper caste movements shifted in a more radical and secular direction, toward Marxism. The attraction was strong. But although they were lured by the egalitarian ideals, few actually joined the Communist movements. It is an absence explained in part by the dominantly upper caste background of most Punjabi Communists, and in part by ideological differences: within the outlook of the leaders of the Punjabi Marxist organizations lie concepts of social order and social change that conflict with those held by Untouchables themselves, as articulated by Mangoo Ram, Ambedkar, and others. The Punjabi Marxists, with their materialist view of history, emphasize economic and political sources of oppression. Untouchable activism in the Punjab has regarded culture as the primary form of social oppression, and has utilized cultural symbols in its struggles for protest as well. It is a fundamental difference, and at no point did it become clearer than when many lower caste activists began flirting with Marxism, and the Marxists attempted to lure them in return.

Outwardly, the relationship between Untouchable activists and Marxists are congenial. According to L. R. Balley, the Communist parties in the Punjab are closest in ideology to his own Republican Party of India, and there has been some crossing back and forth of leaders and voters between his party and the Communists.[1] Members of Scheduled

1. Interview with Lahori Ram Balley, Jullundur, November 14, 1973.

Caste communities sit on both branches of the Communist party's executive boards, and a number of them have had experience in the Ad Dharm and Ambedkar movements.[2] There are also organizations within the Communist parties that appeal especially to the lower castes. But in spite of the outward appearance of lower caste involvement, and in spite of the natural community of interests, the general participation of lower caste activists in the Communist movements is small, not at all proportionate to the numbers of Untouchables in the general population.[3]

From the point of view of Marxist theory this is an anomaly, since the lower castes are the Punjab's most oppressed workers. They constitute virtually all of the agricultural laborer class, and many argue that the essential unity among Untouchables is indeed one of class rather than caste.[4] Regardless of the fact that the Chamars were traditionally leatherworkers and the Chuhras sweepers, their primary occupation in most of the rural areas of the Punjab is in fact the same: farm labor. Census reports indi-

---

2. Interview with Satwant Singh, chairman of the executive committee of the Communist Party of India (Marxist), Punjab branch, Jullundur, June 10, 1971; and interview with Gurbax Singh Diwan, general secretary of the Communist Party of India, Punjab branch, Chandigarh, June 4, 1971.

3. According to leaders of the Punjab branch of the CPI(M), 16 percent of their 4,000 members were from the lower castes, but this statistic appears to include many nominal members. Moreover, only one of the eighteen members of their central committee in the Punjab belonged to the lower castes. Party statistics indicate that the lower caste percentage of their membership is only slightly less than what it is in the general population, but the lower caste influence on the leadership of the movement is minimal. I was told, moreover, that the one lower caste person on the central committee was the leader of the special branch formed by the party specifically to attract members of the lower castes. His leadership, evidently, was limited to that; none of the regular party leadership directly reflected the interests of the lower castes.

4. The argument over whether the lower castes constitute a separate class in the Marxist sense continues to be debated. The major statement in favor of the class character of the lower castes is that of G. S. Ghurye, *Caste and Race in India* (Bombay, 1969). For a discussion of the issue in the Punjabi context, see Juergensmeyer, "Cultures of Deprivation: Three Case Studies in the Punjab," *Economic and Political Weekly*, February 1979.

cate that this has been the case at least since the middle of the nineteenth century, and there is some indication that in this century the Chuhra and Chamar castes have tended to become even more involved in agricultural labor.[5] A few families are tenant farmers or have some other rights of tenancy on the land they till, often as sharecroppers,[6] but most lower caste laborers are landless and seasonal, lacking not only tenancy rights but even the security of knowing that they will be employed throughout the year. And in both these respects things seem to be getting worse rather than better.[7] In the nineteenth century, because of British policies that encouraged large landholdings, the tenancy system gained wide frequency. But during this century, as land control has become more centralized under mechanized modern farming techniques and absentee landlordism has been discouraged, tenant cultivation has become increasingly less common.[8] Efficient decentralized landholdings do not need tenants—they rely on wage labor instead—and as the lower caste laborers who had formerly

5. For instance, a comparison of the 1921 and 1911 census statistics in the Punjab show a significant increase in the numbers of lower caste respondents listing their occupations in farm labor categories, and a significant decrease in those claiming their traditional caste occupations (*1911 Government of India Census*, Punjab, vol. 20, chap. 12, subsidiary table 8, p. 542; *1921 Government of India Census*, Punjab, vol. 20, chap. 11, sec. 4, p. 362).

6. For a description of lower caste economic conditions in North India earlier in this century, see Sir Malcolm Darling, *The Punjab Peasant in Prosperity and Debt* (London, 1925 [reprinted 1947]), p. 159; and G. W. Briggs, *The Chamars* (London, 1920), p. 57.

7. Evidence of this trend is indicated in early census returns where, for example, the numbers of "farm servants and field laborers" rose by 174.9 percent in the same ten-year period (1901–1911) that the income from the rental of agricultural land decreased by 9 percent (*1911 Government of India Census*, Punjab, vol. 20, chap. 12, subsidiary table 7). For recent evidence of the continuation of this trend, see citations in chapter 20, notes 18, 20, and 22.

8. Absentee landlordism was discouraged through the Punjab Alienation of Land Act, 1900, which prohibited nonagricultural castes from owning land. The intention was to keep the moneylenders from taking over huge amounts of mortgaged farmland. For a study of the act, and its various effects on Punjab society, see N. G. Barrier, *The Punjab Alienation of Land Bill, 1900* (Durham, N.C.: 1965).

been tenants became wage laborers, they took a step downward in status and security. It is true that in many cases the wages of daily labor are somewhat better than the income lower caste laborers may have had previously as tenants, but the conditions are far worse.

Considering all this, one might think that the lower castes were ripe for recruitment into Marxist organizations: they were conscious that they made up the laboring class, that they were exploited, and that their labor conditions were growing steadily worse. Some of the leaders of the Ad Dharm movement and the Ambedkar movements have seen these adverse conditions as contributing greatly to the success of their own efforts. Why did such conditions not strengthen the Communist movements, whose analyses focused on just such factors in an even more direct way?

Some of the leaders of the Marxist movements in the Punjab, in discussing this issue, have—with some ambivalence—blamed the Ad Dharm and Ambedkar movements for the lower castes' lack of interest in the Communist parties. Yet they felt that the lower caste movements did serve some useful functions. Satwant Singh, for instance, the chairman of the executive committee of the Communist party of India (Marxist) in the Punjab, observed that "the Ad Dharm movement gave [Untouchables] a sense of unity, and Ambedkar's Republican party helped to weaken the grip of the Congress party on the lower castes."[9] But others are disturbed by the fact that the lower castes, instead of participating more fully in the Marxist movements, have tended to seek out their own movements.

However, even after the Ad Dharm had disappeared from the scene and the growth of the Ambedkar movements slackened, Untouchables still failed to be attracted to Communist groups in substantial numbers. Some of the Communist leaders reason that lower caste people, being less well educated and less politically conscious than the average, find it difficult to understand a rather abstract political philosophy that is devoid of cultural and religious symbols.[10] But there remains the embarrassing fact that

9. Satwant Singh interview.
10. Gurbax Singh Diwan and others at the headquarters of the Communist Party of India, Punjab branch, Chandigarh, June 4, 1971.

most lower caste leaders who are educated and politically conscious have also found the Communist movements unappealing. The matter is complex and basic enough that one must examine the general relationship between Marxist movements and traditional social structure in order to explain the limited appeal of the Marxist cause, and this means viewing Punjab Marxism in situ, in the towns and villages of the region.

The town of Jandiala in Jullundur district is fairly typical of Marxist areas of the Punjab.[11] In this town of approximately 7,000, over half of the population are Jats of the Johl subcaste. The Johls in this area tend to be Marxist; in Jandiala they have adapted the two major parties of the national Communist movement—the Communist Party of India (CPI) and the Communist Party of India (Marxist)—to traditional alignments among themselves. Theirs is an old and quaint town set on a hill above a large village pond; the architecture shows the influence of the Mughal period. But flying from the flagpole in the central square is the hammer and sickle: the Communist parties have come to dominate the politics of the town.

What difference has this made to the Scheduled Castes? Local Communist leaders claim that they have been vigorous in their attempts to involve the lower caste people and have made special efforts to show equality. One of the party leaders made this point by explaining that he allowed a lower caste girl to work in the kitchen of his house, where she would ordinarily not be permitted to go because her ritual impurity would defile the food. But there were more meaningful efforts as well: in party matters, for example, lower caste Communists are regarded with a greater measure of respect. Perhaps the most prominent lower caste participants in the Marxist movements are the youngest, students at the local college. A large number of them wear Lenin buttons, and although they deny it, some are rumored to have been active in leadership in the Maoist

11. Jandiala was one of the six locales included in the case studies mentioned in chapter 1. Information on Jandiala comes from these studies, which were conducted over a ten months' period in 1970–1971. For a description of the systematic approach to these studies, see the appendixes to Juergensmeyer, "Political Hope."

Naxalite cadres of adjoining village areas. Through party contacts some of the young people from the Chuhra caste have set up a flour mill.

Nonetheless, the overwhelming majority of the lower caste people in Jandiala have shown very little interest in communism. In only one of the seven lower caste areas of the town are Communist party representatives regularly returned in the elections. The single Communist lower caste section of Jandiala is a Chuhra area (they call their caste Valmiki, incidentally, a Hindu term, even though they term their place of worship a *gurdwara* and most of them adopt the appearance of Sikhs). The Chamars, who in Jandiala are called Ad Dharm, have a sprinkling of CPI supporters in one of their areas and another Chamar neighborhood leans toward the CPI(M), but the rest support the Congress instead. Whereas over 50 percent of the upper castes in Jandiala vote for the Communist parties, no more than 20 percent of the lower castes follow suit.

One of the old Chamars gave a very simple explanation for this lack of support for the Marxists: "They are our class enemies." And indeed the Communist parties in Jandiala are dominated not by the proletariat but by the landowning and ruling castes. Some lower caste people see this in caste rather than class terms, regarding the Marxist parties as analogous to the Akali party, a political group that expresses the communal interests of Jat Sikhs. But in whatever terms they perceive the political base of Marxist influence, few see any natural association between the Marxist cause and their own. The Ad Dharm Chamars tend to claim that the Chuhra Valmikis vote for the CPI and the CPI(M) only because they are pressured into it, and indeed one lower caste member told me that he voted for the Communist party because he feared reprisals from the upper castes if he did not. Thus, in the town of Jandiala the revolutionary image of Marxism is severely stained with caste and sectarian interests.

South of Jandiala, near the border of Punjab and Haryana in an area where the Marxist parties also fare well, the situation is quite different. There, in village Bimla,[12]

12. "Bimla" was also one of the locales included in the case studies described in chapter 1. The name has been changed.

where the lower castes serve as badly mistreated servants and laborers for large landholding families which dominate the area, the lower castes have turned to Marxism on their own initiative. The parliamentary constituency adjoining theirs is one that has been reserved for Scheduled Caste candidates, and in recent years a lower caste candidate running on the ticket of the Community Party of India has been elected. He is regarded as something of a folk hero among Untouchables in the entire region, and the Communist parties are seen as potential liberators. Many of the lower caste laborers in village Bimla have taken part in protest movements and attempts at land seizure, but usually they have done so in villages other than their own, where they will not be identified by their upper caste employers. In fact, despite the outspokenly pro-Communist sentiments among the Untouchables of village Bimla, few votes have actually been cast for Communist candidates. The reason is simple: members of the Scheduled Castes fear reprisals if they do not vote for the same party (usually the Akali) that the upper caste people support. In one of the earlier elections, the voting registrar announced that Communist party candidates had earned a significant number of votes. Since it was a village of only four hundred voters, the Communist voters were quickly identified as being from the lower caste community. Those suspected of having voted Communist were beaten, and the whole lower caste community was punished by being denied access to the fields of the upper caste landlords for several weeks, an act tantamount to denying them access to their toilets. Thus any direct support for the Marxist parties on the part of the lower castes has to be covert: some of the militant lower caste youth are rumored to have joined the Naxalite guerrillas who have been involved in several violent attacks on landlords and police stations in the area.

The Naxalite movement of Maoist revolutionary Marxism is the only Communist movement in the Punjab to have attracted a significant amount of lower caste support. Punjab police officials who have investigated the movement confirm the observations of many lower caste political leaders, that militant lower caste youths are the mainstay of the Naxalite movement in one of its centers of activity in the Punjab, Bhatinda and Patiala districts.[13] In this region, as in village Bimla, there are large landholdings in which the lower castes receive the brunt of a generally depressed economic situation. In the remaining area of the Punjab where Naxalites have been active—the region comprising Jullundur, Hoshiarpur, and Gurdaspur districts—their members have been students and young teachers from upper castes, usually Jats, the rebellious sons of Punjab's heartland.[14] Among the Naxalites in the Punjab, contacts between these Jat students and the lower caste rural youth, who are the backbone of the movement elsewhere, have not always been harmonious: lower caste people complain about the Jats' tendency to take control, and the Jats regard the lower castes as insufficiently schooled in Marxist theory. One should remember, however, that the total number of Naxalites in the Punjab is not great, probably less than a few hundred, hence the total number of lower caste youth involved even in this expression of Marxism is very small. And the sort of sympathy for the Communist cause that one encounters in village Bimla is similarly atypical. Most lower caste Punjabis respond to the Communist parties as they do in Jandiala—with an indifference bordering on suspicion.

This is a matter of concern and embarrassment for many Communist party leaders, who need the support of the lower castes, not only to bolster their numbers but also to provide them with ideological justification in a society where landless laborers are probably the group subjected to the most severe economic oppression. The origins of this lower caste disinterest in communism, however, are understandable. From the very beginning the Communist strength in the Punjab has come from "middle class" small

13. Prakash Chand, deputy inspector-general, Punjab Police, Chandigarh, May 28, 1971.

14. My information on Naxalites in the Punjab comes from interviews with Prakash Chand and other police, and with lower caste and Marxist observers who wish not to be identified by name. For descriptions and analyses of the nationwide Naxalite movement in India, see Mohan Ram, *Maoism in India* (Delhi, 1971); and Manoranjan Mohanty, *Revolutionary Violence: A Study of the Maoist Movement in India* (New Delhi, 1977).

landowners and craftspersons, primarily in central Punjab. These have been Jats, by and large, who have been drawn to the Communist movements because of their stress on rural collectivization rather than because of the promises they held out to the economically disinherited. Once incorporated, they effectively became the Communist movement in the Punjab, stamping it with an identity radically different from anything that seemed sympathetic to the Untouchables.

This process was not a simple one. The Communist party in the Punjab has its origins in three separate historical currents, which only later coalesced into a single political body.[15] One of these was the radical, political side of modern Sikhism, especially the Akali and Singh Sabha movements and those that agitated for *gurdwara* reforms in the early decades of this century. A second base for the Communist party in the Punjab was the Naujawan Bharat Sabha, the group identified with the nationalist martyr Bhagat Singh. The third predecessor was the Kirti party, which was composed of former Gadarites. At least one Untouchable, Mangoo Ram, had once been a member of the Ghadar party, but its composition was overwhelmingly Jat, as was that of the other precursors to the Communist party in the Punjab.

In a loose way, these groups functioned collectively as the Communist party from the time of their founding, in the mid-1920s, but it was not until the mid-1930s that efforts were made to unite them formally. This was stimulated by a movement that took hold in rural areas early in the 1930s, agitating for the cancellation of debts. It had the effect of uniting the various Marxist groups temporarily, but important differences of personality and ideology persisted. Baba Gurmukh Singh and his Kirti party remained

15. My information on the history of the Punjab Communist parties comes from interviews with Satwant Singh and Pandit Kishori Lal, June 10, 1971; Gurbax Singh Diwan; and Sohan Singh Josh, one of the founders of the Punjab Communist party, September 14, 1973. See also Tilak Raj Chadha, "Punjab's Red and White Communists," *Thought*, June 14, 1952, and the documentary records of the party available at the headquarters of the CPI in Chandigarh and the CPI(M) in Jullundur.

to one side, vigorously nationalist and uncompromisingly revolutionary, while Baba Sohan Singh Josh welded the remainder into a fledgling Communist party, building on the fact that many of them had been together in prison in 1934 following the Meerut Conspiracy case. The newly formed Communists were less single-mindedly nationalist than the Kirti party, since they had misgivings about the nationalist leadership being provided by the Congress and preferred to follow the lead of the Soviet Union and the international Communist movement in matters of policy. And the Kirti party, for its part, was unwilling to relinquish control over its considerable treasury, allegedly amassed from the contributions of Punjabis living in the United States.[16]

These two factions of Marxists did not become effectively united until 1942, when they were all thrown together in prison as an act of detention by the British during World War II; at that point the Punjab Marxists joined forces with Indian Communists throughout the nation.[17] Even so, real differences of personal style and ideological position continued to divide the party, and when the unity of the Communist party throughout India was shattered in 1964, its Punjabi branch split into the divisions which had been there all along.[18] Interesting, however, is the fact that all factions of the Punjab Community party regard themselves in some sense as heirs to the old Gadar party. For instance, the CPI(M) has chosen to locate its state head-

16. Chadha, "Punjab's Red and White Communists."

17. For a general overview of the historical developments in the Communist Party of India, see Gene D. Overstreet and Marshall Windmiller, *Communism in India* (Berkeley and Los Angeles, 1959) and Muzaffar Ahmad, *Communist Party of India: Years of Formation* (Calcutta, 1959). On the split between the CPI and the CPI(M), see John B. Wood, "Observations on the Indian Communist Party Split" (*Pacific Affairs*, Spring 1965). For more recent analyses of the Communist parties, see Bhabani Sen Gupta, *Communism in Indian Politics* (New York, 1972), and Mohan Ram, *Indian Communism: Split Within a Split* (Delhi, 1969).

18. This was true in other parts of India, as well; the 1964 split should not be read as a simple difference of opinion between electoral and nonelectoral strategies, or Moscow and Peking. See Wood, "Observations on the Indian Communist Party Split."

quarters adjacent to the grounds of the Desh Bhagat Yadghar, a memorial and residence for old members of the Gadar party in Jullundur city. And on the wall inside the office, next to Lenin's portrait, hangs the portrait of Dr. Bhag Singh, who received his Ph.D. from the University of California, Berkeley, and was associated with the Gadar party there. As for the CPI, its veteran leader in the Punjab, Sohan Singh Josh, has undertaken a three-volume history of the Gadar party, which he considers to be his party's political predecessor.[19] And the Gadar party has also figured in the self-understanding of the newest branch of Communists, the revolutionary Communist Party of India (Marxist/Leninist). These activists claim that one of the first revolutionaries of their group to be killed by the police in the Punjab was an eighty-five-year-old former member of the Gadar party, Bhuja Singh.[20]

Despite the disagreements and schisms that divided the Punjabi Communist movement, then, the Gadar party provided a measure of common heritage. Even more important was the social bond that united almost all Communists in the Punjab: they were predominantly rural and overwhelmingly Jat. As such, they became attracted to Marxism primarily because of the scientific socialism they saw represented in the Soviet Union, with its emphasis on collective farming. For small landholders in central Punjab who were threatened by the power of the large landowners to the west and the financial demands of Hindu moneylenders in the city, the idea of collectivizing agriculture and nationalizing credit made a great deal of sense. The Communist vision was for them a vision of a modern, mechanized agriculture, cooperatively owned and controlled by the people who were currently farming the land: the Jats. They had had a tradition of cooperation and solidarity within their *biradari,* their caste brotherhood, so the Marxist notion of solidarity among the rural peasantry struck a familiar and responsive chord. Thus from the earliest days

19. Sohan Singh Josh, *Hindustan Gadar Party, A Short History* (New Delhi, 1977).
20. I have heard this account from several different sources, each of whom did not wish to be named in print.

the Kisan Sabha (the farmers' union) of Jats was the backbone of the Communist organization in the Punjab.

The question of mobilizing the landless labor (predominantly Untouchable) did not even arise until after 1947.[21] At that time, when the Punjab was partitioned between Pakistan and an independent India, there was a great scramble for the land that had been left behind in Eastern Punjab by the Muslims who went to Pakistan. Some of the Untouchables felt that this was their opportunity to acquire land for themselves, and since the alternative would have been to give the land to Hindus from West Punjab, the Communists backed the demands of the Untouchables. Moreover, after independence the Communists had more to gain politically from the Untouchables than they had had before: Untouchables were allocated a larger number of reserved seats in the legislature by the new government. Urged on by these factors, the Communists began taking seriously the notion that Untouchables, as the laboring class in the rural areas, should be the bulwark of Marxist movements, whereas in earlier years the Jat Sikhs, who were the mainstay of the Communist movements, evidently regarded *themselves* as analogous to the European peasantry. On this understanding there had been no room for Untouchables in an ideology that pitted them, the peasantry, against the large Hindu and Muslim landlords. Only recently have these "peasants" realized that there was indeed another class even more oppressed than they, for whom Marxist ideology should have had its appeal. Like the Blacks in the United States, the Untouchables had been invisible elements of society, even to those who were most sensitive to issues of social oppression and conflict. The realization that the Untouchables had been inadvertently left out of the Marxist movements in the Punjab was a matter of embarrassment and considerable political reflection among the leaders of the Communist parties.

The Khait Mazdur Sabha (Agricultural Laborers' Union) was established to correct that error. It has gained its greatest strength in two areas: the Ad Dharm's old strong-

---

21. Satwant Singh and Diwan interviews.

hold, Jullundur district and environs, where the Scheduled Castes were more sophisticated politically and more inclined to join Marxist movements on ideological grounds; and the semidesert areas of the Punjab (especially Sangrur, Bhatinda, and Ferozepur districts), where a tradition of tenant farming was being eroded by new methods of agriculture, and lower castes felt that they were becoming rapidly more oppressed than before.[22]

After the split between the two branches of the Communist party, the Khait Mazdur Sabha split as well, with both branches claiming from thirty to forty thousand adherents. But membership has been sporadic. Only a fraction of the members of either Khait Mazdur Sabha actually belong to a Communist party; most of those who are counted as members of the organization have simply participated in its mass rallies and agitations at one time or another. Especially popular have been the attempts at land seizure, campaigns in which large numbers of landless laborers have occupied unused land owned by large landlords. There have been several waves of sit-ins to claim such land; one of the largest was in 1970, when thousands of protestors were jailed in the Punjab. Virtually all of the members of the Khait Mazdur *sabhas* are from lower castes. The general secretaries of the two *sabhas* sit on the executive councils of their parent bodies, the Communist Party of India and the Communist Party of India (Marxist); they are the only Untouchables to do so.

In recent years both branches of the Communist party in the Punjab have recognized that the recruitment of Untouchables into the party should be one of their major priorities. To accomplish this, they have initiated appeals for the redistribution of land in small plots to landless labor. This runs athwart their past emphasis on the collectivization of land, but represents the leadership's recognition that Untouchables will never support that program until they first have land of their own. Without it Untouchables feel disenfranchised. The other issue on which the Communists have begun supporting the lower castes is the

22. Master Hari Singh, head of Department of Agricultural Workers, Communist party of India, Punjab branch, Chandigarh, June 4, 1971.

demand for a minimum wage for agricultural workers throughout the year, for except in harvest seasons there is a surplus of laborers and therefore a miserably low wage-scale.

The party is also making new efforts to recruit lower caste members directly. In the past when Communist workers came out to recruit in the villages, they would stay with their comrades and supporters in the upper caste areas of the village. Needless to say, this created an adverse image among the lower castes. Now the practice is to send out lower caste recruiters when possible; and if upper caste recruiters are despatched, they are urged to stay in the lower caste areas of the village. In addition, an attempt has been made to change the political awareness of the rank and file of the Communist party so that it takes into account lower caste concerns. According to one of the Marxist leaders, "We cannot simply fight on *behalf* of the Untouchables. That would be paternalism similar to that of Gandhi and the Congress. Instead, we have to show that we and they are united in a common cause."[23]

Perhaps the greatest problem in gaining lower caste support for the Communist parties has been the image set by the patterns of the past. In many villages in central Punjab, the prejudice against Untouchables has been fueled by economic as well as social motives. There has been the feeling among the middle caste Jat peasantry that the lower castes were in collusion with the Hindu *bania* moneylenders, since moneylenders would often circumvent legal restrictions against their owning and controlling land by using the lower castes as fronts. On occasion the lower castes have indeed looked to the *bania* merchants and moneylenders when they needed support in conflicts with landholders, many of whom were Jats, and for that reason they have tended to ally themselves with the political parties of the *banias*—the Congress and the Jan Sangh—rather than those of the Jat Sikh landholders—the Communist parties and the Akali Dal. Satwant Singh, general secretary of the Punjab branch of the Communist Party of India (Marxist) used to maintain that the Communists

---

23. Diwan interview.

would gain support from the lower castes only after the breakup of the Congress party,[24] but when that happened in the 1977 elections, there was no noticeable realignment in favor of the Communists.

However well the Marxist movements may have served as examples of revolutionary strategy and ideology, they ultimately seem something alien to the lower castes. It is not simply that they are dominated by Jats or that their interest in agricultural collectivization is not directly relevant to the lower castes: there is also something alien in the Marxist social vision. Marxist social analysis, based on a European concept of society, is not easily able to incorporate the issue of caste as the crucial index of oppression in the villages. According to Gurbax Singh Diwan, general secretary of the Punjab branch of the Communist Party of India, "the lower castes are more easily mobilized around social issues than economic ones."[25] "Social issues" mean caste, and since in India the concept of caste is based on religious ideas, most members of the lower castes sense that only a reconception of religion will make a new social order possible. One way of reconceiving the role of religion is to envision a totally secularized society; another is to create a new religious movement. Revolutionary Untouchables have usually found the latter a more compelling option than the former. One is left, then, with an odd situation: Marxism among lower caste Punjabis has been hampered not so much by religion as by the Marxists' inability to see in religion a potentially radical vehicle of social change.

24. Satwant Singh interview.   25. Diwan interview.

19 Radhasoami and the Return of Religion

Secular and religious versions of social protest have continued to compete with one another as the activist members of Untouchable castes have chosen one form, then the other, throughout this century. But old secular dreams, and old religious visions, have become replaced in time with newer ones. In the 1940s many members of lower castes began another return to religion, although not a religious movement of their own making, nor a traditional one of upper castes, for that matter. The lure came from the new guru movements, especially one called Radhasoami.

In Jullundur, one finds a Radhasoami fellowship hall *(satsang ghar)* established directly across the road from the old Mission Compound church, as if taunting it. Since the 1940s the Radhasoami crowds have grown remarkably. They are now larger than at the Mission church and, with their loudspeakers, noisier. The Satsang Ghar is a new building, and the dramatic expansion of the Radhasoami movement, established in the Punjab in the early years of this century, is also very recent. Radhasoami has attracted a wide following among members of the lower castes, including some who had been involved in the Arya Samaj, Ad Dharm, Ambedkar, and Valmiki Sabha movements, and a few Christians as well. There is a certain poignancy in the adjacent locations of the Jullundur quarters for Radhasoami and the church, for in the early decades of the century it had been Christianity that was lively and expanding, Christianity that made remarkable strides in the conversion of lower castes. Now, in both regards, the mantle has been passed to Radhasoami. Like Christianity and the other mass movements, Radhasoami and the newly revived intercaste guru movements akin to it provide, along with spiritual nourishment, new expressions of social change and cultural identity.

In some ways, however, the Radhasoami movement is not new at all. Its lineage of gurus, now fragmented into several branches in Uttar Pradesh, the Punjab, and elsewhere in India, began in 1861 in Agra with the teachings of Shiv Dayal Singh, who came from an urban, middle-caste Punjabi family which had settled there.[1] Parts of Dayal's teachings were more or less original, in particular his emphasis on the primacy of an eternal sound current, to which the guru and various meditation practices provided access for devotees, and his arrangement of a hierarchy of realms of consciousness into which followers could expect to ascend. Other aspects of the master's teachings, however, and much of the poetry, symbolism, and language of the faith, were taken over from the Sant tradition of medieval Hinduism. The Radhasoami movement claims a kinship to Nanak, the first guru of the Sikhs, and also to Sant Ravi Das, the sixteenth-century saint who figured so prominently in the mythology of the Ad Dharm movement.[2]

1. My information on the founder, the origins, and the history of the Radhasoami movement comes primarily from original documents of the movement, including Swami Dayal Singh, *Sar Bachan; Souvenir in Commemoration of the First Centenary of the Radhasoami Satsang (1861–1961);* Anand Swarup, *Diary of Sahabji Maharaj;* and Sawan Singh, *Spiritual Gems;* and from interviews with leaders of the movement at the Dayalbagh and Soamibagh centers near Agra, and at the Beas center in the Punjab, and the official reports from those centers. See also Mark Juergensmeyer, "Radhasoami as a Trans-National Religion," in Jacob Needleman and George Baker, eds., *Understanding the New Religions* (New York, 1979); A. P. Mathur, *The Radhasoami Faith: A Historical Study* (Delhi, 1974); and accounts of the Radhasoami movement in J. N. Farquhar, *Modern Religious Movements in India* (New York, 1924); and Philip Ashby, *Modern Trends in Hinduism* (New York, 1969).

2. Writings of the Radhasoami movement frequently refer to the broader tradition in which they stand as "Sant Mat," the tradition of devotion to a formless god that is principally identified with great medieval Hindu figures such as Kabir, Dadu, Nanak, and others. See Juergensmeyer, "The Radhasoami Revival of the Sant Tradition," in Karine Schomer and W. H. McLeod, eds., *The Sant Tradition of India* (Berkeley, 1981).

Radhasoami, however, claimed that the Sant tradition had not ended in the medieval period, but was very much alive in gurus of the present day. The particular master to whom one gave credence depended on which lineage one followed. The oldest lineage is the one based in Agra, but another has gained the largest following, the one established in the *dera* (spiritual center) near the village of Beas, along the banks of the river of that name, midway between the cities of Jullundur and Amritsar. It was the Beas branch of Radhasoami which made such a successful appeal for devotees from the lower castes.

Radhasoami is not the only guru movement in the Punjab, of course, and not the only one to have attracted lower caste followers.[3] In the Punjab it is common for holy men to establish themselves as gurus, give mantras, perform initiations, and solicit followers from a variety of castes. In rural areas these local gurus are everywhere. They set aside the formality and social strictness of the more traditional forms of Hinduism, Sikhism, and Islam, and unlike the holy men one finds at the lower caste *deras* of Ravi Das, they lay little stress on any links they might have with the high tradition. At most of these local *deras* one finds persons of mixed religious affiliation, of mixed economic status, and of mixed social origin. But some gurus have had an especially wide appeal among the lower castes, including Guru Sat Nam, leader of the Sachasauda movement in Sirsa, Klaranwala Sant of Ludhiana, Sant Nahar Singh of Malout, and the leaders of Kotakapura movement of Ferozepur.[4]

The associations they inspire are free-lance religious movements in the sense that they have influence only in restricted local areas and their eclectic teachings tend to change in conformity with the whims of whatever guru happens to be in charge. But they also carry on the medieval Sant tradition in that they preach a form of salva-

   3. A list and summary description of all religious movements with a significantly large lower caste involvement in the Punjab, drawn from ethnographies, census reports, and my own interviews, is included as an appendix to "Political Hope," pp. 586–596.
   4. These are all new movements, the largest of which is the Sachasauda movement, based in Ferozepur district, Punjab; its origins are in Radhasoami, and the others also have been influenced by it.

tion that depends upon the raising of spiritual consciousness rather than the performing of social obligations and religious rituals dictated by custom and duty. Furthermore, like the Sants, they deny the efficacy of anthropomorphic representations of the divine and are relatively unconcerned about caste restrictions, which gives them an air of concern about social reform.[5] In many ways Radhasoami, like Nirankari, another large guru movement that substantially resembles it, is simply one of these local guru movements writ large,[6] but there are considerable differences as well.

Size itself is important. According to the statistics of the movement itself, there are over a half million Radhasoami adherents in the Punjab alone,[7] and the ubiquitous visibility of the movement increases the impression of size and vitality that it projects. Since mid-century the number of local *satsang ghars* has steadily expanded until today any town of the most modest population is likely to have one.[8] But there are other factors than size and the systematic or-

5. There is some controversy as to whether the spiritual equality preached by the Sant tradition implied social equality as well. In modern India, however, the Sants are familiarly regarded as precursors to Gandhi and other recent advocates of social reform. See, for example, V. Raghavan, *The Great Integrators: The Saint-Singers of India* (New Delhi: 1966).

6. The main similarities between Nirankari and Radhasoami are that both trace the origins of their ideas to the Sant tradition, both have living masters, and both have evolved within the last century into large, aggressively expanding organizations. The Nirankari movement (named after the quality of formlessness which its members regard as inherent in the divine nature) is found in two branches, both based in the Punjab. One of them, the Sant Nirankaris, is more closely related to Sikhism, whereas the other, the Gurbachan Singh Nirankaris, has recently been at odds with the Sikhs. The riots that resulted provoked in 1977 an official proclamation from the headquarters of the Sikhs *(hukum-nama)* banning the Gurbachan Singh group of Nirankaris. Gurbachan Singh himself was assassinated in 1980. For an excellent history and analysis of the other branch of Nirankaris, see John Webster, *The Nirankari Sikhs* (Bombay: Macmillan, 1979).

7. The total number of persons initiated into Radhasoami, according to the movement's own records through 1977, is 531,559 (sources: Annual Reports of the Radhasoami Satsang, Beas), a figure that is matched, they claim, by a similar number of those seeking admission.

8. The Annual Reports of the Radhasoami Satsang, Beas, list 260 local chapters in Punjab and elsewhere in India.

ganization of the movement's teachings that distinguish it from its less prosperous cousins. One of these is economic. Both the Agra and Beas branches of Radhasoami have large landholdings in which self-contained colonies have been established. These differ from one another in tone and intent, but the scale of the enterprise in both cases is notable. The Agra branch has been more self-contained, emphasizing the growth of industries, educational institutions, and modern farms in Agra itself, all done in a collective manner.[9] The Beas branch has devoted greater attention toward projecting itself outward, making the idealistic city it founded in Beas the hub of an organizational network of international proportions.[10] In both cases, however, there is a modernity and a cosmopolitan quality about Radhasoami which sets it apart as something unusual. An emphasis on science and on progressive social and moral values figures prominently in Radhasoami teachings of all stripes,[11] and the efficient, fair-minded conduct of its organization has given many the impression that it is indeed the harbinger of a new and attractive social order. This has given Radhasoami much the same image and appeal that Christianity and the Arya Samaj possessed earlier, especially among villagers and more particularly rural members of the lower castes, whose only access to the modern world is through the social constructs of modern religious societies.

In almost all of the villages and town neighborhoods that I visited to gauge the effect of the Ad Dharm and other

9. At the height of Dayalbagh's industrial development in the 1930s, the community had dozens of factories producing a variety of goods from handkerchiefs to hunting knives, microscopes to toilet soaps. Some of the impetus behind this expansion was provided by Gursarandas Mehta, the Spiritual Master of Dayalbagh from 1937 to 1975, who had been an engineer before heading the movement. After India's independence, government restrictions and a change of leadership in Dayalbagh resulted in a decrease in economic activities and a stabilization of the community.

10. There are over sixty overseas branches of the Beas Radhasoami movement, largely in South Africa, England, and America. The numbers of foreign members have expanded exponentially in recent decades, averaging over a thousand new initiates yearly since 1970 (Annual Reports of the Radhasoami Satsang, Beas, 1966–1977).

11. The concept of science as a metaphor for spiritual exercises was developed within Radhasoami most fully by a recent master of the Beas branch, Jagat Singh. See his *Science of the Soul* (Beas, 1959).

lower caste movements, Radhasoami has come to be a significant presence.[12] In only one place did I find an Untouchable community that had no Radhasoami followers, and that was understandable because the village is located near the Rajasthan and Haryana borders, far from the center of both the Punjab and Radhasoami. Elsewhere the movement is strong. In village Nallah, for example, where I had talked with old Kishan Lal, an early follower of the Ad Dharm movement, I discovered that his own son-in-law and a nephew had become ardent Radhasoami devotees. Kishal Lal's son-in-law told me that he first found out about Radhasoami when a carpenter with whom he worked in a small factory in a town ten miles away told him about the ideas of the faith and the great center of the movement at Beas. What impressed him even more, however, was that soon after their first conversation the carpenter made a special trip to his house to describe the tenets of the faith further. It had been the first time that someone from outside the Untouchable castes, even someone of such middling status as a carpenter, had ever visited his family's home and eaten food prepared in their kitchen. It was, then, not just the new ideas of the movement or its living guru or modern organization, but its real egalitarianism that impressed Kishan Lal's son-in-law. And when he visited the Radhasoami *dera* at Beas, he was so moved with the power he perceived in the physical presence of the master, Charan Singh, and with the enormity and enthusiasms of the crowds, that he requested and received initiation soon thereafter. From that time on, he has displayed pictures of the Radhasoami guru proudly on his walls, brought his wife and cousin into the movement with him, and attended *satsang* services regularly in the town where he works. At *satsang* he has the opportunity of associating socially with shopkeepers, people he meets in the market, and his fellow workers. Thus Radhasoami has for him some of the same lure that the Ad Dharm had had for his father years before—a broader perspective from which to see his

12. For a description of these village studies, see the accounts earlier in this book and in "Political Hope," chap. 2. The appeal of Radhasoami to lower caste people has also been noted by Satish Saberwal, "Harijans and Inequality: Politics in Urban Punjab," unpublished paper, p. 6.

world and a new network of associations to go with it. There is, of course, a difference: Radhasoami is not a lower caste movement per se. But its vision of a utopian community, already in the process of being realized, substitutes handily for an assault on caste institutions through overtly political means.

In Allahpind, where most of the Chuhra caste are Christians, there is also a large Radhasoami following. Only one of the Christians has joined the movement, but several families of Ramdasia Chamars have done so, as has virtually the whole of another Untouchable caste, the Mahasha. Allahpind lies only twenty miles from Beas, so the attraction of Radhasoami is not surprising. It is noteworthy, however, that only members of lower castes have been initiated, and of them the large majority are Mahasha. This is all the more significant in light of the fact that the Mahasha caste received its name from an earlier wave of conversion in its home area of Sialkot,[13] one that also had an intercaste element. The Mahashas had been won over to the Arya Samaj. Some claimed that they had been Meghs prior to that, an Untouchable caste of slightly higher status than the Chamars; others reported, however, that they had been Doms before they were converted, and therefore were closer in status to the Chuhra. Whichever is true, the Mahashas became involved after conversion in occupations that were less degrading than most of those practiced by the lower castes: they took up weaving and blacksmithery, and some of them became carpenters. But after the great era of the Arya Samaj passed, most of them forgot the teachings of the movement and the values of the association, and today the younger generation does not even know its name. When Radhasoami appeared on the scene, then, there was once again a place for something that would fulfill the religious and social needs that the Arya Samaj had formerly satisfied.

The Mahasha Radhasoamis became quite devoted to the faith, the more ambitious of them traveling to the Beas *dera*

---

13. The term Mahasha ("Great Hope") was meant to signify a rebirth from Untouchable to Arya Samaj caste status.

for *satsang* once a month, and others attending weekly *satsang* in a town fifteen miles away. A middle-aged Mahasha widow known only as Asha, for instance, is one of the most loyal devotees in Allahpind. Asha not only attends the monthly *satsangs* at the *dera* herself, but takes along her children as well and arranges for someone to help carry an infirm aunt, so that all might receive the nourishing blessings of the *darsan* ("sight") of the guru. For Asha, Radhasoami is faith and magic and healing, as well as an emblem of her caste identity. Other Mahashas participate in the movement in hopes of obtaining other sorts of benefits. Some find the weekly *satsang* in the town nearby useful for making business contacts, and a few claim that their associations with upper caste Radhasoami *satsangis* are of advantage in securing support for their children's education. So, in tangible benefits as well as symbolic ones, the Radhasoami *satsang* has replaced the Arya Samaj as the Mahasha's means of upward social mobility. Unlike the Arya Samaj, however, Radhasoami seems to fit the spiritual temper of the Mahashas, satisfying their taste for gurus and divine healings.

In both Nallah and Allahpind villages the only Radhasoami devotees are members of the lower castes, but the town of Jandiala presents a more mixed picture. There the Radhasoami *satsang* gathers approximately 300 members from a population of 7,000, about half coming from the relatively less poor Ad Dharm (or, as it is sometimes called, Ramdasia) sector of the Chamar caste—people who work in offices and shops as menial employees. The other half of the Radhasoamis are drawn from artisan and shopkeeper castes. There are also a few Brahmans (a caste without much prestige in the Punjab) and several members of the dominant Jat caste, belonging to the Johl subcaste. As one upper caste political leader put it, however, "they are rather peculiar Jats."[14]

Every week the Radhasoami group meets underneath a tree near a shop owned by one of its members, propping up a picture of the guru and listening to his discourses on a

14. Interview with S. S. Sekhon, principal of Khalsa College, Jandiala, March 29, 1971.

portable tape-recorder. One of the leaders of the *satsang* services is a young Ramdasia, Jai Singh, a lean and bright-eyed fellow who wears a beard and a turban and works as a postman, a job he received through the government's policy of reserving positions for Scheduled Castes. Jai Singh is more ambitious than his position indicates, however, and attends night classes in the local college, in the hope of eventually receiving a certificate that will allow him to become a schoolteacher. He reports that the main appeal of Radhasoami for him is not the aura of the guru, but the scientific notions of meditation and levels of spiritual consciousness, whose intricacies he is fond of expounding. It is obvious, in addition, that he warms to his role as a leader of the local *satsang* fellowship. In his home, a one-room brick and mud affair which he shares with his wife, two children, an elderly mother, and occasionally the family buffalo, Jai Singh has posted various pictures to represent his several affiliations. Prominently displayed are a photograph of Charan Singh, the guru of the Beas branch of Radhasoami, and pictures of Ravi Das and Karl Marx. Jai Singh describes the importance of these three by explaining that it was Charan Singh who gave him spiritual fulfillment, Ravi Das who gave him a sense of social pride, and Karl Marx who held out the possibility of political change.

A large number of lower caste Radhasoami followers can also be found in the cities, but the social composition of the group differs considerably from what one finds in the villages. In villages Radhasoami is almost entirely a lower caste phenomenon, whereas in urban areas it appeals to a more mixed group—members of the emerging middle class and particularly those who live in newer sectors of the city, where traditional ideas have a weaker hold. For these people, uprooted from the places and groups that had formerly been their home, Radhasoami provides a sense of fellowship and a community that counteracts the social isolation of an urban environment—a social role not unlike that played by religious sects, secret societies, and fraternal orders in other parts of the world, including the urban West.

In suburban areas of Jullundur, for example, Radhasoami has a sizeable following that increases as years go by.

These suburban Radhasoami communities include upwardly mobile Scheduled Caste residents of the area who are employed in government agencies and large business concerns, and who blend into the Radhasoami fellowship as equals. Even in Boota Mandi, the old stronghold of Ad Dharm support and Ravi Das identity, some of the younger members of the richest families have become members of the Radhasoami faith. In fact, the first person in Boota Mundi to become an initiate of the Beas guru was none other than Chanda Ram Mehay, the younger brother of Sundar Das, who was a founder of Boota Mandi and a leader of the Ad Dharm. Chanda Ram Mehay succeeded subsequently in bringing the rest of his family into Radhasoami, and because of their devotion there are greater and greater evidences of the faith in Boota Mandi: more and more one sees pictures of the guru, and some shops close on Radhasoami festival days. In addition, large numbers of Boota Mandi residents, even those not initiated into Radhasoami, take part in special occasions at the *dera* in Beas. Thus, even in the successful lower caste culture of Boota Mandi, Radhasoami's egalitarian religious society offers a compelling alternative to more traditional affiliations.

There is indeed a conscious attempt to promote a sense of egalitarian unity in the Radhasoami fellowship, a unity evident especially at the times of the great festivals, the *bandharas,* which are held at the Radhasoami *dera* at Beas, usually on the birth or death anniversaries of the Radhasoami gurus.[15] On such occasions as many as 150,000 persons converge for a two- or three-day series of *satsang* services.[16] The sheer number of participants is an awesome sight, and one wonders at the ability of the Radhasoami organization to provide comfortably for the food and shelter of so many people, settling them in huge sleeping-halls

---

15. Information on life in the Beas *dera* comes from my studies of it in December 1970, January–May 1971, November 1973, and July 1978.

16. Estimates by S. L. Sondhi, general secretary of the Radhasoami Satsang Beas, in July 1978, confirmed by my own estimates, which are based on the numbers of meals served (approximately 8,000 each in two dozen twenty-minute shifts) and include a factor for others not eating in the halls provided.

and feeding them with mountainous portions of *chapattis* (thin wheat bread), vegetables, and lentil soup in dining halls big enough to serve thousands in a single shift. Members of the lower castes are easily absorbed in the crowd and become very much a part of it. Yet there are distinctions, and some areas of discrimination.

In the earlier years of the Radhasoami *dera* a separate dining hall was maintained for the lower castes. The present guru abolished that, but followers who do not wish to avail themselves of the free dining provisions and are able to pay a modest rupee or two are still able to take their meals in a separate hall. This dining hall does not cater directly to caste scruples, but it does have the effect of making some distinction between the poorer and richer members of the movement—the lower castes being, of course, among the former. Even more dramatic distinctions are evident in the arrangements made for lodging—one can sleep on simple canvas stretched on the ground or in handsome hotels and cottages. The wealthier followers, such as the Mehay family from Boota Mandi, have no worry about the problem of housing, since they have purchased their own house (or rather, made a long-term lease: there is no private property at the *dera*). But the cost of an average dwelling at the *dera* begins at Rs. 8,800 (except for a few of the old places, which can be leased for Rs. 3,500), and this is well beyond the means of the average villager, much less most of the members of the lower castes.[17] Hence, most of the lower caste people who reside permanently at the *dera* are not house owners but servants: from the standpoint of wealth and privilege, the Radhasoami *dera* is not an egalitarian place at all. Moreover, members of the lower castes are not represented in positions of leadership in the movement in a ratio at all proportionate to their membership in the movement as a whole. The present guru estimates that half the adherents of Radhasoami in the Punjab come from the lower castes, and the percentage may actually be much higher,[18] yet only one lower caste person has ever served on the seventeen-member executive Trust Committee. That

17. Interview with K. L. Khanna, general secretary of Radhasoami Satsang, Beas, February 26, 1972.
18. Interview with Charan Singh, Spiritual Master of Radhasoami Satsang, Beas, April 2, 1971.

was Sadhu Ram, a Congress party member of parliament who had also been a member of the Ad Dharm and Ambedkar movements, and after his death there has been no lower caste representation on the Trust Committee at all.[19]

Nonetheless, lower caste participation in Radhasoami has been increasing, and has been cheerfully welcomed by the present master.[20] Cynical outside observers have suggested, however, that the present guru may be trying to expand his numbers with easy conquests, and provide a free labor force for the *dera*'s ambitious building program. According to the Ambedkarite, L. R. Balley: "The Radhasoami Colony is a rest house for the rich, with Scheduled Castes to do the work."[21]

Whatever the master's motives may be, the Scheduled Castes have had their own reasons for wanting to join Radhasoami. I asked a sampling of the lower caste members of Radhasoami about their religious and social views,[22] and I found that their perceptions of the problem of Untouchability were distinctly different from those of their counterparts outside of the movement. The majority of them blamed caste prejudice on Hindu religious concepts; the non-Radhasoami lower caste respondents felt that the problems of the lower castes followed from their poverty and lowly occupations. Radhasoami, then, had provided a religious solution for persons who felt that their problems had indeed been religious. It separated them from Hinduism and put them in a society ostensibly without caste, giving them new friends and a somewhat altered social status. At the same time it afforded them a new dignity, at least by inference, placing them in closer contact with the higher economic and social status of other members. And it was the religious nature of Radhasoami that had made this alteration possible.

For a movement to be religious, in India, does not mean that it lacks social significance. Quite the opposite: because Radhasoami is a religious movement it is capable of chang-

19. The present Spiritual Master at Beas says he is currently looking for a suitable replacement for Sadhu Ram (Charan Singh, July 10, 1978).
20. Charan Singh, April 2, 1971.
21. Interview with L. R. Balley, Jullundur, November 14, 1973.
22. The questions included in the survey and the tabulation of the answers are given in an appendix to "Political Hope," pp. 581–582.

ing the assumptions upon which old social structures are based. Like Christianity, the Valmiki Sabha, the Arya Samaj and the Ad Dharm, it has been able to make the kind of appeal that the Marxists cannot, an appeal that radically shifts the religious bases of social values and thereby reconceives society as well. Radhasoami took off from where the four earlier movements left off, resuscitating a religious vision of an alternative society. The Marxist approach—to remove the grip of religion on social values by discouraging religious belief altogether and thereby make those values susceptible to change—continues to have a certain fascination, in part because it seems to avoid the dilemma of shifting from one illusory construction to another; and the Marxists have not been the only ones to approach social change in these terms. Indeed, much of the momentum of post-independence India has been precisely in the direction of creating what in the West is called "the secular society," in which not only would government be free from the political control of religious organizations, but social values would be liberated from religious assumptions as well. This secular vision has had a certain influence in independent India, especially upon the lower castes, who have the most to gain from the demise of traditional religious values. But the fact that movements such as Radhasoami have continued to exist in post-independence India and indeed have expanded is clear indication that the secular outlook is not altogether convincing. To a degree, India's independence has meant the rejection of religion, but it has also shaken the foundations in such a way as to require the rediscovery of basic beliefs about society, and with them the security of new religious associations.

PART V Revival Post-Independence

20 The Ex-Untouchables of Post-Independence Punjab

On August 15, 1947, India received her independence, and on January 26, 1950, freedom of a sort came to the Untouchables. On that date the Constitution of India was officially ratified, and with it Article 17, which "abolished Untouchability in all of its forms."[1] The chairman of the drafting committee of the constitution was none other than Dr. Bheem Rao Ambedkar, India's most accomplished leader from the Untouchable castes, and the document he shaped transformed Untouchables into ex-Untouchables. By law they were touchable and free. Changes in social attitudes, customs, and opportunities, however, are not accomplished by fiat, and in many respects India still awaits the social revolution which the wording of the Article would imply. Still, Article 17 did mean something. It laid the legal basis for civil action against obvious forms of discrimination—access to temples, for example—and it gave a constitutional impetus to government reforms, such as the provisions for reserved places for lower castes in housing, education, and government jobs.[2] Article 17 also did something else: it made explicit a point of view that had touched India's independence movement in several ways—the conviction that a modern, progressive society is an egalitarian one as well, and one committed to secular social values.

1. Article 17, in Part III, "Fundamental Rights" of the *Constitution of India*. The entire article is only two sentences long, and avoids defining untouchability or suggesting how its abolition might be enforced.
2. See Marc Galanter, *Competing Equalities: The Indian Experience with Compensatory Discrimination* (Berkeley and Los Angeles, 1982).

In consequence, independence has brought a new era into the lives of the castes that had been called Untouchable. The government sided with them in two important ways: pledging to protect and promote their basic human rights, and, more profound, committing itself to a vision of a secular society that would thwart the Hindu social values on which the concepts of caste and untouchability were based.[3] The latter especially was the dream of the first prime minister, Jawaharlal Nehru, but it has been echoed a number of times in the words of his daughter, Indira Gandhi. This secular vision, however, has not been the only image of modern India, and independence was not the only major event of 1947. Something else happened that year: a religious state was created in the subcontinent, Pakistan, and that has had immense repercussions in Indian religious politics and helped to spark new affirmations of an Indian society dedicated to religious ideals.

In the Punjab the creation of Pakistan was the more shattering event of 1947. The dividing line between India and West Pakistan slashed directly through the Punjab, along the river Ravi, severing abruptly what had been, despite major divisions of religion and caste, a reasonably homogeneous culture, society, and economy. The division caused massive social dislocations as Muslims living in East Punjab moved to the West, and Hindus and Sikhs who had made their homes in the West traveled east. There was a certain logic to the division, for the bulk of the Punjab's Muslims had lived in the western regions, and the eastern areas tended to be Hindu and Sikh. But many families had to move, suddenly, violently. An estimated four million people were uprooted, and in the anger and confusion of the shift, old animosities flared and religious riots ensued.[4] Thousands were killed.[5] Memories of those bitter years lingered on in

---

3. See Donald Smith, *India as a Secular State* (Princeton, 1963).
4. The most authoritative work on partition is Penderel Moon's *Divide and Quit* (London: 1961). For a fictional account of its effect in the Punjab, see Khushwant Singh's *Train to Pakistan* (New York: Grove Press, 1956).
5. Some estimates of the number killed run into the hundreds of thousands. A more conservative estimate is that of Penderel Moon (*Di-*

tensions between religious communities which have sullied the relations between India and Pakistan since and aggravated the religious communalism within India as well. Thus the Punjab emerged from 1947 with two contradictory experiences: the secularism brought by India's independence, and the religious communalism institutionalized by the partition of the Punjab. And the lives of many people from the lower castes were more deeply touched by the latter than by the former.

Partition affected them in various ways. In most cases they did not have to move from one side of the Punjab to the other, since in general the lower castes had accommodated themselves to the religious identity of the dominant religious community where they lived. In western Punjab (which became Pakistan) they had become Julahas and Mochis—Muslim equivalents of Chamars—just as they had come to be known by Hindu and Sikh caste names (Ramdasia, Balmiki, Mazhabi, and the like) in the eastern, Indian Punjab. Many of the Chuhra caste in what became Pakistani Punjab had converted to Christianity; they maintained that identity after partition and were joined by many others of their caste who also converted in order to appear to be less Hindu. All of these groups stayed where they were. Others, however, usually Chamars and other castes of relatively higher status, found it necessary to abandon their homes. Some living in the Pakistani part of the Punjab had become so identified with Hinduism or Sikhism that they had to move to the east, and a shift in the reverse direction was required of Julahas and Mochis who had lived in the Indian Punjab. In village Allahpind,[6] for example, which lies just to the east of the dividing line, no Muslims now remain, despite the fact that they had owned the land and given the village its name (Allahpind, the "village of Allah"). They were replaced by Jat Sikhs from western Punjab and lower caste Meghs who had become converts to the Hindu

---

vide and Quit, p. 293). Moon estimates over 120,000 dead, half in each side of the Punjab.

6. Allahpind was included in the village studies undertaken in 1970–1971, described in previous chapters. The name has been changed, but the actual name is also of Muslim origin.

Arya Samaj in Sialkot district, which had become part of Pakistan.

Even though most of the lower castes did not have to move from one part of the Punjab to another, some displacement was caused simply by the confusion that reigned. In the general anarchy some of the lower caste villagers were divested of what little property or land they had, either by newcomers or by upper caste neighbors who seized the opportunity to increase their own holdings. A large refugee camp that was established near Amritsar to care for dislocated lower caste Punjabis, for instance, was populated mostly by locally uprooted people rather than by refugees from western Punjab. Another kind of dislocation was caused by the severing of traditional ties and understandings that the lower castes had developed with Muslim landowners and shopkeepers; these had to be forged entirely anew when Hindu and Sikh landowners and shopkeepers settled in their villages. The sweeper caste Christians in village Allahpind, for example, report that their relationships with Muslim landowners were much more generous than those that have grown up between them and the refugee Jat Sikhs who took their place. The major effect of the partition on the lower castes, however, had nothing to do with any of these particular instances of discomfort and change. Much more critical were the radical shifts in social climate and the patterns of communal discord which, though they did not begin with partition, were exacerbated by it, and from 1947 on set the Punjab reeling.

Prior to partition there had been a delicate balance between Muslims, Sikhs, and Hindus, with the lower castes caught in the middle. But in the events of 1948 that balance went askew. The partition of the Punjab went a long way toward solving one communal problem—it gave the Muslims a separate state—but it severely exacerbated another, and caught the lower castes in the cross fire once again. With the Muslims largely gone, the Indian Punjab was left primarily to the tenancy of Hindus and Sikhs, and the Hindus were clearly dominant. Only in the central districts could the Sikhs claim majorities, and narrow ones at that. The fear of being reabsorbed into Hinduism in a Hindu-dominated Punjab led to mounting pressures for a Sikh state. Khushwant Singh voiced the apprehensions of his community in the concluding lines of his *History of the Sikhs*, in which he described the doom that would befall the Sikhs as a religious community if they did not have their own political entity:

> The only chance of survival of the Sikhs as a separate community is to create a state in which they form a compact group, where the teaching of Gurmukhi and the Sikh religion is compulsory, and where there is an atmosphere of respect for the traditions of their Khalsa forefathers.[7]

The politics of the Punjab, post-independence, has largely revolved around this issue. The Sikh political organization, the Shiromani Akali Dal, became a formidable minority party, able to offer or withhold votes at strategic junctures, and through mergers with the Congress to exercise a direct influence on the policies of government.[8] From 1930 to 1965 the party was under the direct or indirect control of Master Tara Singh, and for the most part enjoyed the support of the Shiromani Gurdwara Parbandhak Committee, the central committee that controls Sikh shrines and holy places.

The Sikhs suffered much in partition and felt slighted by the major concerns of the times. These feelings were suppressed initially by the need to adjust to life in the new Punjab and the new India. Later, however, they reemerged. Sentiment for a Sikh state became particularly strong at the time of the States Reorganization Act in the mid-1950s, when the princely states of the Punjab were merged with the rest of the province. It was tempered, however, by two factors: the steady defection of Akali leaders into the Congress,[9] and the appearance of a uniquely adept politician

---

7. Khushwant Singh, *History of the Sikhs*, vol. 2 (Princeton, 1966), p. 305.
8. The most comprehensive study of Sikh politics and the Akalis is Baldev Raj Nayar, *Minority Politics in the Punjab* (Princeton, 1966).
9. Among them was Hukum Singh, who as an Akali had been a militant spokesman for Sikh separatism and who became the Speaker of the Lok Sabha after his conversion to the Congress.

as the Congress chief minister, Pratap Singh Kairon.[10] And when major Sikh campaigns for a new state were mounted in 1961, including fasts-unto-death by Master Tara Singh, Kairon was able to contain them and ameliorate the sentiments that inspired them.[11]

But the situation was different in 1965. Kairon was followed as Congress chief minister by Ram Kishan, a relatively weak figure who fell increasingly out of favor with the Congress high command in Delhi. There is reason to believe that the Congress leadership in Delhi at the time preferred to have strong Congress parties in two separate states rather than limp along with one ridden by factions in a unified Punjab.[12] Moreover, a new Sikh leader, Sant Fateh Singh, had effectively replaced Master Tara Singh, and the Sant was a more skillful politician. Pressure for a Sikh state mounted again, the Sant went on a fast-unto-death, and in 1966 the Indira Gandhi government announced a decision to divide the Punjab once more: into a Punjabi Suba (the Punjabi-speaking Punjab) and a new state, Haryana, comprising the rest of the Punjab. The former had a narrow majority of Sikhs. In the years since,

---

10. Kairon, sometimes known as the "strong man of the Punjab," had studied political science at the University of Michigan. Despite his abundant political abilities, his administration was rife with rumors of corruption and nepotism, and a court order forced him to resign in 1964. He was assassinated on the Grand Trunk Road as he was driving from Chandigarh to Delhi on February 6, 1965. (See also Khushwant Singh's brief biography in *History of the Sikhs*, vol. 2, pp. 286–287.)

11. The 1960–1961 Punjabi Suba agitation is described in Nayar, *Minority Politics,* pp. 247–269.

12. A series of articles in Indian newspapers during 1965 and 1966 indicate that the central Congress high command was looking for a way to reorganize its own party in the Punjab (e.g., *Hindustan Times,* October 5–10, 1965; *Times of India,* August 3 and October 31, 1966). The *Hindustan Times* reported on December 24, 1965, that according to one view the solutions to the "Punjabi Suba and Ram Kishan issues intertwine." One rumor of the Punjabi Suba settlement was that the Akalis were to merge en masse with the Congress afterwards. For further discussion of this issue, see Juergensmeyer, "Regional and National Integration in India: A Conceptual Approach, with Application to the Punjab," M.A. thesis, University of California, Berkeley, 1968. The thesis includes a case study of the Punjabi Suba decision.

Sikh political strength has been amply demonstrated: the Akali party has frequently been successful in controlling the Punjab legislature and has produced forceful politicians such as Prakash Singh Badal and Gurnam Singh to serve as chief ministers.

The Untouchable castes opposed the creation of a Punjabi Suba.[13] Just as they had resisted the creation of an independent India if there were no safeguards for Scheduled Caste rights, similarly they opposed any efforts to restructure the Punjab in such a way that the dominant groups— Jat Sikhs in Punjabi Suba, and Jat Hindus in Haryana— would be able to rule over them unchecked by competition. A political scientist, Baldev Raj Nayar, summarized the situation at the time in these words:

> The Harijan [Scheduled Caste] Sikhs oppose the demand for Punjabi Suba because of their fear that, as an economically and socially underprivileged group, they would come under even greater political domination by the non-Harijan Sikhs . . . The Harijans have opposed the demand for the Hariana State because of their fear of being dominated by Jat Hindus. The Harijans of Hariana area prefer to live in the larger state of Punjab where there is a larger number of groups whose demands and aspirations have to be accommodated and aggregated.[14]

Their opposition, however, had no effect, and even government benefits assigned specifically to them, as one such

---

13. This position was confirmed in the survey I took in 1970–1971, in which the allegiance of Scheduled Castes to their own community rather than to a regional identity (such as Punjabi Suba) is indicated in the answers to questions regarding the desirability of a new nation. The majority (60%) of upper caste respondents favored a new nation composed solely of the Punjab, but only 45 percent of the Scheduled Castes would support such a nation. However, the Scheduled Castes responded more positively to the idea of a nation composed of their caste community. Sixty percent of the Scheduled Castes found such an idea attractive, as against a mere 27 percent among the upper castes. For a complete text of questions asked and a breakdown of answers given, see Juergensmeyer, "Political Hope," pp. 567–580.

14. Nayar, *Minority Politics*, pp. 326–327.

writer has claimed, came to be drawn into the struggle between Sikhs and Hindus:

> By the Scheduled Castes Order 1950–51, while all Hindu untouchable castes were given special privileges, only four sub-castes of untouchable Sikhs were included in the list. The sub-castes excluded from the schedule showed little reluctance in abandoning the Khalsa [Sikh] tradition and declaring themselves Hindus in order to claim benefits.[15]

As the issue of repartitioning the Punjab came to a head, the census again became a political event. The Sikhs rested their argument for an independent state on linguistic grounds: since most people in central Punjab spoke and wrote a different language from what pertained in surrounding areas—Gurmukhi-script Punjabi—that area should be established as a separate state. To bolster their position, Sikh activists put members of the Scheduled Castes in the region under great pressure to register their language as Punjabi in the 1961 census, regardless of their religious affiliations. Untouchables who wore the Sikh insignia were under additional pressure to recognize the authority of the Akali Dal. If they did not, they were told, they would be responsible for "destroying the right of the Akali Dal to speak in the name of the total Sikh Community."[16] This pressure was most intense at the village level, and many Untouchables found that if they tried to stay neutral in the Hindu-Sikh dispute, they were in trouble with both. Occasionally the tensions were so great that the lower castes migrated in large groups to urban areas.[17] It was a difficult time, and the confusions of communal competition were made worse by economic imbalances that apparently increased as the rural economy developed.

In absolute terms the economic situation of the Scheduled Caste villagers after independence was not much better

15. Khushwant Singh, *History of the Sikhs*, p. 304.
16. Nayar, *Minority Politics*, p. 326.
17. Lahori Ram Balley, editor of *Bheem Patrika* (Hindi edition), Jullundur, April 3, 1971, interview.

than it had been before, and in relative terms, gauged against the increase in living standards of the upper castes, it may well have been worse. As we observed earlier, village Untouchables in the Punjab are virtually synonymous with the economic class of landless laborers. As such, they have seldom had either the means or the occasions to take advantage of the opportunities for economic development, such as they were, that a modernizing India offered. They eventually benefited from the process, but as the economist V. M. Dandekar has demonstrated, the wealthier 40 percent of the population would have to increase its present standard of consumption almost 300 percent before the next to lowest 10 percent of the population (mostly lower caste) would be able to raise its standards the 50 percent necessary to reach the minimum standards set by the United Nations—and even that process would not be completed, at the present rate, until "some time after 1990–1991."[18] "Indeed," as Dandekar concluded, "it seems that the rich must grow immensely richer before the poor may secure even the desirable minimum."[19]

In the 1960s it seemed that the "Green Revolution" would enable the Punjab to give the lie to Dandekar's pessimism. But time has made it clear that the Green Revolution has simply introduced a special case into Dandekar's overall projections. Early in the Green Revolution the lower castes did benefit somewhat from the greater production of food grains, but in more recent years the gap between the upper castes and landless laborers has become more severe than ever before, and the long-range forecast does not seem more hopeful. "At first glance," according to Francine R. Frankel, "it appears that the position of agricultural laborers improved" in the Punjab.[20] But she explains that the landlords' resentment over the higher wages

18. V. M. Dandekar and Nilakantha Rath, *Poverty in India* (Bombay, 1971), pp. 49–51. The Dandekar study was commissioned by the Ford Foundation.
19. Ibid., p. 49.
20. Francine R. Frankel, *India's Green Revolution: Economic Gains and Political Costs* (Princeton, 1971), p. 35.

exacted by laborers at harvest time in fact caused a loss, as landlords curtailed fringe benefits that had always gone to laborers in the traditional *jajman* system. As mechanization increases and hand labor is less needed, Frankel predicts that "the laborers will have lost their major advantage, and their best prospect of realizing significant gains from the green revolution."[21] A study by a team of Indian economists in the area Frankel has studied concludes that although agricultural laborers do reap some benefits from the Green Revolution, they do not benefit as much as the higher sectors of society. And it continues to be the pattern that "labour households, which belong mostly to the scheduled castes . . . fail to earn sufficient income to meet their barest consumption needs."[22]

In the years after independence the lower castes living in the villages of the Punjab came to exemplify a familiar paradigm for potential revolution: they are a class of people with rising expectations who have suddenly had to face conditions relatively or absolutely worse than those they had known before. In addition, they find themselves in a strategic location much like the one they occupied when the Ad Dharm movement was generated in the 1920s: communal tension between the upper castes potentially gives them a leverage with political opportunities. But although the conditions for revolution exist, as yet only preliminary movements have been made toward reestablishing effective organization. And there are obstacles; one of them is the matter of leadership. The educated leadership stratum of the Punjab lower castes has been lured away by another vision of new India than that offered by radical social movements: the lure of Model Town and the rewards which meritocratic urban India grants to ambitious, independent individuals. Yet in time some of this urban group,

21. Ibid., p. 39.
22. G. S. Bhalla, *Changing Structure of Agriculture in Haryana: A Study of the Impact of Green Revolution, 1969–70,* Report Prepared by the Haryana Agricultural Project Team, Department of Economics, Punjab University (Chandigarh: The Economic and Statistical Organisation, Planning Department, Government of Haryana, 1972), p. 93.

in India and in new locations abroad, began to rediscover a need for religious identity which has provided them with the basis for challenging anew the prevailing social values, an identity that has made it possible again for them to join forces with their caste fellows in the villages. But before that could happen, they had to test out modernity and explore the limits of their new world.

21 The Lonely Modernity of Model Town

In India's best-known Hindi novel, the author, Premchand, tells about the elation which a villager's son feels at the prospect of going to the city to seek work. The adventurous son "would return home only when he had enough money to silence the tongues of the village; and then his mother would realize that he was not a blemish on the family name, but rather its crowning glory." And then, Premchand tells us, "revelling in these delightful fancies, he dozed off."[1]

A similar dream brought thousands of lower caste villagers into the cities of the Punjab after independence. Many came out of motives as personal as those described in Premchand's novel. Others came hoping to escape the social unrest created by communal politics and the economic frustrations of continuing poverty. Still others were attracted by what the cities specifically had to offer: India's decisive push in the direction of industrial expansion after independence had created a flood of new employment opportunities, as had also the blossoming of new bureaucracies, both governmental and private. But beyond all this was something else—the lure of the image of city life itself. That lifestyle, which Premchand's novels so eloquently portray, was relatively loose and independent, providing opportunities to individuals regardless of their social sta-

1. Premchand, *The Gift of a Cow: A Translation of the Hindi Novel, Godaan,* trans. Gordon C. Roadarmel (Bloomington: Indiana University Press, 1968 [originally 1936], pp. 166–167).

tion. The image of the city was much more liberal than the reality, but the fact remains that cities have been places of relative liberation, especially for villagers from the lowest castes. My village surveys show that the lower castes are more inclined than others to prize a system in which rewards are based solely on one's abilities, as against a system in which social or family considerations are primary.[2] The city seems to enshrine these same values, and there are jobs to be had. So many from the lower castes have made the move.

A great proportion of the unskilled, uneducated village poor have had to content themselves with makeshift labor camps, which have sprouted up in vacant areas in the cities and at their edges. From there they go to their jobs as construction laborers, rickshaw men, sweepers, and office peons. Initially at least, these crowded, dirty, and dismal huts are not regarded as permanent residences even by their occupants, who hope, like the son in Premchand's novel, to return in "crowning glory" to their home villages as people of means. But what wealth they find is quickly siphoned off by urban living, and most of them remain, amid their fading hopes and routinized squalor. Others, however, those with education, have had a different experience: they have been lifted as if by magic beyond the realm of rickshaws and construction gangs, and have found themselves placed by government examination in various positions of responsibility in its many agencies. These Scheduled Caste members live largely in the new suburban areas of the cities, areas with names such as Naya Abadi ("New Settlement"), Friends' Colony, Gandhi Camp, and Model Town. For them the dream of the city has come true.

The new, educated ex-Untouchable is something for which the government can take considerable pride. Government policies after independence, spurred on not only by the constitutional mandate to erase untouchability but also by the need to garner lower caste votes for the parties

---

2. For the precise statement of the survey question and a statistical tabulation of the responses, see Appendix B to Juergensmeyer, "Political Hope."

in power, produce benefits of unprecedented proportions for the lower castes. Almost 200,000 lower caste children in the Punjab have been supported by government scholarships in middle and high schools since independence.[3] These schools are not only educational institutions, they are instruments of socialization, preparing students for entry into a meritocratic society where rewards, like grades, will go to the most capable. To match the expectations raised by the social equality of school society, the government has established quotas that regulate the minimum number of jobs to be reserved for members of the Scheduled Castes in government agencies. By the mid-1970s over 12 percent of Punjab government employees (almost 20,000 persons) were drawn from the lower castes, a percentage almost equal to the proportion of Scheduled Caste people represented in the general population.[4] The distribution of lower caste employees in higher positions, however, is another matter, since only 2 percent of government employees at the highest levels (Class I) are from the Scheduled Castes, as compared with 30 percent of the lowest occupations (Class IV). But the total numbers are still worthy of note.[5]

3. Department of Social Welfare, Government of India, *Report of the Committee on Untouchability, Economic and Educational Development of the Scheduled Castes and Connected Documents*, Government of India, 1969 (the Elayaperumal Report), p. 363.
4. Ibid., p. 193; figures are projected into the 1970s.
5. The exact number of Scheduled Caste state government servants in 1971 was given as 18,819, or 12 percent of the total number. The breakdown by class (from supervisory to menial) is as follows:

Class of Service	Total Number of Scheduled Castes	Percentage of Total Number of Government Servants
I	18	2.6
II	125	4.4
III	10,640	9.2
IV	8,036	29.2
Total	18,819	12.88

SOURCE: Personal letter from the Superintendant of Social Welfare, Welfare of Scheduled Castes and Backward Classes Department, Government of Punjab, May 14, 1971.

What have all these advantages in education and employment meant to the lower castes? Many villagers are unimpressed; they have received few of the benefits themselves and wonder what the point is in helping so small a minority. Upper caste voices are often equally pessimistic about the effects of the government's policies, but from a different perspective. They argue that persons should not be rewarded simply on the basis of social position, even if they have traditionally been oppressed, for to dispense such benefits creates a vested interest in maintaining lower caste identity, thus buttressing the concept of untouchability. This, of course, was Gandhi's argument when he reacted to the notion of separate electorates for Untouchables in 1932, and it has been often voiced since independence. In 1968 one of India's most liberal newspapers, the *Times of India*, editorially rejected the recommendations of a parliamentary report advocating increased benefits for the lower castes. According to the *Times*, "Harijans are being formed into a new caste by being sorted out for special favors."[6] Peculiarly, the *Times* seems to ignore the fact that the lower castes have been kept separate all along.

When members of the lower castes argue against the government benefits, by contrast, their arguments reflect a concern not for the general fragmentation of society, but for the integrity and progress of their own community. Some Ambedkarite and Christian political leaders, for example, contend that when the government takes the best and brightest of lower caste youth for its own agencies and then prohibits government workers from being active in

---

6. *Times of India*, December 27, 1968. Other recent writings on this issue include Satish Saberwal, "Harijans and Inequality: Politics in Urban Punjab," unpublished paper given at the Indian Institute of Advanced Study, Simla, n.d.; Satish Saberwal, "The Reserved Constituency: Candidates and Consequences," *Economic and Political Weekly*, July 1972; Marc Galanter, "Who Are the Other Backward Classes?" *Economic and Political Weekly* 13 (October 12, 1978); and Galanter's book, *Competing Equalities* (Berkeley and Los Angeles, forthcoming). See also a section of the *Economic and Political Weekly* 14, Annual Number, February 1979, devoted to this issue.

political organizations, it deprives lower caste organizations of their best hopes for leadership.[7] They see government jobs and the pleasant middle-class life that goes with them as forms of co-optation; the government takes those most capable of rebelling against lower caste injustice and buys them off. Some lower caste political leaders are poignantly adamant about this point, since they feel that their own personal ambitions had to be sacrificed in order to fulfill their commitments to lower caste political organizations. They too could have been undersecretaries and government clerks, they too could have moved to Model Town, but instead they stayed to work with their own people.[8]

Those who did become undersecretaries and government clerks, and who did move to Model Town or some place like it, see the matter differently. They feel that they deserve their rewards and are glad to have been given them. In Jullundur's Model Town, for example, the lower caste residents seem almost defiantly proud of their achievements, not the least of which, in their eyes, is the sheer fact of living in Model Town. And at first glance it seems an egalitarian paradise indeed. It is a pleasant area with neat tract houses fronted by small yards and gardens and arranged along concentric semicircular streets; at the hub lies an occasionally functioning fountain surrounded by multicolored mosaic tiles. The physical layout of the colony announces its most fundamental social characteristic; these are homes built for nuclear families, not the sprawling joint-family multidwelling enclaves that one finds in the villages. The homes in Model Town, both upper caste and lower, all look equal and much the same, the living rooms crowded with furniture, a television, and plastic decorations.

There is very little evidence of religion in Model Town. Village dwellings are crammed with pictures of gods and of traditional religious heroes. But the walls of Model Town are adorned instead with pictures representing a mountain

7. Interviews with L. R. Balley, April 3, 1971, and Amar Nath Singh, April 26, 1971.
8. Ibid.

scene in Kashmir or a quiet moment in an English village, and the calendars display Hindi movie stars and sari-clad ladies reclining against their bicycles. In some of the homes, lower caste ones especially, there are religious pictures too, but of a deliberately eclectic selection: Guru Nanak might be rubbing shoulders with Shiva, and Sant Ravi Das staring across the room at Lakshmi, the goddess of wealth. In one lower caste home the religious pantheon also includes Jesus, portrayed with a glowing red heart. Part of the reason for the deliberate attention to a variety of religious identities, according to one lower caste life insurance employee who wears the turban and beard of the Sikhs, is that not everyone in one's office knows one's caste background. If one's fellow workers were to come to tea, there would be no need to surprise them by an inordinate number of pictures of Sant Ravi Das. This man was quick to inform me that he is quite proud of his caste and cultural background, and supports lower caste religious and political organizations as much as a person in his situation can. But he seems to share the feeling of embarrassment and fear of disclosure that one finds among many lower caste moderns of Model Town, although one of their upper caste colleagues insists that "everybody knows who and what they are—look what happens at marriages."

Marriages do indeed pose a problem. There is little leeway in choosing a marriage partner; the family will almost certainly select someone of the same caste, if at all possible someone whose economic status is firm. But when it comes to listing guests to be invited to the occasion, serious dilemmas arise. Lower caste families are hesitant about inviting friends from the office for fear of being rebuffed, just as upper caste people hesitate to extend invitations to them for fear of offending less broad-minded relatives. Difficulties such as these are symptomatic of a whole order of social problems encountered by the Model Town moderns of lower caste. In Harold Isaacs' perceptive series of interviews with suburbanized Scheduled Caste members in Delhi, "ex-Untouchables," as he called them, he found that their success in transferring their old identities into modern

Indian society was only partial.[9] According to Isaacs, such people inhabit a double world—public acceptance and integration on the one hand, and on the other, a private life shared only among those who also bear their clandestine identities.

A survey of "ex-Untouchables" has also been made by a sociologist from Punjab University, Suneila Malik, who interviewed Scheduled Caste members in both the traditional ghettos and the middle-class suburbs of Ambala, a city on the border between Haryana and the new Punjab state. In general, her conclusions are not surprising. Suburban Scheduled Caste people have relatively little association with their caste fellows, do not visit their relatives regularly, shun marriage gatherings, and eschew lower caste organizations; they all are well educated and well aware of the benefits available to them from the government.[10] However, the answers to two of Dr. Malik's questions introduced something unexpected. When asked "Do you think in ordinary social intercourse an educated member of Scheduled Caste will be treated as an equal to a high caste person of the same educational qualifications?" the middle-class respondents tended to answer "no," whereas Scheduled Caste people living in the ghetto more frequently offered the optimistic "yes."[11] And when asked, "Do you still find yourself excluded from the social groups to which you feel your occupational and economic status entitles you?" the middle-class respondents were again the ones who felt the greater discrimination.[12]

These answers are poignant. They reveal that the very people who would have liked to detach themselves from their former identities and become absorbed into the world of Model Town and the middle-class image are precisely the ones who feel most sharply the persistence of their Scheduled Caste identity as it continues to be projected

    9. Harold Isaacs, *India's Ex-Untouchables* (New York, 1964).
   10. Suneila Malik, "Social Consequences of Social Mobility Among Scheduled Castes," Ph.D. dissertation, Punjab University, Chandigarh, 1971.
    11. Ibid., table 19, p. 74.   12. Ibid., table 18, p. 70.

onto them by the society at large. Paradoxically, government benefits that are intended to free the Untouchables have the effect of ushering them into a new society in which their sense of alienation is even more acute.

Politicians, through the policies they have established, can claim much of the credit for bringing Untouchables to Model Town, and the Congress party, which has ruled over post-independence India almost without interruption, has enjoyed the greatest measure of popularity among the educated lower castes. More than a party, it is itself a symbol of the new society that many of its policies are aimed at bringing about. Like Model Town itself, the Congress has the image of egalitarian opportunity, and like Model Town, the image is more pleasant than the reality. The Congress has strived, however, to maintain its image and to encourage the involvement of the lower castes, and for several reasons. One is ideological: the Gandhian and modern ideologies that the Congress claims as its own require it to prove its egalitarianism. Another is strategic: the party aims to win the support of the large blocks of middle- and lower-class voters. And a third follows from India's political structure: the principle of reserved constituencies means that Congress needs to be able to attract Scheduled Caste people with some political acumen to run for office in such constituencies.

Over the years most of the leaders the Congress has been able to locate have been veterans of the old lower caste movements. Master Gurvanta Singh, undoubtedly the most influential Scheduled Caste member of the Punjab Congress party in recent years, began as an Ad Dharmi, joining the Congress in time for the 1952 elections.[13] Other old Ad Dharmis in Congress have included the late Sadhu Ram, M.P., the follower of Radhasoami who first joined the Scheduled Caste Federation, then switched to Congress in 1946;[14] the late Sant Ram, M.L.A., who joined the Con-

---

13. Interview with Gurvanta Singh, Jullundur, May 8, 1971. He was a supporter of the old Kairon faction of the Punjab Congress party, and for years was the party's vice-president.
14. Interview with Sadhu Ram, Jullundur, June 24, 1971.

gress in 1945;[15] and Mangoo Ram himself, who served a brief term as a Congress M.L.A. after independence. The only Congress member of the Assembly to have been recruited from the Balmikis, Bhagat Guran Das from Hoshiarpur, is active in the Valmiki Sabha.[16]

Other lower caste politicians have entered the Congress directly through the Scheduled Caste organizations it sponsors—the Harijan League, the Depressed Classes League, the Bharat Dalit Sevak Sangh, and the Harijan Sevak Sangh. They, like the organizations that brought them into the party, have been around for some time.[17] Prithvi Singh Azad, for example, chairman of the Punjab branch of the Harijan Sevak Sangh, joined the Congress in 1921 and has served in the Assembly or the Legislative Council off and on since that time.[18] The Scheduled Caste leaders of Congress are organized into a "Harijan Cell."[19] Its mission is to formulate policy for Untouchables' welfare and develop strategy for increasing the Congress's lower caste support, but many say that its real concerns lie more with the latter than the former.[20]

It is not just the Harijan Cell that has been more responsive to the demands of the party than to its lower caste

15. Interview with Sant Ram, Member of the Punjab Legislative Assembly, Jullundur Municipal Hospital, June 12, 1971 (in Punjabi).
16. Interview with Gurvanta Singh, May 8, 1971.
17. The first Congress-supported Scheduled Caste organization in the Punjab was the All-India Suppressed Classes League, constituted in 1929 (interview with Lala Mohan Lal, former secretary of the Harijan Sevak Sangh, 1932–1947, in Jullundur, May 1, 1971). Later, the lower caste arm of the Punjab Congress party became the Bhartiya Depressed Classes League, which had its offices in the residence of Sadhu Ram, M.P., in New Delhi, and received 90 percent of its funds yearly—almost 150,000 rupees—from a government grant (interview with K. Ananda Rao, office secretary, Bhartiya Depressed Classes League, June 24, 1971).
18. Interview with Prithvi Singh Azad, M.L.A., Kharar, Rupar District, Punjab, April 13, 1971. Prithvi Singh Azad was made a member of the cabinet again in 1973.
19. Interview with Onkar Chand, office secretary, Punjab Congress Committee, Chandigarh, June 10, 1971.
20. Interviews with L. R. Balley, Jullundur, April 3, 1971, Bhagwan Das, Ambedkar Mission Society, New Delhi, June 21, 1971.

constituency; as much could be said of all Scheduled Caste members of the Congress. That is the nature of a party system based on constituencies that include a cross section of the population and not just a portion of it. This may be a sign of democratic politics, but it also means that the Scheduled Caste leaders in Congress are scarcely the most militant spokesmen of their communities. It may well be true that the Scheduled Castes have in general been treated more favorably by the party of Gandhi than by any other. But from their perspective it remains his party and the party of upper castes, not theirs. The Scheduled Caste voice in Congress has always been filtered through a leadership of the Congress's own choosing.

The other political parties in the Punjab—the Akalis and the Jan Sangh—have also made a flurry of appeals to the Scheduled Castes, but until 1977 the lower castes consistently voted Congress.[21] Congress was seen as the only secular, neutral party among the major contenders, since the Akalis were in close alignment with rural Sikhs, and the Jan Sangh served the cause of urban Hindus, and that was determinative: the Scheduled Castes paid more attention to a party's general policies than to the particular candidates it put forth.[22] This meant, however, that their loyalty to the Congress was only conditional; if ever Scheduled Caste aims were better served by another political force, there was the possibility that lower caste support would be with-

---

21. In fact the Akali governments were generous with positions for Scheduled Castes. In the cabinets of Prakash Singh Badal, several Scheduled Caste politicians had positions. During the 1971 elections a "Punjab Scheduled Caste Board" was set up in Jullundur as an Akali front, and Swami Shudranand, one of the old founders of the Ad Dharm movement, was brought in to be its leader (interview with Sohan Lal, office secretary of the Punjab Scheduled Caste Board, Jullundur, June 10, 1971). The Swami protested, however, that he personally is adamantly opposed to the Akalis (interview with Swami Shudranand, Jullundur, May 15, 1971).

22. In answers to my survey question, 70 percent of the Scheduled Caste respondents indicated that party policies directed their votes, whereas considerably fewer upper caste respondents indicated that that was of primary importance. (Questions and tabulation of responses given in Appendix B to "Political Hope.")

drawn from the Congress. This happened in the elections of 1977, but Mrs. Gandhi was able to recover Untouchable support in 1980. The gap between the Scheduled Caste rank and file and those of its leaders who had assumed positions of responsibility in political parties—all of them, not just the Congress—has been wide enough to leave room for considerable fluidity of choice and for the growth of other political styles and other political movements. At times, indeed, the gap has seemed a chasm. One lower caste villager said of a politician from his caste, "He has left our *qaum* and joined the Congress *qaum*."

The lure that the Congress and Model Town have held for the lower castes is essentially the same: both succeed by providing retreats from the cultural traditions and religion of Untouchables. The Congress has offered an alternative to the politics of religious communities, and Model Town has functioned as an escape from societies based on religious values, on caste. In neither case, however, has the retreat been entirely successful for lower caste people, and the ensuing sense of disappointment has been much the same in both cases. Untouchables have not been accepted into the new worlds they chose as completely as they had hoped, for the worlds themselves are not as new as they had been led to believe. Cut off from the lower caste cultures they have rejected, Scheduled Caste moderns experience the alienation that de Tocqueville called "the loneliness of democracy." Their urban, individualistic society has become separate from that of the traditional laborers who, whether they live in the villages or in the new labor camps that have sprung up around the cities, remain economically disadvantaged, socially oppressed, and politically disenfranchised. Each of these societies needs something from the other: the traditionalists need the vision of change that the society of achievement makes possible, and the modernists, in their alienated isolation, need the comfort and identity of their cultural heritage. Thus the ingredients exist for a plausible, if tenuous, sharing of interests, and this has laid the basis for recent efforts to reassert the cultural identity of Untouchables and revive the religion of the lower castes.

22 Ravi Das in Wolverhampton

The journey from the village to Model Town is a long one, but Untouchables in recent years have undertaken bolder journeys still—emigrations to various parts of the world, especially to certain areas of Great Britain. These are courageous acts. Yet in some ways the individuals who have chosen to live in expatriate communities are not as isolated as those who have tried to blend into urban society back home in India, for in Britain there is little question of blending—neither into British society generally nor into the established societies of upper caste Indians who have made Britain their home. By default lower caste communities remain intact. Like the leather merchant families of Boota Mandi, they have achieved much but are still regarded by many as aliens: outcastes in Boota Mandi, outsiders in Britain. Untouchables in Boota Mandi have responded to this sense of social exclusion with a defiant pride that could be molded into militant movements for cultural integrity and political awareness, and in the expatriate communities in Britain the response has been much the same. These lower caste people have surrounded themselves with the same symbols of communal unity and honor they had known in the Punjab, half a world away.

Between 1950 and 1968, before more rigorous immigration policies were imposed, hundreds of thousands of Indians emigrated to Britain, a remarkably large percentage of them Punjabis.[1] More remarkable still, there was a heavy

---

1. About 300,000 Indians emigrated to England during the first twenty years after Indian independence, when Indians automatically re-

representation from the Scheduled Castes, especially from Chamar subcastes. There are no exact figures, but Indian consular officials estimated that the percentage of Scheduled Caste immigrants within the total Punjabi community was as high as 10 percent;[2] the rest are largely Jat Sikhs. One would not ordinarily expect Chamars to have access to international travel in such large numbers, and indeed in this case it was only that a fortunate selection of officials worked in their favor. Until 1952 it had been difficult for Chamars to thread the maze of upper caste bureaucracy and obtain the necessary emigration papers. In that year, however, the first Scheduled Caste gazetted officer in the Punjab, Ishwar Das Pawar, became the undersecretary for passports in the Punjab government and began handing out passports to Scheduled Caste applicants with an unaccustomed generosity. Pawar estimated that he helped five hundred Scheduled Caste applicants to emigrate each year.[3]

Most immigrants came from the Jullundur *doab* and settled in the industrial areas of England: London, Birmingham, and the Midlands. On the whole, life is better for the Scheduled Castes in England, but in some ways it is disturbingly the same. All of the new immigrants tend to be lumped together in ghettos. There are areas of Birmingham and London which could easily be mistaken for Amritsar or old Lahore, with the men in turbans, the ladies in *silvar-kamiz*, Hindi movies at the cinema, Ravi Das and Guru Nanak on the walls. Other features of life also remain the same: the Jat Sikhs do not hesitate to remind the Chamars that they are still Chamars, even in England. Most of the Chamars prefer to be called Ad Dharmi or Ramdasia, but many Jat Sikhs insist on calling them Chamar, even as a form of personal address. A pub on West End Road, Southall, in the suburbs of London, has come to be known pejoratively as the Chamar-wali pub because

---

ceived commonwealth status and were allowed into the country. For an excellent recent study of the British Indian community see Arthur Helweg's forthcoming *Sikhs in England*.

2. Indian High Commission, London, August 2, 1971.

3. Interview with Ishwar Das Pawar, Punjab Civil Service, retired, Chandigarh, April 9, 1971. Pawar points out that the total number of emigrants was much higher, however, perhaps 5,000 per year, so the overwhelming majority were still upper caste.

of its clientele,⁴ and fights between Jat Sikhs and Chamars have broken out in factories and pubs all over industrial England. Some say there even have been killings.⁵

The British seem to notice these matters very little. In an anti-Indian mood it has made little difference whether the people in question are Chamar or Jat. Theirs has been an impartial discrimination. The lower caste immigrants, in turn, have been largely indifferent to British attitudes. Chamars who have grown up with the experience of caste and racial prejudice are unlikely to be startled by new forms of ill treatment. But the upper caste Sikhs have been genuinely irritated, and have taken out their irritation on each other and on the Chamars. The Jat Sikhs have separated into rival camps. There are Amritsar Jats and Doaba Jats and Malwa Jats from Ludhiana, each with their own *gurdwaras*. The artisan caste Sikhs also maintain separate *gurdwaras*, one for the Ramgarhias (carpenter castes) and another for the Bhartras (traditionally an astrologer caste). And the Chamars feel unwelcome in any of them.⁶

The Chamars, who came to Britain expecting to find life different, take offense at the upper caste Sikhs' attitudes toward them. They earn as much as the Jat Sikhs, sometimes more, and occasionally find themselves placed by the British in command over them—a Chamar foreman superintending a Jat Sikh work crew—much to the displeasure of the latter. On occasion the Jat Sikhs have tried to explain the intricacies of Indian propriety to their British factory managers and have protested that they cannot be expected to work under Chamars, but at least in one such instance the Chamars have retaliated with a law suit.⁷ The Scheduled Castes can afford to act more bravely in Britain,

4. Interview with Chanan Ram, London, August 4, 1971.
5. Ibid.
6. Interview with Mangu Ram Jaspal, Wolverhampton, August 1, 1971. Other Ad Dharmis said they were allowed inside the *gurdwaras*, but were not treated equally. They insisted on having the right to vote in *gurdwara* elections, since "anyone who believes in the Granth is supposed to have the right to vote"; but voting did not seem to help: "certain candidates told us if we voted for them, they would give us equal status. But after the elections, they forgot about us." (Interview with Gurmit Singh, Ravi Das Sabha, Wolverhampton, August 1, 1971.)
7. Interview with Mangu Ram Jaspal, August 1, 1971.

since they have now entered a new context for competing with the Jat Sikhs. In the Punjab the cards were stacked against them, but in Britain they have a fresh start, and the ideology of Ad Dharm has prepared them to take advantage of it. By using the term Ad Dharm as the name of their community, the British Chamars have claimed equality with the Sikhs as a *qaum,* a religious community. Ad Dharm legend makes this very specific by setting Ravi Das on the same plane as Guru Nanak, and the Ad Dharmis feel the competition keenly. As one leader said, "Wait and see. In ten years, you'll find the Sikhs on the bottom and Ad Dharm on top."[8]

In 1956 the Ad Dharm Chamars made the first move toward proving to the British Sikhs that they were a *qaum* of equal status and heritage by organizing associations of Ravi Das *sabhas* in Birmingham and adjoining Wolverhampton.[9] These associations were intended not only to counteract the Sikhs, but to provide support and assistance for the masses of new immigrants, many of whom had only passing familiarity with the English language.[10] Eventually, an attempt was made to establish a central organization with a secular name, the Indian Welfare Association, but it was hard to reach an agreement on what its nature should be. There were three distinct points of view: one group wanted to strengthen the cultural traditions associated with Ravi Das, another group was interested in community fellowship and the prospects for advancing the status of the Chamars in British secular society, and a third group was concerned about finding ways to maintain Scheduled Caste identity in nontraditional ways.[11]

8. Ibid. One indication of the Ad Dharmis' competition with the Sikhs is their insistence on using the term *guru* rather than *sant* for Ravi Das, equating him implicitly with Guru Nanak.
9. Ibid. In Birmingham, the organizers of the Ravi Das Sabha were Bhagat Ram Sohpal, Moti Lal Baloo, Master Santa Singh, Baryam Singh, Sharda Ram, and to a lesser extent, Gurmit Chand Suman, Mani Lal, and Devi Chand. In Wolverhampton, the organizers were Sawan Chand, Sham Lal, Charan Dass, Aram Chand, and Harcharand Dass, who was the first president.
10. Ibid.
11. Chanan Ram, August 4, 1971.

Most of the people in this third group were Ambedkarites and Buddhists. When Ambedkar became a Buddhist in 1956, the idea did not take hold deeply among the Scheduled Castes of the Punjab; but in England, where tradition had a looser hold and the concept of voluntary religion was more familiar, the idea appealed to large numbers of Chamars. They formed their own association, the Indian Republican Group of Great Britain, and ran candidates in British elections.[12] Dr. Ambedkar memorial committees were established in Wolverhampton and London, and Indian Buddhist societies were constituted in London and Birmingham. There were also Ambedkar Buddhists in the Ravi Das *sabhas,* and that was the problem: the Ravi Das people claimed the Ambedkarites had no business being there. The Ambedkarites, however, felt that the Ravi Das *sabhas* were for all people of Chamar caste, regardless of religious preference. They saw the Ravi Das *sabhas* as analogous to the caste associations that the Chuhras had established in England—such as the Valmiki *sabhas*[13]— and argued that they should be available to any Chamar, Ambedkarite or not.

The Ravi Das organization managed to effect a partial solution to this problem of identity by shuffling around the names. On the local level the organization continued to be called Ravi Das Sabha to please the traditionalists, but on the central level the designation was changed to the Indian Welfare Association so that modernists and Ambedkarites would also feel welcome.[14] Even so, relations between the Ravi Das and Ambedkar elements in the association remained uneasy, and a growing hostility erupted in 1965 as a fight over control of the organization's assets, a total of almost £6,000. The issue was in litigation for years.

12. In the May 9, 1971, election two Republican candidates contested in the Southall, Ealing Borough constituency, along with seventeen other candidates. The Republican candidates received 265 votes out of the 42,000 votes cast.

13. Chanan Ram, August 4, 1971. The Indian Christian Fellowship was also primarily Chuhra, but included a variety of castes. The Indian Christian fellowships were in Southall, Bedford, and Birmingham.

14. Mangu Ram Jaspal, August 1, 1971; and Chanan Ram, August 4, 1971.

Another result of the schism was a new name, the Indian Mutual Support and Social Association, West Midlands, Ltd., registered with the British government in 1965, and specifically excluding Ambedkarites.

According to one account, the fight was provoked by the political situation in India: the Ravi Das people supported the Congress, and the Ambedkarites stood behind the RPI.[15] Another version claims that the Ambedkarites were trying to turn the local association into community centers, and wanted the organization to be named in such a way as to reflect that concern.[16] But beneath the conflict about names lay the old issue of social strategy—whether to attempt to assimilate into a wider, egalitarian culture, or to consolidate and dignify the heritage with which they had been identified. The Ambedkarites opted for the former, and the Ravi Das people for the latter. One Ravi Das supporter stated the issue succinctly: "The Ambedkarites think the name makes all the difference. But our religion *is* our economic position. We have to unite behind our own tradition first, then we can fight effectively."[17]

Once the Ambedkarites had been excluded from the Ravi Das organization, things went more smoothly. Harcharan Das, grandson of Labu Ram, one of the founders of the original Ad Dharm movement, became its general secretary, and the name was again changed to reflect revised priorities. It became the Ravi Das Cultural Association. At last the matter of identity seemed to be solved, and the organization became stable: it continued strong in the Birmingham-Wolverhampton area and expanded with the establishment of branches in Bedford and Coventry. The new movement reached its high point with the opening of a Ravi Das temple in Wolverhampton in 1968.

The new Ravi Das temple immediately became the pride of England's Ad Dharmi Chamars. It occupies a small, soot-darkened building at 181 Dudley Road, which was built as

15. Chanan Ram, August 4, 1971.
16. Mangu Ram Jaspal, August 1, 1971.
17. Ibid.

an Anglican church in 1887.[18] But by the 1960s Christianity had fallen on hard times in England and the little Anglican church on Dudley Road found itself in a changing neighborhood with no one to attend. The city took it over, and it was from the Municipal Council that the Ravi Das Sabha rented the building at a modest £300 per year, of which the Municipal Council contributed half. It needed £3,000 worth of repairs at the outset, including a new social hall built onto the back, a kitchen, patches in the roof, a green wall-to-wall carpet in the *satsang* hall (the old sanctuary), and pink paint for the walls. The new occupants hung some colorful and striking pictures: two of Ravi Das, one of Guru Nanak, and a small one of Rishi Valmiki, to show hospitality to the Chuhras.

The main activities in the Ravi Das temple are worship and socializing. At Sunday morning worship services, perhaps a hundred or more participants squat on the green carpets, wearing turbans or a head-covering: it is a point of pride that "Ambedkarites who try to come in with their bare heads and their shoes on are tossed out."[19] The worship follows the form of Sikh religious gatherings. First there are songs—verses from Ravi Das's poems and Punjabi folk tunes, all of which are held to be "songs associated with our *qaum*."[20] Then come readings from Ravi Das and Guru Nanak, the latter being revered as a general religious figure of the Punjab rather than as a Sikh. Finally, there is a little sermon about religious living, social unity, and the like. A *sabha* committee plans the worship, a volunteer reads the sacred books, and flowers and *prasad* are brought by the women. Another worship service is held on Wednesday evenings especially for the women.

Prominent among social functions at the temple are Western-style marriages, which, unlike the traditional In-

18. The information about the Ravi Das Temple is from an interview with Amar Chand, general secretary of the Guru Ravi Das Sabha, United Kingdom (Central Body), at the Ravi Das Temple, Wolverhampton, August 2, 1971.
19. Mangu Ram Jaspal, August 1, 1971.
20. Amar Chand, August 2, 1971.

dian variety, take only one or two hours, after which the wedding party retires to the social hall for cake and champagne. The men of the temple hold business meetings each Sunday following the regular services to discuss politics and the activities of the *sabha*. These activities are several, but central to them all is the promotion of respect for Ravi Das, who is regarded as "guru." The *sabha* prints pamphlets about Ravi Das to distribute to the British and to promote Ravi Das philosophy among the Scheduled Castes, and when the Indian government issued a new postage stamp honoring "Sant Ravi Das," it waged a protest against the omission of the title Guru before his name. Reviving an aspiration of the old Ad Dharm movement, the *sabha* also hopes to compile a Ravi Das Granth, capable of rivaling the Sikh scriptures, which would include the verses of Ravi Das already in the Sikh Granth and supplement them with other Ravi Das poems and the poetry of *bhakti* saints such as Nam Dev and Kabir.[21]

Another activity of the Ravi Das Sabha is its continuing protest against the use of the term "Untouchable." When the *Daily Telegraph* announced Jagjivan Ram's ascension to the Congress party presidency in India with the headline "India Makes Untouchable President," for instance, the *sabha* generated a series of critical letters in response.[22] It regards the term "Harijan" with a similar disdain, feeling that it, too, perpetuates attitudes of subservience and discrimination. The *sabha* does cooperate with other Indian groups on national issues such as support for flood victims and famine relief in Bihar and Maharashtra, but its most ambitious projects focus on the Punjab. The Ravi Das Sabha in Britain has urged the Indian government to establish a chair in Ravi Das studies at Punjabi University, Patiala, and has drawn up plans for its own college in Phagwara, fifteen miles from Jullundur. Furthermore, it

21. Mangu Ram Jaspal, August 1, 1971. The new Ravi Das Granth is being prepared by Ranki Ram of Birmingham. The attempt is reminiscent of Hari Das's compilation of Ravi Das scripture at the beginning of this century, prior to the establishment of the original Ad Dharm (see chap. 4).
22. Amar Chand, August 2, 1971.

has succeeded in establishing a new organization in the Punjab, orchestrated and financed from Wolverhampton, which, though initially intended as a welfare association, has in fact served as the nucleus for the revival of the old Ad Dharm movement itself.

The most significant figure in organizing this new Ad Dharm is a man with a significant name—Mangoo Ram, or as he prefers to spell it, Mangu Ram. He is not related in any way to his famous forebear in the movement, and has made the distinction clear by adding Jaspal to his name. His background parallels that of many of the activists in the new Ad Dharm.

Mangu Ram Jaspal was born in 1928 in a village near the town of Nakodar, fifteen miles south of Jullundur.[23] His family was not especially distinguished, even within its own caste. When Jaspal was seven years old, his mother went to work as a common laborer, a fact which left a deep impression on young Jaspal's mind. When he was young, the original Ad Dharm movement occasionally held rallies near his home village, but his family had only been involved to the extent of registering their religion as Ad Dharm in the census and offering prayers to Ravi Das.

Jaspal received government scholarships in secondary school and went on to enroll in the city college in Jullundur, where he attended classes at night in order to work days as a clerk in the government-supported Cooperative Society. Upon graduation he married and began raising his own family. Sometime during the 1950s his younger brother left home and settled in England, where many other people in their area and caste had emigrated. The lure was great, so in 1960 Mangu Ram Jaspal quit his job and joined his brother in Birmingham, leaving his family at home.

By 1967, after working as a welder and the operator of a steel press, Mangu Ram Jaspal had saved enough money to bring his family to England. They moved to a comfortable but modest home in a working-class neighborhood in Hands-

23. This life history comes from interviews with Mangu Ram Jaspal in Jullundur, January 31, 1971; September 20, 1975; and Wolverhampton, August 1, 1971.

worth, on the outskirts of Birmingham. They bought a large flowered sofa and a television set; Jaspal took pictures of the television and sent them to relatives in Jullundur. By that time, however, a good many of the relatives had also moved to England. Jaspal estimates that they numbered almost a hundred, the whole exodus having begun with his brother in the early 1950s.

In December 1969, Mangu Ram Jaspal returned to the Punjab, not to visit but to establish a newspaper and to revive the Ad Dharm Mandal. The experience in England had changed him—not perhaps in the same way that the original Mangoo Ram's Gadar experience in California had revolutionized him, but it had given him perspective, imagination. It was the idea of developing projects in the Punjab which first fired the enthusiasm of Jaspal. In 1969 he met with five other members of the Ravi Das Sabha at Wolverhampton and Birmingham and began formulating some plans.

The racial situation in England and changing immigration policies at the time gave Indians the distinct impression that they might not always be welcome in Britain and that they had better build up their bases in the home country. Mangu Ram Jaspal, therefore, had purchased seventeen acres of farmland in the Punjab, and he and the other five Ad Dharmis began discussing plans for establishing a collective farm near Jullundur. The meetings continued, and the idea of a collective farm expanded into other projects: a college, a newspaper, a new organization, a political party. Jaspal and his friends did not have much money individually, but collectively they commanded a modest sum, and when British pounds were translated into rupees that amount became a fortune.

Not all of the Ad Dharmis in the Wolverhampton temple were as enthusiastic about the new schemes as Mangu Ram Jaspal, but some aspects of the plan aroused definite interest. The idea of establishing a Ravi Das college similar to the Khalsa colleges of the Sikhs and the D.A.V. colleges of the Arya Samaj was particularly attractive.[24] And the plan to build a temple in honor of Ravi Das in his birth-

---

24. Amar Chand, August 2, 1971.

place, Benares, was almost equally popular. There was also a scheme for buying scores of bicycles so that volunteers could invade the villages, bringing the message of Ravi Das and *qaum* unity to the masses.

To give their ideas solidarity, Jaspal and his associates established their own registered corporation, the Punjab Service Cooperative Society, Ltd.[25] The corporation was to be the parent body behind the newspaper, the farm, the college, and other projects. It provided a rubric that enabled the founders to sell shares and "Qaum Savings Bonds" that would underwrite the aims of the corporation. These were announced somewhat as follows: to establish preachers [*pracharak*] to spread the idea of an economically self-sufficient *qaum*; to build meeting places and temples in the villages; to create job opportunities for Ad Dharmis; to print a newspaper and establish a press; and to build educational institutions and send students to foreign countries in the hope of producing a hundred Ph.D.'s every year. In addition, the corporation dedicated itself to exposing the wrong-doings of bad and selfish leaders, creating a social revolution in cooperation with other *qaums*, and in general promoting good will. But it stopped short of advocating the constitution of a new political party.

Jaspal began campaigning for support among the Ravi Das *sabhas* in England. The main selling points among his *qaum* brethren there concerned the hard economic facts: Britain appeared to be on the brink of a recession, and Indians were in positions too tenuous to guarantee continued employment. If British Ad Dharmis had any hope of a financial future, Jaspal argued, it lay in investment and in constructing an economically viable community in India to which they could return when it became necessary. The campaign was effective. Eighty-six members of the Ravi Das *sabhas* in England agreed to pledge five shillings a week for the Cooperative Society's support.

When Mangu Ram Jaspal returned to the Punjab in December 1969, he returned with high expectations and the Wolverhampton money. He purchased a house in Jullun-

25. Mangu Ram Jaspal, January 31, 1971. Information about the other activities of the corporation described in this chapter also come from this interview.

dur's Model Town to use as an office and community center, installed one of his brothers there as office manager, and began looking for an editor for the newspaper. Before long he was able to enlist the services of Chanan Lal Manik, a newspaperman who had formerly worked for Master Gurvanta Singh, who set up operations in the office at 615 Model Town and by February 17, 1970, had produced the first issue of the *Ravidas Patrika*.[26] Its cover boasted a two-color full-page picture of Ravi Das receiving the word *soham* from some mysterious source in the sky.[27] Pictures of the founders were inside: Mangu Ram Jaspal and two of his Wolverhampton colleagues, Jugindir Lal Khar and Bhagat Ram Sohpal. The newspaper, a sixteen-page weekly printed in Gurmukhi-script Punjabi, continues to be a lively and attractive blending of general news items, poetry and articles extolling the virtues of Guru Ravi Das, and reports of the activities of the new Ad Dharm organization. Originally, the majority of articles were contributed by Ad Dharmis writing in England, and most of the advertisers were also from the Birmingham-Wolverhampton area; half of the subscriptions were sent to England.[28] A regular procession of leaders from the British parent body kept the movement alive in the Punjab, and in 1971 a new association, the Ad Dharm Federation of the United Kingdom, was established to serve as "the political arm of the Ravi Das Sabha and the support for the Indian Ad Dharm Federation in the Punjab."[29] In 1975 Mangu Ram Jaspal took up permanent residence in 615 Model Town as editor of the paper.

Thus the initial impetus for reviving the Ad Dharm movement came not from India but from far away. Yet the issues that face Ad Dharmi Chamars in England are by no

26. Mangu Ram Jaspal, "Ravidas Patrika da Janam" (Birth of Ravidas Patrika), *Ravidas Patrika* 1, no. 1 (Feb. 17, 1970), p. 5.
27. The original Ad Dharm had used *soham* as their sacred word (see chap. 6). The masthead of the *Ravidas Patrika* is similar to a Sikh newspaper published in Jullundur, the *Akali Patrika*.
28. Mangu Ram Jaspal, February 22, 1971.
29. Mangu Ram Jaspal, May 17, 1971. Earlier, from January to May 1971, Swaran Chand from Wolverhampton had spent three months in the Punjab on an organizing trip.

means dissimilar from those their caste fellows encounter in the cities of the Punjab. When Wolverhampton came to Model Town it discovered areas of common interest and yoked these political and social concerns in the name of religion, just as the old Ad Dharm had done so many years before.

23 Ad Dharm Anew

When Mangu Ram Jaspal returned to the Punjab, spurred on by the dream of reviving the old Ad Dharm, he had sufficient local contacts to start the *Ravidas Patrika,* but had to postpone most of his other schemes until he had established broader bases. There are only limited sources of support in lower caste communities, and Jaspal probed them all: the old leadership, the few families with money, the politicians, and the religious figures. All of them initially showed some interest.

The best known of the old leaders was the original Mangoo Ram, then in retirement on his farm near Garhshankar. Jaspal went to Mangoo Ram and attempted to enlist his support by appealing to his sense of history—a successful approach, as it turned out.[1] The old Ad Dharm titan told Jaspal that he was disturbed about the direction of post-independence politics and felt that there was need for a new emphasis:

> Before, we were only interested in removing Untouchability. We have that now, and the government gives us much. We have our people in the government, but they are still treated like slaves. They fear their superiors and the high caste people. . . . We have to organize our people within government, and organize our own political interests. We must make elected parties more responsible. We want them to be fair.[2]

1. Interview with Mangoo Ram, Garhshankar, January 29, 1971.
2. Mangoo Ram, April 17, 1971.

Mangoo Ram agreed to be the titular leader of the new Ad Dharm movement. His colleague and the former general secretary of the Ad Dharm, Hazara Ram, also agreed to lend his name.

Not many Scheduled Caste families have money, but Mangu Ram Jaspal did locate financial support in the town of Phagwara from Bagoo Ram, a retired captain in the Indian army, who joined the organization as manager of the *Ravidas Patrika*.[3] For a time Jaspal also managed to interest Seth Kushi Ram, a leather merchant in Boota Mandi and one of the wealthiest Ad Dharmi Chamars in the Punjab. It was a logical affiliation, since Kushi Ram was the son of Sundar Das, one of the original members of the old Ad Dharm, and Kushi Ram himself had provided Boota Mandi with a Ravi Das school and library. Kushi Ram was interested in an organization that would promote the name of Ravi Das and at the same time wield some political influence,[4] and agreed to join the new Ad Dharm as a member of its advisory committee.

Mangu Ram Jaspal was more cautious in approaching Scheduled Caste politicians.[5] Especially if the new movement aligned itself with the Congress, it stood in danger of losing its independent appeal; Jaspal was afraid the movement might be co-opted before it even began. On the other hand, he could not afford to alienate any significant political force by leaving it out. The most important group from this standpoint was the Ambedkar Republican party, which had already been estranged from the Ravi Das *sabhas* in England, so Jaspal made a concerted effort to include Ambedkar leaders and their wealthy supporters within the new Ad Dharm.[6] He arranged for eight consecutive issues of the *Ravidas Patrika,* beginning with the third, to carry

---

3. Interview with Mangu Ram Jaspal, Jullundur, March 14, 1971.

4. Interview with Manohar Lal Mehay, nephew of Seth Kushi Ram, Boota Mandi, Jullundur, March 16, 1971.

5. Mangu Ram Jaspal expressed his distrust of politicians in the first issue of the *Ravidas Patrika:* "Ravidas Patrika da Janam," February 17, 1970.

6. The wealthy man of Boota Mandi—Seth Kishan Das—had been active in the Ambedkar movements.

pictures of Dr. Ambedkar on the cover; sometimes he was shown alone, sometimes with Ravi Das.[7] But negotiations with the Republican party leaders eventually broke down, and again, as in the English case, nomenclature was a significant point of debate. The Republican party people felt they could not join forces with a group called the Ad Dharm Scheduled Caste Federation. They would have been willing to accept the title Scheduled Caste Federation, since it was reminiscent of the old Ambedkar organization, but Jaspal and Hazara Ram refused to excise Ad Dharm from the name.[8] Nothing was said publicly against the RPI, but Dr. Ambedkar's picture was quietly dropped from the cover of the *Ravidas Patrika*. Behind the issue of names, of course, loomed the larger issue of social vision: the competition between secular and religious versions of ideal social order.

The Ad Dharm name, though it created difficulties for certain politicians, was a definite plus for the religious leaders whom Jaspal approached, and these he saw as his most important base of support. As old Hazara Ram counseled him, "a religious identity is necessary for gathering the people."[9] It was particularly crucial that he be able to attract the allegiance of Sarwan Das, the son of Pipal Das, whose *dera* at village Ballan not far from Jullundur is still the best known Ravi Das holy place in the Punjab. Sarwan Das had succeeded his father there and had taken on the status of Sant himself. He was a man of more far-reaching dreams, however, and hoped somehow to build a temple at the place of Ravi Das's birth, in Shri Govardhanpur on the outskirts of the city of Benares. The cornerstone had been laid in 1967, but money had run out;[10] he was in the process of building his own imposing temple in Ballan, and there was only so much money for temples. Mangu Ram Jaspal came to Sant Sarwan Das with visions of untapped British

7. *Ravidas Patrika* 1, nos. 3–10 (March 3–April 21, 1971).
8. Mangu Ram Jaspal interview, March 14, 1971.
9. Ibid.
10. Chajju Ram, general secretary (publisher), *Sri Guru Ravidas Trust Report, Shiv Govardhanpur, Varanasi, U.P.*, village Ballan, Jullundur, n.d. (hereafter *Ravidas Trust Report*), p. 5.

financial support for completing the Benares temple and for spreading the name and teachings of Ravi Das throughout the Punjab. The idea appealed to the Sant, and on the cover of the eleventh issue of the *Ravidas Patrika* a full-page picture of Sant Sarwan Das replaced that of Dr. Ambedkar.[11]

On December 13, 1970, the first big conference of the new Ad Dharm movement was held at Sant Sarwan Das's *dera* in Ballan.[12] The ostensible purpose of the gathering was to promote the temple in Benares, but as the speakers appeared it became clear that there were other issues on the agenda. One of the primary issues was the renewal of the *qaum* identity. Speakers affirmed that their people were not only separate from the Sikhs, but constituted a distinct community of their own. The old mythology of the Ad Dharm as the original religion of the primordial people of India was resurrected, and the crowds were admonished to keep their own religion and follow gurus of their own, such as Ravi Das, rather than wander off to the gurus of the Sikhs.[13] A great issue was made of the inclusiveness of Ad Dharm, and Rishi Valmiki, the patron saint of the sweeper caste, was given special prominence.[14] This emphasis on Valmiki had become necessary if the new Ad Dharm was to

11. *Ravidas Patrika* 1, no. 11 (April 28, 1970).

12. The Ballan conference is described at some length in the *Ravidas Patrika* issues following the conference—vol. 1, no. 45 (Dec. 22, 1970); no. 46 (Dec. 29, 1970); and no. 47 (Jan. 5, 1971), which has a special foldout section on the Conference: "Ad Dharmi Bharavi lai Subh Sundesh."

13. A long article in the *Ravidas Patrika* admonishes the Scheduled Castes to take advantage of India's freedom of religion and promote their own religion: "Was Ravi Das any less great than the other gurus?" (Bhajan Lal Saroie, B. A. Matric, Pind Sujon, "Dharmanchon Dharm Ad-Dharm," *Ravidas Patrika* 1, no. 44 [December 15, 1970]).

14. The inclusiveness of Ad Dharm and the equality of the followers of Rishi Balmik are consistently emphasized in the *Ravidas Patrika*. See, for example, M. R. Kataria, M.A., M.Ed., "Sarhe Balmik Bhara" (Our Balmik Brothers), *Ravidas Patrika* 1, no. 42 (Dec. 1, 1970), p. 4; and Harnam Singh Lakha (Mogawali) England, "Kuch Ad Dharm Bare" (A Few Things About Ad Dharm), in which he considers the Mazbi Sikhs, Ramdasias, and even the Ambedkar Buddhists as factions within Ad Dharm (*Ravidas Patrika* 1, no. 41 [Dec. 24, 1970]).

win the support of Chuhras, since over the years the term Ad Dharm had come to be construed narrowly as a caste name for some Punjab Chamars.[15]

As at the old Ad Dharm rallies, demands were made on the government, but they were specifically related to the new temple and the Ballan *dera*. The speakers asked for a better road and a bridge across the canal at Ballan, so that people could more easily reach the *dera*, and insisted that a better road be built in Benares to connect the Ravi Das temple there with Benares Hindu University and the rest of the city.[16] The highlight of the conference was an address by old Mangoo Ram, who told the crowds:

> Whatever rights we have now, it is because of the [original] Ad Dharm Mandal. . . . But the young people have not seemed to be capable of carrying the task which we started. . . . During the British rule, we were twice slaves: slaves of the British and slaves of the Hindus. We have gotten rid of the British, now we have to assert our own rights against the upper castes. . . . We were inspired by Ravi Das, Kabir, and Nam Dev. Hinduism is a fraud to us. Ad Dharm is our only true religion.[17]

The occasion served as the public launching for the new Ad Dharm Scheduled Caste Federation, and two new committees were set up.[18] One, the Managing Trust Committee, had specific responsibility for the Ravi Das temple to be constructed in Benares; the other was charged with the general task of organizing the Federation. Seth Kushi Ram was formally made chairman of the sixteen-member Advisory Committee, which had already been constituted, and other names were added, including those of Ishar Das Pawar, the official who had issued so many Chamar pass-

---

15. The emphasis on Balmik did not persuade everyone. Swami Shudranand, for example, refused to join the new Ad Dharm on the grounds that "it is only for Chamars." Interview with Swami Shudranand, May 15, 1971.
16. *Ravidas Trust Report*, p. 7.
17. Ibid., p. 9.
18. Ibid., p. 10.

ports, and representatives from various Valmiki *sabhas*, notably Om Prakash Gill, a member of the Jullundur Municipal Council, and old Fakir Chand.[19] The Advisory Committee drew its membership from Jullundur and Hoshiarpur districts and from Himachal Pradesh. Ad Dharmis from England were purposely excluded and charged instead to set up a support group for the Federation back in Birmingham.[20] The presidency of the federation fell by acclaim to Mangoo Ram, and Hazara Ram became its general secretary. For eighty-five-year-old Mangoo Ram it was a poignant occasion: "After twenty-five years, they are asking me to lead again."[21]

Soon after the Ballan conference there was a series of other conferences, some of which were aimed at stimulating greater government action. In January 1971, for example, there was a conference at Mukerian in Hoshiarpur district, in which demands were raised for Ad Dharm representatives to be included in the new Scheduled Caste Corporation then being established by the Punjab government, for the state welfare minister to be replaced, for land redistribution to move at a greater pace, and for the government's definition of poverty to be raised from a yearly income of Rs. 3,600 to 6,000. And the familiar call for Scheduled Castes to register their religion as Ad Dharm in the census was heard again.[22] This provoked Mangoo Ram to observe that "we're back to where we were in 1925."[23]

The return to 1925 meant a return to an emphasis on cultural identity and communal power. But the mere act of proclaiming these things did not turn them into reality, nor, for that matter, did the mere assumption of the name Ad Dharm restore the enthusiasm and effectiveness of the original movement. Mangu Ram Jaspal had managed to

19. The names are listed on a poster, "Ad Dharmi (Adivasi) Bharawi lai Subh Sundesh" (Good News for Ad Dharm Brethren), *Ravidas Patrika* 1, no. 47 (Jan. 5, 1971).
20. Mangu Ram Jaspal interview, August 1, 1971.
21. Mangoo Ram interview, January 29, 1971.
22. "Mukerian Kanfrans de Mate" (Mukerian Conference Resolutions), *Ravidas Patrika* 2, no. 1 (Feb. 9, 1971). Other meetings were held in Gurdrake (Kangra district) and Phillaur.
23. Mangoo Ram, January 29, 1971, interview.

gather an impressive constellation of names behind his efforts, but he never was able to foster much sense of community or even of common unity, and it was not long before much of his support in the Punjab disappeared. The Boota Mandi people were busy with their own Ravi Das cultural activities and Congress politics (which eventually followed Jagjivan Ram into the new Janata party). Sant Sarvan Das died in 1973, and his successor, Sant Hari Ram, was preoccupied with the temples he had to finish. Even among Jaspal's British colleagues fissures began to appear. He continued to publish the *Ravidas Patrika,* and it is still available today, although its circulation is still confined mostly to British subscribers: it is crowded with pictures of functions at the Ravi Das temple on Dudley Road in Wolverhampton. In 1977 Mangu Ram Jaspal managed to arrange a triumphant tour of England for his famous namesake—Mangoo Ram was ninety-one—and the Ad Dharm Federation continues to exist officially. But it has never been able to enlist the kind of enthusiasm that pushed the earlier Ad Dharm into prominence.

Conditions were different then. Several factors converged in 1925 in such a way as to make the movement possible: communal competition in the Punjab provided a favorable context, a new generation of educated youth had emerged which yearned for its own organization and ideology, and there was a growing momentum of lower caste movements throughout India. The new Ad Dharm movement in 1970 benefited to a degree from the first factor but lacked the other two almost altogether, the ambitious youth and the national momentum.

Later in the 1970s, however, these missing elements reappeared, as a glut of newly educated lower caste youth could not be assimilated into the government's reward system, and the new activist movements of lower caste youth that boiled out of Bombay and the state of Maharashtra threatened to expand into other parts of India. The most militant of the new Maharashtrian lower caste movements was one that deliberately took its name from a similar movement of militant Blacks in the United States; they called themselves the Dalit Panthers. The word *dalit* means "downtrodden" or "oppressed" and was preferred by the movement to any overt reference to their caste name, Mahar, the caste equivalent to Chamars in the Punjab. Their much publicized activities mainly involved protests against lower caste injustices and demands for greater government protection and benefits.[24] They called for a nationwide movement of Dalit Panthers, and elicited a response in the Punjab from at least one person, Santokh Virdi.

In 1974, when Santokh Virdi was a student at a college near his home village on the outskirts of the town of Phagwara, he organized a protest march among his fellow lower caste students against the police handling of an incident in which a person of lower caste had been killed while in jail.[25] When the local newspapers asked him what organization he represented, he told them "Dalit Panthers" without having any real idea of what the phrase meant; he had only read about their activities in the newspapers. The name stuck, and when Dalit Panther leaders in Bombay heard about Virdi's group they sent organizers to Phagwara and drew Santokh Virdi's Dalit Panthers into the national network. The movement lasted for several years, and after graduation from college Virdi and several of his friends worked full time as Panthers. There were only about twenty-five or thirty members of the group, all about Virdi's age, but they managed to attract some financial support and receive publicity for their protest marches. During Indira Gandhi's Emergency in 1976, Virdi's activism became politically suspect and he spent the year in jail. Virdi makes a sharp distinction between his Panthers and the old Ad Dharm movement, of which he is vaguely aware: "We're not like the Ad Dharm. Our movement is not religious, but revolutionary. For religion, let them go to Ravi Das."[26]

In the Boota Mandi section of Jullundur student-age activists have attempted to get their own militant movement

24. See "The Dalit Manifesto" informally published in November, 1973; "Dalit Panthers" in *Economic and Political Weekly* 9, no. 18 (May 4, 1974); and Gail Omvedt and Eleanor Zelliot, "Introduction to Dalit Poems," *Bulletin of Concerned Asian Scholars* 10, no. 3 (July 1978).
25. Interview with Santokh Virdi, Phagwara, August 28, 1978.
26. Ibid.

started, and they also have considered affiliating with the
Dalit Panthers. But they have been somewhat chary of establishing a linkage with the Maharashtrian movement and
have not wanted to abandon Ravi Das, as have other militants; hence they have founded a separate organization.
Still, they retain the word *dalit* in their name to show their
support for the national movement: Dalit Sangarsh Samiti
(Committee for the Struggle of the Oppressed).[27] Although
it was officially founded in 1974, the group did not come
together as a strong organization until 1978, when a burst
of lower caste activism in various parts of India had repercussions in the Punjab. The group held a large demonstration on August 15 of that year in support of naming a
university of Maharashtra after Dr. Ambedkar. The Dalit
Sangarsh Samiti has a varied list of officers and sponsors, including leaders from the three main lower caste communities in Jullundur (Megh, Chamar, and Chuhra) and from
all sections of the city. The main organizer is Sat Pal Mehay,
and once again there are familial connections to the Ad
Dharm: his great uncle was Sundar Das, the president of the
Ad Dharm movement's executive committee in the 1920s.
Sat Pal, a man in his late twenties who works for an insurance company, is a committed initiate into the Radhasoami
faith, but feels an active responsibility for helping his community. According to Sat Pal, the objects of the Dalit Sangarsh Samiti are to "fight the atrocities against lower castes,
spread Ambedkarism and the cultural heritage of our own
gurus, and protect the reservations for lower caste positions
in government jobs."[28]

Sat Pal's cousin, Manohar Lal Mehay, is about the same
age. He is not allowed to become directly involved in the
new organization because he is employed by a bank that is
under government control, and thus is subject to the prohibition of government employees from political activities.
But as a bright and thoughtful person, his leadership behind
the scenes counts for much among the younger educated
activists of his community. Manohar, who has already acquired a motor scooter, is married to an attractive woman

27. Interview with Sat Pal Mehay, August 22, 1978, and Manohar Lal
Mehay, August 19, 1978.
28. Sat Pal Mehay interview, August 18, 1978.

from an Indian family living in Kenya. If and when he abandons his managerial position in the Indian Bank he will be heir to much of the leather business in Boota Mandi. He is a reflective person, and tends to think toward the years ahead: Mangoo Ram and Swami Shudranand, the old Ad Dharm leaders, are his greatest heroes, and he wants in some way to continue their vision. Manohar has in mind a scheme to bring all of the Ravi Das *deras* in the Punjab, some sixty of them, under a central trust committee, somewhat like the Sikhs' Shiromani Gurudwara Parbandhak Committee. He reasons that the SGPC was the source of Sikh power and that only such an entity will make the unity of Ad Dharm similarly visible and potent. Once, in a conversation, he mused, as if talking to himself, "Which is the most useful for our community: religion or politics?" Then he answered his own question: "The thing that made the old Ad Dharm movement work was that it was both. It was proud of who we are, our culture, our religion; and it had some idea of who we might become."[29]

In the various initiatives of the present day the Ad Dharm movement has come full circle. The ideas that spawned it in 1925 live on in the minds of people like Manohar Mehay, who senses in a new generation the same concerns that exercised Mangoo Ram half a century before. The Punjab has changed, the nature of its politics has altered, the attitude toward untouchability has progressively improved, and opportunities for the lower castes have expanded exponentially. Yet the need persists for organizations of cultural and social regeneration which will mobilize lower caste people, provide a base of support for their claims, give them pride in who they are, and excite their imaginations about who they might become.

Earlier in the century the Ad Dharm moved from cultural solidarity to political engagement, a motion paralleled by lower castes elsewhere in India, including the Nadars of Tamilnad[30] and the Jatavs of Agra.[31] But now the trend has reversed, and in the new Ad Dharm there is again a great

29. Manohar Lal Mehay, August 20, 1978.
30. Robert Hardgrave, *The Nadars of Tamilnad*, Berkeley and Los Angeles, 1969.
31. Owen Lynch, *The Politics of Untouchability*, New York, 1969.

emphasis on cultural solidarity, a move echoed in the Valmiki Sabha. The Ambedkarites also have followed the same trajectory, shifting from a concentration on secular politics to the advocacy of a new religion. There are other movements, however, which have hewed more closely to their original goals: Radhasoami and Punjabi Christianity retain their cultural isolation as certainly as the Marxists remain committed to political encounter. Thus in the Punjab no simple line of development in lower caste organization and strategy has emerged. All of the old options are open, and each of them is still being employed. But one pattern is fundamental in every case: a deep yearning to reorder social values and create a world in which people do not have to endure a stigma attached to their names from birth. This is a yearning that touches religious depths, becomes fused with religious symbols, and takes life from social movements that seem for a while almost able to satisfy their expectations.

EPILOGUE: The Social Vision of Religious Movements

The current quandary faced by many young activists from Untouchable castes—whether to turn their people toward religious solidarity or toward political engagement—is an indication of how they, like preceding generations, have perceived these two elements of human identity and aspiration as being interdependent, even interchangeable. The old issues have a way of returning. And the interaction of religion and social vision has been a major theme in this study—sometimes dominant, sometimes muted, but heard time and again in the histories of the Ad Dharm and similar movements against untouchability in the Punjab in this century. The theme has been played in several variations. A central statement of it is that the lower castes perceive their oppression as stemming from a religious concept, untouchability, as much as from political circumstances. As a result they see freedom from oppression not only as liberation from old social alignments, but as a release from old religious ideas as well. A major variant on the theme is the lower caste perception that the fundamental divisions in society are religious. This implies that change in the social order will also have to have a religious character, hence the new religions of Untouchables. And we have also encountered two other variations: the facts that social ambitions tend to be couched in religious language, and that shifts in religious alignment pose serious threats to the old bases of social power.

Neither this theme nor its variations is limited to Untouchables in the Punjab, although we have focused our attention on them. What we have discovered in the Punjab may be found among restless members of lower castes elsewhere in India, and among those who have formed social movements of protest and vision elsewhere in the world. In this chapter, then, we will turn our attention outward to several areas of related concern. One is the continuing problem of integrating Untouchables and other minorities into the larger Indian society. Another is the danger some perceive in using religion as a strategy for social change. And finally there is the matter of religious movements in general, and the question of how adequately they are able to express and preserve social ideals.

UNTOUCHABLE RELIGION AND NATIONAL INTEGRATION

In 1930, when Dr. Ambedkar, Mangoo Ram, and Gandhi stirred the country through their arguments, fasts, and counter-fasts, they were trying to untangle a knot of fundamental confusion: whether the Untouchable castes were to be regarded as a part of the larger Hindu society or as a distinctly separate segment of it. That issue is still unresolved. In 1979, when the Indian parliament debated the proposed renewal of the welfare provisions for Scheduled Castes, it seriously discussed assigning welfare support and special allocations on the basis of economic need rather than lower caste membership, implying that there were no oppressed castes outside the society, only deprived classes within it. The question was this: Should people receive benefits simply on the basis of their cultural affiliations? The dilemma is not unlike the one current in the United States, where special allocations for ethnic minorities are seen, on the one hand, as acts of justice and, on the other, as a form of favoritism, antithetical to egalitarian ideals. In India that issue is compounded by the matter of caste and secularity: frightened at the divisive tendencies already present in Indian society, many people have worried that special benefits given on a caste basis would further entrench the concept of caste and strengthen the notion that some people are to be regarded separately. Even people of good will toward Untouchables, such as Gandhi, were loath to support special benefits for them, fearing separatism.

The old Ad Dharm movement took the opposite position. According to its reasoning, there was no danger of the lower castes drifting farther apart from Hindu society, since they had been banished from it already. The task of the Ad Dharm movement—along with that of Ambedkar, the Valmikis, the Dalit Sangarsh Samiti, the new Ad Dharm, and most of the other movements of Untouchables throughout India—was to retrieve the Untouchables from that social isolation. By solidifying and mobilizing the lower caste people, these movements hoped to engage the larger society and be able to demand Untouchables' rights. The approach worked. The new movements became power bases which could be used for political gain. Without the cultural solidarity which they provided, as we have seen in the later years of the Ad Dharm, political claims did not command the same force: the cultural symbols gave them strength. Yet such an approach may be challenged by those who adopt a broader perspective, those who are haunted by the issue that worries many Indians: whether cultural separatism is good for the society as a whole. Does it lead to social integration? Or is it ultimately fissiparous, divisive?

At first glance it seems hard to avoid the latter conclusion, since Untouchable movements assault the central values of tradition, and in such strident language at that. But if one looks more deeply one discovers elements that do indeed conduce to social harmony. Superficially, for instance, it appears that the lower caste movements adopt legendary heroes primarily in order to symbolize their separate cultural identities, but in fact such figures also face in the direction of the high tradition, so they provide linkages to the social and religious whole as well. This double valence in regard to exemplary or founding figures is perhaps most evident in the Valmiki Sabha, but one can see it also in the Ad Dharm and among the Ambedkar Buddhists, and it also contributes to the appeal exercised by Radhasoami over the lower castes. Rishi Valmiki, Sant Ravi Das, the

Buddha, and the medieval Sants on whom the Radhasoami movement relies are all respected figures in the Great Tradition of the Indian subcontinent. In identifying with them and holding them up for emulation, the lower castes have attempted to elevate their caste status in the eyes of themselves, their peers, and the wider society.

One way of looking at the lower caste use of these figures is to see it as Sanskritization, a term M. N. Srinivas coined to describe the process of emulating the customs of people with higher status in order to achieve greater status for oneself.[1] There is certainly an extent to which this concept applies, although in the case of the Ad Dharm one might call it Sikhization instead, because the role of Ravi Das parallels that of the Sikh gurus, and the new religion is as much an emulation of the religion of Sikhs as it is of Hindus. But in neither case did the Untouchables succeed in becoming like upper caste Hindus and Sikhs—if indeed that was even their intent—although their use of these linkage figures brought them closer to some aspects of the religious tradition of the mainstream. When one considers how great the distance was between the Great Tradition and the parochial religion of village Untouchables, as we discovered in chapter nine, one is impressed with how substantial an access to the larger culture the new movements were able to provide.

In supplying such linkages, of course, the leaders of these movements had little intention that their followers be led through them into a *normative* Hinduism. They positively despised many elements of the old cultural tradition and longed for nothing so much as its hasty demise, to be replaced by an alternative culture in which the lower castes would be seen in a more noble light. In the short run, it is true, the leaders' focus was often more narrow. They craved benefits for their own people and made use of these linkage figures principally in order to solidify support behind their aims. But such figures had a larger import as well: they hinted at a better society for all. And in directing attention to them, the leaders of the new movements not

1. M. N. Srinivas, "A Note on Sanskritization and Westernization," in M. N. Srinivas, *Caste in Modern India and Other Essays* (Bombay, 1962).

The Social Vision of Religious Movements 273

only made specific demands but also—sometimes inadvertently—prepared their followers culturally for access to a wider society, a society reformed. In so doing they created movements that made a significant contribution to societal integration: they provided new perceptions of the social whole, and offered new channels for incorporating the lower castes into them.

The members of the Ad Dharm, for example, wanted to be a *qaum* not so much to remove themselves from the larger society as to enter it—to enter a society they perceived as *qaumik*, comprising large religious communities. In the minds of most people in the Punjab, as we have seen, two different conceptions of society competed with each other: that of *dharmik* order (prevalent among Sikhs and Muslims as well as among Hindus), in which society was stratified into castes of differing statuses, and that of communal society, in which the divisions among Hindus, Muslims, and Sikhs were *qaumik,* each group being equal in status relative to the others. The Balmikis accepted the first model, the one that had traditionally been used to factor the lower castes in (or out), but altered it in such a way that their own caste emerged as nobler, Sanskritized. The Ad Dharm—though different aspects of its program suggest several models of society—tended to place greatest emphasis on the *qaumik* image of the social whole, with the qualification that its own community be added to the others as an equal. To insist on this point was to accept one of several possible ways of entering into *qaumik* society: it could have preferred instead to identify itself with one of the existent *qaums,* perhaps through the medium of the Arya Samaj in the case of the Hindus. The Ad Dharm leaders rejected this possibility, regarding the Samaj as an attempt to shore up upper caste communal identity. The Samaj's facade of social progress was seen as a device behind which lurked the unacceptable baggage of *dharmik* Hinduism—caste consciousness. If society was to be seen as *qaumik,* the Ad Dharm leaders reasoned, they could enter it only as a *qaum* of their own.

But this was not their only alternative. Another model of society found its way into the ideology and imagery of the Ad Dharm: the *panthik* model, an ideal society based on Hindu culture but thoroughly cleansed of caste. This model parallels more closely the aspirations of Untouchable movements elsewhere in India, where the communal model does not predominate as it does in the Punjab. By choosing Ravi Das as its central figure the Ad Dharm not only fastened onto Hindu culture in general but attached itself specifically to one part of that culture, the Sant tradition. The figure of Sant Ravi Das evoked the image of an egalitarian religious society, which many people, especially those of lower caste, associate with his teachings and those of the other medieval Sants. Even though Ravi Das was himself a Chamar, and therefore something of a patron saint for his caste, he has been enshrined with a tradition that symbolizes social equality for all Indians. The Sant tradition has come to be understood as the heritage of all, suggesting a harmonious model of religious society to which all have access.[2] This element of universal access was also one of the features that appealed to Dr. Ambedkar when he chose the Buddha as the central figure of his religion, for many have emphasized the anti-caste, or at least anti-Brahmanical, thrust of the Buddha's teaching.[3] In this respect the Buddha and Ravi Das are parallel figures.

Yet another model of ideal society hidden in the mythology of the Ad Dharm is one which it shares with the other "Adi" movements that appeared in the 1920s (the Adi Dravidas, Adi Hindus, and Adivasis), one in which formerly marginal persons became central. This may appear initially to be separatist in intent, for it regards the Adi people as the only true Indians, and thus contributes to the communal pride of those people who are now regarded as Untouchables and tribals. On the other hand, these "Adi" movements do imagine an ideal and integrated social whole: a society in which traditional hierarchy is turned upside down.

    2. It is this image of the Sant tradition which is promoted in V. Raghavan, *The Great Integrators* (New Delhi, 1966).
    3. For a discussion of this issue, see Padmanabh S. Jaini, "Sramanas: Their Conflict with Brāhmanical Society," in Joseph W. Elder, ed., *Chapters in Indian Civilization*, vol. 1, *Classical and Medieval India* (Dubuque, Iowa: Kendall/Hunt Publishing Company, 1970); and Romila Thapar, *Ancient Indian Social History: Some Interpretations* (New Delhi, 1978).

Those who would accuse lower caste movements like the Ad Dharm of separatism, therefore, are only partially correct, for each of the three models of society that have been operative in the thinking of the Ad Dharm—*qaumik, panthik,* and "Adi"-dominated—has its integrative side. Movements like the Ad Dharm have been separatist only to the extent that they have insisted on separating their followers from old ideas of social integration. They have tried to provide new visions of society in which the upper castes are also invited to play a role: albeit a more humble one than at present.

RELIGION AS A STRATEGY FOR SOCIAL CHANGE IN INDIA

The Marxists and the secular democrats of the Congress party have also propounded new visions of society, but they have not found it necessary to advocate a new religion. From their perspective the social program of the Ad Dharm and the other lower caste movements can be disencumbered of the religious language in which it was framed, without any loss. Indeed, a turn toward religion by a social group is regarded in some quarters of modern India as positively detrimental; some see it as communal, others as anti-political and reactionary. In each of these contentions one finds a central notion—that religion is illusory—and a common conclusion—that by attaching their political ambitions to religious ideas, the Untouchables are hitching their hopes to a dangerous star.

Such contentions reveal a common philosophical stance, an assumption about the separation of religious ideas and social realities that has developed in Western social thought. Yet India's social structure may be regarded as so fundamentally different from that of the West that these contentions simply do not apply. This is the implication of Louis Dumont's cross-cultural studies of Indian and Western social values.[4] This may also be a conclusion one draws

---

4. See Dumont, *Homo Hierarchicus* (Chicago, 1970), and *From Mandeville to Marx; the Genesis and Triumph of Economic Ideology* (Chicago, 1977). The latter is the first of a series projected as a comparison of Western social values with those of India.

in observing the importance of religion for the social strategies of the Ad Dharm and other lower caste movements. But this is not the only conclusion one may draw, and other aspects of the movements seem to be in disagreement with Dumont's observations. Inadvertently, in fact, these Untouchable movements provide an interesting addendum to Dumont's characterization of Indian religion and society, and a qualification to his theory.

Dumont has argued that the religious polarity of purity and pollution that underlies caste encompasses all other polarities, such as those of wealth and poverty, and dominance and submission. Thus, he understands the system of caste to be essential to the maintenance of Hindu society.[5] His argument has been vigorously debated, with the role of Untouchables central to the issue: some have regarded Dumont's position as implicitly Brahmanical, alien to the lower castes;[6] others have attempted to demonstrate that Untouchables do subscribe to the Hindu world view, confirming Dumont.[7] If the leaders of the Ad Dharm were to have entered into this discussion, they would likely have taken a position somewhere in between. They accepted the notion that Hindu society had been structured by caste, and that it was hierarchical, but they did not feel compelled to accept such a society for all time. Instead, they labored at constructing religious superstructures that would give coherence to their alternative visions of the social whole. For they knew—as if they had read Dumont—that if they wanted to create new societies, they would have to create new forms of religion as well.[8]

Their new religious visions were not all the same. Even in a single movement, as we have seen, several notions of social order could be broadcast, each with its accompany-

5. Dumont, *Homo Hierarchicus*.
6. For example, Gerald D. Berreman, "The Brahmanical View of Caste," in T. N. Madan, ed., *On the Nature of Caste in India* (Delhi, 1971).
7. For example, Michael Moffatt, *An Untouchable Community in South India: Structure and Consensus* (Princeton, 1979).
8. Dumont has affirmed that this approach could be understood from within his framework of interpretation (private conversation, Cambridge, Mass., June 7, 1980).

ing religious concepts. But in every case the so-called illusions of religion were functional illusions; they served to interpret and reform social reality. Even when an ideological formulation envisages a secular society in which religious forces are to hold no sway, that image requires an integrated vision of the social whole, an ideology which, by positing a coherent set of relationships between personal fulfillment and social goals, serves as a surrogate for religion.

In the Indian context both secular democracy and Marxist socialism have had to take on some of the roles of traditional religion in attempting to replace it as a value system. They have had to create their own symbolic linkages of action and ideals. Their task in that sense is not much different from that of the new religious movements, including both those which overtly promote social change—such as Gandhi's Sarvodaya movement, the Arya Samaj, the Muslim League, and more recently, the Shiv Sena—and those which disclaim political ambitions but encompass social ideas—such as Indian Christianity and the Radhasoami, Nirankari, Sri Aurobindo, and Satya Sai Baba movements. In each of these, both religious ideas and social values have been altered together, the one affecting the other. And that was precisely what Mangoo Ram and his Ad Dharm colleagues in the Punjab also had in mind.

Mangoo Ram created the illusion of a reality that had not yet come into being and through the sheer power of that illusion tried to make it materialize. At first it seemed a brazen pretense that the lower castes made up a separate religious community, but in the census of 1931 the idea was voted into reality: the Scheduled Castes were declared a religious community indeed, and one with a considerable following at that. In this case the government played a critical role, validating the claims of the movement from outside and providing the independent verification that gave an aura of reality to something that had only been asserted before. This was a role the government had played before when it, along with the world church, gave independent verification to the communal reality of Christianity in the Punjab, elevating it beyond the status of a lower caste movement. The Ambedkar movements, feeling the same need for external confirmation but unable to satisfy it through the political and cultural status quo, legitimized themselves by creating political parties of their own. And in Buddhism, the Ambedkarites have affiliated themselves with a religious tradition whose authority extends far beyond the subcontinent.

All these visions of new social order gained cogency when their claims were legitimated in some way from the outside. But these new ideas also achieved much of their power simply because they were conveyed whole, as religious movements, rather than dispersed in the partial social images presented by religious art, poetry, festivals, and isolated shrines, or parceled out among the programs of various political factions. Movements, particularly religious movements, restructure a total environment. Like drama, they provide for their participants the opportunity of stepping inside the dreams they project and living for a moment in the future, thus enabling their followers to share fully the movement's vision of social wholeness and personal fulfillment. The potency of the lower caste movements, therefore, had much to do with the nature of religious movements itself.

THE SOCIAL CHARACTER OF RELIGIOUS MOVEMENTS

In moments of candor Mangoo Ram has portrayed his role in the development of the Ad Dharm movement simply as that of a strategist who utilized whatever resources were available for mobilizing and inspiring his people: "I just called out the names of our gurus, and our people came running."[9] For some, a confession like this will confirm the suspicion that the Ad Dharm movement and religious movements like it are but the imaginative constructions of a few creative persons. The more cynical will take it as an illustration of a gloomier perspective, that religious move-

9. Mangoo Ram, February 2, 1971.

ments are callous fabrications of their leaders, constructs of clever ideas sold to an unsuspecting audience.

This latter view is not only cynical, however, it is uncharitable toward those who commit themselves to such movements. Indeed, both views discount the acts of creativity and daring involved in choosing to follow something new and uncertain. There is meaning in the old maxim that followers rather than leaders make a movement, for the ideas of the leaders, to ring true to the masses, must touch on deep and widely held sentiments to which their language gives expression. That is to say that regardless of Mangoo Ram's motives in calling out the names of the gurus, it was the response to his call that made the Ad Dharm a movement. Movements are not created by a few leaders: they are stirrings within the social order, upheavals of new awareness and aspiration. The very term "movement" rightly implies this genuinely social dimension. A movement, whether it is regarded as social or religious (we have used the terms almost interchangeably in this study, since religious concepts and social values are so closely intertwined in India), is a coherent shift in the direction of an alternative framework of understanding as undertaken by a social group.

The alternative frameworks which movements present challenge the normative order in two quite different ways: either reversing it or replacing it. Some of the movements that have appeared in this study, in particular the "Adi" movements and the Balmikis, have attempted to thwart the prevailing Hindu tradition as anti-structural reversals of ordinary social order: they have upended social roles and proclaimed the superiority of the lower castes. But most of the movements we have studied move in a counter-structural direction by boldly proclaiming their own alternative conceptions of the social whole.

In that respect these movements are a bit unusual, for most other religious movements in history display an anti-structural rather than a counter-structural character. They allow persons who participate in them an opportunity to deny society, at least for the moments that they spend in the movements, and thereby play an important role in the social fabric, balancing the rigid structures of social order with occasions and collocations that allow for greater freedom. The movements we have selected for this study, however, are all responses to the structural categories of caste and untouchability, so it is understandable that most of them are politically active—directly concerned with affecting social categories and eager to offer counter-structures of their own, rather than departing from them altogether in anti-structural ways. Yet in both kinds of movements we have observed a longing to participate in the mainstream of society and tradition.

That longing has led the movements to play a special role within society—to mediate between the marginal elements and the social core. Although the movements loudly proclaim their distance from the high culture, their very existence allows marginal persons to relate to it, even if only in anger. Perhaps, then, the concept of a cultural tradition should be conceived broadly enough to encompass the contributions of such movements as these to the cultural stream as a whole. After all, movements not unlike those we have studied in the Punjab emerged throughout India's history and have continually revised the tone of the cultural commonwealth. Many of them appear to arise at the periphery of society, but whether separatist or integrative, anti-structural or counter-structural, they interact with the mainstream and bring to the tradition, at various stages of its growth, the vitality of new ideas. Among the movements in our study, some have contributed considerably to the larger social consciousness of the Punjab: the Ad Dharm and the Valmiki Sabha have become a part of the texture of Hindu culture there. Others, the Christians and the Buddhist followers of Ambedkar, are still seen as standing apart; but in their case too, a definite impress of their liberal ideas on the wider culture has been felt.

Most movements, at least initially, hold out the optimistic hope that the challenge they present to tradition will be trenchant enough to replace it altogether, that their counter-structures (and sometimes their anti-structures) will in time become the prevailing structure. It is not an altogether unreasonable expectation: the Protestant challenge to Catholicism emerged triumphant and became the structural religion of many European societies, just as the medieval *panthik* movement of Guru Nanak to which the Sikhs trace their cultural origins blossomed into a major religious tradition. The prognosis for most movements is not so glorious, of course. Some wither into sects within the prevailing tradition, and some stabilize as cults isolated from it, most of them suffering a fate for which Max Weber coined a word: they routinize. Others simply fade in time and pass away.[10] But even those that atrophy or disappear often leave behind the traces of their ideals in the religious symbols and ideas which they once propounded and which have now become part of the mainstream or are kept alive in local cultures. In religion, the social vision lingers on.

At this writing, in 1980, only a few of the movements considered in this study retain significant strength. Others continue in vestigial form as sects or as cultic societies; none of them has fulfilled the promise of restructuring all of society as their bold pronouncements once advertised. Society in the Punjab has not fundamentally changed. Yet the visions of change and new social order persist, either in vestiges of the old movements, in the elements from them which have been appropriated into the main tradition, or in the religious imagery to which the lower castes subscribe.

In the case of the Ad Dharm we have seen all three: it has regenerated in a new form in recent years, it has contributed many of its leaders and social convictions to the major political parties, and it has substantially altered the significance of the traditional veneration of Ravi Das on the part of the lower castes. To revere Ravi Das today is to revere not only a saint but a social reformer; and each new generation that comes into contact with the spirit and language of the Ravi Das *deras* experiences the dreams that animated the Ad Dharm. In a similar way the lower caste devotion to Buddhism and the veneration of Ambedkar himself maintain the founders' social vision, even when that devotion

10. An interesting theoretical discussion of the life cycle of social movements and their absorption into the mainstream of societies is found in Neil Smelser, *A Theory of Collective Behavior* (New York, 1962).

and veneration seem to be the property of only a few. And Christianity, the Valmiki Sabha, and Radhasoami continue to excite the social imaginations of the lower castes in the Punjab. Religion keeps the old illusions alive and saves them for the future, when again they may be fused with political goals and generate a new social power. In the meantime, the religion of lower caste Punjabis holds another kind of social strength: the awesome force of great expectations.

APPENDIX A: The Early Life of Mangoo Ram

Mangoo Ram was born on January 14, 1886, in village Mugowal, Hoshiarpur district, where his father, Harnam Das, had left the traditional Chamar caste occupation of tanning and preparing hides and was attempting to sell tanned hides commercially.[1] Mangoo Ram's mother, Atri, died when Mangoo Ram was three, so the father began to depend heavily on his sons—Mangoo and an older and a younger brother—for assistance. Because the leather trade required some facility in English, Mangoo Ram's father was forced to rely on literate members of the upper castes to read sales orders and other instructions to him. In payment for their reading instructions for an hour, he would have to do a day of crude labor. For that reason, Mangoo Ram's father was eager to have his son receive an early education.

When Mangoo Ram was seven, he was taught by a village *sadhu*, and soon after attended a variety of schools in the Mugowal area (*tehsil* Mahalpur of district Hoshiarpur). He also attended school in a village near Dehra Dun, where his older brother had settled. In most of the schools, Mangoo Ram was the only Scheduled Caste student. He sat at the back of the class, or even in a separate room, and listened through the open door. When he attended high school in Bhajwara, he was forced to stay

1. This account of Mangoo Ram's life is based on the following sources: his brief autobiography, serialized in a Scheduled Caste newspaper in 1971 (Mangoo Rām Bāni Āddharm, Mugowāl, "Meri Videsh Yātrā utte Merā Jivan Birtānt" [My Foreign Travels and My Life Story, in Panjābi], *Ravidas Patrika*, Jullundur, vol. 2, no. 9 [April 6], no. 10 [April 13], no. 11 [April 20], no. 12 [April 27]); and on my seven recorded and transcribed interviews with Mangoo Ram cited in List of Interviews.

outside the building and listen to the classes through the windows. Once when he came inside during a heavy hailstorm, the Brahman teacher beat him and put all the classroom furniture, which he had "polluted" by his presence, outside in the rain to be literally and ritually washed clean. Nonetheless, Mangoo Ram was a good student: he placed third in his class in primary school. But whereas the other good students were encouraged to become *patwaris* ("village record-keepers") or to seek higher education, Mangoo Ram was encouraged to leave school and help his father at a more proper "Chamar task." In 1905, he did quit school; he married, and for three years helped his father develop their leather trade into a thriving business.

In 1909 America was in the air. Scores of upper caste farmers from Mangoo Ram's area of Hoshiarpur had gone to the United States, and those who had not gone were talking about it. Mangoo Ram decided to go also. He persuaded his father that it would be good for the business—he would send money back from America—and his father responded by giving him some of the savings from the family business. Amid assurances from some of the local *zamindars* ("landowners") that he would be employed by their relatives in America, Mangoo and two Chamar friends set off for the new world.[2]

The friends turned back, but Mangoo Ram persevered and arrived in California late in 1909. For four years he picked fruit for the former *zamindars* of his village who had resettled in the San Joaquin valley of California. He was also employed in a sugar mill. Mangoo Ram lived first in Fresno, then in Stockton, Sacramento, El Centro, Vacaville, Visalia, and again in Fresno.[3] He did indeed make money and sent his savings home.

2. Mangoo Ram also may have received loans from the local *zamindars* who were going to America, and wanted Mangoo Ram to work for them; thus, he may have been an indentured servant, a practice that was not uncommon within the immigrant community. However, since the first Punjabi immigrants came to California in 1904 as laborers themselves, it is unlikely that they owned land, as Mangoo Ram stated. More likely, the former *zamindars* from Mangoo Ram's village were labor contractors for American farmowners, and thus contracted for Mangoo Ram's passage and labor.

3. Mangoo Ram also mentioned in an interview (at Garhshankar, November 13, 1973) having lived in "Samar"; but I can find no indication of a town by that name having existed in California.

In 1913 some of the Punjabi settlers in California were forming a militant nationalist organization. Mangoo Ram joined this group, the Gadar movement, as a full-time worker in San Francisco. He was struck by the fact that, as he was later to say, "it was a new society; we were treated as equals."[4] There were not many Scheduled Caste persons in the Gadar movement, however; Mangoo Ram recalls only one other Chamar besides himself.

Initially Mangoo Ram played only a minor role in the organization, but in 1915 he volunteered to be one of five Gadarites to participate in a dangerous mission involving smuggled weapons shipped from California to the Punjab. He was chosen for the task by the man whom he identifies as the "leader of the Gadar party at that time," Sohan Singh Bhakna.[5] The secretary of the Gadar party, whom he remembers as "Godha," sent the five[6] to Los Angeles where they boarded an intermediary boat after collecting all their personal identification. For the rest of the saga, Mangoo Ram would be known by a Muslim pseudonym, Nizamuddin.

4. Mangoo Ram, interview on December 1, 1970. The Gadar movement was briefly described earlier in this book.
5. Sohan Singh Bhakna, a founder of the Communist party in the Punjab, was involved in the original organization of the Gadar party in Astoria, Oregon, but returned to India in July 1914. Lala Hardayal, who was the leading figure of the San Francisco circle, also had left the United States in 1914; and in their place Ram Chandra, Kartar Singh Sarabha, Gyani Bhagwan Singh, and others were sharing leadership of the Gadar party in 1915.

Mangoo Ram's other recollections about the Gadar party include the following: they published a magazine, *Gadar-di-Goonj;* they made a deal with the prime minister of Germany for support; and they sent a shipload of weapons, the *Kariamaru,* to India, which was arrested at Singapore. Mangoo Ram also recalls the Komagatamaru incident, in which Baba Gurdit Singh brought 450 Indians to Vancouver, and after the Canadians refused to let them land, they returned to India, where the British fired upon them in Calcutta harbor. All of these incidents are reasonably accurate, and have been described in detail in the published material relating to the Gadar party.

6. The other four, according to Mangoo Ram, were Hari Singh Badowalia, Charan Das, Harnam Das, and Mahesh Chandar (Mangoo Ram, "Meri Videsh Yatra," April 13, 1971). Government records indicate a "Gambhir Singh" (or "Raghbir Singh") rather than Mahesh Chandar, and Harnam Chand rather than Harnam Das; but the other names are the same.

According to Mangoo Ram, the intermediary boat took them to the Secrorro [sic] islands to rendezvous with the weapons boat, but after thirteen days a military ship from Sydney, the "Man of War," discovered them. Only through the timely intervention of an American warship were they spared. They went to Vera Cruz, Mexico, to receive rations.

There they finally connected with their weapons boat, the *Maverick*; they joined the crew, took on giant turtles for food, and headed for India.[7] They were halted again in Hawaii, where Mangoo Ram witnessed the eruption of volcanoes. Free again, they advanced a bit further, perhaps to Java or New Caledonia.[8] There the Japanese, on behalf of the British, imprisoned them for one year. Eventually, the British decided to hang them, but at midnight the night before they were to be hanged at dawn, fate intervened. The Germans spirited them away in the dark, and the five went their separate directions—Harnam Das and Charan Das to Bangkok; the others, including Mangoo Ram, to Manila. But again, according to Mangoo Ram's memory, the intervention of fate altered their plans. A typhoon appeared, and the ship went to Singapore instead, where British spies, Bela Singh and Bhag Singh, turned Mangoo Ram over to British authorities, who promptly ordered him to be placed before a cannon and shot. Again, however, the Germans whisked Mangoo Ram away, and again he was placed on a ship bound for Manila.[9] When Mangoo Ram arrived in the Philippines he read a news report in

---

7. According to the testimony of other Gadar party and German accomplices, in the trial of *U.S.A. v. Franz Bopp*, et al., 1917–1918, the story was somewhat different. There were two ships chartered by the Germans for sending Gadar arms to India. The *Annie Larson* was the intermediary ship which was to transfer the arms it had brought from San Diego to the *Maverick* during their rendezvous at the Coronado Islands. The rendezvous was unsuccessful; so the *Maverick*, with a cargo of only propaganda, set sail for India anyway. The five Indians on board (including Mangoo Ram) were apprehended when the ship stopped over in Java. Mangoo Ram's recollections apparently have confused the *Annie Larson* with the *Maverick*.

8. In interviews Mangoo Ram claimed that the British arrested them in Java and Sumatra; but in his articles, Mangoo Ram has written, in Gurmukhi script, *krailornian*, which might be Caledonia, or perhaps Carolinian. The government reports indicate they were captured on Java.

9. The only independent verification of this part of Mangoo Ram's story is the fact of the Gadarites' escape and their recapture; the following scholarly account, based on British government records, sums up the

the *Manila Times* indicating that he had been executed for treason by the British in Singapore. Mangoo Ram assumes that one of his captured colleagues had taken on his name to protect him, and that that man had been shot in his place. The news of his alleged death preceded him to the Punjab, where his wife heard the report and promptly married his younger brother, as custom dictated. In the meantime, Mangoo Ram was sequestered in the Philippines in a series of hideouts on various islands. Members of the Gadar party were his benefactors during this period, and Mangoo Ram remembers fondly their hospitality and friendship: he was no longer an Untouchable but a comrade in distress.[10]

The war ended in 1918, and the Gadar party was no longer quite the threat it was earlier when it enraged the British by compounding separatism with sedition through its liaison with the Germans. But Mangoo Ram decided to stay in Manila nonetheless. He met an American, a Mr. Johnson of Marshall Field and Company (a department store in Chicago), who hired him to work in an embroidery factory making shirts for the American market.[11] After six years of that Mangoo Ram was ready to return to India.

---

known information about the voyage: "On board the ship were five Indian revolutionaries from the Ghadar headquarters of San Francisco disguised as Persians. They were Hari Singh, Gambhir Singh, Harcharan Das, Harnam Chand and Mangu Ram. These persons carried an ample supply of revolutionary literature. . . . After some days the ship anchored off the Coronado islands, seventeen miles from San Diego, [then] . . . to proceed to Hilo port in Hawaii, for receiving further orders. . . . The Dutch authorities seized the *Maverick* and arrested the Indians at Anjer. Out of these five Indians four escaped from the custody of the Dutch. They were, however, captured on the coast of Sumatra during their flight and were taken to Singapore" (L. P. Mathur, *Indian Revolutionary Movement in the U.S.A.*, New Delhi: S. Chand and Co., 1970), pp. 112–115 *passim*.

10. Almost forty years later, he was still remembered by old Gadarites in California as "Bhai Mangoo Ram, Chamar, also known as Nizamuddin"; quoted in an article by Ranbir, "Duniya-ki Dusri Tarafse—Upne Bhai ke Nam, Pentiesvan Khat" (From the Other Side of the World—To My Brothers, Thirty-Fifth Letter), *Milap*, Jullundur, October 3, 1953.

11. According to Mangoo Ram, his Gadar connections were discovered while he was in the Philippines, and he was interned for six months during the Prince of Wales's visit to Manila in 1922. Mangoo Ram blames the Marshall Field people for exposing him.

Early in 1925 he set sail, this time on a more pleasant and uninterrupted trip. He arrived in Ceylon in the company of a Christian missionary he had met on board, then traveled through the subcontinent to the Punjab, visiting Madurai, Madras, Bombay, Poona, Sitara, Nagpur, and Delhi. He observed the conditions of the Scheduled Castes en route and was dismayed "to see our people being treated so badly."[12] At the Minaksi Temple in Madurai, for instance, he was told to be careful not to touch the *achut* (Untouchables): people assumed from his dress that he was of decent caste. By the time Mangoo Ram reached the Punjab he was convinced that there was need for social change, and wrote to Gadar party headquarters in San Francisco about the difficult conditions of the Scheduled Castes in India, announcing that their freedom was more important to him than that of the nation itself. According to Mangoo Ram, leaders of the Gadar party at that point designated him to work for the uplift of the Untouchables.[13] Thus, in a new context, the old revolutionary from Fresno continued the Gadar spirit.

Late in 1925, after his return to the Punjab, Mangoo Ram began teaching in a primary school in his home village of Mugowal, a school which Mangoo Ram claims he named the Ad Dharm School. It was in that school, on June 11 and 12, 1926, that Mangoo Ram convened the meeting that formally launched the Ad Dharm movement. Mangoo Ram was elected its first president, a title he has retained for the duration of the movement. In November 1926, when the Ad Dharm organization opened an office in the city of Jullundur, Mangoo Ram took up residence there, where he remained until he became active in politics in the 1940s, at which point he moved to the town of Hoshiarpur. Later, the newly independent government of India presented him with some land near Garshankar, not far away, which he developed into a small farm.

12. Mangoo Ram, "Meri Videsh Yatra," April 20, 1971.

13. Mangoo Ram did not pursue any of his former Gadar connections in the Punjab, to my knowledge, although he would have had ample opportunity to do so. Mangoo Ram said that Bhai Permanand was in charge of the Gadar party in Lahore when he was supposed to bring the weapons on the *Maverick*, but Mangoo Ram never contacted him when he finally did arrive (Mangoo Ram, interview on January 29, 1971). Through the years, Mangoo Ram has kept in contact with one of his fellow companions on the *Maverick*—Hari Singh, of village Badawal near Ludhiana (ibid.). Mangoo Ram also claimed to know the editor of

In 1977, after the Ad Dharm movement had been reestablished, and Mangoo Ram had been again elevated to leadership of the movement, his supporters sent him on a triumphant tour of communities of expatriate lower caste Punjabis in Great Britain. It was Mangoo Ram's first major voyage since returning from America, half a century before. For him the occasion was one of nostalgia, but also one of completeness, for it enabled him to mark the closing phase of his long public career with a trip abroad, just as he had opened it in a similar way many years before. It was to be the last great event before his death on April 22, 1980, at the age of 94.

The pattern of expatriate experience leading to nationalism and political activism when the expatriates return home is replicated in the personal histories of other leaders: the lives of Gandhi, Sri Aurobindo Ghose, Dr. B. R. Ambedkar, the Gadar militants, and other Third World figures such as Kwame Nkrumah and Ho Chi Minh. Seldom, however, has a personal history held such dramatic extremes—from international to provincial politics, from leadership in a secular movement to leadership in a religious one, from an anti-British to a pro-British stance (and then back again), from being a banished Untouchable to being an imposing political figure. The sheer diversity of Mangoo Ram's colorful life would invalidate any claims he might have wanted to make about being a man of the people. His roots were in the village culture of the lower castes, but experience forged him into a modern man. Ultimately, his characteristics were modern ones: eclectic, assertive, uncompromising, optimistic. So also were those of the movement he led and of the proud new breed of ex-Untouchables he came to represent.

Naya Yug, a Ludhiana newspaper founded by old Gadarites; the editor known to Mangoo Ram was Nidhan Singh Alam, who Mangoo Ram claimed first informed Mangoo Ram about the Congress plot to divide up the Scheduled Castes among Hindus and Sikhs—the information which, according to one statement of Mangoo Ram, provoked the founding of the Ad Dharm (Mangoo Ram, interview on April 17, 1971). Whether or not he was in contact with the Gadar people in the Punjab, Mangoo Ram apparently continued to have respect for the party, and considered himself to be carrying on Gadar goals in Ad Dharm; when asked to list the great leaders of India, Mangoo Ram named persons associated with Gadar and similar movements: Lala Hardayal, Barkat Ali, Lala Bhagwan Das, Ajit Singh, and Inder Pratap (Mangoo Ram, interview on November 13, 1973).

APPENDIX B: The Report of the Ad Dharm Mandal, 1926–1931

When this report was published, on May 15, 1931, the Ad Dharm movement was entering its most vibrant phase. It had consolidated its leadership, expanded from central Punjab to the westward desert and eastward mountain areas, and proven its existence as a separate religious community by marshaling almost half a million adherents to record their religious preference as "Ad Dharm" in the 1931 census. It was with a sense of triumph, then, as well as with a desire to propagate its faith even further, that the leadership of the movement compiled this, its first and only report. The language is lively, compelling. The authorship is anonymous, but the style and ideas indicate that the central figure in the movement, Mangoo Ram, was close to the writing.

The report purports to cover the period from January 1926 to April 30, 1931. Its eighty pages contain diverse materials compiled with several purposes in mind. One purpose was financial: to report the sources of funds and their outlay, perhaps in order to quell any suspicion that the movement had received government or other external support, or that their funds had been improperly used. This financial statement runs to some dozen pages. Another thirty pages list the branches of the movement, and members of various committees, a total of over five hundred names with addresses appended, as if to prove the movement's claim to a vast organizational network. Another eight pages are demands for equal rights and economic benefits, directed to the government.

The main part of the report, however, occupying almost thirty pages, is a general statement of the movement as a new religion: its ideology, its mythic origins, its beliefs and symbols, its hopes for the future, and the demands it makes on its followers. In sum, it portrays the new world and the new world view which the Ad Dharm offered to an oppressed but restless community of Untouchables in the Punjab, expressed with a sense of urgency and excitement. In this appendix are included several sections of this general statement: the myth of origins and the religious and moral requirements for followers of the Ad Dharm faith. I have made a translation of the entire report available elsewhere.[1]

The Kishan Steam Press, on Railway Road, Jullundur, printed a thousand copies of the original report. I was able to locate only one extant copy, however, which was made available to me by L. R. Balley of Jullundur, whose grandfather, Inder Ram, was a missionary in the movement. I wish to express my great appreciation to Mr. Balley for his kind cooperation. The original version, written in Urdu, in Arabic script, and containing a polyglot vocabulary of Urdu, Hindi, Punjabi, and English words, was translated with the assistance of Surjit Singh Goraya and Hassan Hamdani. I accept responsibility for this final English version, however, and any mistakes it may contain.

PREFACE

[p. 1] In India[2] one-quarter of the population is Untouchable,[3] people who have been enslaved by the high caste Hindus for the last 5,000 years. These poor people have been dethroned from their political and religious status to such an extent that their souls have been crushed—crushed so hard that they have lost their identity. If you reflect upon these people's condition, you will realize everyone knows about it, even little children, all over the world. To shed more light on their beginnings is like rechewing old food. The historians have written tons of books about it, enough books to fill London. We are not concerned about

1. Juergensmeyer, "Political Hope," Appendix F.
2. The classical term, *Bhārat*, is used; elsewhere the Report uses the term *Hindustan*.
3. *Achūt*, a term which in other contexts also means "untouchability."

the historical origins of the Untouchables; we should put the Untouchables on the path of progress rather than telling them about their past and inflaming them. We are not trying to inflame the Untouchables into a holy war against any other community [*qaum*]. That would be twice as bad as untouchability. That is why we do not join those organizations which say they want to do away with untouchability and the whole system of castes; these movements would mislead the Untouchable into obliteration.

The fact of the matter is that before the British, all other groups ruling India mistreated the Untouchable. The present plight of the Untouchable is due to the way these invaders treated them. The Untouchables are the descendants of the original people. They are the original children of paradise [*dharm-khand*] and the motherland, and were living a peaceful and spiritual life in their own land when they were attacked and slaughtered with a double-edged sword by the bloodthirsty invaders. However, as Kabir has said, "whoever cuts someone else's throat will someday have his own throat cut."

[*p. 2*] Today the slayers are now lying along with their victims, having been slaughtered with Fate's own[4] double-edged sword: they have fallen under the rule of a government which has taken practical steps to crush the old order. Untouchability is so well entrenched that it seems no power in the world can shake it. After all, as Guru Nanak has said, "Whatever is done, is done by Him, there is nothing in the hands of us human beings."

Anyone with an inclination to oppress the Untouchables has been, is now being, or will be punished by Fate. It is our belief that all creatures are created by God [*parm-ātmā*], and if the strong oppress the weak, then let the task of punishment rest in the hands of God [*ishwar*]. We should go about our work. Unfortunately, the proud people of the high castes are miles away from these ideals. For this reason there have not been any significant achievements by the organizations which claim to assist the Untouchables. The problems of the Untouchables cannot

4. *Qudrat kā mēlā*. The term refers to a primordial arbitrating and creative force; elsewhere translated also as "Nature."

be understood by the high caste Hindus. So the Untouchables lie in the same miserable condition as before.

These are the organizations that are supposedly helping the Untouchable, but in fact are not: *Antaj Uddhār* (Uplift of the Lowborn), *Patat Uddhār* (Uplift of Untouchables), and *Dayanand Dalit Uddhār* (Swami Dayanand's Uplift of the Oppressed). These organizations are run by high caste Hindus. They collect money like beggars, but they spend it for themselves. They do not spend it for the Untouchables. Ninety-nine percent of the Untouchable people do not even know the names of these organizations. But if you read their reports, they give exaggerated claims of their achievements. The truth is that these organizations are composed of selfish people.

[p. 3] Untouchables have three powers: communal pride [*qaumiat*], religion [*mazhab*], and organization [*majlis*]. These are what everybody wants to take away from us. Whenever they can, these "generous" reform groups try to destroy these powers in order to absorb the Untouchables.

The Ad Dharm Mandal, which was founded in 1925 as a collective organization of all Untouchables in the Punjab, has been actively opposing all these selfish organizations. This Mandal is the protector and defender of these three powers; it has a concrete program. These high caste Untouchable organizations, who shed crocodile tears over the Untouchable, have tried to destroy the Ad Dharm Mandal. They have seduced and bribed some of our preachers [*prachārak*]. But the Ad Dharm Mandal's roots go too deep; we cannot be shaken by this.

A society based on truth cannot be shaken. Despite attacks from all directions, it has led Untouchables to progress step by step. The Ad Dharm has presented the government with many deputations and memorials. For
[p. 4] example, a deputation was sent in 1928 to John Simon, Royal Commissioner. Another deputation was sent to His Excellency Sir Geoffrey Fitzroy de Montmorency, K.C.T.E., K.C.V.O.C., B.E.M.A., I.C.S., Governor of Punjab, Lahore, in Jullundur, 12 October 1929. This day may be marked as the birthday of Untouchables as a people, for we were then recognized as human beings. We

received rights we never had before: we got an 8 percent quota for legislative seats in the legislative assembly of India, and in many provincial assemblies as well. The local government also has recommended 10 percent. The Round Table Conference in London also mentions the need for the rights of the Untouchables. The government's Education Department has also provided many facilities and has been very helpful.

All these items are facts, not exaggerated claims on paper. These are resolutions which have been passed, and regulations which have been put into effect. The day is not far away when the British government will implement these plans.

[p. 5] In addition to the political aspect of Ad Dharm Mandal, Jullundur, which has been very successful, there is even a greater emphasis on social reform. The religious and organizational status of the Untouchable has been raised through our efforts. For example, we are getting education for Untouchable children. As one wise man of the Punjab put it, "Ad Dharm has performed miracles beyond imagination." To us, no talk is worthwhile without action. We are not interested in simply collecting money the way the other groups are doing. They collect money for their own luxuries, for their own names. Our principle is solely humanitarian. As someone has said, "It is only the struggle for humanity's improvement which is worth the pain of having been created." And as Guru Ravi Das[5] has said, "for the spirit of sympathy, the whole body is created."

In short, the founding of the Ad Dharm Mandal is for humanitarian purposes and to fulfil our duty to humanity. We carry the banner of the downtrodden people, and we devote our entire lives to the cause, so that future generations may follow in our footsteps and follow the cause, a cause which has long been neglected. We have made this report for the sole reason of explaining our purposes. So if people ask, "Who are these people? Where did they come from? What are they doing?" they will be able to know. As someone has said, "Those who are truthful do not shout about it. The truth itself is witness to their achievements."

---

5. The name is written with honorifics: Sri Guru Ravi Das-ji.

SECTION I.
The Rise and Fall of the Adi People

[p. 6] Nature [*Qudrat ka Mela*] created human beings from the original source [*adi*] at the time that it created all beings in the earth. The knowledge of moral behavior [*karm-dharm*] was also given to them at that time by Nature. Nature made humans superior to animals, but among humans all were equal.

In the beginning, when Nature created human beings, there was no discrimination. There were no differences and no quarrels. In particular, there were no such concepts as high or low caste. God [*ishwar*] was meditating; all was in harmony. Everyone believed in one *dharm* which Nature had given them through intellect and knowledge; this *dharm* was Ad Dharm. Nature gave birth to these original people in the valleys of the original mountains— the Himalayas.

Later on, the original [*adi*] people spread out. Some migrated to mountains, others to plains. As their numbers increased, so did the search for better places. Some lived in the caves, the mountains, and the plains of Central Asia and the Caucasus mountains. Some groups settled in Europe. Some groups came back to the original land after some time, and were known as Aryans. But there was another group which did not go to the Caucasus mountains or Central Asia, but settled instead in the plains near the original mountains, in the original land. These people are the original [*adi*] people.

[p. 7] Before the Aryans returned, our forefathers had great success in such fields as industry, arts, science, liberal arts, physical and spiritual arts. In brief, they were the most civilized people in the world at a time when others knew nothing of civilization or of science. Our people excelled in knowledge. And in those places where the rivers of knowledge are flowing today, there were only primitives. They lived in trees and caves, ate bark and leaves, and had no spiritual life. They lived as shepherds and hunters and had no sense of communal identities [*qaum*]. This was their condition when the original land, India, was at the peak of civilization. Peoples of the world considered our land the crown of success, and paid tribute to us and our achievements. They respected and bowed down to our kings. There was no enemy, no foe, no fear of foreign invaders, and no sign of internal dissention. As the great Kabir has said, "First God created his light, and from that every human being was created."

During this time of great achievement the Aryans heard about the original land's civilization and came there. They learned the art of fighting from the local inhabitants, and then turned against them. There were many wars—six hundred years of fighting—and then the Aryans finally defeated our ancestors, the local inhabitants. Our forefathers, the inhabitants of our glorious motherland, were pushed back into the jungles and the mountains. Some of them stayed and asked for mercy; they were enslaved. We do not regret that our forefathers were defeated by the Aryans: it mattered little. For in the following years the country was invaded many times, and always the invaders were victorious.

Our forefathers were not only enslaved, they were mistreated. The victors acted like conquerors. The Aryan government practiced so much cruelty and injustice that the original people forgot their own identity. Whatever signs of their glory remained were destroyed. The Aryans exaggerated their own achievements, and the achievements of the local inhabitants were tossed into the dust.

[p. 8] In this period of time Manu was born. He made some regulations and imposed them on the original people. For example, it was he who started the idea of discrimination, stating how different people were to be treated differently. Such principles of injustice were adopted as values by the Aryans to enslave the local people. Books were written to teach humiliation and were taught in the schools as textbooks. Every means of humiliation was used.

From that time onward, hundreds of governments have come and gone, but the original people are still not free. From that time to this time Hindu Aryans have suppressed the original people. Not a single Hindu Aryan has shown the correct path of freedom to these suppressed and oppressed people. On the contrary, each generation has been worse than the one before, and the condition of the original people has gone from bad to worse. Always the Aryans followed the rules of Manu.⁶

Finally Fate decided to change the condition of these poor people. After the Hindu Aryan rule, which was tyrannical, unjust, and discriminatory, the age of Islam came. The Muslims ended the unjust Aryan control and Manu's philosophy with it. They became sympathizers rather than tyrants. They tried their best to get rid of discrimination—this caste system. But unfortunately Hinduism affected Islam, and it too became the prey of discrimination.

[p. 9] After the rise and fall of Islamic government, the flag of British rule began waving in this country. When the British took power, they tried to end the tyranny of injustice and lay the foundations of peace. At about the same time there was a Sikh government in the Punjab, but it did not last very long, because of its tyranny. The people preferred the rule of the British to that of the Sikhs.

Even after the British government was established, the Hindu Aryans and the Sikhs did not change their attitudes. They continued to discriminate against people on the basis of so-called high caste and low caste. They continued to trap people in the cage of discrimination. At this time Christianity came to India. It tried to attract all communities, and especially the low castes, because Untouchables were an orphaned people.

[p. 10] Swami Dayanand saw the progress of Christianity and considered it a threat to Hinduism. He realized that Christianity was digging a hole in the foundation of Hinduism which would destroy Hinduism's whole building. The Swami tried to think of a way to keep the Untouchables within Hinduism. He had to face much resentment from other upper caste Hindus in trying to do this, and did not succeed in his purpose. The Swami was intelligent and farsighted, a true patriot of the Hindu religion [*mat*]. He realized that without a Hindu government the Untouchables were no longer under Hindu power, so he

6. The term *Manu-bhagwan* is used, suggesting that Hindus regarded Manu as a god.

founded an organization called the Arya Samaj. Its sole purpose was to bring all the Hindu organizations together so that the Untouchables would not leave their ranks. They used many false fronts to keep the foundations of the Hindu caste system together.

The Arya Samaj established many other organizations. They preached, they formed new societies, they started the whole movement of reconversion [*Shuddhi*]. They tried everything to obliterate the Untouchables. They seduced thousands of Untouchables in the net of reconversion. They conjured up all sorts of hypocritical arguments, saying that Untouchability was over and there was no discrimination. The poor Untouchable was trapped again by the Hindu Aryan, like falling into the clutches of elephants' teeth. The fact was that the Hindu Aryans were still followers of Manu, full of discrimination. The Untouchables realized they were trapped by these Hindu Aryans, so they wanted organizations of their own. The Untouchables themselves started taking an interest in their own welfare; they did not trust the high caste Hindus. Organizations were made, societies were formed, they chose their own gurus.

So in the beginning of 1925 a society was formed with the name Ad Dharm: Rishi Valmiki, Ravi Das, Kabir, and Nam Dev were named as founders.[7] The first meeting was held in the village of Mugowal, Thana Mahalpur, tehsil Gahrshankar, Hoshiarpur district, on 11–12 June 1926, under the chairmanship of Mangoo Ram.[8] The meeting was attended by people from all sections of the Punjab. All Untouchables attended: Chuhras, Chamars, Ravidasis, Sansis, Bhanjres, Ghadhilias, Burrs, Julahas, Meghs, Chambars, Kabirpanthis, Mahashas, Doms, and other castes. And there were other respectable people in addition to Untouchables, people from other communities: Christians, Sikhs, Muslims, Arya Samajis, and Sanatanis. With all groups present it was a great success. Represen-

---

7. All of them legendary figures in lower caste religious traditions. The honorifics, Maharaj and Bhagwan Satguru, accompany the names of Kabir and Nam Dev respectively.

8. Again there are honorifics: Shriman Babu Mangoo Ram.

[p. 11] tatives of the Untouchables presented their positions eloquently and loudly. They told about all the hypocritical religions [*mazhab*], exposing them for what they are. But the representatives of organizations from the other religions criticized the Ad Dharmis strongly. After a lot of debate and argument, and inspired by the teachings of Rishi Valmiki, Ravi Das, Kabir, and Nam Dev, they decided that the Untouchables should be called Ad Dharm. And from that day on the organization has been called Ad Dharm. Everyone praised the decision; they shook the heavens with cheers. It seemed as if an old tree had come alive, or as if an old flower had burst into bloom. On that day, a completely downtrodden community [*qaum*] began calling itself Ad Dharm.

One hundred distinguished committee members were appointed, and Jullundur was chosen as the headquarters. The full name of the society is: Ad Dharm Mandal of Punjab, Jullundur City.

The Resolutions Passed at Mugowal:

1. a. We declare to the government and all the Untouchable brotherhood that the Ad Dharm Mandal has been formed.
   b. Our greeting is "Jai Guru Dev."[9]
   c. Our faith [*itqad*] follows the teachings of the Ad Prakash.[10]
   d. Our sacred word is *soham*.[11]
2. The founders of our religion are Rishi Valmiki, Guru Ravi Das, Maharaj Kabir, and Bhagwan Sat Guru Nam Dev. And the name of the founders' scriptures has been established as Ad Prakash.

9. Literally, "victory to the divine gurus" or "victory to the divine Guru." In accord with the *sant* tradition generally, the phrase *guru dev* can refer either to the four figures to whom the Ad Dharm looks as founders—Rishi Valmiki, Ravi Das, Kabir, and Nam Dev—or to God himself, the great guru.

10. A number of honorifics are used in the original designation, *Shri guru ad prakash asankh deep granth,* and the term for scripture chosen to characterize the collection is that used by the Sikhs: *granth.*

11. A sanskrit phrase found in the Upanishads, meaning literally "I am it."

[p. 12]

3. This conference represents all districts of the Punjab, and it appeals to all Untouchables in the Punjab to call themselves Ad Dharmis.
4. All the Untouchable brotherhood [*biradari*] should forget about caste and quarrels and get along together. They should not fight with each other. Rather, all Untouchables should start eating together and have social relations with each other. They should eat and drink together.
5. If some other community [*qaum*] attacks an Ad Dharmi, the Ad Dharmis should defend each other.
6. All Ad Dharmis should follow the *rishi*, the *gurus*, the *bhagats*, the *mahatmas*—all the great religious leaders. True worshipers of these saints will not believe in idol worship or the caste system, and will not think some people's practices are better than others!
7. All girls and boys of the Untouchable brotherhood should have compulsory primary education.
8. The *granths* and *shastras*[12] which show Untouchables as slaves should be boycotted. To follow the teachings of such books is a mortal sin.
9. It is legal to eat with Ad Dharmis. Others should eat from Ad Dharmis' hands. And Ad Dharmis should be willing to eat with those who are willing to eat with them.
10. The Minister of Education of the Punjab Government, Lahore, should give special scholarships and education for Untouchable children. Because of our poverty we cannot bear this expense.

[p. 13]

11. Our children should be taken care of by the government, since private schools do not help us or encourage the admission of our children. We should get the same grants that others get, and special schools should be set up for Untouchables.
12. We are agriculturalists; we know our work well. But we are not paid enough in agricultural wages. We cannot take care of our families properly. Vacant

---

12. *Granths* refer to the scriptures in the Sikh tradition; *shastras* refer to sacred writings in the Hindu classical tradition.

lands should be given to the Untouchable community [achut qaum].

13. The government should treat agriculturalists from the Untouchable class on a par with agriculturalists from other communities [qaum], especially in Lyallpur, Sheikapura, Sargoda, Montgomery, and Multon. In these districts there should be more land for Untouchables and more employment.

14. Untouchables should be able to own the houses where they live. The term *rayit-namma*[13] and similar terms should be eliminated. The Land Transfer Act should not apply to Untouchables.

[p. 14] 15. We are not Hindus. We strongly request the government not to list us as such. Our faith is not Hindu but Ad Dharm. We are not a part of Hinduism, and Hindus are not a part of us.

16. Ad Dharm should be listed separately in the census and in other ways be given rights equal to Hindus.

17. We want proper representation on municipal councils and district councils, on the Legislative Assembly, the police and military, and in every other department. We should be separately represented among the officers of these groups as well.

18. India should not be given independence until the Untouchables are free and equal. Otherwise it would be a disgrace to the British rule.

19. The Dayanand Dalit Uddhar Mandal (Hoshiarpur), Patat Uddhar Mandal, Antaj Uddhar Mandal, Achut Uddhar Mandal, and Lahor Achut do not represent Untouchables. They are simply used by upper castes to increase their own power. Ninety-nine percent of the Untouchables have never heard of these organizations. They have been formed by the upper castes for their own interests, and the government should be aware of it. The government should not consider these people to be our representatives.

[p. 15] 20. Red color is the symbol of the Ad Dharm. It is the color of the original inhabitants; the Aryans took it

13. A term used to designate the servant-master relationship.

and prohibited Untouchables from wearing it. We request the government to allow us to wear red colors. In fact, we insist on it: red is our rightful color.
21. Texts like the Laws of Manu, which treat Untouchables as slaves, should be banned and removed. These books have been obstacles in our progress.
22. The city of Jullundur has been chosen as our headquarters, and the government is notified to send any announcements, important documents and correspondence for us to the Ad Dharm Mandal, Jullundur City.
23. This conference assures the government that we Untouchables are true supporters of the English government, true patriots. We have been, are, and will in the future remain loyal well-wishers of the government.
24. All Ad Dharmis should act on these principles. It is their duty to ask their Ad Dharmi brothers to follow them also.
25. The government of the Punjab should issue strict warnings to all branches of government that no one has the right to use Untouchables without paying wages.

[p. 37] *The Basic Principles of Ad Dharm*

1. The essential teachings of the Ad Dharm will always be the same: no one can change them. They can stay alive and persist only through the help of a guru.
2. Every man and woman belongs to the faith, but they may not know it. To live without a guru is a sin.
3. A guru should be someone who truly and rightly knows the teachings of the previous masters. He should be able to distinguish between falsehood and truth. He should be able to bring peace and love within the community.
4. Everyone should be instructed by the lives of previous masters; progress comes from following the masters' examples. The practices of previous masters should not be abandoned. This leads to progress.

5. There should not be any discrimination in regard to eating with other castes.
6. Ad Dharmis should abstain from theft, fraud, lies, dishonesty, looking at someone else's wife with bad intentions, using anything which brings intoxication, gambling, and usurping other persons' property or belongings. All of these things are against the law of nature and therefore the law of Ad Dharm.
7. Every Ad Dharmi has the duty to teach his children current knowledge and also to teach them to be obedient to the present king.
8. Every Ad Dharmi should read the Ad Prakash and act upon it. This is a foremost duty.
9. Ad Dharm does not believe in the caste system or any inferiority or superiority of this sort.
10. To learn and seek knowledge, and to learn and seek progress is compulsory for every man and woman.

[p. 38] *The Duties of the Ad Dharm Organization:*
1. To publicize and propagate Ad Dharm.
2. To take pride in Ad Dharm.
3. To promote the use of the name of the community [*qaum*] and to use the red mark, which is its sign.
4. Ad Dharmis should try to retrieve any property of fellow Ad Dharmis that has been usurped.
5. We should distinguish among Hindus, Ad Dharmis, and the other communities [*qaum*] of India.
6. Those books which have created the problem of untouchability and led to discrimination—books such as the Laws of Manu and other *shastras*—should be completely boycotted and abandoned.
7. We should celebrate the festivals of our own gurus and follow our faith to the utmost.
8. Abandon idolatry.
9. Receive education for ourselves and others in the brotherhood.
10. Boycott those who curse us as "Untouchables" or discriminate against us.

11. Bring all demands of Ad Dharmis before the government.
12. Abandon expensive marriage and the practice of child marriage.

[p. 39] *Ad Dharmi Commandments:*
1. Each Ad Dharmi should know everything about the faith.
2. For the betterment and salvation of one's body—physical and spiritual—one should recite the word *soham*.
3. Each Ad Dharmi should remember Guru Dev for half an hour each morning or evening.
4. When Ad Dharmis meet, their greeting should be "Jai Guru Dev."
5. We should be true followers of the founders, Rishi Valmiki, Guru Ravi Das, Maharaj Kabir, and Bhagwan Sat Guru Nam Dev.
6. A guru is necessary, one who knows about previous gurus and has all the capabilities of being a guru.
7. The wife of a guru should be regarded as one's mother, and the guru's daughter as one's sister.
8. Devotion to one's wife should be a part of one's faith, for therein lies salvation.
9. Every Ad Dharmi should regard his wife as his only wife, and every other woman as his sister or mother.
10. Every Ad Dharmi should abstain from theft, fraud, lies, dishonesty, and usurping the property of others.
11. One should not cause someone else heartache. There is no worse sin than this.
12. Every Ad Dharmi should enthusiastically participate in Ad Dharmi festivals and rituals.
13. There should be equally great happiness at the birth of both boys and girls.
[p. 40] 14. After the age of five, every boy and girl should be given proper religious teaching.
15. Extravagent expenses at weddings are useless. Every marriage should be conducted according to the rituals of our tradition.

16. Ad Dharmis should marry only Ad Dharmis. To marry someone outside Ad Dharm is not legal, but if someone does marry an outsider, he or she should be brought into the faith.
17. All Ad Dharmis, both men and women, should be obedient to their parents.
18. After the death of both parents it is the duty of each Ad Dharmi to cook food and distribute it among the poor.[14]
19. The dead should be cremated, except for those under the age of five, who should be buried.
20. Ad Dharmis do not follow any other law except their own.
21. In the Ad Dharm faith only one marriage is allowed, but a husband may marry after the death of his wife. Also, if the first wife does not bear children, the husband may take another wife, provided he has the consent of the first wife. If this happens, the first wife remains a legal wife, with all the rights she had before.
22. Ad Dharmis should marry their children to the Ad Dharmis of surrounding areas.
23. A girl should be more than twelve years old at the time of the marriage. The boy should be four years older than the girl.
24. It is illegal to receive money for a bride; on the other hand, there should be a dowry. Those who sell their daughters commit a very great sin.
25. Offerings and sacrifices for prayers should be given only to those holy men [*sadhus*] who are Ad Dharmi and who have shown themselves to follow Ad Dharmi principles religiously.

[*p. 41*] 26. It is necessary for each Ad Dharmi to provide primary education to both boys and girls.
27. The girls should be educated especially in household work such as sewing and needlework.
28. Young girls and boys should not be sent out to cut grass and gather wood.[15]

14. *Āndān*, a common religious act of social service.
15. That is, they should be given education rather than be used as child labor.

29. It is the duty of parents not to allow young widowed daughters to remain in their household, because a young widowed daughter is a cause of disgrace.[16]
30. If an Ad Dharmi widow with children wants to hold a commemoration of her deceased husband, but cannot afford it, then the Ad Dharm Mandal of Jullundur and its members will help her.
31. It is not good to cry and beat oneself at a death or funeral. To do so is to anger Guru Dev.
32. Among Ad Dharmis sons and daughters should receive an equal inheritance.
33. To eat the meat of a dead animal or bird is against the law of Ad Dharm.[17]
34. To use wine or any other intoxicants is a sin, except in the case of sickness.
35. It is legal to eat food offered at non–Ad Dharm[18] marriages, but the food should be decent, and not leftovers.
36. Cleanliness is important. It guarantees good health.
37. It is forbidden to practice idolatry and worship statues, and one should not believe in magic, ghosts, or anything of the sort.
38. Ail Ad Dharmis should forget notions of caste and untouchability and work toward the unity of all people in the world.
39. Each Ad Dharmi should help a fellow Ad Dhami in need.

[p. 42] 40. One Ad Dharmi must not work at a place where another Ad Dharmi works until the first Ad Dharmi has been paid his wages.
41. If Ad Dharmis enter into a dispute with one another, they should attempt to come to some agreement by themselves or within the community. If no agreement

---

16. A young widow is often considered inauspicious in India. This injunction, then, may be construed as an attempt to make the lower castes look more proper in the eyes of others in society.

17. This requirement of vegetarianism was not followed by all Ad Dharmis. Some leaders of the movement, in fact, advocated meat-eating as a way of demonstrating their independence from upper caste mores.

18. That is, upper caste.

is accomplished, they should refer the case to the Ad Dharm Mandal, Jullundur, and the Executive Committee will take action.
42. Ad Dharmis should open shops and businesses in every village.
43. Every Ad Dharmi should be a missionary for the faith.
44. Ad Dharmis should call themselves such and register in the census as "Ad Dharmi."
45. A red turban on the head is mandatory, for it is the color of our ancestors.
46. Every Ad Dharmi should work hard for the progress and peace of the community [qaum].
47. Ad Dharmis should organize themselves into cadres [jate-bandi] called martyrdom cells [shaheedi-jata].[19] They should work hard on the Ad Dharm's projects.
48. Each Ad Dharmi should separate himself from Hindus, Sikhs, and members of other religions.
49. Each Ad Dharmi should be a good citizen, a patriot loyal to the present government, and should follow the laws of the land.
50. Ad Dharmis have the obligation to consider the Ad Dharm Mandal of Punjab, city of Jullundur, as their rightful representative, and to recognize that the programs of the Ad Dharm are for their benefit.

[p. 43] 51. It is the duty of every Ad Dharmi to trust the Ad Dharm Mandal of Jullundur, and to share its work.
52. All local branches of the Ad Dharm should be certified by the Ad Dharm Mandal of Jullundur, and those which are not certified should not be considered genuine.
53. All Ad Dharmis should save their fellow Ad Dharmis from fraud and selfishness on the part of other communities. If such a situation arises, the Mandal should be informed.
54. Each Ad Dharmi should report any difficulty concerning the community to the Mandal in Jullundur.

19. A term used to describe bands of religious militants who, in Sikh and North Indian Muslim traditions, gave their lives willingly in dangerous expeditions against a religious enemy.

55. Ad Dharmis should subscribe to the *qaum*'s newspaper, Adi Dankā. They should receive it regularly, read it regularly, and help support it regularly.
56. Anyone violating the laws of the Ad Dharm or of the guru, or who insults these laws in one way or another, will be liable to punishment, even the greatest punishment—being banished from the community [*qaum*].

LIST OF INTERVIEWS

Aggarwal, R. C., director, Social Welfare and Welfare of Scheduled Castes and Backward Castes, Punjab government. Chandigarh, April 6, 1971.

Akhtar, A. U., director of Social Welfare, Punjab government (Pakistan). Lahore, July 2, 1971.

Azad, Prithvi Singh, former M.L.A. Kharar, April 13, 1971. Chandigarh, November 12, 1973.

Badhan, J. C., Ambedkarite leader. Jullundur, March 28, and May 16, 1971.

Balley, Lahori Ram, Ambedkarite leader and editor of *Bheem Patrika*. Jullundur, December 1970; April 1 and 3 and May 3, 1971; November 14, 1973; August 16, 1978.

Barkat, Masih, principal of Foreman Christian College. Lahore, June 28, 1971.

Bhardwaj, I. S., Jullundur municipal commissioner. Jullundur, May 2, 1971.

Campbell, Rev. Ernest, missionary and former Punjab social worker. New Delhi, October 20, 1970; June 12, 1972; November 7, 1973.

Chand, Amar, Ad Dharm leader. Wolverhampton, U.K., August 2, 1971.

Chand, Prakash, deputy inspector-general, Punjab Police. Chandigarh, May 28 and June 15, 1971.

Chandra, Vimal, deputy commissioner for Scheduled Castes and Tribes. New Delhi, June 20, 1971.

Chaudhry, Bashir A., lecturer, Department of Social Work, Punjab University. Lahore, June 29, 1971.

Chawla, Rabindra Nath, secretary of Harijan Sevak Sangh. Delhi, June 26, 1971.
Das, Bhagwan, general secretary, Ambedkar Mission Society. New Delhi, April 1, June 21 and 24, 1971; November 14, 1973; August 12, 1978.
Das, Harcharan, cashier of Guru Ravi Das Sabha, U.K. Wolverhampton, August 2, 1971.
Das, Principal Ram, president of Dayanand Salvation Mission, former principal of DAV College. Hoshiarpur, April 18, 1971.
Das, Sant Sarwan, spiritual leader of Ravi Das *dera*. Ballan, April 25, 1971 (in Punjabi).
Das, Seth Kishan, first president of Scheduled Caste Federation, Punjab. Jullundur, November 16, 1973.
Daskawie, Dr. M. A. Q., Christian Study Centre. Rawalpindi, Pakistan, July 2, 1971; October 26, 1973.
Din, S. F. (also spelled Deane), former Deputy Chairman, Upper House, Punjab government. Chandigarh, June 5 and 6, 1971.
Diwan, Gurbax Singh, general secretary of the Communist Party of India, Punjab. Chandigarh, June 4, 1971.
Emile, A. G., legal counsel for the United Church of North India. Chandigarh, June 5, 1971.
Gaikwad, B. K., member of Parliament, Republican Party of India. New Delhi, June 24, 1971.
Garg, Shri R. P., deputy director, Northern Zone, Backward Classes Welfare, Government of India. Chandigarh, February 2, 1971.
Gill, Om Prakash, member Municipal Corporation. Jullundur, May 5, 1971 (in Hindi).
Gill, R. L., president, Valmiki Sabha (Charan Das group). Jullundur, May 1 and 28, 1971.
Jadoun, Baba Ram, general secretary of Radhasoami Satsang (Dayalbagh). Agra, November 9, 1973.
Jaspal, Mangu Ram, publisher of the *Ravidas Patrika*. Jullundur, January 31, February 22, March 14, April 26, May 17, 1971; September 20, 1975; August 20, 1978. Wolverhampton, U.K., August 1, 1971.
Khanna, K. L., general secretary, Radhasoami Satsang, Beas, Dera Baba Jaimal Singh. Beas, December 10, 1970; January, February 26, and May 25, 1971.

List of Interviews

Kharat, R. G., president of Bombay Pradesh, Republican Party of India. New Delhi, June 24, 1971.

Lal, Pundit Kishori, leader of Communist Party of India (Marxist), Punjab branch. Jullundur, June 10, 1971.

Lal, Lala Mohan, former secretary, Harijan Sevak Sangh. Jullundur, May 1, 1971.

Lal, Rattan, general secretary, Jullundur Safai Muzdoor Union. Jullundur, May 27, 1971.

Lal, Sohan, office secretary, Punjab Scheduled Caste Board. Jullundur, June 10, 1971 (in Punjabi).

Lal, Sudashan, acting general secretary, Guru Ravi Das Sabha, U.K. Wolverhampton, August 2, 1971.

Loehlin, Rev. Clinton, former missionary and Sikh scholar. Marysville, California, August 10, 1972. Berkeley, California, March 27, 1974.

Love, Paul, Presbyterian missionary. Batala, March 21, 1971.

Mahabir, Miss M., headmistress, Methodist Mission Primary School. Batala, March 20, 1971.

Mal, Rev. Yaqub Chajju, pastor of the Church of North India. Jullundur, December 1970; January and April 1971.

Malhotra, S. L., Professor of History and Gandhian Thought, Punjab University. Chandigarh, April 28, 1971.

Masih, Johann, pastor of the Union Church. Chandigarh, March 24, 1971.

Mehay, Manohar Lal, president, Ravi Das Youth Club, Boota Mandi, Jullundur, March 16, April, and May 15, 1971; August 19, 1978; July 23, 1979.

Mehay, Sat Pal, leader of the Dalit Sangharsh Samiti. Jullundur, August 22, 1978.

Nahar, Hari Krishan, former president of Valmiki Navyuk Mandal. Jullundur, May 4, 7, 15, and 27, 1971.

Pawar, Ishwar Das, Punjab Civil Service, retired. Chandigarh, April 9, 1971.

Prashad, C. L., pastor of Batala Christian Missionary Society Church. Batala and Amritsar, March 21, 1971.

Rai, Yashwant, former deputy minister, Punjab government, and leader of Valmiki Sabha. Chandigarh, April 7, 1971.

Ram, Chanan, former president, Republican Party of India, Punjab branch. London, U.K., August 4, 1971.

Ram, Mangoo, founder-leader of Ad Dharm Mandal. Garhshankar, December 1, 1970 (with the assistance of Santokh Singh, in Punjabi); January 29, 1971 (with the assistance of Anil Puri, in Punjabi); February 2, 1971 (with the assistance of Devinder Singh, in Punjabi); April 17, 1971 (with the assistance of Mohinder Singh and Devinder Singh, in Punjabi); November 13, 1973 (with the assistance of Bharat Bhushan Babbar, in Punjabi); July 28, 1978 (with the assistance of Manohar Mehay, in Punjabi). Jullundur, May 12, 1971 (in Punjabi).

Ram, Rullia, former Ad Dharmi. Jullundur, March 28, 1971 (in Punjabi).

Ram, Sadhu, M. P., member of Ad Dharm, Scheduled Caste Federation, and Radhasoami. New Delhi, June 24, 1971 (in Punjabi); November 7, 1973 (with the assistance of Mrs. Promilla Ahuja, in Punjabi).

Ram, Sant, B. A., founder-leader, Jat Path Thorak Mandal. Purani Bassi, April 18, 1971.

Ram, Sant, M. L. A., Punjab Congress Party. Jullundur, June 12, 1971 (in Punjabi).

Rao, K. Ananda, office secretary, Bhartiya Depressed Classes League, June 24, 1971.

Saky, P. P., Receptionist and Director of Public Relations, Nirankari Colony. Delhi, June 25, 1971.

Sadhoo, son of Sundar, Christian leader. Sarai Khas, February 28, 1971.

Salvation Army officials, Booth Tucker Hall. Batala, March 20, 1971.

Sekhon, Principal S. S., writer and principal of Khalsa College. Jandiala, Jullundur district, March 29, 1971.

Sharma, Vijay, secretary, Jullundur district Jan Sangh. Jullundur, May 26, 1971.

Shastri, Sohan Lal, Ambedkarite leader. New Delhi, June 25, 1971.

Shudranand, Swami (Shiv Charan), a founder of Ad Dharm Mandal. Jullundur, April 15, May 15, and June 10, 1971 (in Punjabi).

Singh, Amar Nath, general secretary, Bharatiya Masihi Dal. Saranasi, Jullundur, April 26, 1971.

Singh, Bhagat, *bhagat* of Gugapir sect. Village Badal, Ferozepur district, May 9, 1971 (in Punjabi).

Singh, Charan, Spiritual Master of Radhasoami Satsang, Beas. Dera Baba Jaimal Singh, Beas, December 18, 1970; February 26 and April 2, 1971; July 10, 1978.

Singh, Guprite. Badal, May 9, 1971. Chandigarh, May 31, 1971.

Singh, Gurmit, leader of Ravi Das Sabha. Wolverhampton, U.K., August 1, 1971.

Singh, Gurvanta (also spelled Gurbanta), vice-president, Congress Party, Punjab, and former Ad Dharm leader. Jullundur, January 31 and May 8 and 26, 1971 (in Punjabi).

Singh, Master Hari, Punjab Communist Party of India, head of Department of Agricultural Workers. Chandigarh, June 4, 1971.

Singh, Hazara, custodian of Gadar party records. Jullundur, June 7, 1971.

Singh, Brigadier Manmohan. Jullundur, June 10, 1971.

Singh, Dr. Ram, principal of Baring College. Batala, February 24, 1971.

Singh, Satwant, chairman, executive committee, Communist Party of India, Punjab branch. Jullundur, June 10, 1971.

Sondhi, S. L., an administrator of Radhasoami Satsang. Beas, February 26, 1971.

Virdi, Santokh, founder-leader of Punjab Dalit Panther organization. Phagwara, August 28, 1978.

GLOSSARY OF INDIAN TERMS

abadi *(ābādī)*: neighborhood, section of a city
achut *(achūt)*: untouchable, an Untouchable
Achutistan *(achūtistān)*: land of the Untouchables
ad, adi *(ādi)*: ancient, original
adivasi *(ādivāsī)*: literally, original dwellers; a name given to tribal peoples
Akali *(akālī)*: literally, immortal; a group of Sikh loyalists
andolan *(āndolan)*: social movement
Arora *(aroṛa)*: an urban merchant caste in the Punjab
Arya *(ārya)*: pertaining to the Aryans, an ancient Indo-European people; also refers to the modern Hindu reform movement, Arya Samaj
ashram *(āśram)*: literally, refuge; a religious retreat
Baba *(bābā)*: title used for a respected old person
badshah *(bādśāh)*: king, emperor
Balmiki *(bālmīki, vālmīki)*: a designation of the Chuhra caste using the name of Rishi Valmiki
bandhara *(bandhārā)*: a great festival

bania *(baniyā)*: merchant, the merchant class
basti *(bastī)*: neighborhood, section of a city
Bazigar *(bāzīgar)*: a lower caste, traditionally entertainers
begar *(begār)*: forced labor
bhagat *(bhakta)*: literally, devotee; in the Punjab a title for a religious singer or holy man
Bhagwan *(bhagavān)*: God
bhai *(bhāī)*: brother; also used as a title of respect
bhajan *(bhajan)*: a religious song
bhakti *(bhakti)*: religious devotion
bhang *(bhaṅg, bhāṅg)*: a marijuana drink
bhangi *(bhaṅgī)*: a term used in some areas for the Chuhra caste
Bharat *(bhārat*, Skt. *bhārata)*: India
Bharatiya *(bhāratīya)*: Indian
bhawan *(bhavan)*: building
Bhil *(bhīl)*: a tribal group, in the Punjab regarded as lower caste nomads
biradari *(birādarī)*: brotherhood
bodhisattva *(bodhisattva)*: for Buddhists, an enlightened being who remains available for inter-

315

cession and guidance in this world

Brahman *(brāhmaṇ)*: the highest caste, traditionally priests

Chamar *(camār)*: an Untouchable caste, traditionally leatherworkers

chapatti *(capāttī)*: thin wheat bread

Chuhra *(cuhḍā)*: an Untouchable caste, traditionally sweepers

dal *(dal)*: group, party

dalit *(dalit)*: downtrodden, oppressed

danka *(ḍankā)*: a kind of drum

darshan *(darśan,* Skt. *darśana)*: literally, sight, seeing; the auspicious sight of a religious figure or deity

D.A.V. (Dayanand Anglo-Vedic): term used by the Arya Samaj to name educational institutions after its founder

dera *(derā)*: literally, camp; a sacred compound, residence of a holy man

desh bhagat *(deś-bhakta)*: patriot

dev *(dev,* Skt. *deva)*: god, God

dharm *(dharm,* Skt. *dharma)*: moral order; sometimes also translated as religion

dharm-khand *(dharm-khaṇḍ)*: the realm of righteous behavior

dharmik *(dharmik)*: pertaining to *dharm*

doab *(doāb, doābā)*: the area between two rivers

dravida *(draviḍ)*: the land, people, and language family of South India

faqir *(fakīr)*: a holy man, originally a Muslim ascetic

Gadar, Ghadar *(gadar)*: literally, mutiny; a militant movement of expatriate Punjabis headquartered in the United States

ghar *(ghar)*: house, building, hall

ghi *(ghī)*: clarified butter

gotra *(gotra)*: subcaste

Granth *(granth)*: scriptures, such as the Adi Granth of the Sikhs

Gujjar *(gujar)*: a cow-herding caste, dominant in some areas of the Punjab hills

gurdwara, gurudwara *(gurudvārā)*: literally, the threshold of the guru; a meeting hall for Sikh worship and technically any place which houses the Sikh scriptures

Gurmukhi *(gurumukhī)*: literally, from the mouth of the guru; the script in which the Punjabi language is written

guru *(guru)*: spiritual teacher, especially the ten great teachers of the Sikh tradition

Harappa *(harappā)*: one of the chief cities of the ancient Indus Valley civilization

Harijan *(harijan)*: literally, people of God; term applied by Gandhi to Untouchables

hatha yoga *(haṭh yog,* Skt. *haṭha yoga)*: a physical and spiritual discipline

Hindi *(hindī)*: the major, Sanskrit-based language of North India

iktar *(ektār)*: a one-stringed instrument

Ishwar *(īśvar,* Skt. *īśvara)*: the Lord, God

jai *(Jay,* Skt. *jaya)*: literally, victory; a term of salution: hail!

jajman *(jajmān,* Skt. *yajamāna)*: the granter in the granter-

Glossary

grantee relationship that pertains in rural India; the network of such traditional reciprocal relationships as a whole
jangal *(jangal)*: wasteland
Jat *(jāt)*: the dominant caste of rural Punjab
Jatav-kshatriya *(jātav-kṣatriya)*: a movement of lower caste people *(jātav)* who claim to be members of a higher *varṇa*, the *kṣatriya*
Julaha *(julāhā)*: a weaver; the weaver caste
karma *(karm,* Skt. *karma)*: literally, action; the Hindu concept that actions are rewarded in kind, either in this or in a subsequent life
karm-dharm *(karm-dharm,* Skt. *karma-dharma)*: proper spiritual and moral behavior
khalsa *(khālsā)*: originally, the army of the faithful in the Sikh tradition; by extension, a true Sikh
Khatri *(khatrī)*: an urban merchant caste in the Punjab
khet *(khet)*: field
kirti *(kīrti)*: glory
kisan *(kisān)*: farmer
kranti *(krānti)*: revolution
lala *(lālā)*: an affectionate honorific; in the Punjab, associated with the Arya Samaj
Lok Sabha *(lok sabhā)*: the lower house of India's national parliament
Mahar *(mahār)*: a large Untouchable caste in Maharashtra
mahasha *(mahāśā)*: literally, great hope; term given to members of the Megh caste by the Arya Samaj

mahatma *(mahātmā)*: literally, great-souled; holy man
majlis *(majlis)*: organization
mandal *(maṇḍal,* Skt. *maṇḍala)*: literally, circle; a group or an organization
mandi *(maṇḍī)*: marketplace
mantra *(mantra)*: a religious incantation
Manu *(manu)*: the legendary author of the traditional Hindu social code
masih *(masīh)*: Messiah
masihi *(masīhī)*: Christian
mat *(mat)*: persuasion, opinion; hence, religious point of view
mazhab *(mazhab)*: belief
Mazhabi *(mazhabī)*: literally, religious; term given to members of the Chuhra caste who became Sikhs
Megh *(megh, meng,* or *mihngh)*: a lower caste, traditionally weavers
mela *(melā)*: fair, festival
Mirasi *(mirāsī)*: a lower caste, traditionally entertainers
mirdang *(mṛdaṅg)*: a kind of drum
M.L.A.: member of the legislative assembly, which is the parliament of an Indian state
mochi *(mocī)*: shoemaker; the shoemaker caste
mohalla *(muhallā)*: neighborhood, section of a city
moksha *(mokṣa)*: liberation, especially the liberation of the soul at the end of a cycle of rebirths
M.P.: member of the parliament, which is India's national legislative body
muni *(muni)*: sage
munshi *(munśī)*: a title referring to a teacher

murdabad *(murdābād)*: term used in slogans to mean "destroy"

muzdoor *(mazdūr)*: unskilled labor

Nadar (Tamil *nāḍār*): a large Untouchable caste in Tamil Nadu, South India

nath yoga *(nāth yog,* Skt. *nātha yoga)*: a tradition of spiritual practice traceable to the early medieval figure Gorakh Nath

naujawan *(naujavān, navajavān)*: new youth

navyug *(navayug)*: new age

Naxalite *(naksalbandhī)*: a term designating a member of the Communist Party of India (Marxist-Leninist), after an area in West Bengal where an uprising against landlords occurred

nirguna *(nirguṇ,* Skt. *nirguṇa)*: literally, devoid of qualities; concept of God as beyond attribution

pahul *(pāhul)*: Sikh initiation vows

panchayat *(pañcāyat)*: a governing council consisting traditionally of five members

panth *(panth)*: literally, path; religious group following a lineage of spiritual masters

panthik *(panthik)*: pertaining to *panth*

parameshwar *(parameśvar)*: the supreme lord; God

patrika *(patrikā)*: newspaper, publication

patwari *(paṭvārī)*: village record-keeper

pind (Punjabi: *pind)*: village

pracharak *(pracārak)*: preacher

pradhan *(pradhān)*: literally, chief; a leader

prakash *(prakāś)*: light, illumination

prasad *(prasād,* Skt. *prasāda)*: blessed food

pundit *(paṇḍit)*: Brahman teacher

Punjabi *(panjābī)*: pertaining to the Punjab; a person who lives in the Punjab; the language of the Punjab

qaum *(qaum)*: religious community; a people

qaumiat *(qaumiat)*: communal unity

qaumik *(qaumik)*: pertaining to *qaum*

Qudrat ka Mela *(kudrat kā melā)*: glory of nature, Fate

Rajasthani *(rājasthānī)*: pertaining to the state of Rajasthan, adjacent to the Punjab

Rajput *(rājpūt)*: the dominant caste of the Punjab hills

Ramdasia *(rāmdāsī)*: a name given to people of the Chamar caste who become Sikhs

rishi *(ṛṣi)*: sage

R.S.S. (Rashtriya Swayamsevak Sangh, *rāṣṭrīya svayamsevak sañgh)*: National Society for Self-protection, a right-wing Hindu organization

sabha *(sabhā)*: an assembly or society; a religious or social movement

sachkhand *(sac khaṇḍ)*: realm of truth; term used by Guru Nanak to describe the highest realm

sadhu *(sādhu)*: ascetic, holy man

safai *(saphāī)*: cleaning, cleanliness; hence, sanitation work involving cleaning and sweeping

Glossary

salvar-kamiz *(salvār-kamīz)*: loose blouse and baggy trousers worn by Punjabi women

samaj *(samāj)*: society, organization

samaji *(samājī)*: member of a *samāj*, such as the Arya Samaj

samiti *(samiti)*: committee

sanatan *(sanātan)*: eternal, ancient

sangat (Punjabi: *sañgat*): society, group; Hindi *sañgh*

sangh *(sañgh)*: association, society

sangharsh *(saṃgharṣ)*: struggle

sansi *(sānsi)*: a nomadic group regarded as lower caste in the Punjab

sant *(sant)*: literally, good or saintly; one of a group of medieval religious poet-saints; a title used for a holy man in the Punjab

sarangi *(sārañgī)*: a multi-stringed, bowed instrument

sarvodaya *(sarvoday,* Skt. *sarvodaya)*: literally, service to all; a social service movement established by Gandhi

Sat Guru *(sadguru)*: true guru

satsang *(satsañg)*: gathering of the faithful; communal worship

satyagraha *(satyāgraha)*: literally, truth-force; a term coined by Gandhi to describe his method of conflict resolution

seth *(seṭh)*: title of respect usually referring to a wealthy person

sevak *(sevak)*: servant, especially in the sense of religious or social service

Shaiva *(śaiv,* Skt. *śaiva)*: pertaining to or devoted to Śiva

shakta *(śākta)*: pertaining to Śakti, the Goddess conceived as power or energy

shastra *(śāstra)*: traditional treatise, as for instance the *dharmaśāstras*

shloka *(ślok,* Skt. *śloka)*: a common Sanskrit verse form; more generally, verse

shuddhi *(śuddhi)*: purification; an Arya Samaj rite affirming (or reaffirming) a person's Hindu purity

Sikh *(sikh)*: a North Indian religious tradition originating in a *panth* following Guru Nanak

Sikhistan *(sikhistān)*: land of the Sikhs

Singh *(siṃh)*: literally, lion; the name of the tenth guru in the Sikh tradition; thereafter a name used to designate all male Sikhs

soham *(so'ham)*: literally, "I am It"; a Vedantic phrase referring to the primacy of the soul

suba (Punjabi *sūba)*: a province, a state

Swami *(svāmī)*: a holy man; a title implying spiritual achievement

swaraj *(svarāj)*: self-rule, independence

tehsil *(tehsīl)*: subdistrict

thana *(thānā)*: precinct

uddhar *(uddhār)*: uplift, salvation

U.P. (Uttar Pradesh, formerly United Provinces): state in North India

updeshak *(upadeśak)*: missionary

Urdu *(urdū)*: North Indian language related to Hindi and associated with Islam

Vaishnava *(vaiṣṇav,* Skt. *vaiṣṇava)*: pertaining to or devoted to Viṣṇu or one of his avatars

varna *(varṇa)*: literally, color; one of the four classical groups into which castes *(jātis)* are organized

vidya *(vidyā)*: knowledge

-wala, -wali *(-vālā, -vālī)*: pertaining to

yadav *(yādav,* Skt. *yādava)*: an Untouchable caste of Western U.P.; see also *jatav-kshatriya*

yadghar *(yādghar)*: memorial hall

zamindar, zamindara *(zamindār)*: landowner

zindabad *(zindābād)*: term used in slogans to mean "long live"

BIBLIOGRAPHY

THEORETICAL CONSIDERATIONS

Bendix, Reinhard, and Lipset, Seymour Martin, eds. *Class, Status and Power: Social Stratification in Comparative Perspective.* New York: Macmillan Free Press, 1966.

Berger, Peter, and Luckmann, Thomas. *The Social Construction of Reality.* Garden City, N.Y.: Doubleday, 1966.

Cantril, Hadley. *The Politics of Despair.* New York: Collier, 1962.

Cohn, Norman. *The Pursuit of the Millennium.* New York: Harper, 1961.

DeVos, George, and Wagatsuma, H., eds. *Japan's Invisible Race: Caste in Culture and Personality.* Berkeley and Los Angeles: University of California Press, 1966.

Dollard, John. *Caste and Class in a Southern Town.* Garden City, N.Y.: Doubleday, 1957.

Douglas, Mary. *Purity and Danger: An Analysis of Concepts of Pollution and Taboo.* London: Routledge and Kegan Paul, 1966.

Dumont, L. *From Mandeville to Marx: The Genesis and Triumph of Economic Ideology.* Chicago: University of Chicago Press, 1977.

Geertz, Clifford. "Ideology as a Cultural System." In David Apter, ed., *Ideology and Discontent.* New York: Free Press, 1964.

Gurr, Ted. *Why Men Rebel.* Princeton, N.J.: Princeton University Press, 1970.

Gurvitch, George. *The Social Frameworks of Knowledge.* Translated by Margaret A. Thompson and Kenneth A. Thompson. New York: Harper Torchbooks, 1966.

Gusfield, Joseph R., ed. *Protest, Reform and Revolt: A Reader in Social Movements.* New York: John Wiley, 1970.

Hobsbawm, E. J. *Primitive Rebels: Studies in Archaic Forms of Social Movement in the 19th and 20th Centuries.* New York: Norton, 1958.
Johnson, Chalmers. *Revolutionary Change.* Boston: Little, Brown, 1966.
Kardiner, Abram, and Ovesey, Lionel. *Mark of Oppression.* Cleveland: World, 1962.
Kautsky, John H. *Political Change in Underdeveloped Countries.* New York: John Wiley, 1967.
Kuper, Leo. "Plural Societies: Perspectives and Problems." In Smith and Kuper, eds., *Pluralism in Africa.* Berkeley and Los Angeles: University of California Press, 1969.
Lanternari, Vittoria. *The Religions of the Oppressed.* New York: Mentor, 1965.
Lasswell, Harold D. *Politics: Who Gets What, When, How.* New York: Meridian Books, 1958.
Latham, Earl. *The Group Basis of Politics.* Ithaca: Cornell University Press, 1952.
Lewy, Guenter. *Religion and Revolution.* New York: Oxford University Press, 1974.
Litt, Edgar. *Ethnic Politics in America.* Glenview, Ill.: Scott, Foresman, 1970.
Marx, Karl. *The German Ideology.* Edited by R. Pascal. New York: International, 1939.
Mead, George Herbert. *On Social Psychology.* Chicago: University of Chicago Press, 1958.
Moore, Barrington, Jr. *The Social Origins of Dictatorship and Democracy: Lord and Peasant in the Making of the Modern World.* Boston: Beacon Press, 1966.
O'Dea, Thomas F. *The Sociology of Religion.* Englewood Cliffs, N.J.: Prentice-Hall, 1966.
Redfield, Robert. *The Little Community.* Chicago: University of Chicago Press, 1956.
Schutz, Alfred. *Collected Papers, I: The Problem of Social Reality.* Edited by M. Nathanson. The Hague: M. Mijhoff, 1962.
Selznick, Philip. *The Organizational Weapon.* Berkeley and Los Angeles: University of California Press, 1963.
Smelser, Neil J. *Theory of Collective Behavior.* New York: Free Press, 1962.
Smith, M. G., and Kuper, Leo, eds. *Pluralism in Africa.* Berkeley and Los Angeles: University of California Press, 1969.
Thrupp, Sylvia, ed. *Millennial Dreams in Action.* The Hague: Mouton, 1962.

Toennies, Ferdinand. *Community and Society.* Translated by Charles P. Loomis. East Lansing: Michigan State University Press, 1964.
Valentine, Charles. *Culture and Poverty.* Chicago: University of Chicago Press, 1968.
van den Berghe, Pierre L. *Race and Racism.* New York: John Wiley, 1967.
Wallace, Anthony. "Revitalization Moments." *American Anthropologist* 58 (1956).
Wilson, Bryan. *Religious Sects: A Sociological Study.* New York: McGraw-Hill, 1970.
Worsley, Peter M. *The Trumpet Shall Sound: A Study of "Cargo" Cults in Melanesia.* London: MacGibbon and Kee, 1957.

INDIA: SOCIAL AND RELIGIOUS CHANGE

Ashby, Philip. *Modern Trends in Hinduism.* New York: Columbia University Press, 1969.
Babb, Lawrence Alan. *The Divine Hierarchy: Popular Hinduism in Central India.* New York: Columbia University Press, 1975.
Berreman, Gerald D. "Race, Caste, and Other Invidious Distinctions in Social Stratification." *Race* 13, no. 4 (April 1972).
―――. "Social Categories and Social Interaction in Urban India." *American Anthropologist,* no. 74, 1972.
Béteille, André. *Castes Old and New.* Bombay: Asia Publishing Company, 1969.
Bettelheim, Charles. *India Independent.* New York: Monthly Review Press, 1968.
Biswas, P. C. "Present State of the Problem of Correlation Between Racial and Caste Differentiation in India." *Anthropologist* 12, nos. 1 and 2 (March and August 1965).
Cashman, Richard Ian. "The Politics of Mass Recruitment: Attempts to Organize Popular Movements in Maharashtra, 1891–1908." Ph.D. dissertation, Duke University, 1969.
Chattopadhyaya, Sudhakar. *Evolution in Hindu Sects.* New Delhi: Munshiram Manoharlal, 1970.
Chopra, Kusum. "Changes in the Economic Structure of Rural India." Ph.D. dissertation, University of Colorado, Boulder, 1969.
Conlon, Frank Fowler. *The Emergence of the Saraswat Brahmans, 1830–1930: A Study of Caste and Social Change in Modern India.* Berkeley and Los Angeles: University of California Press, 1977.

Dandekar, V. M., and Rath, Nilakantha. *Poverty in India.* Bombay: Indian School of Political Economy, 1971.
Desai, A. R. *Social Background of Indian Nationalism.* Bombay: Oxford University Press, 1948.
Dumont, Louis. *Homo Hierarchicus: The Indian Caste System and Its Implications.* Translated by Mark Sainsbury. Chicago: University of Chicago Press, 1970.
Farquhar, J. N. *Modern Religious Movements in India.* New York: Macmillan, 1924.
Frykenberg, Robert Eric, ed. *Land Control and Social Structure in Indian History.* Madison: University of Wisconsin Press, 1969.
Fuchs, Stephen. *Rebellious Prophets: A Study of Messianic Movements in Indian Religions.* Bombay: Asia Publishing House, 1965.
Fürer-Haimendorf, Christoph von. *Morals and Merit: A Study of Values and Social Controls in South Asian Societies.* London: Weidenfeld & Nicholson, 1967.
Ghurye, G. S. *Caste and Race in India.* Bombay: Popular Prakashan, 1969.
Gumperz, John J. "Religion and Social Communication in Village North India." *Journal of Asian Studies* 23 (June 1964). Reprinted in Edward Harper, ed., *Religion in South Asia.* Seattle: University of Washington Press, 1964.
Harper, Edward B. *Religion in South Asia.* Seattle: University of Washington Press, 1964.
Kothari, Rajni, ed. *Caste in Indian Politics.* Delhi: Orient Longmans, 1970.
Lal, Pyare. *The Epic Fast.* Ahmedabad: Karnatak Printing Press, 1932.
Lannoy, Richard. *The Speaking Tree: A Study of Indian Culture and Society.* New York: Oxford University Press, 1971.
Lewis, Oscar. *Village Life in Northern India.* New York: Random House, 1958.
Madan, T. N., ed. *On the Nature of Caste in India: A Review Symposium on Louis Dumont's Homo Hierarchicus, Contributions to Indian Sociology.* New Series, 5. Delhi: Vikas, 1971.
Majumdar, R. C. *Struggle for Freedom.* Bombay: Bharatiya Vidya Bhavan, 1969.
Mandelbaum, David C. *Society in India.* 2 vols. Berkeley and Los Angeles: University of California Press, 1970.
Marglin, Frédérique Apffel. "Wives of the God-King: A Study of the Rituals of Some Temple Courtesans in India." Ph.D. dissertation, Brandeis University, 1980.

Marriott, McKim, ed. *Village India: Studies in the Little Community.* Chicago: University of Chicago Press, 1955.
Mathur, L. R. *Indian Revolutionary Movement in the U.S.A.* Delhi: S. Chand, 1970.
Mayer, Adrian C. *Caste and Kinship in Central India: A Village and Its Region.* Berkeley and Los Angeles: University of California Press, 1970.
Moon, Penderel. *Divide and Quit.* London: Chatto and Windus, 1961.
Munz, Peter, and Gupta, Brijen. "Revolution and Tradition in Modern Indian History." *Journal of Indian History* 44, Part 1 (April 1966).
Nimbark, Ashakant. "Men in the Middle: Marginality of a Village, a Caste and a Political Ideology in Transitional India." Ph.D. dissertation, New School for Social Research, 1966.
O'Malley, Lewis Sydney Steward. *Popular Hinduism, the Religion of the Masses.* Cambridge, England: The University Press, 1935.
Omvedt, Gail. *Cultural Revolt in a Colonial Society: The Non-Brahman Movement in Western India, 1872–1930.* Bombay: Scientific Socialist Education Trust, 1976.
Orans, Martin. *The Santal: A Tribe in Search of a Great Tradition.* Detroit: Wayne State University Press, 1965.
Rao, M. S. A. *Social Movement and Social Transformation: A Study of Two Backward Classes Movements in India.* Delhi: Macmillan, 1979.
———, ed. *Social Movements in India* (2 vols.). New Delhi: Manohar Publications, 1979.
Rudolph, Lloyd I., and Rudolph, Susanne Hoeber. *The Modernity of Tradition: Political Development in India.* Chicago: University of Chicago Press, 1967.
Sanghvi, L. D. "Perspectives for Study of Racial Origins in India." *Anthropologist,* Special Volume 1, 1969.
Sebring, James Marshall. "Caste Ranking and Caste Interaction in a North Indian Village." Ph.D. dissertation, University of California, Berkeley, 1968.
Silverberg, James, ed. *Social Mobility in the Caste System in India.* The Hague: Mouton, 1968.
Singer, Milton. *When a Great Tradition Modernizes: An Anthropological Approach to Indian Civilization.* New York: Praeger, 1972.
Sitaramayya, Pattabhi B. *The History of the Indian National Congress.* 2 vols. Bombay: Padma Publishers, 1946.

Smith, Donald Eugene. *India as a Secular State.* Princeton, N.J.: Princeton University Press, 1963.
Srinivas, M. N. *Caste in Modern India and Other Essays.* Bombay: Asia Publishing House, 1962.
———. *Social Change in Modern India.* Berkeley and Los Angeles: University of California Press, 1966.
Thapar, Romila. "Ethics, Religion and Social Protest in the First Millennium B.C. in Northern India." In *Ancient Indian Social History,* Delhi: Orient Longman, 1978.
Wadley, Susan Snow. *Shakti: Power in the Conceptual Structure of Karimpur Religion.* Chicago: Dept. of Anthropology, University of Chicago, 1975.
Weber, Max. *The Religion of India: The Sociology of Hinduism and Buddhism.* Translated by Hans Gerth. New York: Free Press, 1968.
Whitcomb, Elizabeth. *Agrarian Conditions in Northern India,* Vol. 1. Berkeley and Los Angeles: University of California Press, 1972.

PUNJAB

Archer, J. C. *The Sikhs in Relation to Hindus, Muslims, Christians and Ahmadiyyas.* Princeton, N.J.: Princeton University Press, 1946.
Barrier, N. G. *The Punjab Alienation of Land Bill 1900.* Durham, N.C.: Duke University South Asia Series, 1965.
———. *The Sikhs and Their Literature.* Delhi: Manohar Book Service, 1970.
Crooke, William. *An Ethnographical Hand-Book For the North-Western Provinces and Oudh.* Allahabad: North-Western Provinces and Oudh Government Press, 1890.
———. *Natives of Northern India.* London: Archibald Constable and Co., 1907.
———. *The Popular Religion and Folk-Lore of Northern India.* 2d ed., rev. and illus. Delhi: Munshiram Manoharlal, 1968.
———. *Tribes and Castes of the North-Western Provinces and Oudh.* 2 vols. Allahabad: North-Western Provinces and Oudh Government Press, 1890.
Darling, Malcolm Lyall. *The Punjab Peasant in Prosperity and Debt.* London: Oxford University Press, 1925 (reprinted 1947).
Eglar, Zekiye. *A Punjabi Village in Pakistan.* New York: Columbia University Press, 1960.

Frankel, Francine R. *India's Green Revolution: Economic Gains and Political Costs.* Princeton, N.J.: Princeton University Press, 1971.
Heeger, G. A. "Politics of Integration: Community, Party and Integration in the Punjab." Ph.D. dissertation, University of Chicago, 1972.
Helweg, Arthur. *The Sikhs in England.* Delhi: Oxford University Press, 1980.
Ibbetson, Denzil; MacLagan, E. D.; and Rose, H. A. *A Glossary of the Tribes and Castes of the Punjab.* Lahore: Civil and Military Gazette Press, 1911.
Jammu, Parkash Singh. *Changing Social Structure of Rural Punjab.* Delhi: Sterling Publishers, 1977.
Josh, Sohan Singh. *Hindustan Gadar Party, A Short History.* New Delhi: People's Publishing House, 1977.
Juergensmeyer, Mark. "The Ghadar Syndrome: Immigrant Sikhs and Nationalist Pride." In *Sikh Studies: Comparative Perspectives on a Changing Tradition,* edited by Mark Juergensmeyer and N. G. Barrier. Berkeley: Berkeley Religious Studies Series, 1979.
———. "The International Heritage of the Ghadar Party: A Survey of the Sources." *The Sikh Sansar* 2, no. 1 (March 1973).
Kessinger, T. G. *Vilyatpur, 1948–1968.* Berkeley and Los Angeles: University of California Press, 1974.
Latifi, M. *History of the Punjab from the Remotest Antiquity to the Present Time.* New Delhi: Eurasia Publishing House, 1964.
Lavan, Spencer. *The Ahmadiyah Movement: A History and Perspective.* Delhi: Manohar Book Service, 1974.
Leaf, Murray J. *Information and Behavior in a Sikh Village: Social Organization Reconsidered.* Berkeley and Los Angeles: University of California Press, 1972.
McLeod, W. H. *The Evolution of the Sikh Tradition.* Oxford: Clarendon Press, 1972.
———. *Guru Nanak and the Sikh Tradition.* Oxford: Clarendon Press, 1968.
Malhotra, S. L. *Gandhi and the Punjab.* Chandigarh: Punjab Publications Bureau, 1970.
Mathur, Laxman Prasad. *Indian Revolutionary Movement in the United States of America.* Delhi: S. Chand Publishers, 1970.
Morrison, Charles, "Dispute in Dhara: A Study of Village Politics in Eastern Punjab." Ph.D. dissertation, University of Chicago, 1965.
Nayar, Baldev Raj. *Minority Politics in the Punjab.* Princeton, N.J.: Princeton University Press, 1966.

Pettigrew, Joyce. *Robber Noblemen: A Study of the Political System of the Sikh Jats.* London: Routledge & Kegan Paul, 1975.
Pradhan, Mahesh Chandra. *The Political System of the Jats of Northern India.* London: Oxford University Press, 1966.
Raulet, Harry M., and Uppal, Jogindar S. "The Social Dynamics of Economic Development in Rural Punjab." *Asian Survey* 10, no. 4 (April 1970).
Reinhardt, William W. "The Legislative Council of the Punjab, 1887–1912." Ph.D. dissertation, Duke University, 1969.
Saberwal, Satish. *Mobile Men: Limits to Social Change in Urban Punjab.* New Delhi: Vikas, 1976.
Sharma, Sri Ram. *Punjab in Ferment in the Beginning of the Twentieth Century.* Patiala: Punjab University Department of Punjab Historical Studies, 1966.
Singh, Harbans, and Barrier, N. G., eds. *Punjab Past and Present: Essays in Honour of Dr. Ganda Singh.* Patiala: Punjab University Press, 1976.
Singh, Khushwant. *A History of the Sikhs.* 2 vols. Princeton, N.J.: Princeton University Press, 1963 and 1966.
Tandon, Prakash. *Punjabi Century 1857–1947.* Berkeley and Los Angeles: University of California Press, 1968.
Temple, R. D. *The Legends of the Punjab.* 3 vols. Patiala: Language Department, Punjab University, 1963.
Uppal, J. S. "Implementation of Land Reform Legislation in India: A Study of Two Villages in the Punjab." *Asian Survey* 9, no. 5 (May 1969).
Van den Dungen, P. H. M. "Changes in Status of Occupation in 19th Century Punjab." In D. A. Low, ed., *Soundings in Modern South Asia History.* Berkeley and Los Angeles: University of California Press, 1968.

UNTOUCHABLES

Ahmad, Karuna. "Towards Equality: Consequences of Protective Discrimination." *Economic and Political Weekly,* Annual Number, February 1979.
Anant, Santokh Singh. "Caste Hindu Attitudes: The Harijans' Perception." *Asian Survey* 11, no. 3 (March 1971).
Bathwal, C. P. "Representation of Scheduled Castes in Parliament and State Legislatures." *Economic and Political Weekly* 4, no. 36 (September 6, 1969).
Béteille, André. "The Future of the Backward Classes: The Competing Demands of Status and Power." In *Perspectives,* supplement to the *Indian Journal of Public Administration* 11

(1965). Reprinted in *India and Ceylon: Unity and Diversity*, edited by Philip Mason. London: Oxford University Press, 1967.

Bhandarkar, R. G. "The Depressed Classes." *The Indian Review* 14 (1913).

Briggs, George W. *The Chamars*. Calcutta: Associated Press; London: Oxford University Press, 1920.

——. *The Doms and Their Near Relations*. Mysore: Wesley Press, 1953.

Chandidas, R. "How Close to Equality are Scheduled Castes?" *Economic and Political Weekly* 4, no. 24 (June 14, 1969).

Chowdhury, J. N. *A Comparative Study of Adi Religion*. Shillong: North-East Frontier Agency, 1971.

Cohen, Stephen P. "The Untouchable Soldier: Caste, Politics and the Indian Army." *Journal of Asian Studies* 28 (1969).

Cohn, Bernard S. "Chamar Family in a North Indian Village: A Structural Contingent." *Economic Weekly* 13 (1961).

——. "Changing Traditions of a Low Caste." In *Traditional India: Structure and Change*, edited by Milton B. Singer. Philadelphia: American Folklore Society, 1959.

Dushkin, Lelah. "The Policy of the Indian National Congress Toward the Depressed Classes: An Historical Study." M.A. thesis, University of Pennsylvania, 1957.

——. "Scheduled Caste Policy in India: History, Problems, Prospects." *Asian Survey* 7, no. 9 (September 1967).

Foot, Isaac. "The Round Table Conference, the Future, and the Depressed Classes." *Contemporary Review* 139 (1931).

Fuchs, Stephen. *The Children of Hari*. Vienna: Herold, 1950.

——. "The Religio-Ethical Concepts of the Chamars in Northern India." *Missiology: An International Review* 4, no. 1 (January 1976).

Gaekwar of Baroda, His Highness the. *The Depressed Classes*. Madras: G. A. Natesan, n.d.

Galanter, Marc. *Competing Equalities: The Indian Experience With Compensatory Discrimination*. Berkeley and Los Angeles: University of California Press, 1982.

——. "Who Are the Other Backward Classes?" *Economic and Political Weekly* 13, October 12, 1978.

Hardgrave, Robert. *The Nadars of Tamilnad*. Berkeley and Los Angeles: University of California Press, 1969.

Hazari [pseudonym]. *Untouchable: The Autobiography of an Indian Outcaste*. New York: Praeger, 1971.

Huq, Afzal. *Pakistan and Untouchability*. Lahore: Muktaba-i-Urdu, 1941.

Isaacs, Harold. *India's Ex-Untouchables.* New York: John Day, 1964.

Juergensmeyer, Mark. "Cultures of Deprivation: Three Case Studies in the Punjab." *Economic and Political Weekly,* Annual Number, February 1979.

———. "Political Hope: The Social Movements of North India's Untouchables, 1900–1970." Ph.D. dissertation, University of California, Berkeley, 1974.

———. "What If Untouchables Don't Believe in Untouchability?" *Bulletin of Concerned Asian Scholars* 12, no. 1 (March 1980).

Khan, Mumtaz Ali. "Impact of the Constitutional Protection and Safeguards on the Scheduled Castes of Satnur Village." *All-India Congress Committee Economic Review* 20, no. 21 (May 15, 1969).

Lambert, R. D. "Untouchability as a Social Problem: Theory and Research." *Sociological Bulletin* 7, no. 1 (March 1958).

Lynch, Owen. *The Politics of Untouchability: Social Mobility and Social Change in a City of India.* New York: Columbia University Press, 1969.

Mahar, J. Michael, ed. *The Untouchables in Contemporary India.* Tucson: University of Arizona Press, 1972.

Malik, Suneila. "Social Consequences of Social Mobility Among Scheduled Castes." Ph.D. dissertation, Punjab University, Chandigarh, 1971.

Mehta, Subhash Chandra. "Persistance of the Caste System: Vested Interest in Backwardness." *Quest* 36 (January 1963).

Miller, R. J. "They Will Not Die Hindus: The Buddhist Conversion of Mahar Ex-Untouchables." *Asian Survey* 7, no. 9 (September 1967).

Moffatt, Michael. *An Untouchable Community in South India: Structure and Consensus.* Princeton, N.J.: Princeton University Press, 1979.

Omvedt, Gail, and Zelliot, Eleanor. "Introduction to Dalit Poems." *Bulletin of Concerned Asian Scholars* 10, no. 2 (July–September 1978).

Oomen, T. K. "Strategy for Social Change: A Study of Untouchability." *Economic and Political Weekly* 3, June 22, 1969; rejoinder in January 25, 1970, issue.

Ouwerkerk, Louise. *The Untouchables of India.* London: Oxford University Press, 1945.

Panchbhai, S. C. "The Levels of Regional and National Identification and Intergroup Relations Among Harijans and

Adivasis." *Indian Anthropological Society Journal* 2 (March 1967).
Parvathamma, C., and Jangam, R. T. "India's Scheduled Castes M.P.'s: A Socio-Economic Profile." *Journal of Karnatak University* 5 (1969).
Patwardhan, Sunanda. "Changing Religious Behavior and Traditions of Scheduled Castes." *Deccan College Research Institute Bulletin* 28 (1967–1968).
Ping, Ho Kwon. "Revolt of the Landless Peasants." *Far Eastern Economic Review,* January 12, 1979.
Pushparaj, P. K. *As an Untouchable Feels Untouchability.* Delhi: Servants of Untouchables Society, 1933.
Ramu, G. N. "Untouchability in Rural Areas." *Indian Journal of Social Work* 29 (July 1968).
Rao, M. S. A. *Social Movements and Social Transformation: A Study of Two Backward Classes Movements in India.* Delhi: The Macmillan Company of India, 1979.
Rath, R., and Sircar, N. C. "The Cognitive Background of Six Hindu Caste Groups Regarding the Low Caste Untouchables." *Journal of Social Psychology* 51 (1960).
Saberwal, Satish. *Mobile Men: Limits to Social Change in Urban Punjab.* New Delhi: Vikas Publishing House, 1976.
———. "The Reserved Constituency: Candidates and Consequences." *Economic and Political Weekly,* July 1972.
Sachchidananda. *The Harijan Elite.* Faridabad: Thompson Press (India), 1977.
Schermerhorn, R. A. "Scheduled Caste Welfare: Public Priorities in the States." *Economic and Political Weekly* 14, no. 8 (February 22, 1969).
Shah, Ghanshyam. "Studies on Politics of Scheduled Castes and Scheduled Tribes." New Delhi: Indian Council of Social Science Research, 1971.
Sharma, Ram Sharan. *Sudras in Ancient India.* Delhi: Motilal Banarsidas, 1958.
Simmons, Ruth. "The Berwas of Delhi: Social and Political Mobility in a Caste of Ex-Untouchables." Ph.D. dissertation, University of California, Berkeley, 1971.
Singh, Mohinder. *The Depressed Classes.* Bombay: Hind Kitab, 1947.
Srivastava, R. K. "Gandhi and the Problem of Caste and Untouchability." *Indian Political Science Review* 4, no. 1 (October 1969–March 1970).

Vatsa, Rajendra Singh, ed. *The Depressed Classes of India: An Enquiry into Their Conditions and Suggestions for Their Uplift.* New Delhi: Gitanjali Prakashan, 1977.
Verba, Sidney; Ahmed, Bashiruddin; and Bhatt, Anil. *Race, Caste, and Politics: A Comparative Study of India and the U.S.* Beverly Hills: Sage Publishing Co., 1971.
Youngson, Rev. J. "The Chuhras." *Indian Antiquary* 25 and 36.

See also the bibliography by Eleanor Zelliot in J. Michael Mahar, ed., *Untouchables in Contemporary India.* Tucson: University of Arizona Press, 1972.

MOVEMENTS AGAINST UNTOUCHABILITY

Ad Dharm

Ad Dharm Mandal, 1926–1931. Official Report, Jullundur: Kishan Steam Press, 1931, in Urdu. English translation in Mark Juergensmeyer, "Political Hope."
"Ad Dharm: Revolt of the Untouchables." *1931 Punjab Census Report*, vol. 20, chap. 11.
Ādi Dankā [Newspaper of the Ad Dharm Mandal]. Jullundur, January 19, 1932; February 2, 1933; October 4, 1938; August 7, 1937; September 7, 1937; and May 9, 1939.
Bhatt, G. S. "Trends and Measures of Status Mobility among Chamars of Dehradun." *Eastern Anthropologist* 4 (1961).
Briggs, George W. *The Chamars.* Calcutta: Associated Press; and London: Oxford University Press, 1920.
Goyal, Prem Prakash. "An Inquiry into the Impact of Urbanism on the Magico-Religious Beliefs and Practices of Raidas Chamars of Dehra Dun." M.A. thesis, D.A.V. College, Dehra Dun, 1961.
Jigyasu, Chandrika Prasad. *Shri 108 Svāmi Achhūtānandji Harihar* [Biography of Swami Achutānand, Founder of the Ādi Hindu Āndolan]. Lucknow: Hindu Samaj Sudhar Karyalay, 1960.
Juergensmeyer, Mark. "Ad Dharm: Religion of Untouchables." *Times of India*, October 12, 1975.
Kumaraswami, T. J. "The Adi-Dravidas of Madras." *Man in India* 3 (1923).
Loehlin, Rev. Clinton H. "Notes on Study of Ādi Dankā." Unpublished research notes, c. 1940.
———. "The Punjab 'Ad Dharmis.'" *United Church Review*, December 1937.

Manik, Chanan Lal. "Adi Dharm Bāri" ["About Ad Dharm"]. *Ravidās Patrikā* 1, no. 46 (December 29, 1970).
"Mugowāl Zilā Hoshiārpur de Ād Dharm Skūl: Waddā Bhwāri Diwan" [Mugowal, Hoshiarpur District, in the Ad Dharm School: Huge Public Meeting]. Poster announcing the first Ad Dharm conference. Jullundur: Kishan Steam Press, 1927, in Panjabi. English translation in Mark Juergensmeyer, "Political Hope."
Rama Naidu, M. B. *The Adi Dravida: His Cult, Past and Present*. Presidential Address at the Adi Dravida Conference, Chidambaram, April 21, 1921.
Ram, Mangoo. "Meri Videsh Yātrā utte Merā Jivān Birtānt" [My Foreign Travels and My Life Story]. *Ravidās Patrikā*, Jullundur, vol. 2, nos. 9 through 12 (April 16–27, 1971), in Panjabi.
———. Personal Correspondence: D. A. Bryan, Secretary to the premier, Punjab, to Chaudhri Mangoo Ram, M.L.A., Office Zamindara League, Kutchery Road, Hoshiarpur, Punjab, January 29, 1947; The Governor, Lahore, to Mangoo Ram, May 29, 1939; The Governor, Lahore, to Mangoo Ram, April 10, 1946; K. H. Henderson, Secretary, Punjab Civil Service, Lahore, to Mangoo Ram, February 18, 1947; S. Afzoalali Hosni (Unionist party), to Mangoo Ram, April 19, 1936; Akhtar Husain to Mangoo Ram, February 18, 1947; D. B. N. Shivaraj, President, All-India Scheduled Castes Federation, to Mangoo Ram, June 24, 1946; Sir Sikander Hyat Khan, to Mangoo Ram, March 7, 1934; Mangoo Ram to the Governor of the Punjab, Jullundur City, August 2, 1930; Mangoo Ram to the Prime Minister, British Parliament, London (telegram), October 1931; Revenue Minister, Punjab, to Mangoo Ram, February 17, 1947; Viceregal Lodge, Simla, to Mangoo Ram, May 21, 1931; The Viceroy, Simla, to Mangoo Ram, May 4, 1936.
Ranbir. "Duniya-ki-Dusri Taraf-se—Upne Bhai ke Nam, Pentiesvan Khat" [From the Other Side of the World—To My Brother, Thirty-Fifth Letter]. *Milap*, Jullundur, October 3, 1953, in Urdu.

The New Ad Dharm

"Ad Dharmi Bharāvi lai Shubh Sundesh" [Beautiful News for Ad Dharmi Brethren]. *Ravidās Patrikā* 1, no. 47 (January 5, 1971).
Aurora, Gurdip Singh. *The New Frontiersmen: A Sociological Study of Indian Immigrants in the United Kingdom*. Bombay: Popular Prakashan, 1967.

"Bhari Khed" [Very Sad]. *Ravidās Patrikā* 2, no. 2 (February 16, 1971).
"Dhanowāli dā Shalāghā Yug Faislā." Editorial in the *Ravidās Patrikā* 2, no. 12 (April 27, 1971).
"Guru Ravidās Kālaj Wāli Grāundh Wich Bhāri Samāgam" [Big Meeting on the Guru Ravi Das College Grounds]. *Ravidās Patrikā* 2, no. 19 (June 15, 1971).
Jaspal, Mangu Ram. "Ad Dharmi Bharāwān nu Kush Khabari" [Good News for Ad Dharm Brothers]. *Ravidās Patrikā* 2, no. 19 (June 15, 1971).
———. "Ravidās Patrikā da Janam" [Birth of *Ravidās Patrikā*]. *Ravidās Patrikā* 1, no. 1 (February 17, 1970).
Kataria, M. R. "Sārhe Balmik Bhara" ["Our Balmik Brothers"]. *Ravidās Patrikā* 1, no. 42 (December 1, 1970).
Lakh, Harnam Singh. "Kuch Ad Dharm Bāre" [A Few Things About (the new) Ad Dharm]. *Ravidās Patrikā* 1, no. 41 (December 24, 1970).
"Mūkeriān Kānfrans de Mate" [Mukerian Conference Resolutions]. *Ravidās Patrikā* 2, no. 1 (February 9, 1971).
Ram, Chajju, General Secretary. *Sri Guru Ravidas Trust Report, Sri Govardhanpur, Varansi, U.P.* Ballan, Jullundur District, n.d., c. 1971.
Ram, Sadhu. "Halkā Phillaur de Votrān dā Dannwād" [Thanks to All the Voters of Phillaur]. *Ravidās Patrikā* 2, no. 9 (April 6, 1971).
"Samājwād lai Sunhiri Samān." *Ravidās Patrikā* 2, no. 4 (March 2, 1971).
Sarlie, Bhajan Lāl. "Dharmanchon Dharm Ad-Dharm." *Ravidās Patrikā* 1, no. 44 (December 15, 1970).
Singh, J. D. "Immigrants." *Tribune,* Ambala, January 27, 1971.

Ravi Das and the Sant Movements

Attari, Ishar Singh, ed. *Eh Janam Tumari Lekhe.* Jullundur: Panjabi Sabikya Board, n.d.
Azad, Prithvi Singh. *Ravidās Darshan.* Chandigarh: Sri Guru Ravidas Sansthan, 1973.
Barthwal, Pitambar Datta. *The Nirguna School of Hindi Poetry: An Exposition of Medieval Indian Santa Mysticism.* Benares: Indian Book Shop, 1936.
Bhandarkar, R. G. *Vaisnavism, Śaivism and Minor Religious Systems.* Strassburg: Karl J. Trübner, 1913.
Briggs, George. *Goraknath and the Kanpatta Yogis.* Delhi: Motilal Banarsidass, 1973 (reprint of the 1938 edition).
Chaturvedi, Parashuram, *Uttrī Bhārat kī Sant-Paramparā* [The Sant Tradition of North India], Allahabad: Leader Press, 1952.

Deming, Wilbur S. *Ramdas and the Ramdasis.* Calcutta: Association Press, 1928.
Greeven, R. *The Heroes Five (Panchon Pir).* Allahabad: Pioneer Press, 1898.
McLeod, W. H. *Guru Nanak and the Sikh Religion.* Oxford: Clarendon Press, 1968.
Orr, William G. *A Sixteenth-Century Indian Mystic: Dadu and His Followers.* London: Lutterworth Press, 1947.
Rāe Dāsi kī Bānī [Sayings of Guru Ravi Das]. Allahabād: Belvedere Press, 1908.
Raghavan, V. *The Great Integrators: The Saint-Singers of India.* New Delhi: Ministry of Information and Broadcasting, Government of India, 1966.
Ravi Das. *Nit Naim Bānī* [Moral Sayings]. Jullundur: Guru Ravidass Printing Press, n.d.
Schomer, Karine, and McLeod, W. H. *The Sant Tradition of India.* Berkeley: Berkeley Religious Studies Series, 1981.
Sharma, B. P., ed. *Sant Guru Ravidās-Vānī.* Chandigarh: Sant Guru Ravidas Foundation, 1979.
Singh, Darshan. *Sant Ravidas and His Times.* Delhi: Kalyani Publishers, 1978.
Singh, Padam Gucharan. *Sant Ravidas Vicharak aur Kavi* [Sant Ravi Das, Thinker and Poet], n.p, n.d.
Vaudeville, Charlotte. *Kabir,* vol. 1. Oxford: Clarendon Press, 1974.
Westcott, G. H. *Kabir and the Kabir Panth.* Calcutta: Association Press, 1907.

Arya Samaj

Barrier, N. G. "The Arya Samaj and Congress Politics in the Punjab, 1894–1908." *Journal of Asian Studies,* May 1967.
Das, Ram. *All India Dayanand Salvation Mission Report, 1969–70.* Hoshiarpur, Punjab: Dayanand Salvation Mission, 1970.
Dua, Veena. "Arya Samaj and Punjab Politics." *Economic and Political Weekly* 15 (October 24, 1970).
Graham, James Reid. "The Arya Samaj as a Reformation in Hinduism with Special Reference to Caste." Ph.D. dissertation, Yale University, 1943.
Jones, Kenneth W. *Arya Dharm: Hindu Consciousness in 19th-Century Punjab.* Berkeley and Los Angeles: University of California Press, 1976.
Rai, Lajput. "The Depressed Classes." *Indian Review,* May 1909 and 1913.

———. *On the Upliftment of the Depressed Classes.* Lahore, n.p., 1914.

Ram, Sant (B.A.). *Mere Jiwan Anubhav* [My Life Experiences]. Varanasi: Om Prakash Beri, Hindi Pracharik Prakashan, n.d.

Sahni, Lala R. R. "Self Revelations of an Octagenarian." Unpublished manuscript in the Punjab State Archives of Patiala, Punjab, 1942.

Punjab Christianity

Anderson, Howard E. *Gospel Romance in the Huts of the Punjab.* New York: Revell Co., 1925.

Annett, E. A. *Conversion in India: A Study in Religious Psychology.* Christian Literature Society for India, 1920.

Asimi, Alfred A. "Christian Minority in West Punjab." Ph.D. dissertation, New York University, 1964.

Asirvadham, E. "The Depressed Classes and Christianity." *National Council of Churches (India) Review,* December 1935.

Bandy, C. "The North Indian Presbyterian Mass Movement." *International Review of Missions,* April 1919.

Bowen, John. *Missionary Incitement and Hindoo Demoralization: Including Some Observations on the Political Tendency of the Means Taken to Evangelize Hindoostan.* London, n.p. 1821.

Brush, Stanley. "Protestants in the Punjab: Religion and Social Change in an Indian Province in the Nineteenth Century." Ph.D. dissertation, Department of History, University of California, Berkeley, 1971.

Burditt, J. F. *Work Among the Depressed Classes and the Masses.* Bombay: Education Society's Steam Press, 1893.

Campbell, Ernest Y. *The Church in the Punjab: Some Aspects of Its Life and Growth.* Nagpur: National Christian Council of India, 1961.

Cavalier, A. R. *In Northern India.* London: Zenana Bible and Medical Mission, 1899.

Christian Missionary Society (CMS). *Mass Movement Surveys.* India, 1927 (a series of pamphlets).

Clarkson, Rev. W. *India and the Gospel: An Empire for the Messiah.* London: John Snow, 1851.

Coleman, Fred L. "The Sudra and the Gospel." M.A. thesis, Union Seminary, New York, 1933.

Dubois, Jeane Antoine. *Letters on the State of Christianity in India: In Which the Conversion of the Hindoos Is Considered*

Impracticable. London: Longman, Hurst, Rees, Orme, Brown, and Green, 1823.
Gordon, Andrew. *Our Indian Mission*. Philadelphia: Andrew Gordon, 1888.
Hayter, O. C. G. "Conversion of Outcastes." *Asiatic Review* 26 (1930).
Hayward, Victor, ed. *The Church as Christian Community: Three Studies of North Indian Churches*. London: Butterworth Press, 1966.
Heinrich, J. C. *The Psychology of a Suppressed People*. London: George Allen & Unwin, 1937.
Hunt, W. S. *India's Outcastes: A New Era*. London: Church Missionary Society, 1924.
Koshy, Ninan. *Caste in the Kerala Churches*. Bangalore: Christian Institute for the Study of Religion and Society, 1968.
Lucas, E. D., and Das, Frank Thakur. *The Rural Church in the Punjab*, c. 1938.
Luke, P. Y., and Carman, John B. *Village Christian and Hindu Culture: Study of a Rural Church in Andhra Pradesh, South India*. London: Lutterworth Press, 1968.
Macduff, A. R. *The Utmost Bound of the Everlasting Hills*. London: Nisbet & Co., 1902.
Macnair, J. "Problems Raised by the Indian Mass Movements." *The East and the West*, October 1924.
Madras, Henry. "The Mass Movement Towards Christianity in the Punjab." *International Review of Missions* 2 (1913).
Noble, W. *Floodtide in India: An Eyewitness' Account of the Mass Movements*. London: Cargate Press, 1937.
Pathak, Sushil M. "American Protestant Missionaries in India: A Study of Their Activities and Influence 1813–1910." Ph.D. dissertation, University of Hawaii, 1964.
Philip, P. *The Depressed Classes and Christianity*. Calcutta: National Christian Council, 1925.
Philip. P. O. "The Harijan Movement in India in Relation to Christianity." *International Review of Missions* 24 (1935): 162–177.
Phillips, Rev. G. E. *The Outcastes' Hope: Work Among the Depressed Classes in India*. London: Student Volunteer Missionary Union, 1912.
Phillips, Godfrey. *The Untouchables' Quest: The Depressed Classes of India and Christianity*. Foreword by B. R. Ambedkar. London: Edinburgh House Press, 1936.
Pickett J. Waskom. *Christian Mass Movements in India: A Study With Recommendations*. New York: Abingdon Press, 1933.

——— . *Christian Missions in Mid-India: A Study of Nine Areas, With Especial Reference to Mass Movements.* Jubbulpore: Mission Press, 1938.
Stevenson, Margaret Sinclair. *Without the Pale: The Life Story of an Outcaste.* Calcutta: Association Press, 1930.
Streefland, P. H. *The Christian Punjabi Sweepers: Their History and Their Position in Present-Day Pakistan.* Publication no. 6 of the South and South East Asia Department of Anthropological and Sociological Centre, Amsterdam: University of Amsterdam, 1973. Reprinted by the Christian Study Centre, Rawalpindi, Pakistan. See also J. J. van der Linden's review of the book in *Al-Mushir* 16, no. 1–3 (Jan.–March 1974) (Rawalpindi, Pakistan).
——— . *The Sweepers of Slaughterhouse: Conflict and Survival in a Karachi Neighbourhood.* Assen, The Netherlands: Van Gorcum, 1979.
Webster, John C. B. *Christians and Sikhs in the Punjab: The Village Encounter.* Special number of the *Bulletin of the Christian Institute of Sikh Studies.* Batala, Punjab: Baring Union Christian College, December 1977.
——— . *The Christian Community and Change in Nineteenth Century North India.* Delhi: The Macmillan Company of India, 1976.

Ambedkar Movements

Ambedkar Buddhist Mission. *Constitution of the Ambedkar Buddhist Mission.* Jullundur, Punjab: Ambedkar Buddhist Mission [mimeographed], 1966.
Ambedkar, B. R. *Annihilation of Caste.* Amritsar: Ambedkar School of Thoughts, 1936.
——— . *Thus Spoke Ambedkar: Selected Speeches.* 3 vols. Edited by Bhagwan Das. Jullundur: Bheem Patrika Publications, 1969.
——— . *The Untouchables: Who They Were, and Why Did They Became [sic] Untouchables?* Lucknow: National Herald Press, 1948.
——— . *What Congress and Gandhi Have Done to the Untouchables.* Bombay: Thackur, 1945.
——— . *The Shudras: Who They Were and How They Came to Be the Fourth Varna of the Indo-Aryan Society.* Bombay: Thackur, 1946.
Bharill, Chandra. *Social and Political Ideas of B. R. Ambedkar.* Jaipur: Aalekh Publishers, 1977.

Bheem Patrikā. Ambedkar weekly periodical, edited by L. R. Balley, Jullundur, in Panjabi. *Bheem Patrika,* English language edition, edited by Bhagwan Das, Jullundur.

Fiske, Adele M. "Religion and Buddhism Among India's New Buddhists." *Social Research* 36 (Spring 1969).

———. "Scheduled Caste Buddhist Organizations." In J. Michael Mahar, ed., *The Untouchables in Contemporary India.* Tucson: University of Arizona Press, 1972.

Gandhi or Ambedkar. Foreword by Radhakrishnan. Madras: Gandhi Era Publications, 1945.

Joshi, Barbara Ravenell. "The Buddhist Movement in U.P.: Autonomous Low Caste Mobilization." Unpublished paper presented to the annual conference of the Association for Asian Studies, March 26, 1977.

Kuber, W. N. *Ambedkar: A Critical Study.* New Delhi: People's Publishing House, 1973.

Kulkarni, A. R. "Dr. Ambedkar and Buddhism." *Maha Bodhi* 58 (1950): 338–346.

Leel, K. C. *Ambedkari Āndolan-me Punjābiyō kā Rol* [The Role of Punjabis in the Ambedkar Movement]. Jullundur: Bheem Patrika Press, n.d. (circa 1977).

Miller, R. J. "'They Will Not Die Hindus': The Buddhist Conversion of Mahar Ex-Untouchables." *Asian Survey* 3, no. 9 (September 1967).

Nayar, Baldev Raj. "Religion and Caste in the Punjab: Sidwan Bet Constituency." *Economic Weekly,* August 4, 1962.

Republican Party. *Election Manifesto of 1957.* Delhi: B. D. Khobaragade, 1957.

Robbins, Jeanette. *Dr. Ambedkar and His Movement.* Hyderabad: Dr. Ambedkar Publishing Society, 1964.

Scheduled Castes Federation. *Election Manifesto of the All-India Scheduled Castes Federation.* New Delhi: P. N. Rajbhoj, General Secretary, 1951.

Zelliot, Eleanor. "Background of the Mahar Buddhist Conversion." In *Studies on Asia,* edited by Robert K. Sakai. Lincoln: University of Nebraska Press, 1966.

———. "Buddhism and Politics in Maharastra." In *South Asian Politics and Religion,* edited by Donald Smith. Princeton, N.J.: Princeton University Press, 1966.

———. "Dr. Ambedkar and the Mahar Movement." Ph.D. dissertation, Department of South Asia Studies, University of Pennsylvania, 1969.

———. "Learning the Use of Political Means: The Mahars of Maharashtra." In Kothari, Rajni, *Caste in Indian Politics.*

New York: Gordon and Breach, 1970 (published in India by Orient Longman, 1970).

———. "Religion and Legitimation in the Mahar Movement." In *Religion and Legitimation in South Asia* edited by Bardwell Smith. Leiden: Brill, 1978.

Sweeper Movements

Das, Bhagavan. *Mai Bhangi Hu* [*I Am a Sweeper*]. Jullundur: Bhim Patrika Publications, n.d. (1977?).

———. *Valmiki Jayanti aur Bhangi Jati* [*The Sweeper Caste and Valmiki's Birthday*]. Jullundur: Bhim Patrika Publications, n.d.

Greevens, Col. R. *Knights of Brooms*. Benares: Medical Hall Press, 1894.

Griswold, Harvey D. *Insights into Modern Hinduism*. New York: Henry Holt, 1934.

———. "Religion of the Chuhra." C.M.S. Movement Quarterly, 1918.

Hanes, W. P. "The Chuhras of the Punjab." *Church Missionary Review,* June 1920.

Mahar, Pauline Moller. "Changing Religious Practices of an Untouchable Caste." *Economic Development and Cultural Change* 8.

Prabhakar, K. K. *Social Mobility Among the Sweepers of India.* Edited by B. K. Roy Burman, Census of India. New Delhi: Office of the Registrar General, Ministry of Home Affairs, c. 1962.

Ratan, Ram. "A Study in Magic and Medicine: Treatment by Poison-Sucking Among the Bhangis." In *Vanyajati* 3 (1955).

———. "The Changing Religion of the Bhangis of Delhi." In L. P. Vidyarthi, ed., *Aspects of Religion in Indian Society.* Meerut: Kedar Nath Ram Nath, 1961.

Strickler, J. H. "The Religion and Customs of the Chuhra in the Punjab Province, India." M.A. Thesis, Department of Sociology, University of Kansas, Lawrence, 1926.

Youngson, Rev. J. "The Chuhras." *Indian Antiquary* 35 and 36.

Radhasoami

Dayalbagh Herald. Weekly publication of the Radhasoami Satsang Sabha (Dayalbagh).

Farquhar, J. N. *Modern Religious Movements in India*. New York: Macmillan, 1924.

Griswold, Harvey D. *Insights Into Modern Hinduism.* New York: Henry Holt, 1934.
Johnson, Julian. *With A Great Master in India.* 5th ed. Beas: Radhasoami Satsang (Beas), 1971.
Judgement in Suit: Dayalbagh vs. Soami Bagh. Agra: Radhasoami Satsang Sabha (Dayalbagh), 1965.
Juergensmeyer, Mark. "Radhasoami as a Trans-National Movement." In Jacob Needleman and George Baker, eds., *Understanding the New Religions.* New York: Seabury, 1979.
―――. "The Radhasoami Revival of the Sant Tradition." In Karine Schomer and W. H. McLeod, eds. *The Sant Tradition of India.* Berkeley: Berkeley Religious Studies Series, 1981.
Mathur, Agam Prasad. *The Radhasoami Faith: A Historical Study.* Delhi: Vikas Publishing House, 1974.
Memorandum, Rules and Regulations of Association of Radhasoami Satsang (Beas). Beas: Radhasoami Satsang (Beas), 1957.
Misra, Pandit Brahm Sankar [Maharaj Sahab]. *Discourses on Radhasoami Faith.* Agra: Radhasoami Satsang Sabha (Dayalbagh), 1960.
Radhasoami (Beas) Satsang, Annual Reports. Beas: Radhasoami (Beas) Satsang, 1957–1972.
Sahabji Maharaj as Others Saw Him. (Personal Accounts of Anand Swarup.) Agra: Radhasoami Satsang Sabha (Dayalbagh), 1969.
Sarup, Sir Anand [Sahabji Maharaj]. *Diary of Sahabji Maharaj.* Part 1. (English translation.) Agra: Radhasoami Satsang Sabha (Dayalbagh), 1973.
―――. *Yathārtha Prakāsa.* Part 1. (English translation.) Agra: Radhasoami Satsang Sabha (Dayalbagh), 1954.
Singh, Charan. *St. John, The Great Mystic.* Beas: Radhasoami Satsang (Beas), 1970.
―――. *Spiritual Discourses.* Beas: Radhasoami Satsang (Beas), 1964.
Singh, Jagat. *Science of the Soul.* Beas: Radhasoami Satsang (Beas), 1959.
Singh, Kirpal. *A Brief Life-Sketch of Hazur Baba Sawan Singh-ji Maharaj.* Delhi: Ruhani Satsang, 1949.
Singh, Sawan. *Spiritual Gems.* Beas: Radhasoami Satsang (Beas), 1959.
Singh, Swami Dayal. *Sar Bachan.* 2nd ed. Translated by Sewa Singh. Beas: Radhasoami Satsang (Beas), 1955.
Souvenir in Commemoration of the First Centenary of the Radhasoami Satsang (1861–1961). Agra: Radhasoami Satsang Sabha (Dayalbagh), 1962.

Marxist Movements

Ahmad, Muzaffar. *Communist Party of India: Years of Formation.* Calcutta: National Book Agency, 1959.

Chadha, Tilak Raj. "Punjab's Red and White Communists." *Thought,* June 14, 1952.

Choudhary, Sukhbir, ed. *Peasants' and Workers' Movement in India, 1905–1929.* New Delhi: People's Publishing House, 1971.

Franda, Marcus F. "India's Third Communist Party." *Asian Survey* 9, no. 11 (November 1969).

———. *Radical Politics in West Bengal.* Cambridge, Mass: M.I.T. Press, 1971.

Gough, Kathleen. "Peasant Resistance and Revolt in South India." *Pacific Affairs* 40, no. 4 (Winter 1968).

———. "Class and Agrarian Change: Some Comments on Peasant Resistance and Revolution in India." (Rejoinder to Shah.) *Pacific Affairs* 42, no. 3 (Fall 1969).

Gough, Kathleen, and Sharma, Hari, eds. *Imperialism and Revolution in South Asia.* New York: Monthly Review Press, 1973.

Gupta, Bhabani Sen. *Communism in Indian Politics.* New York: Columbia University Press, 1972.

Mohanty, Manoranjan. *Revolutionary Violence: A Study of the Maoist Movement in India.* New Delhi: Sterling Publishers, 1977.

Nanda, B. R., ed. *Socialism in India.* Delhi: Vikas Publications, 1972.

Natarajan, L. *Peasant Uprisings in India (1850–1900).* Bombay: People's Publishing House, 1953.

Overstreet, Gene D., and Windmiller, Marshall. *Communism in India.* Berkeley and Los Angeles: University of California Press, 1959.

Petrie, Sir David. *Communism in India, 1924–1927.* Calcutta: Editions India, 1928.

Ram, Mohan. *Split Within a Split.* Delhi: Vikas Publications, 1969.

———. *Maoism in India.* Delhi: Vikas Publications, 1971.

Wood, John B. "Observations on the Indian Communist Party Split." *Pacific Affairs* 38 (Spring 1965).

GOVERNMENT REPORTS

Great Britain, Indian Franchise Committee, 1932. *Report of the Indian Franchise Committee, 1932.* 5 vols. London: H.M.S.O., 1932.

Great Britain, First Indian Round Table Conference, London, 1930–1931. *Indian Round Table Conference, 12th November, 1930–19th January, 1931, Proceedings.* London: H.M.S.O. Cmd. 3778, 1931.

Great Britain, Second Indian Round Table Conference, London, 1931. *Indian Round Table Conference, 7th September, 1931–1st December, 1931, Proceedings.* London: H.M.S.O. Cmd. 3997, 1932; *Proceedings of the Federal Structure Committee and Minorities Committee.* London: H.M.S.O., 1932.

Great Britain, Indian Statutory Commission (1928). *Review of Growth of Education in British India.* (Auxiliary Committee of Indian Statutory Commission, Chairman, Sir Philip Hartog.) London: H.M.S.O., Cmd. 3407, 1929.

Great Britain, Indian Statutory Commission (1928). *Report of the Indian Statutory Commission.* 17 vols. London: His Majesty's Stationary Office, 1929–1930.

Great Britain, Government of India (Constitutional Reforms). *Addresses Presented in India to His Excellency the Viceroy and the Right Honourable, the Secretary of State for India.* London: H.M.S.O., Cmd. 9178, 1918.

Great Britain, Government of India, The Reforms Committee (Franchise, 1918). *Evidence Taken Before the Reforms Committee.* 2 vols. Calcutta: Government of India, 1919.

Great Britain, Government of India, Registrar General. *Punjab Census Report, 1881.* Lahore, 1882. *Punjab Census Report, 1891.* Lahore, 1892. *Punjab Census Report, 1901.* Lahore, 1902. *Punjab Census Report, 1911.* Lahore, 1912. *Punjab Census Report, 1921.* Lahore, 1922. *Punjab Census Report, 1931.* Lahore, 1932. *Punjab Census Report, 1941.* Lahore, 1942. *United Provinces Census Report, 1911.* Lucknow, 1912.

Government of India, Commission of Scheduled Castes and Tribes. *Annual Reports.* New Delhi: Government of India, 1951 to the present.

Government of India, Department of Social Welfare. *Report of the Committee on Untouchability, Economic and Educational Development of the Scheduled Castes and Connected Documents* [The Elayaperumal Report]. New Delhi: Government of India, 1969.

Government of India, Office of the Registrar General. *Punjab Census Reports, 1951; Punjab Census Reports, 1961; Punjab Census Reports, 1971.*

Government of India, Office of the Registrar General, Ethnographic Studies. *Chambers, Khatiks, Nats, Pernas, Kolis or Koris, Sikligars and Sapelas.* Census of India, 1961.

———, Office of Registrar General, India, Ministry of Home Affairs. *Mallah of Delhi.* Census of India, 1961.

———, Office of the Registrar General, Ministry of Home Affairs. *Sikligar of Delhi.* New Delhi: Census of India, 1961.

———. *Social Mobility Movements Among Scheduled Castes and Scheduled Tribes of India.* n.d.

———. *Study of Customary Rights and Living and Working Conditions of Scavengers in Two Towns.* Monograph Series, vol. 1, part 2-D. New Delhi: Manager of Publications, 1966.

———. *Vanna: A Scheduled Caste of Madras.* Census of India, 1961, vol. 1, Ethnographic Study no. 4. New Delhi: Office of the Registrar General, India, Ministry of Home Affairs.

Government of India, Parliamentary Report. *Report of the Backward Classes Commission.* 3 vols. (Kalelkar Commission Report), New Delhi: Government of India Press, 1956.

Government of India, Planning Commission. *Report of the Committee on Distribution of Income and Levels of Living.* (The Mahalanobis Committee Report), February 1964.

Government of Punjab, The Board of Economic Enquiry Punjab (India). Publication no. 121. *Farm Accounts in the Punjab 1967–68.* Jullundur City: Swan Printing Press, 1970.

———. Publication no. 122. *Family Budgets.* Jullundur City: Swan Printing Press, 1970.

Government of Punjab, Department of Scheduled Castes and Backward Classes' Welfare. Letter to Mark Juergensmeyer from the Superintendent, Social Welfare, May 14, 1971, itemizing numbers and percentages of Scheduled Castes actually employed in each of the four categories of Punjab government service.

Government of Punjab. *District Gazeteers: Amritsar District* (A. MacFarquhar, ed.). Chandigarh: Government Press, 1947.

———. *Jullundur District.* Lahore: Government Press, 1935.

———. *Statistical Tables.* Lahore: Government Press, 1933.

———. *Jullundur District Handbook* (R. L. Anand, ed.). Chandigarh: Government of Punjab, 1966.

———. *Gurgaon District Gazeteer.*

———. *Hissar District Gazeteer.*

———. *Imperial Gazeteer.*

Government of Punjab, Election Commission. A. N. Kashyap, Commissioner. *Report on General Elections in Punjab, 1967.* Chandigarh: the Government Press, 1968.

Government of Punjab, Finance Department. *Punjab on the March 1971.* Chandigarh, 1971.

Government of Punjab, Legislature Reports. *The Report of the Evaluation Committee on Welfare, Regarding the Welfare of Scheduled Castes, Backward Classes and Denotified Tribes in Punjab State.* (The "Brish Bhan Report"). Chandigarh: The Secretary to Government, Punjab, Welfare Department, 1966.

Government of Punjab, Public Relations Department, Research and Reference Section. *Facts About Punjab.* Chandigarh: Director, Information and Publicity, Punjab, November 1970.

Government of Haryana, Planning Department. G. S. Bhalla, *Changing Structure of Argiculture in Haryana: A Study of the Impact of the Green Revolution, 1969–1970.* Report prepared by the Haryana Agricultural Project Team, Department of Economics, Punjab University. Chandigarh: The Economic and Statistical Organization, Planning Department, Government of Haryana, 1972.

NEWSPAPERS AND PERIODICALS

Ādi Dankā, weekly newspaper of the Ad Dharm movement. Sant Ram "Azad," editor. In Urdu. Jullundur, from 1927 to 1938. Selected issues in the possession of Mangoo Ram, Garhshankar, Punjab.

Bheem Patrika, weekly journal of Ambedkar Mission Society. L. R. Balley, editor. In Hindi. Jullundur, from 1960 to the present. English version, Bhagwan Das, editor. New Delhi, from 1973 to the present.

Dayalbagh Herald, weekly journal of Radhasoami Satsang Sabha (Dayalbagh). Babu Ram Jadoun, editor. In English. Agra, from 1970 to the present.

Hindustan Times. New Delhi, 1965 to the present.

Indian Social Reformer. Indian Social Conference, Bombay, founded in 1890.

Mitra's Annual Register (Indian Annual Register). N. N. Mitra, editor. Calcutta, The Annual Register Office, 1918–1947.

Northern Indian Patrika. Allahabad, 1966.

R. S. Greetings, bimonthly magazine of the North American Sangat, Radhasoami Satsang (Beas). Published by the Seva Trust, Waukegan, Illinois.

Ravidās Patrikā, weekly newspaper of the new Ad Dharm movement, Chanan Lal "Manik," editor, Mangu Ram "Jaspal," proprietor. In Panjabi. Jullundur, from 1970 to the present.

Statesman. New Delhi, from 1965 to the present.

Times of India. New Delhi, 1965 to the present.
Tribune. Lahore, 1921–1935.
Tribune. Ambala, 1965 to the present.
Valmik Sundesh, monthly journal of the Punjab Valmik Sabha. Nahal Chand Chetta, editor. In Urdu. Amritsar, 1970 to the present.

INDEX

Achutanand, Swami, 24n, 25–26
Achutistan, 144–145, 145n, 147
Achut Uddhar Mandal, 38, 65, 301
Ad Dharm, 1, 6, 55, 192–193, 196, 204, 208–209, 212–213, 217, 220, 232, 241, 248, 250, 252–254, 257, 262, 266–267, 269, 271, 273–278, 280; activities of, 72–76, 109–114, 126–129, 134–140, 142–152; alliance with Christians, 182–184; alliance with Sweepers, 170–173; All India Ad Dharm Mandal, 70; as a caste name, 108, 153, 198, 215, 246–248, 262; Brahmans in, 50; composition of, 77–80; decline of, 151–155, 159, 161–164; education in, 120–121; factions in, 64, 68–70; finances of, 55–59, 110, 113, 149, 290; Hoshiarpur group, 41n, 70; ideology of, 130; Jains in, 50; Jullundur group, 41, 70; leaders in, 36–40, 62, 110, 118, 146, 152, 164–165, 177n, 217, 219, 267, 279; modern values in, 115, 119–123; Muslim support, 147–151; mythology of, 46–50, 71, 89, 182, 261, 291–299; name of, 24, 26, 260, 263; Naujawan Santokh Sabha in, 61; origins of, 22, 30, 35–42, 288, 293, 298–299; poetry of, 76, 110, 112, 120–122, 136; religion of, 45–53; revival of, 258–264; schools of, 288; social values in, 303–308; symbols of, 53–54, 62, 83–91, 110, 112, 138, 301; theology of, 120; women in, 110, 121, 304–306; worship in, 52

Ad Dharm Federation of the United Kingdom, 256

Ad Dharm Report, 40n, 58, 61, 69, 74, 125, 138, 147n, 148, 148n, 170, 290–308

Ad Dharm Scheduled Caste Federation, 260, 262, 264

Adi Danka, 56, 56n, 69, 149, 308

Adi Dravidas, 24, 274

Adi Hindus, 24, 25, 274

Adi Purkh, 51

Adivasis, 274

Ad Prakash, 121, 299, 303

Ahmad, Mirza, 148n

Ahmadiyya movement, 28, 40, 148, 148n

Ahmed, Dr. Feroz-ud-din, 148n

Aiyodhidas, Pandit, 25

Akali Dal, 31, 144, 206, 227, 230

Akali party, 198, 227, 227n, 229
Alam, Nidhan Singh, 289n
Ali, Barhat, 298n
Allahpind, 190, 214–215, 225–226
All India Depressed Classes Association, 23
All India Depressed Classes Conference, 136
All India Depressed Classes Federation, 23, 125
All India Suppressed Classes League, 242n
Ambedkar, Dr. Bhim Rao, 26, 39n, 46, 70, 104, 127, 127n, 139, 145n, 153, 162–163, 168, 193, 219, 223, 260–261, 266, 270, 274, 281, 289; biography of, 159–165
Ambedkar Mission Society, 167
Ambedkar movements, 147, 169, 192–193, 196, 208, 249–250, 268, 271, 278
Ambedkar, Yeshwant Rao, 163n, 171n
Amritsar, 79
Antaj Uddhar Mandal, 65, 293, 301
Aroras, 169, 174
Aryans, 47–49, 71, 182, 295–297
Arya Samaj, 2, 28n, 30–31, 35, 42, 49–50, 55, 57, 64, 67–68, 70, 73–74, 80, 121, 124, 132, 139–140, 144, 155, 170, 177, 181, 208, 212, 214–215, 214n, 220, 226, 254, 273, 277, 297–298; conversion into, 38–39; history of, 38–39; schools, 37–38, 41, 65, 147n, 254; Untouchable organizations in, 38, 64–66, 293, 298–301; Untouchables in, 26–27, 40–41, 43
Aurobindo, Sri, 43, 277, 289
auspiciousness, 96, 96n

Azad, Prithvi Singh, 74n, 126n, 242n
Azad, Sant Ram, 41n, 55, 153

Babb, Lawrence A., 96n
Babbar Akalis, 31
Backward castes, 20
Badal, Prakash Singh, 229, 243
Badowalia, Hari Singh, 285n
Bahishkrit Hitkarini Sabha, 168n
Bala Shah, 101, 171–172, 176, 186
Balley, Lohori Ram, 137n, 145n, 163, 165–166, 168n, 193, 219, 230n, 238, 242n, 291
Balmik Ad Dharm Mahasabha Akalianwala, 60
Balmik, Rishi. *See* Valmiki, Rishi
Balmiki Gate, 174, 177, 179
Balmikis, 101, 180, 271. *See also* Chuhras
Baloo, Moti Lal, 248n
Barkat, Dr. Masih, 191n
Bazigars, 16
Begar, 14, 25, 135, 302
Berreman, Gerald D., 276n
Bhagavad Gita, 113
Bhakna, Sohan Singh, 285
Bhakti, 4–5, 85–86, 105, 252
Bhanjres, 45, 298
Bharat Dalit Sevak Sangh, 242
Bharati Muzdoor Sangh, 178
Bhartiya Depressed Classes League, 242n
Bhartiya Masihi Dal, 190–191
Bhartras, 247
Bheem Patrika, 163, 166
Bhil, 45
Bimla, 198–200
Biradari, 300
Blacks in the United States, 15, 56, 204, 264
Bombay Presidency Social Reform Association, 23

Index 349

Boota Mandi, 94n, 115–119, 146, 217–218, 245, 259, 264–265, 267
Brahmans, 88–89, 103, 105, 178, 215, 284; in Ad Dharm, 50; Untouchable, 102
Briggs, George, 94, 98n
British: anti-Indian nationalism of, 286; army cantonments of, 36; army of, 117, 134, 179; ideology of, 22; in India, 12, 14, 29, 49, 125, 132–141, 154, 160, 186, 202, 297; policies of, 73–74, 126, 132–141, 195; prejudice against Indians, 247, 254
Bryan, D. A., 155n
Buddhism, 4, 161–164, 166, 249, 278, 280–281
Buddhists, 261n, 271
Burrs, 298

Calcutta, 117–118
California, 42, 284–285
Campbell, E. Y., 187n
Caste, 184, 219, 237, 276; concept of, 2–3, 12, 15, 71, 105, 207; identity, 16; in Punjab, 6, 181–192; names of, 12; racial origins of, 47n
Caste and class, 16, 18, 20, 135, 194, 194n, 204
Census, 31
Census of 1931, 61, 72, 80
Census policies, 92–93
Chamars, 1, 12–13, 16–17, 35, 42–43, 45, 51, 59–60, 62–63, 79–80, 86, 89–90, 100n, 102, 107–109, 117, 119, 122, 134n, 153, 155n, 160, 169–170, 172, 177, 177n, 182, 194–195, 198, 214, 224, 246–247, 249, 256, 259, 262, 265–266, 274, 283–285, 298; Klare subcaste, 117–118, 123; Mehay subcaste, 117–118, 123; occupation of, 18
Chamba, 60
Chambras, 298
Chand, Amar, 251
Chand, Aram, 248n
Chand, Devi, 248n
Chand, Harnam, 287n
Chand, Mahatma Fakir, 60n, 171, 263
Chand, Prakash, 200
Chand, Prem, 151n
Chand, Ram, 55
Chand, Sawan, 248n
Chand, Swaran, 256n
Chand, Thakar, 35, 41, 56, 68–69, 146
Chandar, Mahesh, 285n
Chandra, Ram, 285n
Chinese shoemakers, 117
Chopri, Duni Chand, 165
Christendom, 180, 184, 186–187
Christianity, 5, 44, 49, 52, 67, 77, 179–180, 208, 212, 220, 297; concept of, 93; conversion into, 26–27, 182; in England, 251; in India, 237; in Pakistan, 191–192, 225; in Punjab, 31, 77, 268, 277, 280, 282
Christian League, 191
Christians, 1, 73, 77, 133, 179–180, 184–185, 193, 208, 214, 226, 298; communities of, 183; converts of, 122; missionaries of, 55, 121, 172, 181, 188
Chuhras, 1, 11, 13, 16, 45, 60, 60n, 63, 73, 79–80, 96, 122, 134n, 155n, 161, 169–172, 174, 179, 181–182, 193–195, 198, 214, 224–225, 249, 249n, 262, 266, 273, 298; customs of, 101, 104, 177; Gill subcastes, 175;

Chuhras, (con't.)
  Kalyana subcastes, 175; Nadar subcastes, 175; occupation of, 18; Sabbarwal subcastes, 175; Sondi subcastes, 175. *See also* Mazhabi Sikhs
Class: *See* caste and class
Communalism, 29, 139, 143, 226–230, 232, 234, 264, 275
Communism. *See* Marxism; Communist party
Communist party, 193–207. *See also* Naxalites
Congress party, 23, 28, 30–31, 125–127, 136, 138, 140, 145–146, 149–150, 153–154, 159, 165, 177, 177n, 196, 202, 205, 207, 207n, 228, 228n, 241–244, 252, 259, 264; Harijan cell of, 242–243

D.A.V. colleges, 27
Dadu, 86, 209
Dadupanthis, 86
Dalit Panthers, 264–266
Dalit Sangarsh Samiti, 226, 271
Dandekar, V. M., 231
Das, Bhagat Guran, 242
Das, Bhagwan, 167, 242n, 289n
Das, Charan, 248n, 285n, 286
Das, Harcharand, 248n, 250, 287n
Das, Hari, 252n
Das, Harnam, 146n, 283, 285n, 286
Das, Hiran, 85, 87
Das, Pipal, 84–85, 260
Das, Principal Ram, 35, 145n, 171n
Das, Ravi. *See* Ravi Das
Das, Sarwan, 84–85, 260–261, 264
Das, Seth Kishan, 59, 59n, 116–117, 117n, 118–119, 126n, 145n, 146, 147n, 151n, 152–153, 161, 164, 259n

Das, Sundar, 117–119, 217, 259, 266
Das Thakar, 37
Daskawie, Dr. M.A.Q., 191n
Dayal, Swami. *See* Shiv Dayal Singh
Dayanand Dalit Uddhar Mandal, 38, 69–70, 293, 301
Dayanand, Swami. *See* Saraswati, Swami Dayanand
Depressed Classes League, 242
Depressed Classes Mission, 159
Depressed Classes Mission, Lahore, 125
Desh Bhagat Yadghar, 203
Dharm, 2–3, 6, 96, 98, 100, 108, 119, 123, 209, 266, 273, 295
Dharmik identity, 2–6, 93–94, 109, 113, 115, 123, 273
Diwan, Gurbax Singh, 194n, 201n
Doms, 298
Dumont, Louis, 3, 5, 11n, 13, 97n, 275–276

Education, 135–136, 185, 236–237, 255, 283, 303, 305
Elections, 145–152, 244
Equality, 121, 130, 132, 187–188, 193, 213n, 217–219, 241, 261, 300
Erikson, Erik, 72

Frankel, Francine R., 231
Fresno, 284
Fuchs, Stephen, 4n, 98n
von Fürer-Haimendorf, Christoph, 103

Gadar party, 30–31, 30n, 36, 39n, 43, 133, 154, 201–203, 254, 285–288
Gait, Edward, 73

Index

Gait circular, 73n
Galanter, Marc, 273n
Gandhi, Indira, 176, 224, 228, 244, 265
Gandhi, Mohandas K., 4–5, 13, 16, 23, 28, 31, 43–44, 72, 124–131, 139, 142, 149, 154n, 161, 163–164, 171, 206, 237, 241, 243, 270–272, 277, 289
Ghadhilias, 298
Gill, Om Prakash, 171n, 175, 177, 263
Gill, Ram Lal, 178–179
God: concept of, 51, 100
Gogapir, 53n, 102, 102n
Government of India Act, 23, 26, 29, 136, 143, 149
Green Revolution, 231–232
Gujarat, 79
Gujjar, 108
Guru, 52–53, 302, 304, 308
Gypsies, 16

Hamdard Hindu Injamin Ahmadiya, 148
Harappan civilization, 48
Hardayal, Lala, 285n, 289n
Harijan, 13, 16, 252
Harijan League, 242
Harijan Sevak Sangh, 131, 242
Harijan Social Forum, 178
Haryana, 228
Henderson, K. H., 154n
Hinduism, 4, 5, 84, 105, 113, 120, 124, 176, 208, 210, 225–226, 262, 272, 296–298, 301; concept of, 64–65, 92–94, 96; definition of, 1, 3; deities of, 172; reform movements of, 148; tradition of, 51
Hindus, 72–74, 143, 174, 180, 182, 187–188, 219, 224, 226, 230, 243, 272–273, 296; as a qaum, 50; customs of, 96n; use of the term, 26, 181
Hoshiarpur, 35, 62–63, 69–70, 72, 77, 87, 146, 153, 200, 263, 288
Husain, Akhtar, 151n, 154n, 155n

Independence (of India), 220, 223–224, 301
Indian Ad Dharm Federation in the Punjab, 256
Indian Christian Fellowship, 249n
Indian Franchise Commission, 139
Indian Immigrants: in Britain, 36, 116, 179, 245–246, 245n, 246n, 254–256; in New Zealand, 59; in Singapore, 59; in the United States, 36, 42–43, 202, 284–285; policies affecting, 245n, 246n, 254–256
Indian Mutual Support and Social Association, West Midlands, Ltd., 250
Indian National Congress. *See* Congress party
Indian Republic Group of Great Britain, 249
Indian Statutory Commission. *See* Simon Commission
Indian Welfare Association, 248–249
Iqbal, Sir Muhammad, 144
Isaac, Harold, 239–240
Islam, 2, 5, 210; conversion into, 27. *See also* Muslims

Jaini, Padmanabh S., 274n
Jainism, 4
Jains: in Ad Dharm, 50
Janata party, 264
Jandiala, 197–200, 215

Jan Sangh, 177–178, 206, 243
Jaspal, Mangu Ram, 258–260, 262, 264; biography of, 253–256
Jatistan, 144n
Jat Path Thorak Mandal, 39, 39n
Jats, 5, 108, 144n, 175, 198, 200, 203–204, 206, 229, 246–248; Jolh subcastes, 197–215
Jinnah, Muhammad Ali, 144, 151
Josh, Sohan Singh, 201n, 202–203
Julahas, 225, 298
Jullundur, 35–36, 55–56, 62–63, 72, 77, 79, 84, 87, 115, 117–118, 126, 146–147, 153, 170, 174–175, 179, 189, 200, 205, 208, 216, 238, 243n, 246, 254, 263, 265–266, 288, 302

Kabir, 51, 85–86, 102, 105, 252, 262, 292, 296, 298–299, 304
Kabirpanth, 86, 298
Kairon, Pratap Singh, 153, 154n, 177n, 228, 228n
Kangra, 60, 79
Kapurthala, 77
Karma, 97–99
Karmic retribution, 71, 98n, 99
Kataria, M. R., 261n
Khait Mazdur Sabha, 204–205
Khalsa Diwan, 28
Khalsa, Gopal Singh, 146n
Khan, Sir Sikander Hyat, 149–151, 149n, 150n
Khan, Zafarulla, 149
Khanna, K. L., 218n
Khar, Jugindir Lal, 256
Khatris, 169, 174–175
Kirti party, 201–202
Kisan Sabha, 204
Kishan, Ram, 228n
Kishori, Juggal, 146n
Klaranwala, Sant, 210

Komagatamaru incident, 285n
Kotakapura movement, 210

Lahor Achut, 301
Lahore, 77
Lal, Bakshi, 60n
Lal Beg, 101, 171, 172
Lal, Chunni. *See* Thapur, Chunni Lal
Lal, Hari, 107–109
Lal, Kishan, 213
Lal, Lala Mohan, 170, 242
Lal, Mani, 248n
Lal, Pandit Kishori, 201n
Lal, Shadi, 177n
Lal, Sham, 248n
Land Alienation Act, 29, 29n, 36, 126, 195n
Landless laborers, 18, 169, 194–196, 204–205, 231–232
Landlordism, 195n
Landlords, 205, 231–232
Landowners, 226
Land redistribution, 154
Land Transfer Act, 301
Leather industry, 134–135
Leather trade, 36–37, 42, 59, 116–119, 283–284
Leatherworkers. *See* Chamars
Loehlin, Clinton, 56, 183, 188n
Lower castes. *See* Untouchables
Lyallpur, 62–63, 67, 70, 77, 79

McLeod, W. H., 87n, 105n
Mahar, 160, 265
Mahashas, 214, 214n, 298
Mal, Reverend Y. C., 189
Mal, Samuel, 191
Malhotra, S. L., 74n
Malik, Suneila, 240
Manik, Chanan Lal, 41n, 256
Manu, 49, 161, 296, 298, 302–303
Manusmrti, 161

Marglin, Frédérique Appfel, 97n
Marijuana, 19, 121
Marriott, McKim, 96n
Martin, Reverend S., 181
Marxism, 193–194, 196–207, 216
Marxists, 166, 220, 268, 275, 277
Masihi Sangat, 191
Masihi Sevak Sangh, 191
Mazhabi Sikhs, 92, 134n, 225, 261
Meghs, 27, 214, 225, 266, 298
Mehay, Chanda Ram, 217
Mehay, Manohar Lal, 117, 259, 266–267
Mehay, Sat Pal, 266
Mehta, Gursarandas, 212n
Mirasis, 16
Mochis, 225
Model Town, 232, 235, 238–239, 245, 249, 256–257
Montgomery, 77
Moore, Barrington, 4
Morley-Minto Reforms, 29
Mormans, 29n
Mughul governments, 49
Mukand, Bal, 173
Multan, 77
Muslims, 72–74, 92, 117, 125, 132, 143, 147, 174, 192, 224, 226, 273, 298, 307n; as a qaum, 50; customs of, 96n, 101; Untouchable, 14, 23
Muslim landlords, 148–149
Muslim landowners, 29
Muslim League, 144, 150–151, 150n, 277

Nadar, Hari Krishan, 171n, 174
Nadar, R. K., 178
Nadars, 24, 267
Nala, 213, 215
Nam Dev, 252, 262, 299, 304
Nanak, Guru, 209, 209n, 239, 251, 281, 292

Narcotics, 19
Nationalism, 30–31, 68, 74, 140; ideology of, 22
Nath, Gorakh, 104
Nath Yoga tradition, 104–105
Naujawan Bharat Sabha, 201
Nayar, Baldev Raj, 229
Nehru, Jawaharlal, 154, 224
Nehru, Motilal, 126
Nehru Report, 127
New Zealand, 59, 59n
Nirankaris, 211, 211n, 277
Nizamuddin, Khasa Jusid, 148

Omvedt, Gail, 265n
Opium, 121

Pakistan, 144, 150–151, 150n, 191, 204, 224, 224n, 226
Panchayats, 18–19, 110
Panth, 2, 6, 87, 87n
Panthic League, 150
Panthik: identity, 2–6, 109, 113, 273; movements, 107, 132
Paraiyan Mahajana Sabha, 25
Paramanand, Bhai, 39n
Patanga, B. L., 178
Patat Uddhar Mandal, 65, 293, 301
Pawar, Ishwar Das, 60n, 67n, 246, 246n, 262
Permanand, Bhai, 288n
Philippines, 387
Politics: definition of, 142
Pollution, 11–13, 18, 71, 96n, 99, 100, 119, 188, 276, 284
Poona Pact, 143, 164
Poverty, 15, 18, 219, 234, 263, 276; culture of, 15, 15n
Prasad, Rajendra, 154n
Pratap, Inder, 281
Premchand, 234–235
Presbyterian church, 183

Punjab: cities of, 234; castes in, 13, 16–21; characteristics of central districts, 35–36, 72; partition of, 224–230, 230n; politics of, 227–230, 241–244; religion of, 2–3, 5–6, 14; Republican party in, 165, 259, 260; social strata, 18, 281; Untouchables in, 14, 15n
Punjab Scheduled Caste Board, 243n
Punjab Service Cooperative Society, Ltd., 255
Punjabi Suba, 228–230, 230n
Purity, 11, 12n, 13, 18, 71, 96n, 99, 119, 276

Qaum, 2, 6, 46–47, 50, 53–55, 62, 67, 70–71, 74, 76, 107–108, 110, 112, 120, 132, 140, 143, 155, 241, 251, 255, 261, 273, 292, 295, 300–301, 303, 307–308; definition of, 45
Qaumik identity, 2–6, 109, 113, 273
Qaum Savings Bonds, 255

Radhasoami, 208–220, 266, 268, 271, 277, 282
Raedasis. *See* Ravi Das, panth
Rai, Basant. *See* Rai, Vasant
Rai, Vasant, 35, 37–38, 41, 56, 68, 69, 70, 127
Raj, Lala Hans, 56, 146n, 170n
Raj, Lala Mulk, 170n
Rajah, M. C., 24, 26, 136–137, 139, 159
Rajputs, 61, 79
Raksha Dal, 173
Ramanand, 85, 88
Ram, Bagoo, 259
Ram, Chanan, 145n, 154n
Ram Das, Guru, 89–90
Ramdasias, 214–216, 225, 246, 261

Ramdasis. *See* Ravi Das, panth
Ram, Gandu, 60n, 171
Ram, Hari, 41n, 55, 264
Ram, Hazara, 41n, 146n, 206, 263
Ram, Inder, 291
Ram, Jagjwan, 145n, 252, 264
Ram, Mali, 59
Ram, Mangoo, 37, 41, 50, 55, 57–58, 60n, 61, 67–68, 70, 85, 109–110, 123, 126–129, 126n, 127n, 133, 136, 137n, 139, 145–155, 145n, 151n, 154n, 161–163, 183, 193, 242, 254, 258, 262–264, 267, 270, 277–279, 287n, 298; biography of, 42–44, 283–289
Ram, Munshi Jhandoo, 111
Ram, Ranki, 252n
Ram, Sadhu, 37, 67n, 70, 149, 153, 161, 164, 219, 241, 242n
Ram, Sant, B.A., 38, 39n, 145n, 170n
Ram, Sant, M.L.A., 171, 173, 177n, 241, 242
Ram, Seth Kushi, 126, 259, 262
Ram, Sharda, 248n
Ramgarhias, 247
Ravi Das, 51, 53n, 61, 100, 102, 105, 112, 147, 153, 153n, 155n, 209, 216–217, 239, 255–256, 260, 262, 266, 272, 294, 298–299, 304; as a symbol, 83–91, 115–116, 119, 248, 248n, 251, 259, 271, 274; *deras*, 83–85, 87, 88n, 267, 281; myths about, 87; panth, 87, 89–90; temple in Benares, 260–262, 264; temple in England, 250–252, 264; veneration of, 52, 85, 163, 252–254, 261, 264, 281; writings of, 52, 84, 87, 111, 251–252
Ravi Das College, 254

Index

Ravi Das Cultural Association, 250
Ravi Das High School, 152
Ravidasis. *See* Ravi Das, panth
Ravidas Patrika, 256, 258–261, 264
Ravi Das Sabhas, 87; in England, 248–252, 248n, 254–255, 259
Religion: concept of, 1–3
Religious movements, 2, 20, 207–208, 210n, 220, 268, 277–282
Republican party, 153, 160, 164–166, 193, 196; in Punjab, 165, 259–260
Round Table Conference, 127, 160, 294

Sachasauda movement, 210
Sachkhand, 120
Safai Muzdoor Sanga. *See* Sweepers Union
Sai Baba, Satya, 277
Sanatanis, 298
Sanitation workers, 175
Sansis, 45, 298
Sanskritization, 272
Sants, 51, 83–86, 102, 104–105, 209–210, 272, 299n
Sant tradition, 210, 274
Sant synthesis, 105n
Sarabha, Kartar Singh, 285n
Saraswati, Swami Dayananda, 38, 47, 297
Sarvodaya movement, 277
Sat Nam, Guru, 89–90
Satnamis, 86, 298
Scheduled Castes: definition of, 14. *See also* Untouchables
Scheduled Caste Corporation, 263
Scheduled Caste Federation, 147n, 151n, 153, 161–164, 166, 241, 260

Separate electorates, 127–129, 164, 237
Shahpur, 79
Shakta cults, 105
Shastri, Sohan Lal, 171n
Sheikhapura, 77
Shiromani Akali Dal. *See* Akali Dal
Shiromani Gurdwara Parbandhak Committee, 227, 267
Shiva, 101
Shivaraj, D.B.N., 153n
Shiv Narayans, 86
Shiv Sena, 277
Shuddhi, 27, 49–50, 64
Shudranand, Swami, 35–37, 39–41, 56, 67n, 68–69, 110, 118, 126n, 137n, 148, 154n, 243, 262, 267
Sikhism, 2, 6, 51, 84, 89, 105, 162, 201, 210, 225; Untouchables in, 27–28, 66, 90, 92–93, 108
Sikhistan, 144, 145n
Sikhization, 272
Sikhs, 72–74, 76, 132, 143, 145, 148n, 149–150, 181, 188, 198, 208, 210, 211n, 224–230, 239, 243, 247–248, 251, 254, 261, 267, 272–273, 281, 297–298, 307n; as a qaum, 50; customs of, 96; gurus of, 83–90; reform movements of, 148
Simon Commission, 25n, 125, 136–139, 293
Singh, Amar Nath, 189n, 238
Singh, Baba Gurdit, 285n
Singh, Baba Gurmukh, 201
Singh, Baryam, 248n
Singh, Basant. *See* Vasant Rai
Singh, Bela, 286
Singh, Bhag, 203
Singh, Bhagat, 102, 201
Singh, Bhuja, 203

Singh, Chaudhry Prem, 146n
Singh, Darbara, 177n
Singh, Dasandha, 59, 59n
Singh, Gambhir, 287n
Singh, Gopal, 151n
Singh, Gurnam, 229
Singh, Gurvanta, 37, 146, 147n, 151n, 152–153, 177n, 241, 242n, 256
Singh, Gyani Bhagwan, 285n
Singh, Hari, 205n, 287n, 288n
Singh, Hukum, 227n
Singh, Jagat, 212n
Singh, Khushwant, 227
Singh, Master Charan, 213, 216, 218n
Singh, Master Santa, 248n
Singh, Master Tara, 228
Singh, Mohtan, 173
Singh, Mulla, 151n
Singh, Mullan, 146n
Singh Sabha, 2, 28, 55, 80, 201
Singh, Sant Nadar, 210
Singh, Satwant, 194n, 196, 201n, 205
Singh, Shiv Dayal, 209
Singh, Sundar, 139
Singh, Vasant. *See* Vasant Rai
Smelser, Neil, 280n
Snakes, 102, 104
Social movements. *See* religious movements
Soham, 52, 299, 256n
Sohpal, Bhagat Ram, 248n, 256
Sondi, S. L., 217
South India: Untouchables in, 24, 25
Soviet Union, 203
Spirits, good and evil, 94–97, 100, 108, 113
Srinivasan, R. B., 160
Srinivas, M. N., 272
States Reorganization Act, 227

Suman, Gurmit Chand, 248n
Sweepers. *See* Chuhras
Sweepers Union, 173–177

Thapur, Chunni Lal, 60–61, 170, 173
Thapar, Romila, 274n
Times of India, 237
Tradition: concept of, 280
Tribal religion, 103

Unionist party, 31, 147, 149–151, 150n
Untouchability: government policies against, 223, 235–237; policies related to, 23; protests against, 160, 245, 258, 264–266, 269, 303; stigmas of, 1, 5, 14, 17, 42, 54, 283–284, 288
Untouchables: as a term, 17–18, 124, 252; benefits for, 136, 235–238, 266, 270, 294; Brahman, 103; castes in, 45, 60, 298; customs of, 19, 88–89, 99, 121, 186, 239, 251–252; definition of, 11, 12n, 13–14, 223n; economic conditions of, 118, 175, 194–196, 206, 230–232, 234–235, 255; ex-Untouchables, 223, 235, 239–240, 289; family patterns of, 19; identity of, 20–21, 28, 43, 55, 73–74, 93–94, 123, 127, 180, 187, 229, 233, 239, 244, 263, 267, 291; in British army, 134; in Punjab, 14, 15n; in South India, 24, 25; Muslim, 14, 23; organizations of, 22–26, 68–69; origins of, 104; poverty of, 14; religion of, 6, 28, 92–107, 113–114, 269–275; Sikh, 27–28, 66, 90, 92–93, 108

Valmiki Ashram, 172
Valmiki, Rishi, 53n, 112, 155n, 170, 170n, 172, 176, 251, 261, 271, 298–299, 304
Valmikis. *See* Balmikis
Valmiki Sabhas, 60, 60n, 169–171, 171n, 172, 174, 176–177, 179, 192, 208, 220, 242, 249, 263, 268, 271, 279–280, 282
Valmiki Youth Association, 178

Vaudeville, Charlotte, 105n
Virdi, Santokh, 265

Weber, Max, 4, 98n, 281
Wolin, Sheldon, 143
Women: sexual abuse of, 14. *See also* Ad Dharm: women in

Zamindara League, 154n
Zelliot, Eleanor, 265n

Designer: Barbara Llewellyn
Compositor: Viking Typographics
Printer: Braun-Brumfield, Inc.
Binder: Braun-Brumfield, Inc.
Text: Garamond (VIP)
Display: Garamond (Typositor)